Ethics and Mental Health

The Patient, Profession and Community

Ethics and Mental Health

The Patient, Profession and Community

Michael Robertson

Garry Walter

CRC Press
Taylor & Francis Group
Boca Raton   London   New York

CRC Press is an imprint of the
Taylor & Francis Group, an **informa** business

CRC Press
Taylor & Francis Group
6000 Broken Sound Parkway NW, Suite 300
Boca Raton, FL 33487-2742

Library of Congress Cataloging-in-Publication Data

Robertson, Michael D., author.
    Ethics and mental health : the patient, profession, and the community / authors, Michael Robertson, Garry Walter.
    p. ; cm.
    Includes bibliographical references and index.
    ISBN 978-1-4441-6864-8 (pbk. : alk. paper)
    I. Walter, Garry, author. II. Title.
    [DNLM: 1. Psychiatry--ethics. 2. Ethics, Professional. 3. Mental Health--ethics. 4. Psychotherapy--ethics. WM 21]

RC455.2.E94
174.2'9689--dc23   2013027840

Visit the Taylor & Francis Web site at
http://www.taylorandfrancis.com

and the CRC Press Web site at
http://www.crcpress.com

Contents

Contents

Preface

On a hot July day in 1942, SS-Obersturmführer Franz Stangl was driven from Warsaw toward the village of Bialystok, some 60 or so miles to the northeast of the Polish capital. As the commandant of the Sobibor *vernichtslager* (extermination camp), Stangl was a key figure in Operation Reinhard, which sought to effect the Nazis' complete elimination of Jews from Poland. Along with Chelmno near the Polish city of Lodz, Sobibor was one of the first such industrial killing facilities constructed for the planned genocide.[1]

The commander of Operation Reinhard, SS-Obergruppenführer Odilo Globocnik, had tasked Stangl to investigate problems with a new killing facility, Treblinka. As Stangl's car approached the Treblinka railhead, he was sickened by the revolting, vaguely sweet stench of decomposing bodies in the summer heat. When Stangl arrived at the actual camp, he found corpses strewn throughout the campsite, cattle train carriages filled with the dead and the dying, and piles of victims' belongings. He later described the scene to the journalist Gita Sereny as akin to the horrifying imagery of Dante's *Inferno*.[2] The SS guards at Treblinka randomly shot prisoners and perpetrated other unspeakable acts of sadism and cruelty. Enraged at the shambolic scene, Stangl confronted Treblinka's commandant, the psychiatrist Dr. Irmfried Eberl.[2]

By all accounts, Eberl was frequently intoxicated, he abused and humiliated female prisoners, and was generally derelict in his duties.[3,4] He frequently wandered among the condemned of Treblinka in a doctor's white coat. Eberl had aspired for Treblinka to have the highest killing rate of the Reinhard camps—in the first six weeks of operations, 300,000 people were murdered in Treblinka, most of them Jews from the Warsaw ghetto.[5] Eberl had insisted that transports should continue to ferry the victims to Treblinka, even though hundreds of them perished in the summer heat as the cattle cars banked up on the Treblinka railhead. Eberl's killing teams could not keep pace with his ambitions.[5] Eberl had dedicated little effort to the means of disposal of the remains of Treblinka victims; the industrialized efficiency of the Auschwitz–Birkenau crematoria would not be possible for another year. Eberl opted instead to focus his attention on pilfering the belongings of the dead in defiance of Reichsführer Heinrich Himmler's directive that these were property of the Reich.

This was not Stangl's first encounter with Eberl. The two had met during the Aktion (Operation) T4 program, which sought to rid the Third Reich of its mentally and physically disabled citizens through a network of "euthanasia centers" established in psychiatric hospitals. These centers had purposely built carbon monoxide gas chambers for killing selected patients. In 1940, Eberl had been present at the experimental trial of one such gas chamber at Brandenburg psychiatric clinic, where he had been appointed the clinical director. In the first trial, seven patients were made to strip and enter the chamber, where they were gassed. Several of the victims did not die from the gas but were finished by SS doctors with injections of curare and barbiturate.[4] On the second attempt at the gassing of patients, Eberl had operated the valves for the carbon monoxide tanks.[3]

Soon after this, the perpetrators of the Aktion T4 program embarked on a process of mass killing of patients from many psychiatric hospitals and other facilities around the Reich. In the autumn of 1941, Eberl transferred to a larger euthanasia center at Bernberg. As a matter of routine, the intended victims, identified as appropriate for killing by questionnaires completed by their own psychiatrists, were brought to Bernberg from other facilities. Eberl inspected the victims before each murder, branding some of them with a red marker pen if they had unique physical features that warranted postmortem dissection. At Bernberg, the bloodied dissecting table was adjacent to the gas chamber, so that the victims saw it on the way to their deaths. The victims' remains were cremated and sent to their families with falsified death certificates. At times this was almost comically incompetent; some victims certified to have died from appendicitis had undergone appendectomy in childhood, arousing the suspicion of their families. So efficient was Eberl at killing that many surrounding concentration camps opted to send prisoners to their death at Bernberg under the program Sonderbehandlung (Special Treatment) 14f13.[3,6] Through an agenda of active nonvoluntary euthanasia on a massive scale, Dr. Irmfried Eberl, psychiatrist, had become an accomplished mass murderer.

Eberl was soon relieved of his command. He later served in the Waffen SS as a medic until his capture by Patton's army in Luxembourg in 1945. He continued to work as a doctor in a POW camp before his release in July 1945.[7] He became a family physician in the Ulm area, remarried, and had a son—his first wife had died during the war. In February 1948, a former nurse from Grafeneck, another of the euthanasia centers, reported Eberl to the Tübingen police as a possible war criminal. While he was in custody, the details of Eberl's wartime crimes became apparent, and he hanged himself with a sheet in his cell. Like many fellow Holocaust perpetrators, Eberl was never called to account for his crimes.

Who was the psychiatrist Irmfried Eberl, and what path did he follow to the mass murders at Bernberg and Treblinka? As confronting and potentially distasteful as a detailed consideration of the life of one of history's most despicable characters is, the question of Irmfried Eberl's "moral agency"—put simply—cannot but enlighten us as to the moral agency of contemporary psychiatrists. By *moral agency*, we refer to the processes that lead an individual, possessed of free will, to formulate and act in accordance with a system of values. As we intend to establish, this enlightenment resides in understanding the influence of contextual factors on the behavior of psychiatrists—professionals with *particular* epistemic, personal, disciplinary and institutional values, empowered by societies in *particular* historical and cultural settings. The emphasis on *particular* here is our central thesis.

Irmfried Eberl—Psychiatrist and Dutiful Mass Murderer

To begin to comprehend how a psychiatrist could become the commandant of a place like Treblinka, we must consider the forces that motivated and influenced Irmfried Eberl. As with Hannah Arendt's nuanced judgment of Adolf Eichmann,[8] one of the main architects of the Holocaust, there is little prospect of a simple explanation of Eberl's actions. Rather, we need to understand the confluence of factors that led Eberl to his crimes. To try to understand and come to terms with the crimes of Irmfried Eberl, the psychiatrist, is perhaps to understand the complexity of moral agency of all psychiatrists.

This is the starting point of our exploration of a new approach to psychiatric ethics.

Eberl's Early Life and Personal Background

The youngest of three boys, Irmfried Eberl was born in September 1910 in the Austrian town Bregenz. Irmfried was raised a Catholic. His father worked in a state-run factory and his mother was a homemaker. With the advent of National Socialism, both of Irmfried's brothers and his father joined the Nazi party. Like many Austrians, the Eberls harbored an anti-Semitism, which flourished in the shadow of the rhetoric of Hitler and Goebbels. The family abandoned its Catholic faith due to the Vatican's reactions against Nazism and embraced Protestantism, more in keeping with Germanic values. Irmfried joined the Nazi party as a medical student in Innsbruck. He graduated in 1935. Like his father, who was terminated from his employment as a consequence of his membership in the Nazi party, Irmfried also had limited postgraduate employment options, as these were restricted by the Austrian government because of his Nazism.[7]

In March 1938, Germany annexed Austria in the Anschluss. Austrian Nazis like Irmfried Eberl enjoyed subsequently greater freedom within the expanding Third Reich. Eberl later traveled to Germany, where he worked in public health and later in respiratory medicine. Despite minimal psychiatric training. Eberl took up his first role as a psychiatrist in February 1940 as the medical director of Brandenburg clinic, a euthanasia center established in 1939. Later, in 1941, he took up a similar position at Bernberg clinic, a 132-bed psychiatric hospital on the outskirts of Magdeburg.[9]

Unlike Stangl, who provided an emotionally bland account of his crimes to Gitta Sereny,[2] or Eichmann, who enjoyed the theater of his trial in Jerusalem,[8] Irmfried Eberl left no account of his own moral universe. There are fragments of letters he sent to his then-wife Ruth from Treblinka. In July 1942, Eberl wrote

> I know that I have not written much to you lately, but I could not help this, since the last Warsaw weeks have been accompanied by an unbelievable agitation and likewise here in Treblinka we have reached a pace that is downright breathtaking. Even if there were four of me and each day was 100 hours long, this would surely not be enough … By employing myself ruthlessly, I have nevertheless managed the last days with only half of the personnel at my command. I have deployed my people ruthlessly wherever it was necessary and they have struggled along valiantly. I am happy and proud of this achievement.… Since you represent for me the beautiful part of my life, you should not know everything about it.[10]

This missive to Eberl's wife communicates his use of the "numbing" and "doubling" psychodynamics outlined by the psychiatrist Robert Jay Lifton in his landmark work *The Nazi Doctors*.[6] The letter portrays a man enthralled in the task of killing. Like Eichmann's, Eberl's expressed intention, at least in his public face, was to an almost sacred task on behalf of the *volk* (the German people). Undoubtedly, Eberl would have secreted his abuse of female prisoners and theft of the booty of the victims of Treblinka from the "beautiful part" of his life, yet this is a dissonant observation which undermines the notion of Eberl as dutiful mass murderer. Even more, it emphasizes the complexity of moral agency, with its ample opportunity for self-deception.

It is not helpful to formulate Irmfried Eberl as a sadistic psychopath, as many have.[3,4] There is no one overriding grand narrative of his values; we have a portrait of an unremarkable student from *Mittel Europa,* raised in a family possessed of a latent anti-Semitism and entranced by the seductive rhetoric of Hitler. Yet this does not in itself explain why. The next step is to understand the context of Eberl and his road to mass murder.

The Intellectual Preconditions to Psychiatric "Healing Killing"

Robert Jay Lifton's account of the crimes of the Nazi doctors remains the most compelling portrait of the moral decay of a profession.[6] Like many moral failings, the maleficent acts of German psychiatrists in the Third Reich were gradual in onset. Lifton's account of the evolution from eugenics to genocide commences with the compulsory sterilization of those deemed *lebensunwertes leben*, literally, "life unworthy of life." The next step was the euthanasia of severely disabled infants, progressing to the killing of disabled adults. Once the gas chambers of Bernberg and other facilities outsourced the murder of prisoners from concentration camps, it was inevitable that the killers of Aktion T4 would become functionaries in the Nazis' Final Solution.

The foundation concept in this process derived from a nineteenth-century idea first advocated by the British polymath and first cousin to Charles Darwin, Francis Galton. Like his more famous cousin, Galton was gripped by the notion that heredity could account for the advancement of a species. In evolving his ideas from the perfect domestic pet to humans, Galton coined the term *eugenics* in 1883.[11] Eugenics and the notions of "hygiene" within populations meshed well with the emerging science of medicine in the early twentieth century. Far from just being a preoccupation of German psychiatrists in the interwar period, eugenics first appeared in the writings of Plato and lurked within Western culture over time.[12] Writers such as Malthus predicted that humanity would outstrip resources, necessitating public policies that would not bolster the weaker members of a population.[13]

Regardless, the German version of eugenics emerged in a toxic environment of racial hygiene, postwar resentment of the German defeat in the Great War, and the fragility of the Weimar Republic. In 1904, Alfred Ploetz, a physician, founded the German Society for Racial Hygiene. The emergence of a eugenic discourse in German psychiatry can be credited to the efforts of Ernst Rüdin, the Swiss-born professor of psychiatry at Munich, who was an enthusiastic follower of Kraepelin and Ploetz. Rüdin reframed Kraepelin as a radical racial hygienist and thus mainstreamed eugenics in German psychiatry. Lifton[6] describes Rüdin as "not so much a fanatical Nazi as a fanatical geneticist" (p. 28). Indeed, many German psychiatrists were lured along the road to genocide by a fetish for eugenic solutions to Weimar Germany's many problems.

Germany had lost a generation of young men in the Great War. Many believed that the best of the German blood lay beneath European battlefields, significantly weakening the *volk*. In 1920, Karl Boenhoeffer, the president of the German Psychiatric Association, noted that the value of the life of an individual had diminished in the face of Germany's losses in the Great War.[3] This, more than any other utterance of a psychiatrist in the Third Reich, reflects the critical first step along the road to genocide: the profession's office bearer communicated the renunciation of the foundation value of the physician, that of the value of an individual patient. This departure from Kant's categorical imperative was the critical moral failure that facilitated the horrors that followed. This was by no means an exclusively German phenomenon—the Nazis were emboldened by the practice of compulsory sterilization and unconsented experimentation on certain groups in the United States in the early part of the twentieth century.[14]

One nexus between the enthusiasm for medical genetics and the National Socialist policy of eugenics and later ethnic cleansing was the scientific racism of the physician and biologist Ernst Haeckel. Haeckel's work introduced the notion of racial superiority,[15] one that reflected Hitler's views in *Mein Kampf*.[16] Literary critic and Nazi "groupie" Wilhelm Bölsche introduced Hitler to Haeckel's ideas.[17] Independent of Hitler's embrace of the tenets of racial hygiene, many German universities had established research centers investigating the field prior to his ascension to power. One such center in Frankfurt awarded a PhD to Josef Mengele (the so-called Angel of Death at Auschwitz) for his thesis on the genetics of cleft palate.[18]

The other act of intellectual midwifery for the eugenic policies of the Nazis was performed by the psychiatrist Alfred Hoche. Along with retired jurist Karl Binding, Hoche penned the monograph *Die Freigabe der Vernichtung Lebensunwerten Lebens* (*Allowing the Destruction of Life Unworthy of Living*). Hoche's academic career was always ill-savory. His research interest was the spinal cord activity of prisoners executed by guillotine. Hoche's contribution to this horrid monograph was to argue that severely disabled patients had suffered a "mental death" and represented little more than "human ballast." Perhaps embittered by the death of his son in the Great War, Hoche coldly calculated that each "idiot's … ballast existence" cost Germany 1,300 Reich marks per annum. In a triumph of self-deceit, Hoche and Binding's *opus horribilis* created what Lifton called a medical "as if"—the notion of "healing killing."[6] Lifton's core thesis of the crimes of the Nazi doctors is predicated upon this concept. Put simply, healing killing is the notion that the act of euthanasia of a severely disabled person cures them of their suffering and the *volk* of the impure blood.

Another intellectual foundation of German psychiatry was the influence of Emil Kraepelin, whose reductive biological explanations of mental illness provided more intellectual rigor to the mental hygiene and eugenic underpinnings of German psychiatry. Kraepelin's work, although dwarfed in cultural significance by that of the Jewish Sigmund Freud, had more traction in the domain of more disabling chronic mental illness than the neuroses of polite Viennese or Berliners. It was schizophrenia and intellectual disability, rather than the horse phobia of "Little Hans," that was the stuff of *lebensunwertes leben*. It is intriguing that despite the influence of Freud and the other European psychoanalysts at the *fin de siècle*, German psychiatrists in the Great War had little truck with the concept of "shell shock" in the ranks of the Central Power's troops.[18]

In the aftermath of the murder of more than 70,000 patients by their psychiatrists,[4] we are left with the discomfort of knowing that the intellectual preconditions of this horrid chapter of the history of psychiatry remain in some way viable. While no moral equivalence can be argued for the reductive notions of biological psychiatry and the devaluation of life by Nazi psychiatrists like Irmfried Eberl, the dissonant notion of Darwinian thought remains within psychiatric discourse. In a compelling argument, O'Mathuna avers that five ethical principles emerged from Darwin's *The Origin of Species*,[19] and these formed the basis of social Darwinism and Nazi medical ideology.[20] First, there is relativism to ethics, particularly in regard to the value of human life being absolute. Second, the distinction between humans and animals is blurred. Third, human dignity and the value of life exist in gradations relative to capacity. Fourth, at the lower end of such a ranking, some human life is unworthy, leading to the fifth notion of survival of the fittest becoming an ethical principle. O'Mathuna finds such ideas manifest in contemporary bioethics, particularly in Peter Singer's views of speciesism and utilitarianism,[21-24] questions of resource allocation in the health system, debates over the beginning and end of life and the apparent negotiability of the previously irrefutable notion of the dignity of all human life. This is not to say that every argument in bioethics can be resolved by the intellectual sloth of referring to potential parallels with the Nazi era, but rather to call into critical reflection the notion that psychiatry has learned its lessons from the first half of the twentieth century.

German Psychiatry in the Mid-Twentieth Century

Prior to the Third Reich, German medicine was the most evolved of all professional groups. German medicine was founded upon the tenets of public health, medical education, and research.[25] German physicians were overrepresented in Nobel Prizes for medicine, and their ethical codes for research were as exacting as those derived from the Nuremberg trials in 1946. The medical profession in Germany had been diminished by scandals in 1892 (involving the deliberate infection of prostitutes and orphans with syphilis) and in 1931 (the deaths of 75 children in a hospital in Lübeck, who were administered a flawed tuberculosis vaccine).[26] The Lübeck scandal profoundly undermined the status of medicine in Germany. Julius Moses, a Social Democrat politician and long-time critic of German medicine, described the scandal as an "earthquake" that had all but destroyed the German medical profession "at its very foundations" (p.7).[27] Albert Moll, a neurologist, argued after the 1892 scandal that German physicians had lost perspective through overspecialization and that the scientific method in medicine had created a form of knowledge gap between physicians and the community, leading to alienation between the two and valorization of research over treatment.[28] This latter point had prompted Julius Moses to coin the term *experimental rage* (p. 9)[27] to highlight this core pathology in the soul of German medicine. In this ominous phrase, Moses seemed to be foretelling the crimes of Josef Mengele at Auschwitz and Julius Hallevorden at the Kaiser Wilhelm Institute.[29]

Within the German medical tradition in the twentieth century lay the tension between two forms of *sorge* (care). *Fürsorge* was the care of the ill individual patient, and *vorsorge* was an approach to public health and the overall health and welfare of the *volk*. This apparent dichotomy is reflected in contemporary bioethics discourse on the tension between militant communitarianism and rights-based individual liberalism. In Weimar Germany, the economic and social problems faced by the fragile democratic republic favored the popularity of the racial hygiene and eugenic movements. As such, *vorsorge* won the tug-of-war and became the underlying principle in German medicine in the mid-twentieth century.[30]

Beyond such tensions, there seemed to be somewhat of a crisis in interwar German medicine. In the first instance, German physicians of all stripes assumed a reductive biological view of humanity and of illness. Second, the focus of medicine shifted from the individual to the community. Third, and perhaps most compellingly, the introduction of social welfare and national insurance systems in Weimar Germany emphasized medicine and medical care more as a financial enterprise than had been hitherto considered.[31] This latter evolution, yoked with the growing enthusiasm for biological psychiatry, eugenics, and mental hygiene, made for a highly flammable mixture of ideas underlying modern German medicine. As psychiatry had been traditionally tasked with the care of individuals whose illnesses seldom improved and whose needs seemed endless, it is little wonder that they found themselves at the vanguard of this new medical–economic project.

Like any profession, German psychiatry in the early twentieth century comprised a number of discourses. The biologism of Kraepelin sat in tension with the *Verstehende Psychologie* of Jaspers[32] and the methods of Freud and other psychoanalysts. A renewed enthusiasm for biological psychiatry was buoyed by the apparent success of insulin coma therapy and seizure therapy induced by cardiozol or electrical stimulation.[3] There had been a long-standing tradition of *soziale Psychiatrie* (social psychiatry)[33] in Germany, although the term assumed a polysemous quality in the Weimar Republic.[34] In the calamity of the defeat in World War I, the term had come to mean a shift in focus from the interpersonal and social networks of individual patients to the greater social good of the *volk*. Johannes Enge, a psychiatrist, ironically from Lübeck, wrote in 1919 that psychiatry had a primarily sociopolitical role in protecting the *volk* from "tainted blood" (p.22)[35] through enforced sterilization and exclusion from the community. By the 1930s, this notion had amalgamated with the work of Hoche and Binding, creating the stimulus for the psychiatric eugenic project. It is little wonder that psychiatrists were the most represented group in German society in the Nazi party.[14]

Lifton highlights the eugenic fetish in the Nazification of medicine—a process referred to as *gleichschaltung*. Heinrich Himmler, head of the SS, took a personal interest in the process, championing compulsory membership of the Reich Physician's Chamber and citing the Hippocratic tradition as the basis of the sacred task of the purification of German blood. Within this was a romantic notion of the "cultivation of the genes" to enable the *volk* to realize their "full potential of genetic endowment" (p.30).[6]

Psychiatry in the Weimar Republic

Like many professional groups, psychiatrists had to adapt to the postwar environment in Weimar Germany. Perhaps more than any other time in German history, the Weimar Republic was the most fragile and problematic social system, and its political and economic problems plagued psychiatry in particular.[3]

The Weimar Republic was established in 1919 after the defeat of Germany in the Great War. The fledgling republic was repudiated by many sectors of the population, although it survived attempted coups by extremists from the right and left of politics. The right-wing *Freikorps* (later to morph into the SS) were motivated by the *Dolchstosslegende* (stab-in-the-back legend), which had it that Germany's defeat was brought about by the treachery of Jews and Bolsheviks, many of whom later occupied office in the Weimar Republic. Indeed, it was this mythology of resentment that laid the ground for the Nazis and their genocidal wars on the Jews and the Soviets.

Democracy in Weimar Germany was based on proportional representation and meant many parties with minimal support (like the Nazis) could gain seats and influence legislation. The office of the president was enfeebled by institutional limits and laws that did not always have to conform to the constitution. Indeed, the modern German state was founded in the light of the weakness of Weimar Democracy.[36] The economy of the Weimar Republic struggled under the weight of punitive war reparations, hyperinflation, and unemployment. Germany's economy was by far the hardest hit of any by the Great Depression. The right in German politics, including most industrialists, identified the Weimar Republic with trade unions and the leftist Social Democrats.[36] As the blame for economic calamity was laid at the feet of the political system, it seems little surprise that the right of politics held such appeal by the early 1930s.

Such impecunious circumstances brought into focus the whole question of the cost of the large welfare system in Weimar Germany. The expensive asylum system in Germany was one of many such concerns. The psychiatric hospital system had progressively shrunk throughout the 1920s. This forced German psychiatrists into the role of "essentially control functions" (p.30).[3] Psychiatry in Germany had fallen out of favor, and by the time of the Great Depression, not only were the costly asylums themselves one of many banes of the Weimar treasury, but also the cost of asylums' unproductive and demanding occupants. Rations were reduced in psychiatric hospitals, and more open discussion of sterilization and euthanasia occurred. Historian Michael Burleigh argues that rampant unemployment not only brought about resentment of the cost of providing for occupants of psychiatric hospitals, but also drew entirely unsuitable people into the ranks of psychiatric nursing and asylum orderlies.[3] Given the enthusiastic uptake of National Socialism within medicine, and among psychiatrists in particular, it seems little wonder that by the time of the collapse of the Weimar Republic and the advent of Hitler, psychiatric hospitals became the initial site of the murderous solutions to Germany's problems.

* * *

Prior to integrating our survey of the contextual influences of Irmfried Eberl's moral agency, we should adumbrate the mechanics of the Aktion T4 program. There are many descriptive accounts of this outrage in the history of psychiatry. However, we seek to emphasize how the administrative structure of Aktion T4 facilitated German psychiatrists like Eberl into their crimes.

The name "T4" came from the abbreviation of the Berlin address, Tiergartenstraße 4, where the program was headquartered. The program saw the death of around 70,000 patients,[18] although the journalist Horst von Buttlar estimates that based upon recently accessed documents, the death toll is closer to 200,000.[37]

The first step in the elimination of those least fortunate in German society was the passage of the Law for the Prevention of Hereditarily Diseased Offspring through the compliant Reichstag in July 1933. Following this, a network of sterilization courts provided the necessary appearance of procedural fairness in the forced sterilization of those determined unworthy to reproduce. Far from this being a uniquely Nazi law, similar eugenic statutes of forced sterilization of mentally ill, intellectually disabled, and in some circumstances, African American citizens, had existed in the United States since the early twentieth century.[38]

In 1939, Hitler tasked two of his staff, Reichsleiter Philipp Bouhler, his head of chancellery, and Dr. Karl Brandt, his personal physician, to carry out a program of euthanasia to rid the Reich of those lives unworthy of life. In July 1939, Brandt had facilitated the death of a profoundly disabled child at the behest of the boy's family. Three weeks after the baby was murdered, the Orwellian-named Committee for the Scientific Treatment of Severe, Genetically Determined Illness was established.[39] The Nazi propaganda machine helped manufacture consent for the euthanasia program through the production of films, such as *The Inheritance* (1935) and *The Victim of the Past* (1937), which depicted the waste of these lives. The most remarkable of these films was *Ich Klage An (I Accuse)*, which was released in 1941. This film was the most mainstream and artistic of the genre and depicted the trial of a man accused of murdering his wife, who suffered from multiple sclerosis. So effective was *Ich Klage An* as a propaganda tool that an argument has been made that it in part inspired Clint Eastwood's 2005 Oscar-winning film *Million Dollar Baby*.[40]

The program of psychiatric murder progressed when Werner Heyde, professor of psychiatry at Würzburg, joined Brandt and Bouhler in enacting Hitler's decree. Other senior psychiatrists joined the program and developed a process of identifying victims via questionnaires completed by their treating doctors. Eberl had consulted extensively in the drafting of relevant policies and data-gathering procedures for T4.[3]

As to *why*, there have been numerous attempts at explanation; however, the analysis of Dudley and Gale in 2002[41] correlates most closely with ours. Their thesis is that psychiatrists were led to their crimes by pressure from peers and superiors, unquestioning obedience, racist ideology, and "careerism." Deceptive language, "bureaucratic and technical proficiency," and the enthusiasm for romanticized Darwinian and Galtonesque ideas also contributed. In other words, Dudley and Gale see the profound influence of context on these psychiatrists.

In Formulation—The Moral Agency of Irmfried Eberl

Seeking to comprehend the origins of unspeakable crimes risks diminishing the suffering of the victims and in some way lessening the responsibility of the moral agent. Yet in formulating the moral agency of Irmfried Eberl, we seek to understand this process in extreme form. Within any form of common morality, Eberl's behavior as a psychiatrist would be determined as evil. Just as Aquinas conceptualized evil to be a privation of good, i.e., evil existing as the absence of good, perhaps formulating Eberl's "evil" acts as a psychiatrist might provide an inverse portrait, and understanding of, the "good" psychiatrist.

We have little doubt that Irmfried Eberl was a despicable man. His behavior at Treblinka in particular was sadistic and criminal, even allowing for the moral tone of Nazi Germany. We have little insight into the private world of Irmfried Eberl, other than his family's intrinsic anti-Semitism and the appeal of Hitlerian ideology to the family's values. Eberl's letters to his wife communicate both Lifton's psychodynamic formulations of "numbing" and "doubling" and Eberl's somewhat narcissistic ambitions to be the most effective killer in Aktion Reinhard. As an Austrian, it is possible Eberl sought to be almost hyper-German (like Hitler), in the same manner that the Corsican Napoleon sought to be hyper-French.

Eberl practiced within a profession that was enamored of a biological view of mental illness, infused with the tenets of social Darwinism. In the interwar years, German psychiatry shifted from a focus upon the individual to one of the *volk*. Social psychiatry in Germany had morphed into a militant form of communitarianism, elevating the needs of the community over the individual. As the task of caring for the chronically mentally ill became a source of consternation to the Weimar treasury, this imperative strengthened. German psychiatrists embraced National Socialism more than any of their medical colleagues, although the bulk of the German medical profession fell in with the new regime, whose integration of romanticized notions of racial and mental hygiene, misguided scientific fervor, and the imbuing of doctors with an almost priestly role of social protector was all too irresistible. In the shame and ignominy of a vanquished, humiliated, and economically hobbled postwar Germany, the notion of a Third Reich, the ultimate conqueror of Europe and possessed of a *volk* cleansed of racial and genetic impurity, provided an anodyne. In a deliberate inversion of Nietzsche's conceited notion of the *übermensch* (superman), the prominent Nazi Alfred Rosenberg had championed the term *untermenschen* (subhuman) in referring to those inferior to the *volk* and whose presence represented an existential threat to their future.[42] In interwar Germany, it was little wonder that the task of ridding the *volk* of impurities began with the most disabled.

There is an inherent danger in seeking to provide a reductive or plausible account of Eberl's "evil" actions and, by extension, what might account for the contrary "good" actions of a psychiatrist–moral agent. Our investigation into the origins of Eberl's behavior has identified numerous potential determinants extending from his early environment to the grand narrative of the German *volk*.

One might seek to formulate Eberl's actions much like that of a patient, using the biopsychosocial model of Engel.[43,44] Engel's model argues that human experience arises from the interaction of biological, psychological, and social factors. By analogy, we might propose a comparable model of moral agency identifying *endo* (individual), *meso* (local), and *exo* (larger-scale) factors (Figure 1). While inclusive, this approach risks falling into the same criticisms of Engel's model. Pilgrim has argued that Engel's model merely forces several themes into coexistence, rather than offering genuine theoretical integration.[45] Ghaemi's critique of Engel's approach is more comprehensive, regarding the model as merely eclectic and therefore not intellectually rigorous. In contrast, Ghaemi urges psychiatrists to accept an approach of pluralism.[46] *Pluralism* in this sense is the assumption that phenomena observed empirically require multiple explanations, not one unified explanation. To Ghaemi, human life is characterized by existential situations, or crises, which become opportunities for authentic existence. One might argue that this is most acute in moral deliberation.

Our model posits that the complex phenomenon of moral agency in psychiatry integrates perspectives from different levels that provide a more textured account of its different aspects.

Our concept of moral agency is one of the rational, autonomous being who can evolve a system of values and apply these to either universal or particular applications of "the good life." In this, we are specifically applying Kant's moral philosophy of the "noumenal self."[47] *Noumena* are aspects or matters, such as values, that are known intrinsically without experience in the external world. The paradigmatic example of this in medicine is the Hippocratic injunction applied to any treatment decision made by a physician. Kant's moral agent is the individual who applies a means of understanding the world of events or objects (phenomena). Kant described this process as "transcendental idealism." Our application of the Kantian notion of moral agency to psychiatry is predicated on the noumenal nature of values. Psychiatrists as moral agents apply values to their experience and in doing so formulate understanding and courses of action. We will discuss the nature of values and their conceptual priority to ethics in the next section.

In our model, the noumena of the psychiatrist include individual and collective values and larger-scale influences such as history, grand narratives of state or the people, and politics (Figure 1).

The first noumenal level of our model, the *endo*, comprises the aspects of moral agency primarily manifest in individual values evolved from family, community, and the individual psychology of the moral agent. The second noumenal level, the *meso*, incorporates values derived from the professional existence of psychiatrists. These include the particular values held and advocated by a professional group, the values of an institution, and the values

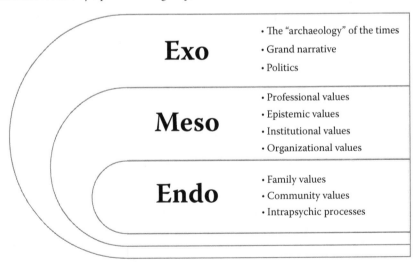

Figure 1 A model of moral agency in psychiatry as a manifestation of the noumenal self.

implicit in the forms of knowledge (epistemic) chosen or evolved within it. The third noumenal level, the *exo*, addresses the broader historical and cultural context of the moral agent and how such factors become innate in the way in which the moral agent deliberates. The "archaeology" of the times describes the journey taken by a group to a particular point or status, both in self-concept and in a broader geopolitical sense. The grand narrative of a community or state becomes an innate part of how individuals or groups conceptualize themselves and their actions. Our use of the term *politics* does not denote a particular ideology or partisan position, but rather the engagement of an individual or group in the life of the state. This derives from the classical notion of the individual vitally engaged in the affairs of the *polis*, the substantive city–state of antiquity.

One other perspective demanding consideration is the phenomenon of the dual role in psychiatry. As we are taking the position that moral agency in psychiatrists is in large measure determined by a distinctly social constitution of values and contextual influences at the meso and exo levels of our model, the obligations of the psychiatrist to his or her community in addition to obligations to his or her patient are often in tension. We have previously argued[48] that much of the discourse in psychiatric ethics exists as a process of the resolution of that tension, and we will revisit this in the third section of this book. In the wrestle between obligations to the *volk* and to each individual patient, the *volk* clearly triumphed over those who went to their deaths in the gas chambers of Bernberg in the moral deliberations of Irmfried Eberl and his Aktion T4 confederates. In this instance, the constellation of factors we have surveyed in coming to understand the noumenal world of Eberl and his crimes saw the needs of the *volk* valued over the lives of those deemed unworthy of life.

New Ethics in Psychiatry—The Profession, the Patient, and the Community

This book is structured in three sections. The first section of the book begins by providing our distilled views regarding current normative theories of psychiatric ethics. We discuss the potential for empirical methods to make codes of conduct more representative of professional values. We then revisit some of our previous work on professionalism in psychiatry to establish the theoretical basis of our proposed methodology for mental health ethics. Next, we consider concepts of justice and the moderate communitarian position before outlining our methodology. From this consideration, we rework the concept of virtue in psychiatrists and the virtuous clinician as the virtuous citizen in a community. Virtuous citizenship resides with the contractarian relationship between professions and their societies. In essence, we argue that mental health professionals exist within a perpetual state of tension brought about by the beneficent influence of Hippocratic injunction, their personal values, notions of social justice, and the potentially harmful influences of their social role, mediated by the social contract as applied to professions. Tension invariably arises through the malleable concept of the *common good*, critical to the professional relationship with society.

In the second section, we apply this consideration to the area of involuntary psychiatric treatment and later address the context of psychiatric practice and the moral agency of psychiatrists. Based upon our arguments regarding the social constitution of psychiatrists as moral agents, we will outline in detail the different influences on the craft of psychiatry to better illustrate the diverse forces that influence moral deliberation and the practice of ethics in mental health. This covers areas as diverse as cultural, economic, scientific, and political domains.

In the third section of the book, we apply our methodology in considering contemporary (as opposed to classic) dilemmas in mental health ethics. In each instance, we will outline in detail the dilemma in the context of mental health implications. We will then apply the methodology in formulating how the mental health clinician would approach the quandary. Our aim is to bring a new perspective to classic dilemmas from the past, to contemporary challenges, and in anticipation, to fresh dilemmas that will inevitably arise.

References

1. Arad Y. *Belzec, Sobibor, Treblinka: The Operation Reinhard Death Camps.* Bloomington: Indiana University Press; 1987.

2. Sereny, G. *Into That Darkness: An Examination of Conscience.* London: Vintage Press; 1983.

3. Burleigh M. *Death and Deliverance.* London: Pan; 2002.

4. Weale A. *The SS: A New History.* London: Little, Brown; 2010.

5. Klee E, Dressen W, Riess V. *The Good Old Days: The Holocaust as Seen by Its Perpetrators and Bystanders.* Old Saybrook, CT: S. Fischer Verlag GmbH; 1988.

6. Lifton R. *The Nazi Doctors.* New York: Basic Books; 1986.

7. Strous R. Dr. Irmfried Eberl (1910–48): mass murdering MD. *IMAJ.* 2009;11:216–218.

8. Arendt H. *Eichmann in Jerusalem: A Report on the Banality of Evil.* London: Faber & Faber; 1963.

9. Friedlander H. *The Origins of Nazi Genocide: From Euthanasia to the Final Solution.* Chapel Hill: University of North Carolina Press; 1995.

10. Holocaust Research Project. http://www.holocaustresearchproject.org/trials/suchomelstat (accessed September 10, 2011).

11. Galton F. *Inquiries into Human Faculty and Its Development.* London: Macmillan; 1883.

12. Lynn R. *Eugenics: A Reassessment.* New York: Praeger; 2001.

13. Malthus T. *An Essay of the Principles of Population, 7th Edition.* London: Reaves and Turner; 1826.

14. Cohen M. Overview of German, Nazi, and Holocaust medicine. *Am J Med Genet.* 2010;152:687–707.

15. Haeckel E. *The History of Creation, 3rd Edition, Volume 1.* London: Trench & Co; 1868.

16. Hitler A. *Mein Kampf.* Munich: Franz Eher Nachfolger; 1930.

17. Gasman D. *The Scientific Origins of National Socialism: Social Darwinism in Ernst Haeckel and the German Monist League.* New York: Elsevier; 1971.

18. Proctor R. *Racial Hygiene: Medicine under the Nazis.* Cambridge, MA: Harvard University Press; 1988.

19. Darwin C. *On the Origin of Species by Means of Natural Selection, or the Preservation of Favoured Races in the Struggle for Life, 2nd Edition*. London: John Murray; 1860.

20. O'Mathuna D. Human dignity in the Nazi era: implications for contemporary bioethics. *BMC Medical Ethics*. 2006;7:2.

21. Singer P. *How Are We to Live*. London: Mandarin; 1994.

22. Singer P. *Practical Ethics, 2nd Edition*. Cambridge: Cambridge University Press; 1993.

23. Singer P. *The Expanding Circle: Ethics and Sociobiology*. New York: Farrar, Straus and Giroux; 1981.

24. Singer P, Kuhse H. *Should the Baby Live? The Problem of Handicapped Infants*. New York: Oxford University Press; 1985.

25. Wynia M, Wells A. Light from the flames of hell: remembrance and lessons of the Holocaust for today's medical profession. *Isr Med Assoc J*. 2007;9:186–188.

26. Sass H. Pre-Nuremberg German regulation concerning new therapy and human experimentation. *J Med Philos*. 1983;8:99–111.

27. Moses J. *Der Totentanz von Lubeck*. Dresden: Madaus. Navad. D; 1930.

28. Killen A. Hypnosis and medical ethics in Germany. 2011; http://www.psychiatrictimes.com/blog/psych-history/content/article/10168/1950721 (accessed September 28, 2011).

29. Annas G, Grodin E, eds. *The Nazi Doctors and the Nuremberg Code: Human Rights in Human Experimentation*. Oxford: Oxford University Press; 1992.

30. Seeman M. Psychiatry in the Nazi era. *Can J Psychiatry*. 2005;50:218–225.

31. Bonah C. "Experimental rage": the development of medical ethics and the genesis of scientific facts. *Soc Hist Med*. 2002;15:187–207.

32. Jaspers K. *General Psychopathology*. Hoenig J, Hamilton M W, trans. Chicago: University of Chicago Press; 1963.

33. Ilberg G. Soziale psychiatrie. *Monatsschr Soz Med*. 1903;1:321–329.

34. Schmeidebach H-P, Priebe S. Social psychiatry in Germany in the twentieth century: ideas and models. *Medical History*. 2004;48:449–472.

35. Enge J. *Soziale Psychiatrie*. Berlin: Adler; 1919.

36. Kershaw I. *Weimar. Why Did German Democracy Fail?* London: Weidenfield & Nicholson; 1990.

37. Buttlar Hv. Forscher öffnen Inventar des Schreckens. *Der Speigel*. October 1, 2003.

38. Rosen C. *Preaching Eugenics: Religious Leaders and the American Eugenics Movement*. New York: Oxford University Press; 2004.

39. Perper J, Cina S. *When Doctors Kill: Who, Why and How*. New York: Springer; 2010.

40. Smith W. Million dollar missed opportunity: what Clint Eastwood's Oscar winning movie could have done. 2005; http://www.discovery.org/a/2431.

41. Dudley M, Gale F. Psychiatrists as a moral community? Psychiatry under the Nazis and its contemporary relevance. *Australian and New Zealand Journal of Psychiatry*. 2002;36:585–594.

42. Rosenberg A. Der Mythus des zwanzigsten Jahrhunderts. http://www.gnosticliberationfront.com/myth_of_the_20th_century.htm.

43. Engel G. The need for a new medical model: a challenge for biomedicine. *Science.* 1977;196:129–136.

44. Engel G. The clinical application of the biopsychosocial model. *American Journal of Psychiatry.* 1980;137:535–544.

45. Beauchamp T, Childress J. *Principles of Biomedical Ethics.* New York: Oxford University Press; 2001.

46. Ghaemi N. *The Concepts of Psychiatry: A Pluralistic Approach to Mind and Mental Illness.* Baltimore: Johns Hopkins University Press; 2003.

47. Kant I. *Critique of Pure Reason.* Project Gutenburg 1787. http://www.gutenberg.org/ebooks/4280.

48. Robertson M, Walter G. The many faces of the dual-role dilemma in psychiatric ethics. *Australian and New Zealand Journal of Psychiatry* 2008;42:228–235.

About the Authors

Michael Robertson, MD, PhD, is clinical associate professor of psychiatric ethics at the Centre for Values, Ethics, and the Law in Medicine at the University of Sydney and a senior consultant psychiatrist. Dr. Robertson has published numerous scientific papers, book chapters, and monographs and has presented at many international meetings in the areas of psychiatric ethics, psychological trauma, coercive psychiatric treatment, and philosophy in psychiatry. In 2007 he conceived and subsequently developed the pioneering "Ethics and Mental Health" course at the University of Sydney. His previous books include *Interpersonal Psychotherapy: A Clinician's Guide.*

Garry Walter, MD, PhD, is professor of child and adolescent psychiatry at the University of Sydney and clinical director of Child and Adolescent Mental Health Services in Northern Sydney Local Health District, Australia. He is also an adjunct professor at Dalhousie University, Canada. As a child and adolescent psychiatrist, in 2002 he completed a doctorate on ECT in young people, which is the subject of his next book (Oxford University Press, 2013; co-edited with Neera Ghaziuddin).

Dr. Walter has published over 300 papers and has received many prestigious research prizes. His major research interests are ethics, genocide and severe trauma, psychiatric stigma, physical treatments in psychiatry, mood disorders, and medical education. He is the long-standing editor of *Australasian Psychiatry,* international editor-at-large of the *Journal of the American Academy of Child and Adolescent Psychiatry,* and a member of several other editorial boards. In 2012 Dr. Walter was appointed a member of the Order of Australia by the country's governor-general for service to medicine in the fields of adolescent mental health, medical education, and publishing.

Section I

New Methodology for Mental Health Ethics

Methods of Ethical Reasoning in Psychiatry

Introduction: Psychiatric Ethics as a Distinct Discourse

Bill Fulford, an English philosopher of psychiatry, dubbed psychiatric ethics the "bioethical ugly duckling."[1] Fulford attributed this to the explosion of high-tech medicine, the arcane nature of psychiatric diagnosis and treatment, and the confronting and difficult nature of ethical issues that occur in day-to-day practice in psychiatry, such as involuntary treatment or breaching confidentiality.

Whether there is a distinct discourse in psychiatric ethics remains the subject of debate. Campbell and collaborators[2] saw psychiatric ethics as having a special status in biomedical ethics, primarily given the effect of mental illness diminishing the autonomy of the patient. These authors have little time for academic debates about the relative merits of one normative theory over another in the field and argue that psychiatric ethics should adhere to basic tenets of beneficence and nonmaleficence. Dilemmas surrounding the impairment of autonomy and the stigmatizing effects of mental illness were at the core of Beauchamp's account of psychiatric ethics.[3,4] American philosopher Jennifer Radden offered a more comprehensive case for the uniqueness of psychiatric ethics,[5,6] arguing that psychiatry differentiates itself from other medical specialties in the unique role of the therapeutic relationship in therapeutic outcome, the vulnerability of psychiatric patients, and the characteristics of the psychiatric therapeutic project as something akin to raising children. As such, Radden argued that the tradition of virtue ethics is profoundly important to the discourse in psychiatric ethics. American psychiatrist Allen Dyer[7] argued that psychiatry's status as a part of the profession of medicine needed reconsideration. Dyer saw that the contemporary physician was defined by his or her technological skills or expertise rather than professional or personal values. Medicine was thus defined as the beneficent application of specialized knowledge to the needs of fellow citizens. Dyer argued that since market forces have interceded in the doctor–patient relationship, a professional relationship has become more an issue of technical services traded in the marketplace, rendering the Hippocratic tradition in medicine little more than a historical footnote. The status of psychiatry and the profession of medicine and medical ethics generally is now partly alienated from the Hippocratic tradition, particularly with the intrusion of third-party payers' doctor–patient relationship.[7]

In this review of the theoretical background to psychiatric ethics, we will define the various normative theories of ethics and their application to the psychiatric enterprise. Theories of ethics are either descriptive or normative. Descriptive ethical theories aim to define *what is*, whereas normative theories aim to define *what should be*. While descriptive ethics are problematic in that they may lack solid foundations other than what has emerged out of a culture or society, normative ethics suffer the problem of justifying *should*s and *ought*s.

The Scottish philosopher David Hume argued that it was impossible to define *should* and *ought*, contending that most humans act ethically in response to their emotions, not their thoughts or values. As Hume proclaimed, "Reason is the slave of the passions."[8] Normative ethics tries to define *should* based upon various methods of reasoning, an approach that the utilitarian philosopher R. M. Hare described as "prescriptivism."[9]

This essential distinction between what ought be done and what is actually done in resolving dilemmas in psychiatric practice is critical to our methodology, as normative theories make claims to be universally applicable, which as we will argue in the following section is unworkable as an approach to psychiatric ethics.

Taxonomy of Normative Theories in Psychiatric Ethics

Many theories of ethics have emerged throughout history; however, (with the exception of virtue ethics) the main ideas in moral philosophy relevant to psychiatry have appeared only since the Enlightenment. This is a reflection of the intellectual theme of liberal humanism, which places human reason, unconstrained by political, theological, or social tyranny, at the center of moral philosophy.

In our survey of the field of normative theories in psychiatric ethics, we have categorized them into three domains of approaches—instrumental, reflective, and integrative (Table 1.1).

Instrumental approaches are those that apply a particular methodology to a dilemma and provide an "output," or a concrete recommendation for a course of action to follow in order to resolve a dilemma. Reflective approaches prompt the moral agent to apply a process of reflection in order to arrive at a position in regard to an ethical dilemma that accords with

Table 1.1 A taxonomy of normative theories in psychiatric ethics

Instrumental approaches

  1. Utilitarian ethics
  2. The ethics of duty
  3. The four principles
  4. Casuistry
  5. Common morality theory

Reflective approaches

  6. Virtue ethics
  7. The ethics of care
  8. The ethics of the Other

Integrative approaches

  9. "Political" ethics and the Rawlsian approach to justice in mental health
10. Postmodern ethics or antimodern ethics

a particular value system or consistent approach to moral action. Integrative approaches are applications of various theoretical ideas to specific aspects of clinical practice or social action. Each of these approaches has strengths and limitations in its application to ethical dilemmas in psychiatry.

Instrumental Approaches to Psychiatric Ethics

Utilitarianism

Introduction

Many philosophers have argued that a "good life" maximizes pleasure, defined as "the absence of pain." This is the moral philosophy of ethical hedonism, which dates from antiquity. One of the first proponents of ethical hedonism, Epicurus, wrote:

> Pleasure is our first and kindred good. It is the starting-point of every choice and of every aversion, and to it we come back, inasmuch as we make feeling the rule by which to judge of every good thing.[10]

Following on from this, the philosophy of "consequentialism" takes the position that the merit of any act is evident in its ultimate consequences. When integrated with ethical hedonism, this approach to moral philosophy holds that the merit of any act is the amount of overall pleasure it generated. This is the philosophy of utilitarianism. Utilitarianism was first articulated by English philosopher Jeremy Bentham,[11] who argued that all humans were beholden to a form of hedonism and as such any moral and political philosophy should aim to maximize pleasure within the population. Bentham's somewhat vulgar form of utilitarianism argued it was better to be a contented pig than an unhappy human. It may be that there is a survival advantage for species that practice utilitarian approaches in that elevating collective over individual needs may help groups thrive in challenging settings of threat or environmental adversity.[12] Indeed, utilitarianism has been so dominant as a moral philosophy in the modern era that it represents the theoretical starting point for all ethical considerations.[13]

Utilitarianism evolved from this into a credible ethical theory through the philosophical works of other British philosophers such as John Stuart Mill[14,15] and Henry Sidgwick.[16] We have summarized the key steps in the evolution of utilitarianism in Table 1.2.

Fundamental Problems of Utilitarianism

One of the initial problems with the concept of hedonistic utilitarianism is the "quantification problem,"[17] i.e., how do we quantify the level of pleasure achieved by a moral act? This invites the considerations of the merits of different pleasures relative to each other. How can an argument be made that staged wrestling matches are less worthy pleasures than a Mahler symphony? There is simply no way to argue that any one form of pleasure is more worthy than another. The quantification problem is better resolved by considering preferences rather than pleasure. This "preference utilitarianism," advanced largely by controversial Australian philosopher Peter Singer,[18] advocates that individuals' or groups' preferences, rather than gratifying pleasures, should be the focus of a utilitarian deliberation.

The first problem with preference utilitarianism is the issue of adaptive preferences, whereby gratification of people's preferences are compromised in that they tend to accept less, because of modest expectations (such as in the parable of the contented slave).[19] The second

Table 1.2 Key concepts in the evolution of utilitarianism

Author	Key concepts	Other issues
Bentham (1748–1832)	Maximizing utility is to maximize the total amount of pleasure in society.[11]	Preferable to be "a contented pig" than an unhappy human. Higher pleasures not preferable to base ones; pushpin is as good as poetry. Runs into the quantification problem, i.e., how to measure pleasure.
Mill (1806–1873)	Cultural, intellectual, and spiritual pleasures are of greater value than physical pleasures in the eyes of a competent judge.[14,15]	Provides foundation for later formulations of "preference" utilitarianism, i.e., the good relates to satisfaction of greatest number of preferences. "Act" and "Rule" utilitarianism distinction later outlined by J.J.C. Smart.[21]
Sidgwick (1838–1900)	Outlines a method of moral philosophy based on Universal Hedonism (utilitarianism).[16]	Sidgwick's ideas provide the foundation of current conception of utilitarianism and highlight some conflicts between personal and collective pleasure. Rejects motivations as a basis of morality, rather sees common sense as the basis of ethical choice.
G. E. Moore (1837–1958)	No true conception of the ethical good could be formulated. Maximizing "ideals," like aestheticism or love preferred to mere pleasure.[22]	Advances the notion of what is later dubbed "informed preferences" and economic views of personal preferences.
R. M. Hare (1919–2002)	Levels of moral thinking— "practical" is utilitarian and "analytic" is more complex.[9,23]	Sees Kant's "Kingdom of Ends" as utilitarian in spirit.[23,24] Advances a form of utilitarianism as a method of psychiatric ethics.[25]
Popper (1902–1994)	"Negative utilitarianism" as the responsibility to prevent the greatest amount of harm or evil.[26]	Argument against negative utilitarianism is the so-called pinprick argument, which states it would be better to painlessly destroy humanity than to allow one person to experience a pinprick.[27] Also criticized by J.J.C. Smart.[28]
Singer (1942–)	Utilitarianism requires equal consideration of those interests, whatever the species.[18] Utilitarian ideas are a form of naturalism— suppressing individual need for that of the collective has survival advantages.[12]	Concept of diminishing marginal utility argued. Adopts a journey model of life, which sees validity of claim to consideration of preferences based in sentience and the stage or capacity to meet life goals. Singer's views are polemic and have led to heated debate, in particular over the manner in which his philosophy appears to validate euthanasia and abortion.[29]

problem is the issue of unexperienced preferences (i.e., ones we will never know existed) and preferences that may be harmful.[13] The third problem is external preferences, in which the individual's desires regarding the distribution of preferences to others are considered. An example of this is the idea that a population is allowed to express preferences for how the law deals with the access of homosexual couples to public funding for assisted reproduction. In the light of this, some have argued that preference utilitarianism as a basis of public policy should be limited to goods that are universally desired or provide basic necessity.[20]

One of the challenges to moral philosophy is the nature of moral truths as compared with factual truths. English philosopher R. M. Hare, a prominent utilitarian, identified the problem of "prescriptivism" in moral reasoning.[9,30] Put simply, prescriptive moral statements containing *should* or *ought* have a different status, and verifiability, than those referring to fact. "You should do A" is a different proposition from "this is an A." As such, Hare sought to define conditions in which prescriptive moral statements could be valid. Hare identified two conditions for prescriptive statements—universalizability and the so-called golden rule. Hare's utilitarianism extended from this approach.[9] Hare distinguished between two levels of utilitarian thinking. The first is the "critical" level of thinking, applying the golden-rule argument—could a particular act be considered as the best approach in all circumstances? The second level of utilitarian thinking is the "intuitive" level that utilizes simple consequentialist principles.[31] In confronting an ethical dilemma, one deliberates *prima facie* using a simple consequentialist approach, i.e., which approach has the best outcome for the most. In Hare's method, one then deliberates at the critical level, considering whether such an act is virtuous, legal, or practical. The conclusions of the intuitive level must therefore be acceptable at the critical level. English philosopher Bernard Williams argued that few people are capable of such deliberation, which gives way to an elitist view that the critical-level utilitarian thinking is the domain of only the enlightened few, or what he described as "government house utilitarianism."[17]

The distinction between intuitive and critical levels has evolved into *act* and *rule* utilitarianism.[21] In act utilitarianism the moral agent decides to act on the basis of what is most likely to maximize utility in a particular instance. Rule utilitarianism, in contrast, is more prescriptive and has the moral agent acting relative to the notion of maximizing preferences generally, rather than in regard to the specific instance.

Evaluating Utilitarianism as a Basis for Psychiatric Ethics

The advantages of utilitarianism as an ethical theory lie in its intuitive appeal, particularly its apparent scientific approach to ethical reasoning.[21] Medical ethicists Tom Beauchamp and James Childress see the strengths of utilitarianism in its output power, practicality, and clarity.[32] They argue that utilitarianism fits well with approaches to public policy. There have, however, been a number of challenges to utilitarianism.

The first is the "replaceability problem."[33] This is based upon a thought experiment involving the utilitarian justification of one healthy person being killed to provide transplant organs for a half a dozen others in need. Another scenario is whether we would kill one man to save dozens of others.[17] Many have argued that these challenges are somewhat "straw man" in nature (i.e., reducing utilitarianism to a simplistic view to justify criticism of it). Utilitarian approaches to ethics work extremely well in common situations, and the elaborate or unrealistic scenarios devised by the critics of utilitarianism are not good arguments against it.[34] Rather than be purely beholden to the principle of utility in a vacuum, the moral agent should also reflect upon the critical level of Hare, such as how a utilitarian act relates to issues such as one's duty to other persons. The alternative is the unrealistic prospect of the "U-Agent,"[35] who is totally devoid of any personal morality and wedded to his or her utilitarian abacus. In reality, physicians incorporate agent-relative values in considering a utilitarian calculation morally wrong if its consequences affront the basic tenets of a healing profession.[36] Workable forms of utilitarianism-based professional ethics require adherence to a process of critical reflection to promote the welfare of others.[37]

The other main criticism of utilitarianism is the notion that moral agents are responsible for all of the consequences of their choices, including the failure to prevent negative consequences and the consequences of consequences, placing an unreasonable burden.[17] The more balanced view appears to be that the responsibility for ongoing consequences of utilitarian choice should diminish over time.[38]

Utilitarianism and Psychiatry

Hare has advanced a version of utilitarianism as a workable basis for psychiatric ethics,[25] applying his previous work in moral theory.[23] Hare argued that utilitarian accounts of psychiatric ethics are often abandoned unnecessarily because of the conflict between agent-relevant duties of psychiatrists toward their patients. Hare suggested that psychiatrists

> need not think like utilitarians; they can cleave to principles expressed in terms of rights and duties and may, if they do this, achieve better the aims that an omniscient utilitarian would than if they themselves did any utilitarian calculation (p. 30).[25]

Peter Singer's writings of utilitarianism introduced a controversial "principle of equality" encompassing all beings (including other species) with interests and, therefore, preferences.[18] While all species prefer to avoid pain, only sentient humans maintain an interest in cultivating their unique individual abilities, through gratifying their informed preferences. Singer considers this distinction as the justification of differential consideration of different preferences. Singer then articulates a concept of "diminishing marginal utility," in which the utilitarian consideration of preferences considers both the *need* as well as the *desire* for the preference. This elaborates into a journey model of life, which measures the merits of how preferences fit within a life journey's goals. A personal interest in continuing to live and not suffer in order to fulfil an individual life journey is the highest order of preference in utilitarian calculations. Singer's utilitarianism thus justifies both euthanasia and termination of pregnancies carrying fetuses with profound deformations.[29]

Extending Singer's views to psychiatry may lead to some unpalatable conclusions. Mental illness, by its very nature, thwarts a life journey's goals compared with other forms of physical illness. Many severe forms of schizophrenia engender profound levels of impairment of individual life projects, particularly where the clinical picture is dominated by negative symptoms or disorganization. Comparing the different prognostic implications of psychiatric diagnoses leads to distinctions made on the value-laden concept of quality of life. Applying Singer's variation of utilitarianism to psychiatry, the preference of a person with severe, intractable schizophrenia to avoid suffering is placed second to the desire of the patient with phobic anxiety to return to university and continue a fulfilling life's journey. Moreover, in the utilitarian-based public policy decisions about the allocation of limited health resources, the diminishing marginal utility doctrine takes on even more significance, as the preferences of many in society are gratified by the mildly disabled returning to employment and contributing to society through individual fulfillment, rather than the preferences of those patients with severe psychiatric disability to avoid or reduce suffering. This also introduces a variant of the quantification problem.

Psychiatrists are in part responsible for the economic aspects of treatment decisions.[39] The international standard measure of utility in this regard is the Disability Adjusted Life Year (DALY) [40] and the Quality Adjusted Life Year (QALY).[41] Singer argues that the use of QALY justifies the favoring of the preferences of those not severely disabled by mental illness,[42] despite the fact that these are insensitive measures applied to psychiatric disorders.[43]

In recent times two factors extraneous to psychiatry may have promoted the position of utilitarianism in psychiatric ethics. First, legislated responsibilities of psychiatrists, particularly in relation to issues of public safety, have effectively trumped any ethical code of conduct intrinsic to the psychiatric profession.[44] Such legal imperatives are invariably utilitarian in nature and have usually emerged in the context of social and political responses to issues such as public safety.[45,46] This has led to utilitarian justifications of the otherwise vexed "double-agent role" in regard to forensic patients.[47]

The other factor promoting utilitarian thinking in psychiatric ethics has been the profound changes to healthcare systems in the face of globalization and financial pressures, particularly in the United States and Australia. Indeed, as Allen Dyer has stated, medicine has become a three-way relationship between doctor, patient, and third-party provider.[7] This issue was given close consideration by psychiatric ethicists Stephen Green and Sidney Bloch, who identified that when applied to mental healthcare decisions in a managed care setting in the United States, the problem emerged that "maximizing the common good encompasses a central limitation—the indifference to the uniqueness of the person."[48] Green and Bloch go so far as to suggest that the psychiatrist may be ethically compromised in submitting to a market-driven approach in the management of mental illness.

Ethics of Duty

Introduction

Deontic refers to duty (from the ancient Greek *déon*, meaning "that which is binding or proper"). The ethics of duty, or deontic ethics, is usually attributed to eighteenth century German philosopher Immanuel Kant. Kant's moral philosophy is outlined in three main works: *Groundwork for the Metaphysics of Morals* (or *Groundwork*; 1785),[49] *Critique of Practical Reason* (1787),[50] and *Metaphysics of Morals* (1797).[51] To Kant, the central ethical question was prescriptive: "What ought I do?" Kant valued human reason, and this dictated that the answer to this question had no reference to a conception of what was good or any concept of virtue. Kant sought, in essence, principles of action, which could be adopted by anyone without any specificity about desires, circumstances, or social relations. In developing a prescription for duties, Kant differentiated between so-called perfect duties, which are required of all moral agents at all times, and imperfect duties. The latter refers to somewhat of a double negative—not neglecting our duties to others in need.

Kant's Ethics

Kant's philosophy is a product of the Enlightenment, the period, beginning in the late eighteenth century around the time of the French Revolution in which the principles of liberty, fraternity, and equality challenged the divine right of kings and religious scholasticism to control society. An intellectual movement, liberal humanism, evolved in tandem with the political changes of the Enlightenment. Liberal humanism (what is now termed *modernism*) was based upon the human capacity for rational thought and was characterized by notions of absolute truth, i.e., that the world can be controlled, represented accurately, and understood. Enlightenment thinkers believed in ordered, linear progress and the idea that history progressed according to an overall idea, theme, or what was termed *metanarrative*. Kant had proclaimed that the motto of the Enlightenment was *sapere aude* (dare to know).

The two key concepts in Kant's ethical philosophy are the notions of individual autonomy and duty. Kant defined *autonomy* as the capacity for free, rational moral choice—the ability of a person to formulate his or her own laws of morality. This is a form Kant described as "practical reason," in which man is not beholden to divine commands or superstition, but rather a notion of secular morality based upon rational thought. Kant rejected other forms of moral action, such as those based upon emotions or filial bonds. To Kant, the sign of a good moral agent is little more than the possession of good will or dedication to duty. The moral worth of an act is its relationship to a good will—not its intentions or consequences. In other words, deontic ethics can be reduced to the notion of doing the right thing for the right reasons.

Kant's conception of autonomy is therefore profoundly different from the more modern conception of autonomy as the right to negative liberty, i.e., the liberty to pursue one's own ends, to satisfy one's desires, and to exercise freedom of choice, without the undue interference of others or of the state. In Kant's "Kingdom of Ends," each moral agent is both a moral self-legislator and also beholden to a common law. Kant did not believe in individual autonomy existing at the expense of the rule of law.

The issue of duty is defined in Kant's ethics as the notion of the "Categorical Imperative" (CI), articulated in *Groundwork*. Kant argued that, in day-to-day dilemmas, we develop maxims that guide decision. The universalizability of moral maxims is tested against the CI.

The CI has multiple formulations.[49] The first formulation articulates the principle of universalizability by directing:

> Act only according to that maxim whereby you can at the same time will that it should become a universal law. (p. 421)

The second formulation of the CI is the injunction:

> Act as if the maxim of your action were to become through your will a universal law of nature. (p. 421)

Arguably, this formulation of the CI seeks to define a relationship between the laws of nature and the moral law.

Kant's third formulation of the CI is often dubbed "the formula of humanity." It reads,

> Act in such a way that you treat humanity, whether in your own person or in the person of another, always at the same time as an end and never simply as a means. (p. 429)

If ethics is a guide to relations between people, then this is the most important of Kant's ethics. The purpose of good actions is respect for people as beings who are intrinsically valuable. To understand how the CI works, one must first define a moral law which is universalizable and in some way naturalistic. Kant wrote of the specific example of lying. Even though a lie may have desirable consequences, it does not occur in accordance with good will and is therefore unethical. Based upon the application of the CI to lying, people develop a set of maxims (specific rules for different situations) that they apply to their moral agency. The third test is whether these maxims value humans intrinsically or not. One can see a contrast here between Kant's view of ethics and that of the utilitarians. It may be quite feasible to lie in the eyes of a utilitarian, if the desired result maximizes preferences or pleasure. To Kant, lying is never permissible, regardless of the consequences.

Kant's formula of humanity is his main argument against suicide. Kant argues that destroying oneself in order to avoid pain or achieve another end violates the formula of humanity. He argues in *Groundwork*.[49]

> To annihilate the subject of morality in one's person is to root out the existence of morality itself from the world as far as one can, even though morality is an end in itself. Consequently, disposing of oneself as a mere means to some discretionary end is debasing humanity in one's person. (p. 423)

The intrinsic value of people, core to the practice of psychiatry, is justified in the fourth formulation of the CI. This defines the "idea of the will of every rational being as a will that legislates universal law"[49] (p. 431). To Kant, people are intrinsically valuable because they are free, rational (or autonomous) agents. This reflects the original view of Aristotle, who saw that human functioning was ultimately based in human capacity for reason. It is also significant in the context of psychiatric ethics, given the impairment of reason that is a fundamental part of severe mental illness. Much of psychiatric ethics is focused upon situations where self-legislation and reason are impaired, so Kant's formula of autonomy is arguably diminished in the context of mental illness. In other words, the formula of humanity, the basis of our ethical obligations to people, is compromised in the context of mental illness.

Kantian Ethics

Contemporary deontic ethics are not specific applications of Kant's writings. Baroness O'Neill of Bengarve[52] distinguishes between Kant's ethics and "Kantian ethics." The distinction lies within the neo-Kantian ideas of writers such as the late American philosopher John Rawls, whose description of liberal autonomy is Kantian in spirit. Moreover, there has been some revisionism in the interpretation of some of Kant's ethics, particularly his use of the phrase *Menscheit*, interpreted as either "humanity" or "man."[53] It has been argued that the phrase "humanity in a person" in his *Groundwork* refers to the characteristics of personhood. Humanity is distinct from animality by the capacity to define ends of intelligent behavior. As such, humanity must be respected even though the most foolish or impaired may "throw away" one's humanity.[53] This latter interpretation appears to factor in the limitations to the formula of humanity posed by mental illness.

Problems with Kantian Ethics

Kant's ethics have numerous limitations. O'Neill lists common criticisms of Kant's ethics (Table 1.3).[52]

Many find the concept of acting purely from duty morally repugnant. Acting from duty does not really countenance compassion for others but is merely fulfilling a responsibility. This would seem an anathema to a psychiatrist dedicated to the relief of human suffering. Moreover, acting merely from duty and denying human impulses such as care, empathy, or compassion may nurture attitudes of objectification toward others. If we have mere obligations toward the psychiatric patients, rather than care or compassion for people who suffer from mental illness, we run the risk of objectifying our patients. Some have argued that examples of the "all-too-obedient soldier, or the good Nazi citizen who overcomes feelings of compassion to turn in the Jews hiding in the neighbour's home" (p. 117) are arguments against Kantian ethics.[54]

Table 1.3 O'Neill's critique of Kant's ethics

1. *Formalism*—The Categorical Imperative is empty or vacuous.
2. *Rigorism*—Deontic ethics are rigid and insensitive sets of rules with no nuance or subtlety.
3. *Abstraction*—The Categorical Imperative is too abstract to guide action.
4. *Conflicting Grounds of Observation*—There is no guide as to what to do when duties come into conflict.
5. *Place of the Inclinations*—Deontic ethics do not account for moral impulses.
6. *No Account of Wrong Doing*—Deontic ethics provide no guide as to wrong actions.

Source: After O'Neill, O., in *A Companion to Ethics* (ed. P. Singer), Oxford, Blackwell, 1991, 175–185.

Kantian Ethics and Psychiatry

Despite the prominence of Kantian ethics in moral philosophy, very little has been written about their specific application to psychiatry. The Kantian concept of autonomy is qualitatively different from the conception usually applied in biomedical ethics; however, the notion of reason as the mark of human function is a useful construct in psychiatry. Aristotle's idea that human flourishing is one of excellence in reason has been argued as a critical issue in understanding mental health and illness.[55,56] The core of mental illness is a harmful dysfunction of that rational capacity, and this has been recently debated as a key ethical issue in the provisions of mental health legislation in the Australian state of New South Wales.[57,58]

Kant's *Menscheit* concept may help us approach patient autonomy in psychiatry in a different way. By way of example, the *Code of Ethics* for the Royal Australian and New Zealand College of Psychiatrists (RANZCP)[44] directs its fellows to "respect the essential humanity" of their patients. The Kantian construct of the human person as a rational being, able to construct maxims of rational moral action, helps us to conceptualize what is involved in this principle. The essence of the humanity of our patients is not in their suffering, their circumstances, or their rights as citizens but in their capacity to legislate moral action. Kant's formula of humanity thus highlights that any action we take in regard to our patients must be beholden to their reason, no matter how deviant it may seem relative to our own. This then guides us as to what the essence of mental illness may be. Jerome Wakefield argued, convincingly, that a theory of mental illness must entail "harmful dysfunction"[59,60] and saw the dysfunction in evolutionary, nonrelativist terms. In the Kantian perspective, the dysfunction is in that of rational autonomy. The rational capacity that facilitates moral action is the function that must be impaired for the patient to be subject to coercive or involuntary treatment. Moreover, the restoration of that reason is the goal of psychiatric intervention. The *Menscheit* concept is not focused upon actions or choices but rather upon the capacity to make such choices.

In terms of duties, one might take the view that codes of ethics are prescriptive duties and, as such, are Kantian in spirit. The proscription by various professional bodies of the exploitation of patients, whether sexual, financial, or for research, is clearly relevant to the third formulation of the CI. Such duties guide action in all circumstances, without regard to contextual factors. The devil is in the detail of the notion of a universal law. For a law to be truly universal is to assert that any psychiatrist at any time would accept such a fact. Prescriptive duties such as RANZCP *Code of Ethics* Principle #2, "Psychiatrists shall not misuse the inherent power differential in their relationships with patients, either sexually or in any other way," or Principle #6, "Psychiatrists shall not misuse their professional knowledge and skills," rely on a question begging argument as to what the term *misuse* means. These are surely the most relativistic of all injunctions, relying on value judgments as to the core concept of *misuse*. While a different category from the charges that Kantian obligations to duty gave oxygen to the projects of "dutiful ethnic cleanser(s)"[61] like Nazi functionaries, the idea that the maxims specified in codes of conduct like the RANZCP's are truly timeless and universal are problematic. In the 1930s, when "mental hygiene" was the dominant paradigm in psychiatry, would the sterilization of mentally ill people to eradicate mental illness from the population be considered a misuse of knowledge? As has been claimed, "The past is another country. They do things differently there."[62]

Principles-Based Ethics

Introduction

Principles-based ethics has become the dominant paradigm in Western medical ethics.[32,63,64] It is a method of ethical reasoning first developed for biomedical ethics by the American philosophers Tom Beauchamp and James Childress. The method owes much to the work of W. D. Ross, who argued that ethical duties were related to *prima facie* responsibilities to irreducible ethical principles.[65] It is also influenced by a form of common morality governing public behavior[66] advocating that when approaching moral dilemmas, physicians deliberate a conflict between four core principles[65]:

1. *Respect for autonomy*: respecting the decision-making capacities of people and enabling individuals to make reasoned informed choices
2. *Beneficence*: considering the balance of benefits of treatment against the risks and costs so as to act in a way that benefits the patient
3. *Nonmaleficence*: avoiding causing harm to the patient, or at least harm disproportionate to the benefits of treatment
4. *Justice*: distributing benefits, risks, and costs fairly and treating patients in similar positions in a similar manner

These four principles, often referred to as the 4Ps, are the cornerstones of Beauchamp and Childress's "principles-based ethics." These four principles have taken on an almost canonical prominence in some quarters, although other authors have advocated the addition of other principles, such as mutuality,[67] confidentiality, or veracity.[67]

Psychiatrists commonly face ethical dilemmas around the issue of involuntary treatment. Within a four-principles approach, these dilemmas can be easily couched in terms of a *prima facie* conflict of the patient's autonomous choice to refuse treatment and the need for beneficence to relieve suffering (Figure 1.1). In many circumstances, the conflict is vitiated by the effects of mental illness, such as psychosis, on the patient's capacity for autonomy, and the scales are therefore tipped toward the beneficent obligation to relieve the patient's suffering. When the patient's autonomy is not so clearly diminished, such as cases involving the involuntary treatment of personality-disordered patients or those who abuse alcohol, the deliberations required become more complex. In those circumstances, a more detailed consideration of the effects of the patient's psychopathology upon autonomy, and the anticipated benefits of treatment, is required.

Autonomy in the 4Ps

Many of the conflicts mediated by the four principles involve clashes with the principle of autonomy in this sense. Autonomy is the principle of individual self-rule or self-governance. It is now enshrined in the liberties and rights of modern liberal states. One author has defined

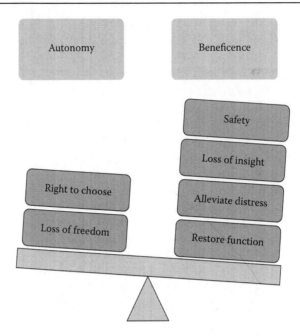

Figure 1.1 The *prima facie* deliberation on the issue of involuntary treatment.

autonomy in terms of "mental state utilitarianism"[68] or a state of self-regulation, based upon reason and self-interest. In the moral philosophy of Beauchamp and Childress there are at least four aspects to autonomy:[69]

1. The capacity to govern oneself
2. The actual condition of self-government
3. A personal ideal
4. A set of rights expressive of one's sovereignty over oneself

Neo-Kantians, such as Harvard professor Christine Korsgaard, see autonomy as the source of all personal obligations, since it relates to our capacity to impose these upon on ourselves.[70] Beauchamp and Childress[32] contend that all theories of autonomy accord with the issues of liberty and agency.

The principle of autonomy is critical in psychiatric ethics. Reason and agency are faculties that can be profoundly affected by mental illness and its treatment.[71] The concept of autonomy in principles-based ethics is focused more on autonomous choice rather than issues of self-governance. Autonomy as one of the 4Ps focuses upon normal choosers who act intentionally, with self-control and understanding of their actions.

While autonomy is ostensibly on a par with the other principles, it tends to prevail in *prima facie* conflicts.[72] Moreover, autonomy is argued to be conceptually prior to the other principles,[73] valorizing it over the others. As prominent bioethicist Robert Veatch has argued,

my own observation is that autonomy has had far and away a pride of place in practice. Justice has given it some competition, but most contemporary theories of justice (for example, Rawls) have an individualistic point of departure anyway; and most renderings of beneficence have had about them the flavor of religion or goody-goodiness, sure losers in the secular world of public policy.[74]

The centrality of autonomy in moral philosophy is predominantly a phenomenon of the liberal West. Given that much of the discourse in bioethics has been Anglo-American, it is clear how autonomy has emerged as a first among equals of principles.

Criticisms of the 4Ps Approach

The undoubted strengths of the 4Ps approach are its clarity and simplicity. In an Anglo-American context, it has dominated the field of bioethics. The approach is not, however, free of significant problems. Many of the advocates of the 4Ps approach have claimed that it represents a universal approach to ethics.[61] It has been advocated as a credible method of medical ethics in cultural settings, including Islamic societies,[75] some African cultures,[76] and in Judaism,[77] but others question its application outside the English-speaking world.

Indeed, patient autonomy, the very center of the 4Ps approach, has been described by Georgetown University medical ethicist Edmund Pellegrino as "a cultural artefact."[78] This position is supported by a series of studies[79–81] that have provided a cross-cultural comparison of autonomy in medical ethics between American and Japanese physicians. In Japanese patients, prioritizing individual autonomy may isolate patients from their families and ultimately compromise patient care.[80] In Japanese culture, diagnostic and prognostic information is often withheld from patients at the request of family members.[79] In the vexed issue of suicide in Japanese culture, issues of autonomy are quite peripheral to the ethical considerations around the area.[81] In African cultures, autonomy is subjugated by communal bonds and responsibilities and is of peripheral relevance in ethical deliberation.[76] In post-Communist Russia, physicians are still primarily beholden to the state, despite attempts to legislate on behalf of patient autonomy.[82] In China, bioethical discourse is revisiting traditional morality as a reaction to "a naïve acceptance of North American and Western European moral philosophical approaches and the bioethical perspectives they produced."[83]

Taking other lines of criticism, American ethicist K. Danner Clouser dubbed the 4Ps approach "principlism" and criticized its apparent vacuity and incoherence.[84] Along with fellow American Bernard Gert, Clouser has also criticized "principlism" as doing little more than providing a checklist of obligations with no specific guidance in mediating a *prima facie* conflict. It is often not clear, for example, where the limits of an ethical deliberation are to be drawn. Gert and Clouser also regard Beauchamp and Childress' assertion that beneficence or nonmaleficence are substantive principles of obligation as being superficial.[85] In response, Beauchamp and Childress have acknowledged Clouser and Gert's critique as being based on a fallacy of relevance—"correct but irrelevant" (p. 390). They responded that the 4Ps had never purported to place their theory on the same footing as other grand ethical theories.[32]

Another critic of the 4Ps is the philosopher of medicine H. Tristram Engelhardt, Jr., who defines the 4Ps as a form of "procedural morality," merely providing a "non-foundational approach" to bioethics.[86] Engelhardt prefers the principle of "permission" rather than autonomy, as permission is constitutive and is philosophically prior to the principle of beneficence. Beneficence is a negotiated or contractarian arrangement, not a universal, foundational principle in Engelhardt's eyes. He describes both autonomy and beneficence as "chapter headings" functioning merely to "indicate the sources of certain moral rights and obligations" (p. 103). If permission is constitutive and beneficence negotiated, then the former is the only substantive component of morality. Moreover, Englehardt does not see justice or nonmaleficence as being substantive, seeing the former as redundant and defining the latter as applied beneficence.

Engelhardt distinguishes between "moral friends" sharing a "contentful" ethics and "moral strangers" who consent to a mutually agreed upon set of rules of behavior. As such, he sees that the 4Ps work only when there is an approximation of views between moral strangers—the 4Ps approach is only "feasible when individuals with the same or very similar moral visions or thin theories of the good and justice have reconstructed their moral sentiments within divergent theoretical approaches" (p. 56). To Engelhardt the method of the 4Ps is a helpful device

1. To resolve moral controversies between individuals with similar moral sentiments but different approaches
2. To explore the ways different theories reconstruct the same set of moral sentiments or intuitions
3. To elaborate differences between moral views and their implications for bioethics
4. To resolve controversies between those who do not share the same moral vision or sense

Others have criticized the 4Ps as "imposing a sort of straitjacket on thinking about ethical issues" that "encourage(s) a one dimensional approach and the belief that this approach is all that ethical thinking requires."[87] By this line of criticism, the method's key strength—its simplicity—becomes its major failing.

Casuistry

Introduction

Casuistry is a method of ethical reasoning that is analogous to the common law based in precedents, which guide subsequent legal judgments. The most comprehensive account of the historical background of the method of casuistry is provided by British philosopher Stephen Toulmin and ethicist and former Jesuit priest Albert Jonsen in their 1988 book *The Abuse of Casuistry*.[88] They argue that the first account of case-based reasoning can be found in the orations of the ancient Roman figure Cicero. In the early Christian church, the idea of case-based or precedent-based dispensation of penance in the confessional is documented in the *Penetentials*. In medieval times, clerics utilized the method of *casus conscientiae* (cases of conscience), which would study and discuss difficult or troubling cases. The method of "high casuistry" reached its apotheosis in the hands of the Jesuits in sixteenth century Europe. The controversial influence of the Jesuits, as well as their reputation for sophistry, made casuistry controversial. Casuistry is a critical component of our methodology in psychiatric ethics.

Method of Casuistry

The modern incarnation of casuistry appears to start with Jonsen and Toulmin's work,[88] who argued that moral reasoning had to be based upon algorithms that are applicable to difficult moral choices. They argued that there are clear sets of moral paradigms (*prima facie* duties) and that precedent or test cases exist, allowing comparison between the matter at hand and the precedent case. As such, casuistic reasoning avoids the perils of moral absolutism and relativism.

Jonsen subsequently articulated a more specific methodology for casuistry,[89–91] defining a case as an "event" or a "happening."[90] He emphasizes that a "case" is a manifestation of a set of circumstances surrounding a set of maxims or principles, the center of a dilemma or quandary. In psychiatry, a case may involve the central maxim of respect for autonomy with circumstances relating to the notion of placing a patient's financial affairs under the control of a third party. The test case, or paradigm, may be that of a patient with a severe, chronic psychotic illness, whose incompetence results in financial exploitation and disadvantage such as homelessness or profound self-neglect. The case at hand may involve a patient whose alcohol abuse is problematic and the imposition of financial restrictions upon the patient primarily aimed at restricting access to alcohol.

The method of casuistry seeks to order the circumstances of the case relative to the central maxims involved. The first task of the casuist is to consider the various components of the situation.[90]

Jonsen's method of analysis nominates four special topics of significance in clinical applications of ethics:[91]

1. *Medical Indications*—assessment of the objective clinical issues in relation to the case
2. *Patient Preferences*—acknowledgment of the individual values and expectations of the patient
3. *Quality of Life*—consideration of the overarching goal of the physician in the alleviation of suffering and the enhancement of quality of life
4. *Contextual Features*—the broad sociocultural, historical, and psychological circumstances in which the case occurs

Jonsen argues that in the method of evaluating the case in question, the casuist proceeds in the order specified. This does not indicate that any one topic is prioritized over another but rather ensures consistency in the method.

Jonsen's method then applies a taxonomic procedure to the cases of relevance to the case at hand. In essence, this taxonomy of cases involves lining up cases in rank order from the paradigmatic case to the case at hand. The order of these cases is determined by their similarities to the paradigm case. As the features of the particular case are identified and the similarities to the paradigm are established, the case is ordered along the line. The further down the order of similarity to the paradigm case, the less "kinesis" the case possesses— Jonsen offers the metaphor of a billiard ball losing kinetic energy the further it rolls from the source of movement. As such, the more distant a case appears to be from the paradigm case in the order of cases, the less applicable are the conclusions of the paradigm case to the case at hand (Figure 1.2).

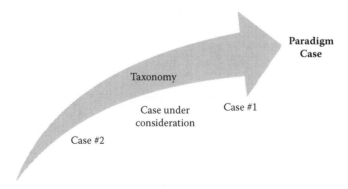

Figure 1.2 The method of casuistry—cases are assembled into a taxonomy of cases, with cases most resembling the paradigm case situated closest to it. When the case under consideration is placed in this taxonomic arrangement, the strength of the conclusion that the case under consideration warrants the same treatment as the paradigm case can be evaluated.

This method is identical to the critical approach of normative analogy, whereby the merits of a proposition (the subject) are compared with those of a precedent proposition (the analog). The subject and analog of the normative analogy are first compared in terms of the presence of similarities between the two. The more similarities between the subject and the analog, relevant to the ultimate conclusion in relation to the analog, the stronger the normative analogy. The second phase of a normative analogy is to identify negatively relevant differences between the subject and the analog. These are the points of difference distinguishing the two entities. The more negatively relevant differences, the less justifiable the position that the conclusion that applies to the subject can be applied to the analog.

An example of a normative analogy is that of the entitlements of people with Type II diabetes to compensation from the fast-food industry compared to that of cigarette smokers with lung cancer from the tobacco industry. In the case of the latter, there is a clear causal link between smoking and lung cancer in addition to the addictive properties of nicotine and the fact that much of this research was withheld from the public. In the former, there is less evidence supporting the addictiveness of fast food, less clear causal relationship between the two (factoring in genetics, inactivity, and so on) and no evidence that the fast-food industry has deceived or misled the public. As such, these claims are less robust.

Criticisms of Casuistry

The most famous critique of casuistry was articulated by Blaise Pascal in his *Provincial Letters* (1656).[92] To Pascal, the method of casuistry had come to represent a form of "Jesuitical excuse-making" by the selective construction of arguments.

Despite the intuitive appeal of the methods of casuistry, it still suffers from the problems of the capacity for sophistry through the selective use of paradigm cases.

American bioethicist John Arras argued that casuistry is unlikely to achieve moral consensus outside of particular settings or moral discourses.[93] The critical issue here is the manner in which any moral discourse is constituted, i.e., who or what determines the paradigm case, its conclusions, and the taxonomy of other cases. Two alternate views of discourse are those of German philosopher Jürgen Habermas[94] and Michel Foucault.[95] In Habermas's view, the "truth" of any consensus achieved through discourse is a function of the plurality and egalitarian composition of the "discursive formation" (group discussion). Foucault takes the alternate approach in that he sees knowledge and power in societies as the same phenomenon, and that the composition of the discursive formation is related to power structures in the society.

Casuistry and Psychiatric Ethics

As with principles-based ethics, casuistry presents an ethical procedure, which lacks a substantive foundation. In order to apply casuistry to psychiatric ethics, we would need to derive a series of paradigm cases upon which to base our casuistic method. The lack of undisputed paradigm cases leads to a reliance on famous cases for paradigms, rather than those that have been carefully reasoned. At present, the only recognizable paradigm case is the infamous "Tarasoff case,"[96,97] which involved a failure to warn a prospective victim of the risk of homicide disclosed in a therapy session. The Tarasoff precedent was articulated primarily by lawyers and academic psychiatrists. To use such legalistic cases is to operate under a suppressed assumption that there is integrity between the law and ethics, a notion many would dispute.

An attempt to define what constitutes paradigm cases, particularly in the light of Arras's critique, would need to be derived from a broad consensus of multiple views of psychiatry, and of mental health generally. This resides on the idea of moral discourse and ethical truths relying upon a free, democratic consensus approach to such knowledge. This assumption leads to problems relating to discourse as a form of knowledge in general, and the type of relationship between power and knowledge described by Foucault.[95] The composition of the discursive formation that attempts to define ethical norms instrumental to the development of paradigm cases is a complex undertaking. Any form of moral discourse in defining paradigm cases would need to be based upon preconditions of equality of access, viewpoints, and communication capacities within the discursive formation. Here is an instance where empirical methods in psychiatric ethics have a role.

Common Morality Theory

Introduction

One potential source of a concept of the good life is the values that are held broadly by a society. Citizens in democratic societies vote for lawmakers, whose legislative proposals represent the wishes of the majority of citizens. Such notions of the good life would therefore move away from criticisms that ethical theories represent "ivory tower" views of life.

Elements of the Common Morality

The philosopher Bernard Gert (see above) coined the term *common morality theory*, which reflects the broad values of citizens living in a stable democratic society.[66,98] Such values can be considered descriptive, as they reflect what people actually do in different situations. According to Gert, his normative moral system is based upon five basic harms—death, pain, disability, loss of freedom, and loss of pleasure. From these five harms, Gert derived 10 ethical maxims reflecting the common morality of a society (Table 1.4).

The first five rules directly prohibit inflicting the five basic harms directly, whereas the second five prohibit actions that may cause those same harms indirectly. These 10 moral rules are not absolute in that their violations are not always wrong.

Applying the Common Morality to Ethical Reasoning

Gert described a two-step method for justification of acts that appear to violate these injunctions. The first step is the establishment of all of the morally relevant facts to give an account of the action. This involves answering a series of questions in relation to the act,

Table 1.4 Gert's 10 maxims from the common morality

1. Do not kill.
2. Do not cause pain.
3. Do not disable.
4. Do not deprive of freedom.
5. Do not deprive of pleasure.
6. Do not deceive.
7. Keep your promises.
8. Do not cheat.
9. Obey the law.
10. Do your duty.

including, What moral rule would be violated? What harms would be avoided, prevented, and caused by the rule violation? And what benefits would be caused by the rule violation?

The second step involves estimating the consequences of everyone knowing that one kind of violation is allowed or the consequences of everyone knowing that another kind of violation is not allowed. The likely harmful and beneficial consequences of the two estimates are then compared. If the general knowledge that such violations are allowed leads to a better outcome than a general knowledge that they are not allowed, then the violation is justified. In other words, there is a quasi-consequentialist feature to this approach.

Gert justified his philosophy by arguing that every rational agent would ultimately endorse adopting a moral system that required everyone to act morally in regard to other moral agents. In essence, Gert's philosophy represents a form of social contract. The basic harms would be seen to be almost universalizable in that all rational people would agree that these are the basic values of stable societies. Gert calls this "the blindfold of justice" in that these rules are independent of religious, nationalistic, or scientific beliefs. Gert's original philosophy has formed the basis of an approach to bioethics. It has been argued that medical ethics is little more than an application of common morality to specific medical ethical dilemmas.[84,99–101]

Reflective Approaches to Psychiatric Ethics

Virtue Ethics

Virtue in Antiquity

Most people understand virtue as a quality of moral excellence. In antiquity, the four cardinal virtues were courage, temperance, justice, and prudence. The concept of virtue, or αρετη (arete), is clearly articulated in Aristotle's *Nicomachean Ethics*[102] as "a settled disposition of the mind determining the choice of actions and emotions, consisting essentially in the observance of the mean relative to us ... as the prudent man would determine it" (Book II, Ch. 6). Aristotle had made a study of great men of his time and attempted to define what it was that made them great. He concluded that the definitive character of mankind was the capacity for reason, and so the "ratiocentric thesis" of the good life was central in Aristotle's thought. Happiness, or ευδαιμονια (eudaemonia), was found in the life of rational excellence.

The Aristotelian concept of virtue is a habit of choosing the "golden mean" between the extremes. In the case of justice, for example, the mean lies between being excessively generous or forgiving and being excessively harsh or austere. As such, the habit of choosing the golden mean is a form of dialectic reasoning in that the synthesis of an action or thought arises from the tension between two alternative views.

Phronesis as a Substantive Ethical Model

The habit of finding the mean requires the capacity for prudence or *phronesis* (practical wisdom) in which the virtuous individual possesses the judgment to find the mean and the practical ability to apply it. Phronesis has a number of components[103]:

1. The citation or acknowledgment of specific ethical principles where appropriate
2. The integration of past experience on the present situation
3. The capacity to argue by analogy from paradigm cases to particular ones

4. The capacity to parallel process other issues to guide moral inquiry by, e.g., psychodynamic implications

5. The capacity to combine all four aspects to formulate a mode of praxis

Applied to psychiatry, virtue involves an integration of its goal (*telos*) and the use of skills (*techne*) to achieve it. The virtuous psychiatrist possesses practical wisdom to find the right actions, in the specific role of alleviating suffering of the ill. American bioethicist Ronald Munson highlighted this distinction, to some degree, in the separation of science and medicine: science and the knowledge it created was instrumental rather than intrinsic to medical practice.[104]

Recent Conceptions of Virtue Ethics

More recent incarnations of virtue theory have provided useful points of reflection. The German Jewish philosopher Hannah Arendt traveled to Israel in 1961 to observe the trial of Adolf Eichmann. Adolf Eichmann was an *Oberstrumbannfuehrer* (Lt. Colonel) in the SS in Nazi Germany. In 1942 he coordinated the Wannsee conference, where the so-called Final Solution to the Jewish Question was resolved. Eichmann was tasked with coordinating the deportation and mass murder of millions of European Jews. After the war, he fled to Argentina, where he lived under an alias. Mossad agents kidnapped him in 1960. He was taken to Israel, where he was tried and convicted of crimes against humanity and then hanged. Arendt published her reflections upon this in her now-famous book *Eichmann in Jerusalem*. Arendt realized that the banality of his evil related purely to the failure to reflect upon the nature of his actions and his mindlessly servile attitudes to duty.[105]

> Except for an extraordinary diligence in looking out for his personal advancement, (Eichmann) had no motives at all … He merely, to put the matter colloquially, never realized what he was doing. (p. 114)

Arendt's later development of the concept of virtue distinguished the virtues of individual life and that of the world of action (*viva activa*).[106] For Arendt, the public and private spheres were distinct, the former moving beyond pure self-interest.[107] This revision of virtue ethics clearly occurs in the context of the totalitarian excesses of the twentieth century and raises an issue that is pertinent to contemporary psychiatric ethics: Can the psychiatrist be truly virtuous without taking part in the public or political sphere?

The virtue ethics of Alisdair MacIntyre[108–110] further develop the concept of the socially situated, contextualized virtue. In Athenian society, the concept of the good—αγαθοζ (agathos)—related to how a man discharged his allotted social functions within the community, or *polis*. As such, the measure of the virtue of a man was his functioning as a successful citizen. In ancient Athens, this involved political action. To hold on to this as the archetype of virtue risks anachronistic versions of the moral philosophies, which are "overwhelmingly the creation of dead-white-male heads of household, including some slaveholders and misogynists."[111] This has been a particular focus of MacIntyre's arguments about the limits of all moral philosophies—that they are situated within a particular culture at a particular point in history. MacIntyre's solution is to emphasize the parts of human existence that are universal, such as birth and death, and the establishment of community, or what the feminist philosopher Martha Nussbaum refers to as nonrelative virtues.[112] As such, MacIntyre sees it as inconceivable that friendliness, courage, and truthfulness would not be valued in any society at any historical point.

MacIntyre's concept of practical wisdom integrates virtue, *telos*, *techne*, and *arete*. He considers practices, which are the exercise of human excellence in the pursuit of a collectively defined good. MacIntyre holds that ancient Greek ethics began with society where evaluative language was tied to the concept of a socially established role. He argues that ethical questions "about ourselves and our actions depend on the kind of social structure of which we are a part" (p. 91).[113] In MacIntyre's view, "bricklaying is not a practice; architecture is. Planting turnips is not a practice; farming is" (p.188).[108] Applied to psychiatry, the practice of the virtuous psychiatrist is the pursuit of expert knowledge, sound judgment, and the other components of clinical skill and the application to the conception of a collective good.

The Virtuous Psychiatrist

Applied to biomedical ethics, various authors and professional groups have provided checklists of desirable virtues in physicians, often extrapolated from the four classical virtues. Beauchamp and Childress[32] list compassion, discernment, trustworthiness, integrity, and conscientiousness. Engelhardt[86] lists tolerance, liberality, and prudence as virtues required of a physician. Pellegrino provides a hierarchy of physician virtues, with the most sublime ones necessitating such selfless superogatory acts that they could not be sustained by even the most devoted physician.[114] Indeed, the main critique of virtue ethics as a moral philosophy in psychiatry is that it seems to have impractical expectations of individuals and places the individual amid a potentially disabling psychodynamic process of identification with the idealized ethical superman.[7] American philosopher Jennifer Radden outlined a list of virtues necessary to a psychiatrist[5] (Table 1.5).

Virtue ethics have been proposed as a foundation of psychiatric ethics,[115] with some argument that the sole virtue of phronesis can provide a comprehensive account of ethics in psychiatry[116] or, at the very least, inform more prescriptive codes of ethics in psychiatry.[117]

More recently, Radden collaborated with American psychiatrist and philosopher John Sadler to argue that the ethical practice of psychiatry depends on the specific character of the practitioner. Akin to our position, they argue that the settings within which psychiatry is practiced, such as different institutions or among specific groups, pose ethical challenges to psychiatrists that warrant a specific discourse on psychiatric ethics. In the view of Radden and Sadler, psychiatric trainees ought to abide by the process outlined in the *Nichomachean Ethics* of cultivating habits that develop sensitivities to domains of gender, race, class, and ethnicity.[118]

We have argued previously that, while virtue ethics are of great importance, there are significant limits to theie instrumental value in psychiatric practice.[119] The virtuous

Table 1.5 The desirable virtues of a psychiatrist

1. Compassion
2. Humility
3. Fidelity
4. Trustworthiness
5. Respect for confidentiality
6. Veracity
7. Prudence
8. Warmth
9. Sensitivity
10. Perseverance

Source: After Radden, J., in *The Philosophy of Psychiatry* (ed. J. Radden), New York, Oxford University Press, 2004, 133–146.

psychiatrist reflects upon his or her motivations and the big-picture aspects of his or her actions, usually based upon a balance of utility and duty. The habit of incorporating this process and finding the golden mean is the pathway to *phronesis*, or practical wisdom; and this, in itself, may provide the psychiatrist with a substantive moral philosophy. As such, virtue ethics can provide a means of informing more practical deliberations, such as those based on consequences, or abiding a social contract.

Ethics of Care

Background

One of the main problems in moral philosophy is the failure to recognize the place of caring or emotional bonds between people as the basis of ethical action. This is the focus of the so-called ethics of care. The status of the ethics of care remains indeterminate. Some have argued it to be a substantive moral theory,[120] whereas other views describe an ethics of care as a virtue, a cluster of virtues, or a version of virtue ethics.[121]

The notion of an ethics of care arose as a reaction to the work of American psychologist Lawrence Kohlberg,[122] whose study of latency age and adolescent boys delineated levels of moral thinking. Kohlberg argued that at an early developmental stage, individuals behave according to socially acceptable norms because they are compelled by the threat of punishment. The next developmental level is a form of psychological egoism or self-interest morality, giving way to a "postconventional" level of moral development characterized by the acknowledgment of a social contract and the development of a principled conscience.

Carole Gilligan[123] argued against Kohlberg's finding, stating that his sample was entirely male and that studies of females reveal that they are more focused on caring for others and maintaining social relationships, rather than defining a rational good. In particular, Gilligan highlighted girls' refusal to make moral decisions out of context, their desire to avoid conflict, and their emphasis on relationships in their thinking. While Gilligan was not dismissive of the male "impartial voice of justice," she argues that the two options are complementary. In some circumstances, abstract ethics of justice are a more apposite point of reflection, whereas in other situations the ethics of care are more appropriate. As such, Gilligan argues that morality is better defined as occurring within a network of caring relationships and not a preoccupation with abstract notions of individual autonomy. Ethics entails, in the view of Gilligan, "situation attuned perceptions" to the needs of others regarding the dynamics of a particular relationship and setting. This distinction is not unique to care ethics, as neo-Kantians, such as Baroness O'Neill, have recognized the distinction between impartial justice and emotional bonds.[124]

The ethics of care can be thus considered as "the rejection of impartiality as the mark of the moral."[125] Turkish-American philosopher Seyla Benhabib sees this as the rejection of the "impartial standpoint" of the "generalised other."[126] In other words, the care approach to ethics emerges not out of the duty or obligations we have to the anonymous, objectified "other," but from emotional or compassionate drives toward another person—a fellow human being. This is akin to the central idea of the moral philosophy of Emmanuel Levinas, who argues that our encounter with the face of another confers an identity of another person, not a philosophical "object"[127] (see below).

Later views of the ethics of care, such as those of New Zealand–born philosopher Annett Baier[128,129] and American educationalist Nel Noddings,[130] focus upon the limits of abstract moral theories such as Kant's and how the ethics of care may add to the perspective of the moral agent. Noddings in particular provides a compelling argument in describing that any mother would violate the Categorical Imperative to lie to save her child.[130] Such actions are motivated by care and not by abstract notions of what is right, although such quasi-emotivism has been argued to leave the moral agent open for exploitation.[131]

Ethics of Care and Psychiatry

The ethics of care has been considered in some depth elsewhere.[119] As with the ethics of virtue, the ethics of care has limited instrumental value in clinical settings. It can certainly inform the ethical standpoint,[114] and English psychiatrist Gwen Adshead has argued that the ethics of care and the other abstract ethical theories offer "two voices in psychiatric ethics."[132]

Apart from its limited instrumental value, the ethics-of-care approach to ethics suffers from an inadequate analysis of the concept of *care*, which has been argued to be "hopelessly vague."[133] In lacking a normative or descriptive account of morality, care-related language defines the concept of care as being constitutive of a moral good. This introduces a form of prescriptivism, which argues that actions are good if they are caring. The argument suffers from a suppressed premise that care is constitutive of an ethical good. Moreover, the prescriptive argument that "one ought care" is weakened by a fallacy of ambiguity—caring about how Manchester United Football Club or the Green Bay Packers fare is not the same as care of your family or patients.[134]

In suggesting that the ethics of care is a substantive moral philosophy, American philosopher Virginia Held[120] argued that it has five defining features: First, "the focus of the ethics of care is on the compelling moral salience of attending to and meeting the needs of the particular others for whom we take responsibility" (p. 10). Second, the ethics of care values emotions and appreciates emotions and relational capabilities that enable morally concerned people in actual interpersonal contexts to understand what would be best. Third, the ethics of care rejects the view that the more abstract the reasoning about a moral problem, the better. Fourth, the ethics of care proposes a novel conceptualization of the distinction between private and public moralities and of their respective importance. Finally, the ethics of care adopts a relational conception of people, which is in stark contrast to the rights-based approaches of modern liberal individualism.

Ethics of the Other

Since the Enlightenment, Western philosophy has been based upon the distinction between the *subject* (the knowing self) and the *object*. This arose from the tradition of Descartes' *cogito*, or the thinking, knowing being, engaged with the phenomenal experience of the universe.[135] In Descartes' original formulation, the knowing "philosophical subject" employed a radical doubt of his or her experience and could only truly know his or her "clear and distinct thoughts." Descartes was suspicious of sensory experience as a means of knowledge, speculating that the senses might well be deceived. If one accepts the premise that post-Enlightenment (or what is termed *modernity*) Western philosophy was based upon the work of Descartes, then the individual, and by extension the moral agent, experiences the world, including other people, with radical doubt. By implication, encounters with others imply a priority of existence of the knowing self over the other. Put alternatively, Western philosophy privileges the existence of the individual over the existence of the other. In extreme circumstances, this leads to the objectification of the other person.

In the light of this conclusion, we formulate the problems of Western moral philosophy in the light of modernity as the distinction between the Self and the Other. This, in our estimation, is particularly important as it is frequently the case that psychiatric patients are cast as the Other by the community.

The notion of the Other has a complex philosophical history. German philosopher Johan Gottlieb Fichte originally emphasized the necessity of interaction with other rational beings in order to achieve consciousness,[136] an idea later evident in Hegel's "Master Slave" dialectic.[137] In this idea, Hegel asserts that a solipsistic I has a self-consciousness that is confronted by an encounter with another I. Perhaps after some resistance, the individual acknowledges the equal status of the other individual. This is a profound confrontation, in that the individual subject becomes aware of his or her existence as an object in the consciousness of the other individual. As Hegel described in *Phenomenology of Spirit*:

> On approaching the other it has lost its own self, since it finds itself as another being; secondly, it has thereby sublated that other, for this primitive consciousness does not regard the other as essentially real but sees its own self in the other. (p. 111)[138]

This interaction breaks down the subject–object distinction in both, and the dialectic process that follows creates an ongoing struggle to dominate. The dialectic process is a new form of awareness of oneself in relation to another. The other enslaves each person's consciousness. The meaning of the master–slave metaphor is that the master requires the slave for his or her awareness of existence as the master and vice versa.

The interplay between the philosophical subject and object is evident in the work of Lacan[139] and Sartre, in that through the gaze of the Other, the philosophical subject becomes Other or object. In other words, the subject becomes object (or Other) through the eyes of another. Sartre refers to this as a sense of "shame." In *Being and Nothingness*[140] Sartre used the metaphor of the eavesdropper to illustrate this point. A person is peering at others through a keyhole; Sartre shows how the subject listening to others behind a door becomes the Other or object when another person sees him eavesdropping:

> But all of a sudden I hear footsteps in the hall. Someone is looking at me …
> I shudder as a wave of shame sweeps over me. (pp. 260–277)

This new concept of himself as an object or image in the mind of the Other is called "being-for-others," or *pour-autrui*. This new experience of the self is not known by the subject but rather lived—the eavesdropper is that object captured in the Other's mind. The shame (or in the case of good acts, pride) is revealed in the Other's look. The shame arises from the helplessness of being objectified and alienated from the eavesdropper's original experience of being self. The shame is the eavesdropper's only access to the Other and the Self is therefore only realized through its "alterity" (otherness).[141]

In the context of madness, Scottish antipsychiatrist R. D. Laing argued that ontology (existence) is defined by "models" in the consciousness of others.[142] The nature of emotions and drives in the mentally ill derive from this form of knowledge about the patient. The knowledge of the patient's experience is in the hands of others and, thus in Laing's view, presents a loss of "radical freedom" for them.

The concept of the Other is most readily associated with the French existentialist Simone de Beauvoir. De Beauvoir's *The Second Sex*[143] agrees with the basic tenets of Fichte, Hegel, and Sartre. De Beauvoir's contribution to the area is her description of the Other as embodied of the "radical alterity" of women. The core of de Beauvoir's thesis is that woman is consistently defined as the Other by man, who takes on the role of the Self. This is a status quo manufactured and perpetuated by existing power structures in society. The position of de Beauvoir is that one is not born a woman but becomes woman through ascribed, socially constructed roles. The woman is passive and alienated. This process was revisited in the estrangement of the elderly from society described in de Beauvoir's *The Coming of Age.*[144]

It is remarkable that de Beauvoir does not linger on psychiatry's complicity in what she described as "the myth of the eternal feminine," unlike later feminist writers such as Lucy Irigaray[145] or Paula Kaplan.[146] What is significant to this discussion is the generalizability of de Beauvoir's thesis to other groups of Others.

The Otherness of the psychiatric patient is manifest in the analytic gaze of the psychiatrist, which categorizes and objectifies experiences as illness through the diagnostic act. The experience of Self as Other or object is mediated through diagnostic labels such as borderline personality disorder or posttraumatic stress disorder. The diagnostic act in psychiatry has instrumental value, but from an existential standpoint reduces the patient's experience of suffering or alteration of state of being as a phenomenon to be explained. This is the essence of psychoanalysis and the psychodynamic framework that many psychiatrists employ in their work. Within the medical model, the emotional or cognitive disturbances experienced are categorized and their origins explained in terms of psychopathological mechanisms. Within the therapeutic relationship, the clinician's experience of attempting to impose an order on the patient's experience creates a form of otherness in that the patient becomes a natural phenomenon to be explained.

In approaching a relation between the self and the experience of another, German philosopher Wilhelm Dilthey distinguished between understanding (*verstehen*) and explaining (*erklären*). Dilthey argued, "the inner experience through which I obtain reflexive awareness of my own condition can never by itself bring me to a consciousness of my own individuality. I experience the latter only through a comparison of myself with others."[147] This necessitated the distinction between *verstehen* as a form of interpretative understanding and *erklären*, or a law-governed explanation more suited to the natural sciences, as two ways to make sense of a phenomenon. This is an interpretive or "hermeneutic" process. The process of *erklären* seeks explanatory hypotheses of phenomena through the establishing of universal laws, whereas *verstehen* seeks to understand the phenomenon by looking for the perspective from which it appears to be meaningful and appropriate. Taking the example of a psychiatrist relating to a depressed patient, *verstehen* and *erklären* are technical terms representing two opposed approaches to a comprehension of human experience.[148] The *erklären* might be represented in the physics of neurotransmitters, whereas the latter is the patient's experience of depression and the meanings they attached to it. *Verstehen* has been defined in terms of the subjective experience of the patient, how that experience is communicated, and the actual object of the experience. In paraphrasing the German philosopher and psychiatrist Karl Jaspers, one author argued that the hermeneutic process in psychiatry is continuous, circular, and tolerant of ambiguity.[149]

While the existence of the problems of the Other poses particular challenges for psychiatric ethics, an alternative view of challenges of the Other is posed by the philosophy of Emmanuel Levinas. Levinas was a Lithuanian Jew who spent most of his life in Paris. Levinas's family perished in the Holocaust, and he spent much of World War II in a forced labor camp. His experience of the Nazi era in Europe exerted a profound effect upon his philosophy. Levinas sees that human values reside within the otherness of persons. While Levinas's philosophy was initially derived from the works of phenomenologists such as Husserl and Heidegger, he became critical of Western philosophy's preoccupation with ontology and epistemology. Levinas's philosophy rejected metaphysics, which reduces other people to merely phenomena to be known. Levinas saw Western philosophy as fundamentally flawed by its rationalism and its need to reduce all phenomena to intelligibility—a process he describes as "totalisation."[150] When applied to others, totalization removes any form of difference between people to a sameness to enhance the power of rationalization. A *person* therefore becomes merely one of a genus *people*. Levinas parted company with traditional existentialism in that he rejected the notion that all things can be reduced to the experience of an autonomous individual. In contrast, he described the need to accept the irreducible nature of all Otherness. In *Totality and Infinity*, Levinas argued for equivalence in the relationship between the Self, or "the Same" (*la Même*), and the Other (*l'Autre*).

A prominent scholar of Levinas, English philosopher Simon Critchley, claimed that Levinas's work was characterized by the "one big idea," namely, the notion that ethics was the first philosophy in being "a relation of infinite responsibility to the other person" (p. 6).[151] Levinas placed ethics as prior to all other philosophy. This "ethics" refers to the responsibility to the Other and the rejection of the Self–Other distinction established in Western philosophy. The "ethics of ethics" is "the study of the manner in which foreignness, inexplicability and unpredictability shape the human condition despite the often arrogant demands of rationalism" (p. 16).[152]

The defining point of Levinas' moral philosophy is that the Other does not reveal itself through perception but rather in the face-to-face encounter with the Other.[150] This face-to-face encounter is violent—causing an "earthquake in the horizon of *la Même*."[153] This ethic of the face-to-face encounter is the most intuitive aspect of Levinas's philosophy; it is much harder to ignore a moral responsibility to another person in a face-to-face encounter than in the abstract. Prosopgnosis, or the ability to recognize faces, is a fundamental human quality, as is the capacity to intuit emotional states as evidenced by facial expression. Conditions such as autism are associated with a degree of prosopagnosia[154] and impairment of empathy, which are arguably preconditions of moral responsibility to the other. American military historian S.L.A. Marshall noted that soldiers were averse to killing men at close proximity, whereas artillery and machine gun crews, firing some distance from the enemy, won most battles.[155]

In his memoir of the Holocaust, *The Drowned and the Saved*,[156] Primo Levi related a telling account of an event in Auschwitz that captures Levinas's point. Dr. Nyiszli, a Hungarian physician who reluctantly assisted Mengele, described the actions of squads of prisoners (*Hilfswillige*) who assisted the SS with the removal of the bodies from the gas chambers. After a group of prisoners was gassed, the members of the *Hilfswillige* found a young adolescent girl who had survived the gas. They tried to revive her and comfort her before an SS officer intervened and killed her. As Levi noted, to survive one erects a *cordon sanitaire* around one's soul, and in doing so denies the reality of what occurs. Levi wrote that in this instance, the *Hilfswillige* "no longer have before them the anonymous mass, the flood of frightened, stunned people coming off boxcars: they have a person."[156]

Levinas was profoundly influenced by the Holocaust and what it meant for moral philosophy. In accounting for the "useless suffering" of Auschwitz, Levinas highlighted that the phenomenon of evil is traditionally defined in the consciousness of perpetrators and victims. He sees the bystanders to such events, who have no responsibility for the crime or its victims, as having the failing of not accepting responsibility of Other to Others. Levinas saw this bystander effect[157] as being at core of the evil of the Holocaust.[158] This failure to recognize the responsibility to the Other is at the core of the evil of Auschwitz. Indeed, Critchley argued that Levinas's ethics are most apparent in the context of such traumatic events.[159]

In projecting the responsibility for the Other into political and social spheres, Levinas's philosophy has been compared to feminist ethics, in that while Levinas's ethics is based on the trauma of the Holocaust, feminist ethics of trauma deals with male domination in society.[160] The totalizing of Western politics is akin to the totalizing effects of male-dominated discourse first elucidated by de Beauvoir.

Thus, the account of the philosophy of the Other reflects that the value and essential humanity of the unique individual patient is imperiled in the totalizing process of psychiatric diagnosis. In referring to or thinking about patients in terms of their disorder, e.g., schizophrenic or borderline, psychiatrists partake of the process of totalization described by Levinas and neglect their responsibility to the patient as Other. The philosophy of Levinas emphasizes that the face-to-face encounter, central to the therapeutic relationship in psychiatry, is the location of ethics. In the light of this, psychiatrists are concerned that the process of psychiatric assessment and diagnosis creates an ontological construct of alien Otherness in patients, which diminishes the patient, much as what Simone de Beauvoir saw happening with women. The second perspective is that the face-to-face encounter with the patient arouses an assumption of the responsibility for the suffering of the patient, as if it were the suffering of the psychiatrist. Although this is a highly individual encounter, in Levinas's work it translates to a broad responsibility for social justice. Thus, in the context of the ethics of Levinas contextualized to psychiatry, there is a link between the individual patient and broad social and political responsibilities.

Integrative Approaches to Psychiatric Ethics

"Political" Ethics and the Rawlsian Approach to Justice in Mental Health

Introduction

Just allocation of limited mental healthcare resources is, arguably, a global issue and forms part of the World Psychiatric Association's *Declaration of Madrid* (1996), which states that "psychiatrists should be aware of and concerned with the equitable allocation of health resources."[161] Several landmark articles in *The Lancet* have also implored psychiatrists to consider issues of just allocation of resources in a global setting as part of their ethical obligations.[162,163]

The American philosopher John Rawls crafted a conception of distributive justice over his career.[164-166] The elements of Rawls's approach to justice related to a hypothetical notion of having moral agents conceptualize an original position in a future social contract, which was presocial and prehistorical. The participant in this social contract would be blinded as to whom they were going to be in this future society through a "veil of ignorance." Based on these constraints, the moral agents would then define a just distribution of goods in this future well-ordered society. Rawls believed that all would operate on the assumption that they would end up the least advantaged person in the society and through a process of constrained maximization allocate resources accordingly. Such resources were not merely wealth, but also freedom, mobility of labor, and equal access to opportunity to achieve fulfilment in life. In Rawls's philosophy, the most just distribution of social goods was one that ultimately benefited the most disadvantaged. This does not necessarily involve equal allocation of resources. This spoke more to equity (a fair share) as against equality in access to social goods. An example of this process might be a small rural community. The government might allocate a sum of money for mental health. The community may decide to use the majority of the funds to recruit good-quality clinicians to the area, with a modest allocation for special welfare payments. Whereas dividing the pool equally among the members of the community with a mental illness may represent equality, it is arguable that the most disadvantaged member of the community would benefit more from having access to capable clinicians, as opposed to having a small fraction of the money.

In stark contrast to Rawls's liberal egalitarianism was the free-market libertarian ideas of writers such as American political scientist Robert Nozick.[167] In the spirit of Adam Smith and Friedrich Hayek, Nozik averred that the only constraint the state should place on the free exchange of resources within a society should be ensuring the legitimacy of the acquisition and subsequent exchanges of property. Libertarianism has become the dominant paradigm in postindustrial developed economies, and many health systems have evolved based upon the principles of such free exchanges of goods and services among individuals.

Rawls's Theory and Mental Health

Rawls's social contract method was ingenious, but there are problems with what he defined as "social goods." Rawls saw that all members of a well-ordered society had equal entitlement to access social goods to have the opportunity to live fulfilling lives. Rawls took the Kantian view that individual fulfillment is a product of autonomy, or rational self-governance. As such, social goods are instrumental in achieving this, and the just distribution of these social goods assists members of society to achieve this autonomous existence. As American philosopher Martha Nussbaum pointed out, such an approach falters when we consider the situation of those whose capacity for autonomy is impaired lifelong. People with disabling chronic schizophrenia may never be truly capable of autonomy, and so their needs are poorly met in Rawls's philosophy. As such, Nussbaum built on the so-called capabilities approach to justice[168] to provide a more workable account of the primary social goods at the center of Rawls's distributive justice.[169]

Postmodern Professional Ethics

Overview

Postmodernism is a term variably used to describe any intellectual activity, from art to architecture, which appears to break with the rationalist traditions of the Enlightenment, or modernism.

French philosopher Jean-Francois Lyotard[170] summarized the core of postmodernism as "incredulity to metanarratives," or the rejection of grand, unified conceptual schemes. Psychiatry is argued to be "a quintessentially modernist project" because of its embrace of scientific paradigms.[171] The postmodern approach to knowledge has been applied to psychiatry,[172] arguing that things are more complex than depicted in science.

Applied to ethics, Australian social scientist Richard Hugman argued that the postmodern approach seeks to move away from overarching theoretical structures into individualizing relationships and have the background of the virtues.[173] Hugman nominates the work of MacIntyre,[108-110] Foucault,[174] and Polish philosopher Zygmunt Bauman[175] as being the key works in postmodern ethics applied to the helping professions.

Bauman's Postmodern Ethics

Zygmunt Bauman's work is, like that of many postmodern theorists, born of disillusionment in the face of the horrors of the twentieth century. Bauman is intellectually indebted to Levinas in that Bauman sees a professional ethic as "a moral party of two" (p. 82). Like

MacIntyre's, Bauman's postmodern approaches to morality are his response to the failings of post-Enlightenment European moral philosophy. He saw the Holocaust as the cataclysmic endpoint of modernity. Indeed as MacIntyre points out, Eichmann was able to reconcile his crimes with his adherence to the deontic tradition of Kant.[113] Bauman insists that our moral responsibility cannot be reduced to the fulfilment of a limited set of socially constructed, arbitrary rules. He takes a position arguing that human morality can be grounded only in the "moral impulse" of the individual.

Bauman's postmodernism is described as follows:

> modernity without illusions … (t)he illusions in question boil down to the belief that the "messiness" of the human world is but a temporary and repairable state, sooner or later to be replaced by the orderly and systematic rule of reason. (p. 32)[175]

Bauman describes the "aporetic" (confused or difficult to verify) nature of human relations, and in the face of this, he rejects the idea of a socially constructed morality. As such, Bauman is critical of bureaucracy and systems. Concerns about bureaucracy are not new. The nineteenth century sociologist Max Weber warned of the destructive effects of large bureaucratic institutions.[176,177] Such institutions focused upon outcomes, rather than values, and as such had lost touch with social values. To Weber, individuals who were subject to the influence of bureaucracies were in an "iron cage," and society had dipped into a "polar night of icy darkness."

Foucault's Postmodern Ethics

Michel Foucault's writings covered many aspects of knowledge and power. His *oeuvre* made frequent reference to psychiatry. In the tradition of postmodernism, Foucault's ethical project rejects the notions of religious, scientific, or conventional moral codes as being the basis of any moral philosophy. Foucault took the view, akin to that of the Ancient Greeks, that traditional morality must be replaced by an ethics based upon the "aesthetics of existence." In essence, Foucault's ethics is primarily concerned with how we decide what kind of person to be and how we seek to be that.[174] Foucault argued that we have to create ourselves as "works of art,"[178] arguing, "Couldn't everyone's life become a work of art? Why should the lamp or the house be an art object, but not our life?" (p. 261).[174] Foucault contends that ethics is the practice

> in which the individual delimits that part of himself that will form the object of his moral practice, defines his position relative to the precept he will follow, and decides on a certain mode of being that will serve as his moral goal. And this requires him to act upon himself, to monitor, test, improve, and transform himself. (p. 28)[179]

Foucault saw that this process is constrained by the fact that many of the practices available to us for such aesthetic realization have been appropriated by the culture in which we live. This process of self-creation involves first our rejecting those forms of identity imposed upon us by society and its institutions. Thus, "Foucault's ethics is the practice of an intellectual freedom that is transgressive of modern knowledge-power-subjectivity relations."[180]

This constitutes a form of secular humanism, in which mankind, not God or other conventional practices, determines what is good or right. In this view, we see that Foucault is extending the humanism of Nietzsche, who rejected religion, in particular Christianity, as a form of slave mentality and called for the ethical superman, or *übermensch*, to rid himself of mundane constraints and take command of his own destiny—what he defined as the "will to power."[181,182] Nietzsche's philosophy has been linked to the excesses of Nazism,[183] although

Foucault arguably distances his philosophy from Nietzsche's in his later work through his concerns about the impact of elitism on disadvantaged groups such as the mentally ill or the homosexual community.[180]

Conclusion

We have argued that different normative theories have strengths and weaknesses, particularly when applied to ethical dilemmas in psychiatric practice. In reality, most psychiatrists utilize approaches from all of the theories, dependent upon circumstance. In the next chapter, we will outline our methodology derived from two theories we will address, social contract theory and communitarianism.

References

1. Fulford K. Psychiatric ethics: a bioethical ugly duckling. In: Gillon R, Lloyd A, eds. *Principles of Health Care Ethics*. Chichester: John Wiley and Sons; 1994:681–695.

2. Campbell A, Gillett G, Jones G. *Medical Ethics, 4th Edition*. New York: Oxford University Press; 2005.

3. Beauchamp T. The philosophical basis of psychiatric ethics. In: Bloch S, Chodoff P, Green S, eds. *Psychiatric Ethics, 3rd Edition*. New York: Oxford University Press; 1999:25–49.

4. Chadwick R, Aindow G. Treatment and research ethics. In: Radden J, ed. *The Philosophy of Psychiatry*. New York: Oxford University Press; 2004:282–295.

5. Radden J. Notes towards a professional ethics for psychiatry. *Australian and New Zealand Journal of Psychiatry*. 2002;36:52–59.

6. Radden J. Psychiatric ethics. *Bioethics*. 2002;16(5):397–411.

7. Dyer A. *Ethics and Psychiatry: Toward a Professional Definition*. New York: American Psychiatric Press; 1988.

8. Hume D. *An Enquiry Concerning the Principles of Morals: The Claredon Edition of the Works of David Hume*. Oxford: Oxford University Press; 1751/1998.

9. Hare R. *Freedom and Reason*. London: Oxford University Press; 1963.

10. Epicurus. Letter to Menoeceus. In: Bailey C, trans. *The Extant Remains*. Oxford: The Clarendon Press; 1926.

11. Bentham J. *An Introduction to the Principles of Morals and Legislation*. London: Althone Press; 1970/1823.

12. Singer P. *The Expanding Circle: Ethics and Sociobiology*. New York: Farrar, Straus and Giroux; 1981.

13. Kymlicka W. *Contemporary Political Philosophy*. New York: Oxford University Press; 2002.

14. Mill J. *Utilitarianism, Liberty, Representative Government*. London: JM Dent and Sons; 1968.

15. Mill J. *On Liberty*. New York: WW Norton; 1859/1975.

16. Sidgwick H. *The Methods of Ethics, 7th Edition*. London: Macmiilan; 1907.

17. Williams B. A critique of utilitarianism. In: Smart J, Williams B, eds. *Utilitarianism: For and Against*. Cambridge: Cambridge University Press; 1973:75–150.

18. Singer P. *Practical Ethics, 2nd Edition*. Cambridge: Cambridge University Press; 1993.

19. Elster J. Utilitarianism and the genesis of wants. In: Sen A, Williams B, eds. *Utilitarianism and Beyond*. Cambridge: Cambridge University Press; 1982:219–238.

20. Goodin R. *Utilitarianism as a Public Philosophy*. Cambridge: Cambridge University Press; 1995.

21. Smart J. Act-utilitarianism and rule-utilitarianism. In: Smart J, Williams B, eds. *Utilitarianism: For and Against*. Cambridge: Cambridge University Press; 1973:9–12.

22. Moore G. *Principia Ethica*. Amherst, MA: Prometheus Books; 1903/1988.

23. Hare R. *Moral Thinking*. Oxford: Oxford University Press; 1981.

24. Hare R. Could Kant have been a utilitarian? *Sorting Out Ethics*. Oxford: Oxford University Press; 2000:147–191.

25. Hare R. *The Philosophical Basis of Psychiatric Ethics*. New York: Oxford University Press; 1993.

26. Popper K. *The Open Society and Its Enemies*. Princeton: Princeton University Press; 1945.

27. "DP". The pin-prick argument. Utilitarianism Resources. 2006; http://www.utilitarianism.com/pinprick-argument.html (accessed October 14, 2006).

28. Smart R. Negative utilitarianism. *Mind*. 1958;67:542–543.

29. Singer P, Kuhse H. *Should the Baby Live? The Problem of Handicapped Infants*. New York: Oxford University Press; 1985.

30. Hare R. *The Language of Morals*. Oxford: Oxford University Press; 1952.

31. Hare R. A philosophical self portrait. In: Mautner T, ed. *The Penguin Dictionary of Philosophy*. London: Penguin; 1997:234–235.

32. Beauchamp T, Childress J. *Principles of Biomedical Ethics, 5th Edition*. New York: Oxford University Press; 2001.

33. Foot P. Abortion and the doctrine of double effect. *Oxford Review*. 1967;5:28–41.

34. Sprigge T. A utilitarian reply to Dr. McCloskey. *Inquiry*. 1965;8:264–291.

35. Brink D. Utilitarian morality and the personal point of view. *Journal of Philosophy*. 1986;83:417–438.

36. Sen A. Rights and agency. *Philosophy and Public Affairs*. 1982;11:3–39.

37. Railton P. Alienation, consequentialism, and the demands of morality. *Philosophy and Public Affairs*. 1984;13:134–171.

38. Smart J. Utilitarianism and the future. In: Smart J, Williams B, eds. *Utilitarianism: For and Against*. Cambridge: Cambridge University Press; 1973:62–67.

39. Singh B, Hawthorne G, Vos T. The role of economic evaluation in mental health care. *Australian and New Zealand Journal of Psychiatry*. 2001;35:104–117.

40. Murray C, Lopez A. *The Global Burden of Disease: A Comprehensive Assessment of Mortality and Disability from Diseases, Injuries, and Risk Factors in 1990 and Projected to 2020*. Washington DC: Harvard School of Public Health on behalf of the World Health Organization and the World Bank; 1996.

41. Williams A. Ethics and efficiency in the provision of health care. In: Bell J, Mendus S, eds. *Philosophy and Medical Welfare*. New York: Cambridge University Press; 1988:111–126.

42. Singer P, McKie J, Kuhse H, et al. Double jeopardy and the use of QALYs in health care allocation. *Journal of Medical Ethics*. 1995;21:144–150.

43. Chisholm D, Healy A, Knapp M. QALYs and mental health care. *Social Psychiatry and Psychiatric Epidemiology*. 1997;32:68–75.

44. Bloch S, Pargiter R. A history of psychiatric ethics. *Psychiatr Clin North Am*. 2002;25:509–524.

45. Adshead G. Care or custody? Ethical dilemmas in forensic psychiatry. *Journal of Medical Ethics*. 2000;26:302–304.

46. Welsh S, Deahl M. Modern psychiatric ethics. *The Lancet*. 2002;359:253–255.

47. Halleck S. The ethical dilemmas of forensic psychiatry: a utilitarian approach. *Bulletin of the American Academy of Psychiatry and the Law*. 1984;12:279–288.

48. Green S, Bloch S. Working in a flawed mental healthcare system: an ethical challenge. *American Journal of Psychiatry*. 2001;158:1378–1383.

49. Kant I. *Groundwork for the Metaphysics of Morals*. Gregor M, trans. Cambridge: Cambridge University Press; 1785/1997.

50. Kant I. *Critique of Practical Reason*. Gregor M, trans. Cambridge: Cambridge University Press; 1787/1997.

51. Kant I. *The Metaphysics of Morals*. Gregor M, trans. Cambridge: Cambridge University Press; 1797/1996.

52. O'Neill O. Kantian ethics. In: Singer P, ed. *A Companion to Ethics*. Oxford: Blackwell; 1991:175–185.

53. Hill T. Humanity as an end in itself. *Ethics*. 1980–81;91:84–89.

54. Baron M. *Kantian Ethics Almost without Apology*. London: Cornell University Press; 1995.

55. Wakefield J. Aristotle as sociobiologist: the "function of a human being" argument, black box essentialism, and the concept of mental disorder. *Philosophy, Psychiatry and Psychology*. 2000;7:17–44.

56. Megone C. Aristotle's function argument and the concept of mental illness. *Philosophy, Psychiatry and Psychology*. 1998;5:187–201.

57. Patfield M. The mentally disordered provisions of the New South Wales Mental Health Act (1990): their ethical standing and the effect on services. *Australasian Psychiatry*. 2006;14:263–267.

58. Robertson M. Mad or bad, have we been had? A response to Patfield (Letter). *Australasian Psychiatry*. 2007;15:77–79.

59. Wakefield J. The concept of mental disorder: on the boundary between biological facts and social values. *American Psychologist*. 1992;47:373–388.

60. Wakefield J. Disorder as harmful dysfunction: a conceptual critique of *DSM-III-R*'s definition of mental disorder. *Psychological Review*. 1992;99:23–39.

61. Campbell A. The virtues (and vices) of the four principles. *Journal of Medical Ethics*. 2003;29:292–296.

62. Hartley L. *The Go-Between*. New York: New York Review Books Classics; 1953.

63. Beauchamp T. Methods and principles in biomedical ethics. *Journal of Medical Ethics*. 2003;29:269–274.

64. Gillon R. Medical ethics: four principles plus attention to scope. *British Medical Journal*. 1994;309:184–188.

65. Ross W. *The Foundation of Ethics*. Oxford: Clarendon Press; 1939.

66. Gert B. *Morality: Its Nature and Justification*. New York: Oxford University Press; 1998.

67. DeMarco J. Principlism and moral dilemmas: a new principle. *Journal of Medical Ethics*. 2005;31:101–105.

68. Atkinson JM. Autonomy and mental health. In: Barker P, Baldwin S, eds. *Ethical Issues in Mental Health*. Cheltenham: Stanley Thornes; 1991:103–126.

69. Feinberg J. Autonomy. In: Christman J, ed. *The Inner Citadel: Essays on Individual Autonomy*. New York: Oxford University Press; 1989:27–53.

70. Korsgaard C. *The Sources of Normativity*. New York: Cambridge University Press; 1996.

71. Radden J. Personal identity, characterization identity, and mental disorder. In: Radden J, ed. *The Philosophy of Psychiatry*. New York: Oxford University Press; 2004:133–146.

72. Dawson A, Garrard E. In defence of moral imperialism: four equal and universal prima facie principles. *Journal of Medical Ethics*. 2006;32:200–204.

73. Gillon R. Ethics needs principles. *Journal of Medical Ethics*. 2003;29:307–312.

74. Veatch R, Gaylin W, Steinbock B. Can the moral commons survive autonomy? (includes commentaries) In search of the good society: the work of Daniel Callahan. *Hastings Center Report*. 1996;26:41.

75. Serour G. Islam and the four principles. In: Gillon R, ed. *Principles of Healthcare Ethics*. Chichester: John Wiley and Sons; 1994:75–92.

76. Kasenen P. African ethical theory and the four principles. In: Gillon R, ed. *Principles of Health Care Ethics*. New York: John Wiley & Sons; 1994:183–192.

77. Steinberg A. A Jewish perspective on the four principles. In: Gillon R, ed. *Principles of Health Care Ethics*. Chichester: John Wiley & Sons; 1994:65–74.

78. Pellegrino E. Is truth telling to the patient a cultural artifact? *Journal of the American Medical Association*. 1992;268:1734–1735.

79. Ishiwata R, Sakai A. The physician-patient relationship and medical ethics in Japan. *Cambridge Quarterly of Healthcare Ethics*. 1994;2:45–47.

80. Miyaji N. The power of compassion: truth telling among doctors in the care of dying patients. *Social Science and Medicine*. 1993;36:249–264.

81. Young J. Morals, suicide, and psychiatry: a view from Japan. *Bioethics*. 2002;16(5):412–424.

82. Tichtchenko P, Yudin B. Towards a bioethics in post-Communist Russia. In: Veatch R, ed. *Cross-Cultural Perspectives in Medical Ethics*. London: Jones and Bartlett; 2000:220–232.

83. Chen X-Y. Clinical bioethics in China: the challenge of entering a market economy. *Journal of Medicine and Philosophy*. 2006;31:7–12.

84. Clouser K. Common morality as an alternative to principlism. *Kennedy Institute of Ethics Journal*. 1995;5:219–236.

85. Clouser K, Gert B. A critique of principlism. *Journal of Medicine and Philosophy.* 1990;15:219–236.

86. Engelhardt H. *The Foundations of Bioethics, 2nd Edition.* New York: Oxford University Press; 1996.

87. Harris J. In praise of unprincipled ethics. *Journal of Medical Ethics.* 2003;29:303–306.

88. Jonsen A, Toulmin S. *The Abuse of Casuistry.* Berkeley: University of Berkeley Press; 1988.

89. Jonsen A. Casuistry. In: Sugarman J, Sulmasy D, eds. *Methods in Medical Ethics.* New York: Georgetown University Press; 2002:104–125.

90. Jonsen A. Casuistry as methodology in clinical ethics. *Theoretical Medicine.* 1991;12:295–307.

91. Jonsen A. Case analysis in clinical ethics. *The Journal of Clinical Ethics.* 1990;1:63–65.

92. Miller R. *Casuistry and Modern Ethics* London: University of Chicago Press; 1996.

93. Arras J. Getting down to cases: the revival of casuistry in bioethics. *Journal of Medicine and Philosophy.* 1991;16:29–51.

94. Habermas J. *The Theory of Communicative Action (2 vols).* Boston: Beacon; 1984.

95. Foucault M. *Discipline and Punish: The Birth of the Prison.* New York: Vintage; 1977.

96. Wexler D. Patients, therapist, and third parties: the victimological virtues of Tarasoff. *International Journal of Law and Psychiatry.* 1979;2:1–28.

97. Stone A. The Tarasoff case and some of its progeny: suing psychotherapists to safeguard society. *Law, Psychiatry and Morality: Essays and Analysis.* Washington DC: American Psychiatric Press; 1984:161–190.

98. Gert B. *Common Morality: Deciding What to Do.* New York: Oxford University Press; 2004.

99. Clouser K. What is medical ethics? *Annals of Internal Medicine.* 1970;80:657–660.

100. Clouser K, Gert B. A critique of principlism. *Journal of Medicine and Philosophy.* 1990; 15(2):219–236.

101. Clouser KD. Some things medical ethics is not. *JAMA.* February 12, 1973;223(7):787–789.

102. Aristotle. *The Nicomachean Ethics.* Oxford: Oxford University Press; 1998.

103. Tallmon J. Casuistry. In: Sloane T, ed. *Encyclopaedia of Rhetoric.* New York: Oxford University Press; 2001:83–88.

104. Munson R. Why medicine cannot be a science. *Journal of Medicine and Philosophy.* 1981;6:183–208.

105. Arendt H. *Eichmann in Jerusalem: A Report on the Banality of Evil.* London: Faber & Faber; 1963.

106. Arendt H. *The Human Condition.* Chicago: University of Chicago Press; 1958.

107. Arendt H. Public rights and private interests. In: Mooney M, Stuber F, eds. *Small Comforts for Hard Times: Humanists on Public Policy.* New York: Columbia University Press; 1977:103–108.

108. MacIntyre A. *After Virtue.* Notre Dame, IN: University of Notre Dame Press; 1984.

109. MacIntyre A. *Whose Justice? Which Rationality?* Notre Dame, IN: University of Notre Dame Press; 1988.

110. MacIntyre A. *Three Rival Versions of Moral Enquiry: Encyclopaedia, Geneology and Tradition*. Notre Dame, IN: University of Notre Dame Press; 1990.

111. Benhabib S. Taking ideas seriously can we distinguish political choices from philosophical truths? *Boston Review.* 2002/2003;27: http://bostonreview.net/BR27.26/benhabib.html (accessed December 22, 2006).

112. Nussbaum M. Non-relative virtues: an Aristotelian approach. In: May L, Freidman M, Clark A, eds. *Ethical Theory: Character and Virtue*. Notre Dame, IN: University of Notre Dame Press; 1988:32–53.

113. MacIntyre A. *A Short History of Ethics*. Milton Park, UK: Routledge; 1998.

114. Bloch S, Green S. An ethical framework for psychiatry. *British Journal of Psychiatry.* 2006;188:7–12.

115. Fraser A. Ethics for psychiatrists derived from virtue theory. Paper presented at: 4th International Conference on Philosophy and Psychiatry. 2000; Firenze.

116. Crowden A. Ethically sensitive mental health care: is there a need for a unique ethics for psychiatry? *Australian and New Zealand Journal of Psychiatry.* 2002;36:52–59.

117. Tobin B. Code of ethics: why we also need practical wisdom. *Australasian Psychiatry.* 1994;2:55–57.

118. Szasz T. *Antipsychiatry: Quackery Squared*. New York: Syracuse University Press; 2009.

119. Robertson M, Walter G. An overview of psychiatric ethics II: virtue ethics and the ethics of care. *Australasian Psychiatry.* 2007;15:207–211.

120. Held V. *The Ethics of Care: Personal, Political, Global*. New York: Oxford University Press; 2006.

121. Veatch R. The place of care in ethical theory. *Journal of Medicine and Philosophy.* 1998;23:210–224.

122. Kohlberg L. *Essays on Moral Development, Vol. I: The Philosophy of Moral Development*. New York: Harper and Row; 1981.

123. Gilligan C. *In a Different Voice: Psychological Theory and Women's Development*. Cambridge, MA: Harvard University Press; 1982.

124. O'Neill O. *Towards Justice and Virtue: A Constructive Account of Practical Reasoning*. Cambridge: Cambridge University Press; 1996.

125. Carse A. The "voice of care": implications for bioethical education. *Journal of Medicine and Philosophy.* 1991;16:5–28.

126. Benhabib S. The generalized and the concrete other: the Kohlberg-Gilligan controversy and moral theory. In: Feder-Kittay E, Meyers D, eds. *Women and Moral Theory*. Totawa: Rowman and Littlefield; 1987.

127. Levinas E. *Totality and Infinity: An Essay on Exteriority*. Pittsburgh: Duquesne University Press; 1969.

128. Baier A. The need for more than justice. In: Hanen M, Nielsen K, eds. *Science, Morality and Feminist Theory*. Calgary: University of Calgary Press; 1987:41–56.

129. Baier A. What do women want in a moral theory? *Nous.* 1985;19:53–63.

130. Noddings N. *Caring: A Feminine Approach to Ethics and Moral Education*. Berkeley: University of California Press; 1984.

131. Card C. Caring and evil. *Hypatia*. 1990;5:101–108.

132. Adshead G. A different voice in psychiatric ethics. In: Fulford K, Dickenson D, Murray C, eds. *Healthcare Ethics and Human Values*. Malden: Blackwell; 2002.

133. Allmark P. Can there be an ethics of care? *Journal of Medical Ethics*. 1995;21:19–24.

134. Allmark P. Can there be an ethics of care? In: Fulford K, Dickenson D, Murray T, eds. *Healthcare Ethics and Human Values*. Malden, MA: Blackwell; 2002:63–69.

135. Goffman E. *Asylums: Essays on the Social Situation of Mental Patients and Other Inmates*. New York: Doubleday; 1961.

136. Fichte J. *Foundations of Natural Right [1796/97]*. Baur M, trans. Cambridge: Cambridge University Press; 2000.

137. Hegel G. *Phenomenology of Spirit*. Oxford: Oxford University Press; 1977.

138. Defoe D. *An Essay upon Projects*. London: Cockerill; 1697.

139. Lacan J. *Écrits: The First Complete Edition in English*. Fink B, trans. New York: W.W. Norton & Co; 2006.

140. Sartre J. *Being and Nothingness: An Essay on Phenomenological Ontology*. Barnes HE, trans. New York: Philosophical Library; 1956.

141. Danto A. *Sartre*. London: Fontana Press; 1991.

142. Laing RD. *The Divided Self: An Existential Study in Sanity and Madness*. Harmondsworth: Penguin Books; 1960.

143. de Beauvoir S. *The Second Sex*. Parshley HM, trans. New York: Vintage Books; 1989.

144. de Beauvoir S. *The Coming of Age*. O'Brian P, trans. New York: WW Norton; 1996.

145. Irigaray L. *This Sex Which Is Not One*. Ithaca: Cornell University Press; 1985.

146. Kaplan M. A woman's view of *DSM-III*. *American Psychologist*. 1983;38:786–792.

147. Dilthey W, ed. *Selected Works—Vol. 4 (1996): Hermeneutics and the Study of History*. Makkreel R, Rodi F, eds. Princeton: Princeton University Press; 1985–2002.

148. Phillips J. Understanding/explanation. In: Radden J, ed. *The Philosophy of Psychiatry*. New York: Oxford University Press; 2004:180–190.

149. Schwartz M, Wiggins O. Phenomenological and hermeneutical models: understanding and interpretation in psychiatry. In: Radden J, ed. *The Philosophy of Psychiatry*. New York: Oxford University Press; 2004:351–363.

150. Levinas E. *Totality and Infinity: An Essay on Exteriority*. Lingis A, trans. Pittsburgh: Duquense University Press; 1969.

151. Critchley S. Introduction. In: Critchley S, Bernasconi R, eds. *The Cambridge Companion to Levinas*. Cambridge: Cambridge University Press; 2002:1–33.

152. Hutchens B. *Levinas—A Guide for the Perplexed*. Wiltshire: Continuum; 2004.

153. Peprzak A. *To the Other: An Introduction to the Philosophy of Emmanuel Levinas*. West Lafayette, IN: Purdue; 1992.

154. van Voren R. Political abuse of psychiatry: an historical overview. *Schizophrenia Bulletin*. 2010;36:33–35.

155. Marshall S. *Men against Fire*. Washington DC: Infantry Journal Press; 1947.

156. Levi P. *The Drowned and the Saved*. London: Abacus Books; 1989.

157. Lavretsky H. The Russian concept of schizophrenia: a review of the literature. *Schizophrenia Bulletin*. 1998;24:537–557.

158. Bernstein R. Evil and the temptation of theodicy. In: Critchley S, Bernasconi R, eds. *The Cambridge Companion to Levinas*. Cambridge: Cambridge University Press; 2002:252–267.

159. Critchley S. *Ethics-Politics-Subjectivity*. London: Verso; 1999.

160. Gottlieb R. Ethics and trauma: Levinas, feminism, and deep ecology. *Cross Currents*. 1994;44:222–241.

161. WPA. World Psychiatric Association. Madrid Declaration on Ethical Standards for Psychiatric Practice. 1996; http://www.wpanet.org/generalinfo/ethic1.html (accessed November 23, 2007).

162. Dhanda A, Narayah T. Mental health and human rights. *The Lancet*. 2007;370:1197–1198.

163. Herrman H, Swartz L. Promotion of mental health in poorly resourced countries. *The Lancet*. 2007;370:1195–1197.

164. Rawls J. *Justice as Fairness: A Restatement*. Cambridge, MA: Harvard University Press; 2001.

165. Rawls J. *A Theory of Justice*. Cambridge, MA: The Bellknap Press; 1971.

166. Rawls J. *Political Liberalism*. New York: Columbia University Press; 1993.

167. Nozick R. *Anarchy, State, Utopia*. New York: Basic Books; 1974.

168. Sen A. Capability and well-being. In: Nussbaum M, Sen A, eds. *The Quality of Life*. Oxford: The Clarendon Press; 1993:30–53.

169. Nussbaum M. *Sex and Social Justice*. New York: Oxford University Press; 1999.

170. Lyotard J-F. *The Postmodern Condition: A Report on Knowledge*. Manchester: Manchester University Press; 1984.

171. Lewis B. Psychiatry and postmodern theory. *Journal of Medical Humanities*. 2000;21:71–84.

172. Bracken P, Thomas P. Postpsychiatry: a new direction for mental health *British Medical Journal*. 2001;322:724–727.

173. Hugman R. *New Approaches in Ethics for the Caring Professions*. Basingstoke: Palgrave Macmillan; 2005.

174. Foucault M. *Ethics: Subjectivity and Truth—the Essential Works of Foucault 1954–1984 (Vol 1)*. Harmondsworth: Penguin; 1997.

175. Bauman Z. *Postmodern Ethics*. Oxford: Blackwell; 1993.

176. Weber M. The profession and vocation of politics. 1919; http://www.ne.jp/asahi/moriyuki/abukuma/weber/lecture/politics_vocation.html (accessed June 19, 2008).

177. Weber M. *Economy and Society. An Outline of Interpretive Sociology*. New York: Bedminster Press; 1968.

178. Foucault M. On the geneology of ethics. In: Dreyfus H, Rainbow P, eds. *Michel Foucault: Beyond Structuralism and Hermeneutics, 2nd Edition*. Chicago: University of Chicago Press; 1983:231–232.

179. Foucault M. *The Use of Pleasure. History of Sexuality. Vol 2*. New York: Pantheon; 1984.

180. Bernauer J, Mahon M. Michel Foucault's ethical imagination. In: Gutting G, ed. *The Cambridge Companion to Foucault*. Cambridge: Cambridge University Press; 2005:149–175.

181. Nietzsche F. *Thus Spake Zarathustra: A Book for All and None*. New York: Modern Library; 1995.

182. Nietzsche F. *Beyond Good and Evil*. New York: Random House; 1967.

183. Russell B. *A History of Western Philosophy*. London: Allen and Unwin; 1961

2

Psychiatric Professional Ethics and the Social Contract

Introduction

Any moral system or law aims to provide a means of a good life. Social contract theory is predicated on the notion that humans will ultimately act in their self-interest—an approach referred to as *psychological egoism*. While there is little doubt that it provides a workable approach to morality, social contract theorists appear to harbor considerable pessimism about both human nature and the nature of moral agency. Social contract theory, or contractarianism, is a moral system that appears to function yet pays little regard to the notion of moral agency in humans. Contractarianism sees a process of ethics by negotiation—a set of agreed upon components of the good, which ultimately serve self-interest.

In Plato's Socratic dialogue *Crito*, Socrates makes a compelling case for his own execution in the light of abiding by the laws of Athens. In spite of the end result of drinking hemlock, Socrates' point is well made in that the community, which permitted his thought to flourish, was best served by adhering to the laws that enabled a civil society. This is likely the first and most paradoxical exposition of the social contract as the basis of moral agency.

Professional ethics represents a variant of this contractarian approach to moral agency. Professionalism as a basis of moral agency in psychiatry is an imperfect approach, but as a system of negotiated morality it has functioned successfully for generations. In this chapter we consider the origins of social contract theory and its manifestation as professional ethics. We conclude by proposing a theory of social justice that is workable for psychiatry.

Social Contract Theory

Book I of Plato's *Republic* contains the story of Gyges, a shepherd from Lydia. Gyges discovers a ring that makes whoever wears it invisible. This provides the perfect setting for Gyges to behave badly and escape punishment. Gyges commits regicide, marries the widowed queen, and assumes great power. The narrator of the story, Glaucon, then argues, likely for the first time in Western literature, that moral agents act out of self-interest. In Glaucon's philosophy, actors in a social system agree to act morally to preserve their own welfare. Glaucon's moral agency is one motivated by fear of punishment for wrongdoing or fear of the dangerous and immoral acts of others. Glaucon's malefactor, Gyges, is perfectly happy in his fraudulent and criminal prosperity. Glaucon has an equally bleak view of the virtuous life, seeing the happiness of the virtuous man as being essentially other-regarding; virtue is not its own reward but rather the approbation of others at being apparently virtuous.

Social contract theorists, like Glaucon, assume that moral agency is motivated primarily by self-interest. In simple terms, the social contract tradition of ethics involves rational individuals choosing to abide by consensual agreements about how to behave toward each other. Ethics is therefore a form of negotiated agreement among individuals within a society. This self-interested approach works on the basis that the actors within the covenant of the social contract all benefit from the agreement.

Since Plato, there have been numerous formulations of the concept of social contract theory, extending from Hobbes's equally bleak picture of human nature to the social justice implicit in the philosophy of the liberal egalitarians such as John Rawls.

Thomas Hobbes

The original notion of social contract theory came from the work English philosopher Thomas Hobbes in his most famous work, *Leviathan*.[1] In the Bible a leviathan is a sea-monster or underwater dragon. Hobbes, initially a royalist, wrote his work in the aftermath of the English Civil War (1642–1651). This was a conflagration that led to a breakdown of civil order, the execution of the despotic King Charles I, and the reconfiguration of English government as a parliamentary democracy with a regent as head of state. At the center of *Leviathan* is the notion that a strong authority, manifest as a powerful sovereign, is required to maintain social order.

Hobbes had a fundamentally mechanistic understanding of human nature and postulated what life would be like without laws or a sovereign, a condition described as "the state of nature." In such a presocial state, there is no right to life, private property, or the protection of law. It is a "war of all against all" (*bellum omnium contra omnes*). According to Hobbes:

> In such condition, there is no place for industry; because the fruit thereof is uncertain: and consequently no culture of the earth; no navigation, nor use of the commodities that may be imported by sea; no commodious building; no instruments of moving, and removing, such things as require much force; no knowledge of the face of the earth; no account of time; no arts; no letters; no society; and which is worst of all, continual fear, and danger of violent death; and the life of man, solitary, poor, nasty, brutish, and short.

> —*Leviathan*, Chapter 13, "Of the Natural Condition of Mankind
> As Concerning Their Felicity, and Misery"

The state of nature is fictional. Hobbes's dystopian vision posits that resources are scarce and that humans are equally motivated by aggrandizement and survival. In the state of nature, humans are roughly equal competitors either through strength or through intellect or cunning. This presents as something of a zero-sum game, as no one competitor is likely to triumph in this internecine conflict envisioned by Hobbes. In the light of this, rational choosers would see that their self-interest is best served by entering into agreements with other competitors in order to obviate threat. This social contract entreats members of the future society to foreclose their "natural liberty" to violence.

Once this agreement is resolved, the voluntary submission gives way to submission to the power of a sovereign, whose role is to enforce the contract. Hobbes argued that without such a presence, individuals would tend to default their obligations and become moral free riders who seek the benefits of the social contract, without abiding by their commitments to fulfill their obligations. Hobbes sees humans being subject to an authoritarian sovereign as entirely defensible in his philosophy. Later contractarians take a less absolute view of social systems. It is clear that Hobbes and his ideas were certainly products of the times.

Jean-Jacques Rousseau

Eighteenth century French polymath Jean-Jacques Rousseau had quite a different view of the state of nature from Hobbes. In *Discourse on the Origin of Inequality* (1754)[2] he wrote:

> Hence although men had become less forebearing, and although natural pity had already undergone some alteration, this period of the development of human faculties, maintaining a middle position between the indolence of our primitive state and the petulant activity of our egocentrism, must have been the happiest and most durable epoch …. The example of savages, almost all of whom have been found in this state, seems to confirm that the human race had been made to remain in it always; that this state is the veritable youth of the world; and that all the subsequent progress has been in appearance so many steps toward the perfection of the individual, and in fact toward the decay of the species. (p. 74)

Rousseau's formulation of social contract theory sees man's state of nature as akin to a halcyon Eden-like existence. To Rousseau, the march of progress, leading to an alteration of subsistence farming to aggregates of humans in cities and the advent of private property, led to a sullying of our natural moral state; he proclaimed famously, "Man was born free, and he is everywhere in chains." Rousseau's formulation of the initial premise of the social contract was as a means of the materially well off attempting to protect their lot. Rousseau's version of the social contract, depicted in the work of the same name,[3] was an attempt to remedy this: we are unable to return to our state of nature; hence, we submit our individual will and renounce our individual rights to a collective will through the agreement or covenant of a social contract. We are, in Rousseau's words, "forced to be free." Rousseau's social contract is in essence a form of classical republicanism, emphasizing sovereignty of the people. In Rousseau's social contract, all forms of tyranny (unlike Hobbes's *Leviathan*) are rejected and governments merely exist to enact the rule of the people. All people submit to the general will, thereby renouncing all forms of natural liberty.

Such a notion of moral agency has its problems. In essence, Rousseau argues that man is inherently good and that rational thought and its associated progress such as in natural science or social progress is corrupting. It seems Rousseau profoundly influenced Saloth Sar, better known as his nom de guerre, Pol Pot.[4] Sar was drawn to communism and was enamored of the notion that the uneducated peasantry represented the true proletariat. Nearly a fifth of Cambodia's population perished under Sar's regime,[5] whose "Year Zero" was intellectually indebted to the reign of terror following the French Revolution. In keeping with Rousseau's ideas about the corrupting influence of the "petulant activity of our egocentrism," teachers, artists, or those who simply wore spectacles were starved, clubbed to death, or buried alive. The breathtaking irony was that the ideas of Rousseau were so instrumental in one of history's most Hobbesian moments.

John Locke

Like Rousseau, English philosopher John Locke did not adhere to such a pessimistic view of humanity as did Hobbes. In his *Second Treatise of Government,*[6] John Locke defined a state of nature quite different from that of Hobbes.

Locke does not see man as bereft of a moral capacity but rather of a political one. Locke's theory of a social contract is predicated upon the notion of the protection of private property—civil society exists primarily for the protection of property, although Locke's definition of property includes "life, liberty, and estate." In the first instance, Locke saw liberty as self-ownership. There has been criticism that, through a linguistic or logic maneuver, Locke had sought to invalidate the concept of slavery and thus was seen as an apologist for the trans-Atlantic slave trade in the eighteenth and nineteenth centuries.

The ceding of any authority to a sovereign in Locke's social contract is therefore to protect private property. Locke's political philosophy sees a political system akin to what is now recognized as the Westminster system of laws, judiciary and an executive. While contemporary democratic forms of government provide national security and the enforcement of laws, arguably the prominent point of interaction between governments and citizenry is in regulation of lawfully conducted economic interactions.

David Gauthier

The modern conception of social contract is evidenced in the work of Canadian philosopher David Gauthier, particularly his classic work *Morals by Agreement*.[7] Gauthier was concerned with the moral free rider problem and in particular the notion that rational self-interest was an inadequate account of moral behavior. Gauthier is most famous for his "prisoner's dilemma" thought experiment. Put simply, two men are charged with committing a crime together and are arrested and then locked in separate cells, with no potential to communicate. Each of them is told the following by their jailers:

- You may either confess to the crime or refuse to confess.
- If one of you confesses but the other does not, then the one who confesses will go free and the other one will be imprisoned for four years.
- If both of you confess, then you will both face three years prison.
- If neither of you confess, then you will both go to jail for one year.
- You are both being told these options.

In this situation, one is safe to assume that both men want minimum periods in prison. Mindful of this, Gauthier produced a matrix (Figure 2.1).

If they both confess, in an attempt to avoid jail, they both face three years. It would seem that both are better off by confessing, either going free, or facing three years (as opposed to four years for not confessing). In the light of this, both will confess and spend three years in jail. The only way for both to achieve the best outcome is to anticipate the other will not confess in the expectation that they will both see it in such terms. The best outcome is

	Prisoner B Confesses	Prisoner B Does Not Confess
Prisoner A Confesses	A&B—3 years	A—free, B—4 years
Prisoner A Does Not Confess	A—4 years, B—free	A&B—1 year

Figure 2.1 Prisoner's dilemma matrix. (After Gauthier, D., *Morals by Agreement*, New York, Oxford University Press, 1986.)

therefore achieved if the interests of both parties are coordinated, rather than both acting in self-interest. This involves choosing a second-best option. The best outcome is clearly for both to act benevolently and face comparatively less inconvenience than acting egoistically and hope to be a moral free rider by evading prison at the expense of the benevolence of the other.

Gauthier's work shows that if everyone acts from self-interest alone, the worst overall outcome will eventuate. Those who act from self-interest while others act benevolently are moral free riders. A successful social contract in Gauthier's model is based upon the notion that morality requires that people be motivated by other-regarding or benevolent concerns, not merely self-interest.

Rawls and the Liberal Egalitarians

Harvard professor John Rawls developed a conception of distributive justice over his career.[8-10] We considered briefly the basic concepts of Rawls's work in the previous chapter. Rawls's notion of the social contract considered more specifically the just allocation of limited resources within what he termed a "well-ordered society." Rawls saw that all members of a well-ordered society had equal entitlement to access social goods in order to have the opportunity of living fulfilling lives. Rawls took the Kantian view that individual fulfilment is a product of autonomy, or rational self-governance. As such, social goods are instrumental in achieving this, and the just distribution of these social goods assists members of society to achieve this autonomous existence. As Martha Nussbaum has pointed out, such an approach falters when we consider the situation of those whose capacity for autonomy is impaired lifelong. People with disabling chronic schizophrenia may never be truly capable of autonomy, and so their needs are not met in Rawls's philosophy. As such, Nussbaum built on what she termed a "capabilities approach" to justice[11] to provide a more workable account of the primary social goods at the center of Rawls's distributive justice.[12] Nussbaum's concept of "capabilities" defined these as the necessary preconditions for a person's capacity to flourish through aspiring to a life characterized by dignity. This is in contrast to Rawls's conception of a life's goal of realizing Kantian autonomy. The capabilities extend from reasonable life expectancy, and sensory and bodily integrity, through to capacity for affiliative behavior, play, and some control over one's environment. Nussbaum thus sees that the ends of just public policy with regard to people with psychiatric or intellectual disabilities, is the guarantee of their basic dignity.[13]

The concept of dignity requires consideration. Definitions of dignity arise in political and moral philosophy, all of which turn on concepts of status and respect. Dignity regularly features in numerous proclamations and statutes of medical bodies. The Latin term *dignitas* was often used in regard to men seeking status in public life in Ancient Rome. Kant's formula of humanity sees humans as intrinsically valuable, although Kant saw this as related to the capacity for practical reason, which is problematic in Nussbaum's approach. Moreover, the concept of value is relative to other entities, so Kant tried to define that human value was intrinsic and not relative. The American philosopher Alan Gerwith conceptualized dignity in terms of both negative rights of avoiding harm and positive rights of achieving a sense of well-being.[14] American philosopher Mortimer Adler, working in the tradition of Aristotelian and Thomistic virtues, saw human dignity as relating to the equality of all humans and their intrinsic value.[15]

Nussbaum's concept of dignity is more intuitive than substantive; it is grounded in "animality" as against Kant's reason. Dignity resides in flourishing, striving, and also vulnerability. Flourishing refers to well-being and enjoyment of a quality of life; in *Frontiers of Justice*, Nussbaum cites examples of people with severe disabilities who derive pleasure from experiences, such as music or interpersonal contact.[13] For the purposes of this discussion, we take Nussbaum's dignity as residing in the intrinsic, nonrelative worth of a person as grounded in his or her capacity for flourishing through pleasurable experience, sense of self-worth, and vulnerability. The last necessitates a moral obligation of just social systems, and indeed moral agents, to ensure that all people are equal and that their vulnerabilities are managed to ensure this.

Returning to Rawls's theories, these have been extended to the specific area of healthcare by American philosopher Norman Daniels.[16] Daniels defines healthcare broadly as encompassing individual medical services, preventive interventions, public health initiatives, workplace safety, and social resources for the chronically ill and disabled. Daniels argues that the right to healthcare carries the implicit assumption that access to healthcare is on par with other civil rights, which equate healthcare with other social goods.

The rationale of providing healthcare paid for by third parties, such as government, is therefore to help restore normal function by decreasing the effect of disease or disability. This compensates for the "natural lottery" in which liability for disease is considered an accident of birth, rather than the individual failings of the sufferer. A guarantee of access to healthcare does not have the goal to enhance well-being or general capability, but merely correcting for the natural lottery. This would address the vulnerability aspect of our conception of dignity.

Daniels and Harvard professor of psychiatry James Sabin have applied these concepts specifically to mental health.[17] They advance a "normal function model" in the light of how mental illness may affect that function. They propose that the goal of mental healthcare is to obviate the disadvantage arising from mental illness, thus making everyone equal competitors for social resources. Their model of justice, achieved through mental healthcare, has three dimensions:

1. A *normal function model* of mental healthcare seeking to create normal competitors for social resources
2. A *capability model* seeking to create equal competitors for resources
3. A *welfare model* addressing the fact that people suffer because of attitudes or behaviors they did not choose and cannot choose to overcome, which should justify access to mental healthcare

The normal function model allows a society to draw a plausible boundary around the scope for insurance coverage. Sabin and Daniels argue that the capability and the welfare models are the most morally substantive but are the most problematic in implementation.

Psychiatry and Social Justice

As we have discussed, the successful operation of the social contract involves rational choosers abdicating certain natural rights in exchange for social goods.

American philosopher James Rachels has been critical of the tradition of the social contract, seeing it as a historical fiction "not worth the paper it was never written on." Rachels has also highlighted circumstances where the social contract process appears to fail:[18]

1. What of those citizens, like the mentally ill, who may be incapable of rational agreement to the social contract process, yet need the protection of the sovereign?
2. What of those members of society who are second-class citizens and do not benefit from the social contract, yet are expected to abide by it?
3. What if the sovereign fails in its responsibilities in enforcing the social contract?

These three scenarios represent specific moral challenges for psychiatrists and provide a framework for considering social justice in regard to their patients. They also represent manifestations of the dual-role dilemma in psychiatry in that they frequently present quandaries that place individual psychiatrists and the profession in a conflicted position. The essence of this conflict is the responsibility to the individual patient versus to society or the community.

The dual-role dilemma has typically been associated with the practice of forensic psychiatry,[19–23] where "obligation to serve the interests of justice" comes into conflict with the Hippocratic principle of *primum non nocere*.[24] In this context, the dual role posits that there is a *prima facie* conflict between the duties of the psychiatrist as *treater* and as *evaluator*. We have reconceptualized the dual-role dilemma elsewhere,[25] defining it as a quandary in which a psychiatrist faces the dilemma of conflicting expectations or responsibilities, between the therapeutic relationship on the one hand and the interests of third parties, such as government or private institutions, on the other.

In contrast to the moral free rider problem, i.e., those who seek to benefit from the social contract without abiding by its requirements, those who cannot necessarily commit to the social contract, by virtue of irrationality or impairment, present a problem for contractarians. Most civilized societies provide some form of decent minimum in terms of basic social goods, such as welfare and some access to healthcare. It is, however, apparent that the mentally ill of most developed societies have failed to benefit from the alleged prosperity of the postindustrial globalized economy. Whether this failure to benefit relates to the incapacity of many people with mental illness, either individually or as a group, to advocate on behalf of themselves or more to the stigma associated with mental illness is unclear. In such circumstances, there is a compelling argument for advocacy by psychiatrists on behalf of their patients.

One of the main questions over the role of psychiatrist's advocacy on behalf of their patients pertains to the limits of such advocacy. Despite the broad canvas of social injustice faced by many people who suffer mental illness, most psychiatrists are more concerned about advocating for their individual patients. Advocacy in this regard addresses the patient's dealings with various social institutions, including health systems and other government utilities such as housing or welfare, insurance systems, the courts, prisons, and citizenship. Psychiatrists also face challenges in dealing with the second problem with the social contract tradition—that of the "second-class citizen." Second-class citizens are, in essence, those members of society who are expected to fulfill the expectations of the social contract without reasonable expectation of the benefits. Second-class citizens may become so either through latent prejudices within a society (often on racial or gender grounds) or through government policy.

The third problem area in relation to social justice operating under the social contract tradition deals with the failure of the sovereign. This failure can take many forms; however, the most common failure faced by people suffering mental illness is the failure to provide adequate services. In the United States, the problem of advocacy has been most acute in the face of the implementation of market forces in healthcare under the auspices of managed care. Managed care has delivered a number of problematic health systems in the United States, leading to calls for psychiatrists to resist the processes in such systems that disadvantage the mentally ill.[26] There is accumulating evidence that managed mental healthcare may adversely affect clinical outcomes,[27] as decisions made on apparent utilitarian grounds of cost containment seem to have the value of reduced access to, rather than improvement of, clinical services.[28] The dilemma faced by psychiatrists, and physicians in general, is to reconcile the needs of the patient with that of society. Such considerations often bring the physician into conflict with the rest of society.[29] The notion of a tension between psychiatrists' obligations to their patients and to third parties is protean and represents another manifestation of the dual-role dilemma.

In the alternate are the ethical responsibilities faced by psychiatrists in resource allocation. While the procurement and protection of access to limited healthcare resources is one issue, the alternative is the need for some form of financial responsibility. Much of the cost of healthcare is decided at the individual clinical level, and while exercising fiscal responsibility should not occur with the dubious goal of aiding health maintenance organizations by diverting health dollars from the clinical setting to corporate profits, the psychiatrist does arguably have ethical obligations to spend mental health dollars wisely.[30] One of the problems associated with this obligation is that of quantification. The international standard measures of utility in regard to healthcare are the Disability Adjusted Life Year (DALY)[31] and the Quality Adjusted Life Year (QALY),[32] despite the fact that these are insensitive measures when applied to psychiatric disorders.[33]

The social contract may fail and lead to social injustice when there is a failure of the sovereign to maintain law and order. This breakdown of law and order may occur as a consequence of some calamity occurring in the state, such as a natural disaster or foreign invasion, or when the sovereign perpetrates oppressive violence against its citizens. These circumstances have been seen in totalitarian regimes, where widespread persecution by the state occurs. A vivid example of this was the human rights violations witnessed in Argentina during the period of the military dictatorship which ended in 1982, documented in the CONADEP (National Commission on the Disappearance of Persons) report.[34] In other circumstances, the sovereign may fail to provide the benefits of the social contract to members of a society who may be part of a persecuted or neglected minority. These groups may be denied the benefits of the social contract as a result of institutionalized racism or on political grounds. Many members of the international community, themselves signatories to international covenants of human rights, are capable of such social injustice.

In these circumstances, the ethical remit of psychiatrists in regard to social justice may extend beyond advocacy for those with established mental illness to all those who are disadvantaged and at risk of developing mental illness. The mental health consequences of politicized violence or denial of the benefits of the social contract arguably represent an area of ethical responsibility for psychiatrists. Moreover, psychiatrists may have ethical responsibilities in the process of restorative justice, in which communities rebuild after such failures of the social contract.

Psychiatrists who live in totalitarian regimes have often been persecuted as a group or for individual actions or beliefs. Individual psychiatrists "disappeared" in Argentina under the dictatorship simply for treating survivors of the regime's torture and imprisonment practices.[35] In other circumstances, such as in the former Soviet Union, psychiatrists have been complicit in persecution of citizens of a totalitarian regime, often confecting politically based diagnoses as justifications for imprisonment.[36]

In modern Australia, psychiatrists face a particular ethical dilemma, which is an exemplar of the problem of the abuse of human rights in otherwise stable and liberal societies. The policy of recent Australian federal governments has been to enact a Draconian approach toward refugees who arrive unlawfully in Australian territory. Part of this process involves the mandatory detention of all "unauthorised illegal entrants," including women and children, in privately operated "detention centres."[37,38] Children detained in these settings have been exposed to suicide attempts and self-injurious behavior by other refugees, compounding their experience of the trauma of the regimes they fled and the perilous voyages made to escape.[39] Given the deleterious consequences of such treatment,[40] it is clear that this represents an instance of the sovereign of a nation violating its obligations under the social contract. While such propositions can be obscured by debates over a nation–state's rights to sovereignty over territory and the status of unlawful entrants under the social contract, the situation faced by psychiatrists in Australia is, quite simply, the perpetration of the abuse of human rights by the state with whom they exist in a contractual professional relationship. Australian psychiatrists face the ethical dilemma of abiding by the reprehensible policy of their society, manifest in the actions of the popularly elected government, or risk politicizing the profession by speaking out against harmful actions by a popularly elected government.[41] Such decisions often invoke the political and moral views of individual psychiatrists, resulting in divisions within the profession.

If advocacy is a core focus of professional ethics in psychiatry, how far can it extend? In most collective groups of psychiatrists, it is apt that there is a divergence of opinion as to the point at which such advocacy becomes inappropriate. The distinction between the advocacy of a psychiatrist as a professional, as opposed to that of an individual citizen, represents a challenge. In an attempt to resolve this, we propose an "onion skin model" of advocacy by psychiatrists[42] (Figure 2.2). In this model, there is a core of expertise possessed by psychiatrists, and therefore actions in this regard are incontrovertibly psychiatric. As one moves to the outer layers of the model, where questions of community attitudes and public policy are situated, the discourse is less psychiatric and more sociopolitical. In such instances, the uncontested role of a psychiatrist as a member of a professional group lies in informing the public debate over matters of policy and community attitudes and less direct political action. The importance of this model is that the further away one gets from the core business of psychiatry—defined as assessment and treatment of symptoms and impairment—the less substantive the role of the psychiatrist in advocacy. The true value of this model is that it

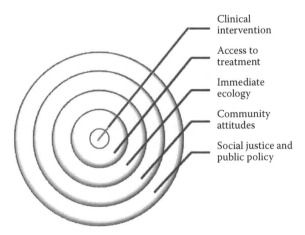

Clinical intervention

Access to treatment

Immediate ecology

Community attitudes

Social justice and public policy

Figure 2.2 The "onion skin" model of advocacy and justice.

avoids the either/or approach to advocacy and, more significantly, provides a coherent basis for levels of advocacy, proportionate to a psychiatrist's expertise.

At the core of the model is the advocacy for best treatment for the patient in a clinical setting. This may include peer review or the advocacy among medical colleagues. The next level describes the capacity of patients to access treatment, whether it is medication, inpatient care, or appropriate psychological management. This may involve representations to third parties or institutional bureaucracies. The next layer describes the scope of advocacy for an individual patient in areas such as access to housing, welfare benefits, access to employment, or other social goods. This advocacy is often achieved through advising government or nongovernment agencies of the clinical aspects of a patient's circumstances. This may also involve providing clinical information to civil or criminal courts. Beyond these is the role of advocacy in attempting to influence unhelpful community attitudes, particularly those which involve stigmatizing patients. Increasingly, dedicated nongovernment agencies have been tasked with this responsibility, resulting in psychiatrists participating in a clinical advisory rather than public advocacy role. The final level sees psychiatrists informing legislatures of the potential psychiatric consequences of specific public policy positions.

Professional Ethics and the Social Contract

The *Oxford English Dictionary*[48] defines *profession* as follows:

> An occupation whose core element is work, based on the mastery of a complex body of knowledge and skills. It is a vocation in which knowledge of some department of science or learning, or the practice of an art founded on it, is used in the service of others. Its members profess a commitment to competence, integrity, morality, altruism, and the promotion of the public good within their domain. These commitments form the basis of a social contract between a profession and society, which in return grants the profession autonomy in practice and the privilege of self-regulation. Professions and their members are accountable to those served and to society.

Traditional notions of professional ethics have evolved from a focus on the doctor–patient relationship, through the Hippocratic tradition and later in the contributions of Thomas Percival[46] and W. D. Ross.[47] The key elements of this definition appear to be the existence of a contract of sorts between a professional group (or individual professional) and society, the promotion of public good, and a number of desirable personal qualities, or virtues. In exchange, the group is accorded professional autonomy and the capacity to self-regulate.[46]

The original Hippocratic tradition was *primum non nocere* (first, do no harm). This holds that any action of a physician must benefit, and in no way harm, the patient. The situation has changed and the Hippocratic tradition in medical ethics has waned[47] due to the presumed effect of the evolution of Western societies into consumer economies,[48] the commercialization of the health system, and technological advances in medicine.[48,49] It has been argued that, in the light of such developments, the craft of medicine has been transformed into a service industry in which technical skills are traded in a marketplace. As such, the notions of the virtuous physician and the Hippocratic tradition have been lost. The scale of the practice of medicine has also increased exponentially. In developed countries, medicine has changed in one or two generations from a cottage industry to one consuming a significant portion of national expenditure.[48]

Professional ethics, arguably, have three core components—specialized training and the acquisition of specialized skills; the provision of expert assistance to those in need and vulnerable; and the virtues of trustworthiness, efficacy, and knowledge, which ultimately enhance the common good and aggregate well-being.[50] A profession is, therefore, a group who possess specialized skills and knowledge applied for a collective good.[51,52]

Several physician's organizations have jointly outlined a series of principles and responsibilities for the medical profession, which integrate the recent influences on medical practice.[52] In this new code, the principles of patient welfare, patient autonomy, and social justice are juxtaposed with the responsibilities of commitment to professional competence, honesty with patients, confidentiality, appropriate relations, improving quality of care, improving access to care, ensuring a fair distribution of finite resources, pursuit of scientific knowledge, and maintenance of trust by managing conflicts of interest and professional responsibilities.

Such aspirational statements have the two themes of physicians possessing a set of desirable virtues and the role of advocacy. These highlight the values of the medical profession. A recent study of Australian psychiatrists[42] suggested that the main values in their work were the value of the patient, the value of sophisticated understanding, the value of reflection, and the value of advocacy. These values are well represented in professional codes of ethics.

Professional ethical autonomy is therefore derived from a tacit understanding that professionals will devote themselves to serving the best interests of society and will self-regulate to maintain high-quality care and beneficent conduct.[46] The tenets of this beneficent conduct have been specified as patient welfare and autonomy, as well as the just allocation of resources.[52]

One of the key elements in this definition of professionalism is the "contract" between the profession and society, in particular what is defined as a "collective good." This collective aspect of professionalism is balanced with the Hippocratic tradition of the individual physician as nonmaleficent healer. There is potential for significant tension between these two traditions of ethics as it is possible that an expected action in the interests of a collective good may be deleterious to an individual patient. The tension between these potentially conflicting roles creates a degree of anxiety about the profession of medicine.[48]

An additional complexity in this mix is provided by the involvement of third parties, a recent phenomenon in the history of medicine brought about by market forces. Such a dilemma has been outlined specifically in the case of psychiatry, with a call to reflect upon the inherent tensions within the notion of medicine as the trade of applied technical skills.[49]

In any setting, the psychiatric profession is thoroughly integrated with the norms of the society in which it exists. Such norms influence both diagnostic and treatment approaches, and exert coercive pressure upon psychiatrists through the imposition of laws that govern many aspects of the way they practice their craft. As such, there is a particularity to the ethics of psychiatry functioning in different sociocultural settings. Such an intricate network of relationships and obligations implores psychiatrists to consider the integration of their own personal sense of an ethical life and the virtues of a physician, the discourses of professional ethics of the psychiatric profession, and the expectations of the social contract.

It has been argued, therefore, that psychiatric ethics is a network of interactions between the individual morality of the psychiatrist, the immediate collegiate relationships of the psychiatrist, and the relationship between the psychiatric profession and the broader society.[53]

There is arguably a "new professionalism" referring to the evolution of medical ethics in the light of a number of changes in healthcare, including the scale of healthcare, the rise of interdisciplinary healthcare and prominence of the biopsychosocial model in mental health, technical progress, increased literacy about healthcare in the community, and public policy and expectations of third parties.

Social Contract and Professional Ethics in Psychiatry

The critical issue in professional ethics and its related dilemmas in psychiatry is that of the social contract. The social contract tradition in medical ethics is problematic in the setting of psychiatry. Society may encourage certain expectations of the psychiatric profession, which are to the detriment of people with mental illness. This places the psychiatric profession in a position of conflict between obligation to a patient and obligation to society in the professional social contract. The clearest example of this relates to public safety. After the rare instance of a person suffering a mental illness harming another person, society may, through its legislators or its institutions, emphasize the expectation that psychiatrists must manage risk more effectively. Putting aside the obvious limits of this as an undertaking, this may result in the psychiatric profession being expected to act more coercively in the treatment of people with mental illness in order to protect the public, rather than provide care for patients. This highlights the fundamental dilemma in the social contract tradition of ethics applied to a professional group, where the presumed common good of society comes into conflict with the interests of the patient.

The other factor influencing the professional landscape in psychiatry has been the emergence of a form of globalized psychiatry. The foundation of the World Psychiatric Association and its ethical proclamations in the wake of the crimes of Soviet psychiatrists[54] avers that the psychiatric profession is a global enterprise that shares a common set of values enshrined in proclamations such as the Declaration of Madrid.[55] Moreover, the effect of commercially successful classification systems such as the American Psychiatric Association's *Diagnostic and Statistical Manual of Mental Disorders* has been the adoption of an approach to the classification of psychiatric disorders that has transcended cultures and created a de facto globalization of the psychiatric profession.[56]

Thus, on two fronts of the social contract, the psychiatric profession confronts ethical dilemmas—those related to just allocation of resources and those related to acting out of self-interest in order to maintain this contractarian relationship. In both instances, there is potential for these imperatives to come into conflict with the values of psychiatrists, in particular those surrounding their relationship with particular patients.

Case Example

A psychiatrist working for a veteran's mental health organization has a patient who is a former serviceman. This patient had served in Afghanistan in a non-front-line role. Like many servicemen, while he had not engaged the enemy in direct combat, nor had he been fired upon, he lived in constant fear of death or injury from suicide bombers or improvised explosive devices.

After he returned home, the patient developed both a depressive illness and alcohol dependence. He had separated from his wife after a series of domestic violence incidents and was the subject of a restraining order. The patient had been discharged from the military on medical grounds, although he was unable to access treatment or benefits from the private mental health service provider retained by the government's Veteran's Administration to provide such care to veterans.

At issue was the nature of the patient's psychiatric problems. It was clear that he had suffered from mood and behavioral disturbances prior to his military service and had in fact enlisted in the army after being charged with assault. His clinical picture since being repatriated was highly indicative of bipolar disorder with comorbid alcohol abuse. He had benefited from mood stabilization medication, and his main problems were unstable accommodation, poverty, and limited access to treatment. The psychiatrist had been seeing the patient and deferring the issue of payment on the expectation that the patient's problems would be recognized by the Veteran's Administration as being related to his military service.

A psychiatrist who was a serving member of the military had reviewed the patient's case. The military psychiatrist also concluded that the patient was suffering from bipolar disorder, which had predated his military service. This resulted in the veteran being denied access to benefits such as a service pension, housing, and access to psychiatric treatment.

The patient's treating psychiatrist was aware that a diagnosis of posttraumatic stress disorder (PTSD) would lead to the patient having access to these benefits and contribute toward his ongoing recovery. The patient described some symptoms that were reminiscent of nightmares and flashbacks; however, a PTSD diagnosis was dubious. The psychiatrist was aware that the budget for the healthcare of veterans was seriously oversubscribed and that there was a responsibility to ensure that the system did not collapse under financial strain.

In essence, the dilemma presented as whether to make an inappropriate diagnosis of PTSD in order to secure benefits for the patient or to adhere to the diagnosis of bipolar disorder and preserve the integrity of the seemingly inflexible veteran's health system. It is possible that the PTSD diagnosis may be at least partly correct; however, it was clear that the patient's problems did not accord with the necessary criteria. The diagnostic dilemma also became a point of friction between the patient and the psychiatrist, as the patient was also contemplating legal action against the military for failing in their duty of care to him.

What is evident in this example is the manifest social injustice faced by the patient and the dual-role problem faced by the psychiatrist. Both parties had to negotiate a relationship with a complex government bureaucracy, which had made an arbitrary decision on diagnostic grounds to deny a person access to important medical and social welfare resources. The psychiatrist faced the dilemma as to whether to make an inappropriate diagnosis in order to subvert what appeared to be a denial of social justice, as the patient needed access to the treatment and other social goods. This seemed particularly unjust, given the patient had chosen, albeit out of self-interest, to serve his country overseas.

In the alternate, the psychiatrist faced a broad responsibility to work within the framework established by the society, through its popularly elected representatives. There was a limited budget for veterans' mental health, and there was a significant number of patients who had more "legitimate" claims. The integrity of the psychiatric profession, particularly in the light of increasing public scrutiny of the area, was also an issue for the psychiatrist to consider. The psychiatrist had a broader option to lobby for change within the system, although it is clear that little would be achieved as isolated acts of direct advocacy. This dual-role responsibility to both the patient and the system is an increasing problem, particularly as third parties, presumably with responsibilities to government and share holders, are tasked with providing mental health care.

Conclusion

In this chapter we have outlined a notion of social justice as the successful operation of the social contract, for the benefit of all. People suffering mental illness are vulnerable within the social contract, particularly when the sovereign fails in its duty. Psychiatrists are conflicted by the tension between their obligations to the patient and those related to the professional social contract. This tension is a fundamental focus of moral action by psychiatrists. We will now expand on the broader social construction of the moral agency of psychiatrists.

References

1. Hobbes T, ed. *Leviathan*. Macpherson C, ed. London: Penguin; 1651/1985.

2. Rousseau J. *The Basic Political Writings*, Second Edition. Cress DA, ed. Indianapolis: Hackett Publishing Company; 2012:74.

3. Rousseau J. *The Social Contract*. 2005; http://etext.library.adelaide.edu.au/r/rousseau/jean_jacques/r864s/ (accessed April 30, 2007).

4. Chandler D. *Brother Number One: A Political Biography of Pol Pot*. Boulder, CO: Westview Press; 1992.

5. Cambodian Genocide Program. http://www.yale.edu/cgp/ (accessed April 17, 2012).

6. Locke J. *Two Treatises of Government*. Laslett, P. ed. Cambridge: Cambridge University Press; 1960.

7. Gauthier D. *Morals by Agreement*. New York: Oxford University Press; 1986.

8. Rawls J. *Justice as Fairness: A Restatement*. Cambridge, MA: Harvard University Press; 2001.

9. Rawls J. *A Theory of Justice*. Cambridge, MA: The Bellknap Press; 1971.

10. Rawls J. *Political Liberalism*. New York: Columbia University Press; 1993.

11. Sen A. Capability and well-being. In: Nussbaum M, Sen A, eds. *The Quality of Life*. Oxford: The Clarendon Press; 1993:30–53.

12. Nussbaum M. *Sex and Social Justice*. New York: Oxford University Press; 1999.

13. Nussbaum M. *Frontiers of Justice*. Cambridge, MA: Bellknap; 2006.

14. Gerwith A. *Self-Fulfilment*. Princeton, N.J: Princeton University Press; 1998.

15. Adler M. *The Difference of Man and the Difference It Makes*. Bronx, NY: Fordham University Press; 1993.

16. Daniels N. *Just Health Care*. Cambridge: Cambridge University Press; 1995.

17. Sabin J, Daniels N. Determining "medical necessity" in mental health practice. *Hastings Center Report*. 1994;24:5–13.

18. Rachels J. *The Elements of Moral Philosophy, 4th Edition*. Boston: McGraw Hill; 2003.

19. Verdun-Jones SN. Forensic psychiatry, ethics and protective sentencing: what are the limits of psychiatric participation in the criminal justice process? *Acta Psychiatrica Scandinavica*. 2000;101(399):77–82.

20. Callahan D, Gaylin W. The psychiatrist as double agent. *Hastings Center Report*. 1974;4:12–14.

21. Strasburger L, Guthiel T, Brodsky A. On wearing two hats: role conflict in serving as both psychotherapist and expert witness. *American Journal of Psychiatry*. 1997;154:448–456.

22. Miller R. Ethical issues involved in the dual role of treater and evaluator. In: Rosner R, Weinstock R, eds. *Ethical Practice in Psychiatry and the Law*. New York: Plenum Press; 1990:129–150.

23. In the service of the state: the psychiatrist as double agent. *Hastings Center Report, Special Supplement*. April 1978:S1–23.

24. Guthiel T. *The Psychiatric Expert Witness*. Washington DC: American Psychiatric Press; 1998.

25. Robertson M, Walter G. The many faces of the dual-role dilemma in psychiatric ethics. *Australian and New Zealand Journal of Psychiatry*. 2008;42:228–235.

26. WPA. World Psychiatric Association. Madrid Declaration on Ethical Standards for Psychiatric Practice http://www.wpanet.org/generalinfo/ethic1.html 1996; (accessed November 23, 2007).

27. Dhanda A, Narayah T. Mental health and human rights *The Lancet*. 2007;370:1197–1198.

28. Herrman H, Swartz L. Promotion of mental health in poorly resourced countries. *The Lancet*. 2007;370:1195–1197.

29. Robertson M, Kerridge I, Walter G. Ethnomethodological study of the values of Australian psychiatrists: towards an empirically derived RANZCP Code of Ethics. *Australian and New Zealand Journal of Psychiatry*. 2009;43:409–419.

30. Green S, Bloch S. Working in a flawed mental health care system: an ethical challenge. *Am J Psychiatry*. 2001;158(9):1378–1383.

31. Green S. The ethics of managed mental health care. In: Bloch S, Chodoff P, Green S, eds. *Psychiatric Ethics, 3rd Edition*. New York: Oxford University Press; 1999:401–421.

32. Thompson J, Burns B, Goldman H, et al. Initial level of care and clinical status in a managed mental health care program. *Hospital and Community Psychiatry*. 1992;43:599–603.

33. Levinsky N. The doctor's master. *New England Journal of Medicine*. 1984;314:1573–1575.

34. Singh B, Hawthorne G, Vos T. The role of economic evaluation in mental health care. *Australian and New Zealand Journal of Psychiatry*. 2001;35:104–117.

35. Murray C, Lopez A. *The Global Burden of Disease: A Comprehensive Assessment of Mortality and Disability from Diseases, Injuries, and Risk Factors in 1990 and Projected to 2020*. Washington DC: Harvard School of Public Health on behalf of the World Health Organization and the World Bank; 1996.

36. Williams A. Ethics and efficiency in the provision of health care. In: Bell J, Mendus S, eds. *Philosophy and Medical Welfare*. New York: Cambridge University Press; 1988:111–126.

37. Chisholm D, Healy A, Knapp M. QALYs and mental health care. *Social Psychiatry and Psychiatric Epidemiology*. 1997;32:68–75.

38. *Nunca Más (Never Again). Report of CONADEP (National Commission on the Disappearance of Persons)*. 1984; http://www.nuncamas.org/english/library/nevagain/nevagain_001.htm (accessed March 31, 2007).

39. Knudson J. Veil of silence: the Argentine press and the Dirty War. *Latin American Perspectives*. 1997;24:93–112.

40. Bloch S, Reddaway P. *Soviet Psychiatric Abuse*. London: Gollancz; 1983.

41. Silove D. The asylum debacle in Australia: a challenge for psychiatry. *Australian and New Zealand Journal of Psychiatry*. 2002;36:290–296.

42. Steel Z, Silove D. Science and the common good: indefinite, non-reviewable mandatory detention of asylum seekers and the research imperative. *Monash Bioethics Review*. 2004;23:93–103.

43. Steel Z, Silove D. The mental health implications of detaining asylum seekers. *Medical Journal of Australia.* 2001;175:596–599.

44. Steel Z, Silove D, Brooks R, et al. Impact of immigration detention and temporary protection on the mental health of refugees. *British Journal of Psychiatry.* 2006;188:58–64.

45. Dudley M, Jureidini J, Mares S, et al. In protest. *Australian and New Zealand Journal of Psychiatry.* 2004;38(11–12):978–979.

46. Percival T. *Codes of Institutes and Precepts Adapted to the Professional Conduct of Physicians and Surgeons.* Birmingham, AL: Classics of Medicine Library; 1985.

47. Ross W. *The Foundation of Ethics.* Oxford: Clarendon Press; 1939.

48. *Oxford English Dictionary, 2nd Edition.* Oxford: Clarendon Press; 1993.

49. Cruess R, Cruess S. Teaching medicine as a profession in the service of healing. *Academic Medicine.* 1997;72:941–952.

50. Pellegrino E. The metamorphisis of medical ethics. *Journal of the American Medical Association.* 1993;269:1158–1162.

51. Cruess S, Johnston S, Cruess R. Professionalism for medicine: opportunities and obligations. *Medical Journal of Australia.* 2002; 177:208–211.

52. Dyer A. *Ethics and Psychiatry: Toward a Professional Definition.* New York: American Psychiatric Press; 1988.

53. Fullinwider R. Professional codes and moral understanding. In: Coady M, Bloch S, eds. *Codes of Ethics and the Professions.* Melbourne: Melbourne University Press; 1996:72–87.

54. Pellegrino E, Relman A. Professional medical associations: ethical and practical guidelines. *Journal of the American Medical Association.* 1999; 282:1954–1956.

55. ABIM Foundation, ACP-ASIM Foundation, EFIM. Medical professionalism in the new millennium: a physician charter. *Annals of Internal Medicine.* 2002;136:243–246.

56. Robertson M, Walter G. Overview of psychiatric ethics VI: newer approaches to the field. *Australasian Psychiatry* 2007;15:411–416.

3

Communitarian Ethics and the Social Construction of Moral Agency

Introduction

Thus far, we have been building an argument that moral agency does not occur in a vacuum. If we revisit the fundamental question of ethics, "How do I live a good life?" we beg the question "What is the good by which I choose to live?" The concept of *good* is elusive, like time—we have a sense of what it is but struggle to find a representative definition. Good is synonymous with excellent, righteous, or even pious. The alternate of good is evil, which is equally difficult to define. In the metaphysics of Plato, the good was a question of the ultimate knowledge, most famously depicted in his "allegory of the cave" in *The Republic*. For Aristotle, good was tied to virtue and happiness. His notion of *arete* referred to a form of moral excellence that was an intrinsic, rather than instrumental, good.

Such approaches to good and by extension the good life assume that good is in some way naturalistic, i.e., that it exists as a natural phenomenon to be known by humans through their reason, rather than through sense experience. Not all views of ethics assume this, and there are compelling arguments that conceptions of the good life are socially, culturally, and historically constructed. In the contemporary West, concepts of liberty, equal representation of views, and even basic concepts of human rights are comparatively recent developments. In this chapter, we explore the notion that the good and, by extension, moral agency are socially constructed. We argue that the best representation of this by a normative ethical framework is ethical communitarianism.

Communitarianism as a Basis of Moral Philosophy

The *Oxford Companion to Politics*[1] defines *communitarianism* as follows:

> A social philosophy that maintains that societal formulations of the good are both needed and legitimate. Communitarianism is often contrasted with classical liberalism, a philosophical position that holds each individual should formulate the good. Communitarians examine the ways shared conceptions of the good (values) are formed, transmitted, enforced and justified.

Communitarianism is a secular moral philosophy that has both moral and political applications. It consists of a unfocused group of theories, which have been divided into militant and moderate forms.[2] The main point of cohesion of the theories is their criticism of the liberal philosophies of John Rawls and his intellectual descendants.[3,4] This may be misleading, as in the eyes of some, the communitarian critique of Rawls is a straw-man argument.[5] Communitarians are particularly concerned about the liberal moral philosophies prioritizing rights and duties over a conception of the good, and by extension the primacy of the individual over the community. In other words, communitarians argue that rights and duties in liberal philosophy exist in their own right, rather than emerging from conceptions of the good. In communitarian eyes, the right to freedom to choose in life without interference (negative liberty) exists in a liberal framework as intrinsically and irreducibly good. To a communitarian, a right to such freedom needs to reflect a value or conception of the good, which exists prior to the conception of that right. The American Declaration of Independence (1776) proclaims rights to "Life, Liberty and the pursuit of Happiness." The authors of that most famous sentence averred that these rights were endowed by their creator. A communitarian would see that this conception of the good, as manifest in these rights, came from the social framework in which the founding fathers lived—a rejection of a despotic and unrepresentative power structure that was alien to migrants to a new world of unfettered opportunity for human excellence.

The militant communitarians include philosophers such as Canadian Charles Taylor,[6–8] American Michael Sandel,[9,10] and ex-patriot Scot Alisdair MacIntyre.[11–13] The militant communitarians saw people's values as constituted by their community's conception of the good. As such, individuals are best able to achieve the good life through community life. In essence, the good person is the good citizen. Communitarians argued for an intersubjective understanding of the values of an individual person, as these are not understandable in isolation. The communitarian concept of community acknowledges that groups can be yoked by a number of phenomena. There are geographical communities of place, communities of memory linked by a historical narrative, and psychological communities, who share common moral sentiments (see below).[14] The last are, effectively, a manifestation of what American bioethicist H. Tristram Engelhardt described as "moral friends" who share a substantive moral philosophy.[15]

The "moderate" communitarians predate Rawls by centuries–G.F.W. Hegel, David Hume, and Aristotle. The moderates occupy an intermediate position between the role of community and the individual in moral and political philosophy. Their moral philosophies permitted concurrent individual and community conceptions of the good life.

Apart from their criticism of liberalism for its emphasis on individual autonomy, the various strands of communitarian thought are conceptually linked in their placing ethical reasoning in the context of a community. Canadian political philosopher Wil Kymlicka[16] saw communitarianism as, ultimately, focused on shared values or understandings of the good. Communitarianism specifically rejects universal approaches to justice. Kymlicka summarized the communitarian argument against the liberal view of the self as having three components. First, individual moral projects occurring outside of the community approximate "Nietzschean nihilism" in terms of morality (p. 221). Second, liberal individualism involves a fundamental violation of self-perception, based largely on American Michael Sandel's argument that the self is constituted by its ends, which are fundamentally embedded in a community.[10] Third, there is by extension the "embedded self argument." This argument arises from Sandel's contention that the question "Who am I?" should be rephrased "Who should I be?" Self-discovery is therefore the process of discovery of one's attachments and commitments within the community.[17]

This is not a new argument. In *The Politics*,[18] Aristotle first argued that the community, rather than the individual, was the source of the good:

> Since we see that every city-state is a sort of community and that every community is established for the sake of some good (for everyone does everything for the sake of what they believe to be good), it is clear that every community aims at some good, and the community which has the most authority of all and includes all the others aims highest, that is, at the good with the most authority. (I.1.1252a1–7)

This ancient conception of the good person as the good citizen in the *polis* defines the good life as the life of the good citizen.

Key Ideas in Ethical Communitarianism

In this section, we will outline the main concepts of ethical communitarianism that provide a critical foundational theory of our ethical methodology.

Alisdair MacIntyre

MacIntyre took the position that Western moral philosophy is in a state of crisis arising from the failure of, what is termed by many the *Enlightenment project*, emphasizing the liberal value of the individual over all others.[11] To MacIntyre, the ultimate origin of this failure was the fact that the proponents of the Enlightenment failed to take account of the "archaeology," or historical development, of values. MacIntyre argued that the kind of virtuous life defined in antiquity had changed in the face of the emergence of liberal individualism in the eighteenth century. To MacIntyre this change led to a redefinition of moral language. The concept of good was recast to individual psychology rather than the form of classical social life described by Aristotle.

MacIntyre's alternative view was that ethics resides in group practices, occurring within a particular cultural and historical context.[19] MacIntyre argued that the paradigm of Kant's moral autonomy arose to prominence in the Enlightenment. Ironically, despite Kant's rejection of emotivism (actions that produce a pleasant emotional response in the actor being defined as moral), it still emerged as a basis of moral philosophy concurrently with his work. In MacIntyre's view, the fundamental flaw of Enlightenment moral philosophy was the assumption of an "ahistorical universalism"—the position that the values of the Enlightenment were timeless and unchanging. The moral failures of humanity in the twentieth century, particularly in civilized Europe, ultimately undermined this view. MacIntyre's critique of modern moral philosophies, such as those of Kant or Utilitarianism, could be summarized as follows[19]:

1. They ignore the dependence of justice and moral reasoning on group traditions.
2. They fallaciously separate facts from values.
3. They promote the atomization or fragmentation of modern man without a means of reintegration.
4. They appear to permit the individual to be at odds with the group.
5. Some groups can predominate over others, thus compromising the philosophy as a basis of the good life.

In contrast to MacIntyre's apparent diplomacy, Turkish American philosopher Seyla Benhabib provided a more specific, *ad hominem,* critique of the work of Enlightenment moral philosophers.[20] Benhabib contended that the philosophical tradition of the Enlightenment is "overwhelmingly the creation of dead-white-male heads of household, including some slaveholders and misogynists." Indeed, this critique of moral philosophy is a prominent theme in the eyes of many communitarians.

G. W. F. Hegel

MacIntyre's thought was indebted to nineteenth century German philosopher Georg Wilhelm Friedrich Hegel. Hegel's work acknowledges the importance of historical processes in philosophy and dialectic methods evident.

Hegel distinguished between *Moralität* (an individual's morality) and *Sittlichkeit* (a community-based morality called linking individuals to their community).[5] In considering the *Sittlichkeit,* Hegel saw morality not as a subjective process but as one embodied in a community of legal relationships, values, and social institutions. We can therefore approach the lives of individuals within a social life in terms of those customs or conventions. In *The Philosophy of Right,*[21] Hegel first argued that *Sittlichkeit* was the process of these customs being internalized by the individual in the process of socialization or acculturation throughout their moral development. Hegel thus defined *morality* as an internalization of values and external legal relations. He then further distinguished two forms of *Sittlichkeit*— that of civil society and that of the family. This represented a contrast of community relations versus filial emotional bonds. This created a sort of dialectic in which the two forms of *Sittlichkeit* help to define modern society. In terms of moral rights, Hegel called for the dialectic between two forms of *Sittlichkeit* to necessitate a form of (individual) reflection upon laws and rules. This dialectic represented the relationship between individual values of the private life and communal values of the social life. This was Hegel's specific rejection of what he termed the "empty formalism" of Kant. This would seem to foreshadow Arendt's observations of Eichmann's unreflective adherence to duty during his trial in Jerusalem.[22]

British political philosopher Dudley Knowles has devised a graphical depiction[23] of the ethical individual in relation to the individual *Moralität* and the communal *Sittlichkeit,* which we have modified (Figure 3.1). In the center of the diagram is the person, the bearer of abstract basic individual rights. Beyond is the moral subject, a responsible agent who has intentional free will and follows rules in pursuit of the good. Beyond this is the ethical individual, contextualized within the normative domains of the family, the civil society and the state. The notion of a moral community or society was outlined by Kant, with reference to the Kingdom of Ends outlined in the third formulation of the Categorical Imperative.[24] Such a state, or *reich,* would be based on moral laws derived from nature, in which there was mutual encouragement to a moral existence.[25] Elsewhere we have argued the notion that such moral communities exist as various aggregates of medical practitioners and within institutions or communities. These moral communities have substantive shared values and balance these with the requirements of the professional social contract.[26]

Charles Taylor interpreted Hegel's ethical project as one of reconciling the ontological tension between the rival notions of man being part of either the natural or social world and of Kant's view of humans as autonomous and self-determining free individuals.[27] Hegel reconciled the two by constructing both the natural and social worlds as expressions or

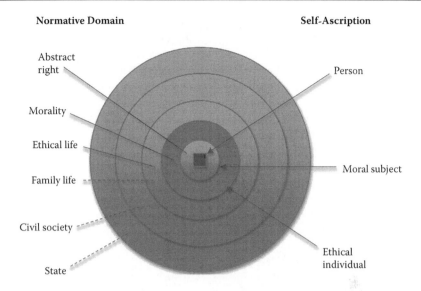

Figure 3.1 Hegel's communitarian ethics. (After Knowles, D., *Hegel and the Philosophy of Right*, London, Routledge, 2002.)

embodiments of a *Geist* (spirit). In doing this Hegel challenged the process of atomization, arguing that any adequate account of the human subject must rely on an understanding of people existing in a network of interactions and becoming individuals only through participation in an intersubjective reality.

Charles Taylor

Charles Taylor saw that Hegel was ultimately wrong, taking the view that Hegel's contribution to moral philosophy was to provide a richer perspective on the individual and his or her relation to society. Taylor's creation of the modern, "post-industrial *Sittlichkeit*" emphasized the relationship of modern man to political and social institutions. This formulation included contemporary issues such as industrial relations, multiculturalism, and the specific role of modern government institutions. In *Sources of the Self*,[6] Taylor argued that modern liberal moral philosophy focuses on what it is right to do, rather than what it is good to be. This appears to be at the core of any communitarian critique of liberalism. Taylor sought to locate morality outside of the individual subject. In this, he saw the role of language as

> a search for moral sources outside the subject through languages which resonate within him or her, the grasping of an order which is inescapably indexed to a personal vision. (p. 510)[6]

Taylor's moral philosophy put moral evaluation at the center of human identity. People understand who they are by the evaluations they make about what is good and how that understanding will direct their lives. Taylor argued that the Enlightenment doctrine of autonomy and self-sufficiency inflict a process of "atomism" on Western culture. This creates a society of disconnected individuals, or "extensionless subjects" with a view of the good as predicated in their individual rights.[28] He rejected this view, arguing that ethical norms make no sense outside of a particular sociocultural and historical context.

Taylor's other key work in this area, *Malaise of Modernity*,[29] attempted to refocus the questions of morality upon shared standards and values. In describing a "culture of authenticity," Taylor argued that we make moral choices based on our individual experience; however, these must be set within the framework of society, nature, and history. Moral choices made from outside these structures lead to a form of soft relativism, which he argues is the primary cause of social malaise.

Daniel Bell

Canadian-born philosopher Daniel Bell attempted to lay out a communitarian "ontology,"[30] arguing that we unreflectively act on the values of our shared social practices, which constitutes the source of our personal identity. Bell is professor of philosophy at Tsinghua University in Beijing and writes from an Asian perspective. To Bell, communities assume various forms. Communities of *place* are defined by geography, whereas communities of *memory* are defined by nationhood, language, or religion. *Psychological* communities are groups of people who participate in common activity and experience a psychological sense of togetherness as shared ends are sought. These are based on face-to-face interaction and are governed by sentiments of trust, cooperation, and altruism in the sense that constituent members have the good of the community in mind and act on behalf of the community's interest.

Bell distinguished *universalism* from *particularism* in terms of ethics.[14] He defined particularism as the claim that there are no defensible moral principles. He argued that the communitarian position, at least in a geopolitical sense, is one of cultural particularism.[31] Arguing from the example of Singaporean society, he argued for particularism along a number of lines. First, cultural factors affect how different societies may prioritize rights. Although a multicultural society, Singapore's ruling class identifies with a Confucian heritage and places greater emphasis upon the value of education than on individual freedom. Second, cultural factors may affect the justification of rights. Third, cultural factors provide moral foundations for distinctive political practices and institutions. In Singapore, political debate focuses on how filial piety is best realized by different legislative approaches. Bell quoted former Singaporean Prime Minister Lee Kwan Yew that Asians have "little doubt that a society with communitarian values where the interests of society take precedence over that of the individual suits them better than the individualism of America" (p. 7).[32]

Bell argued that the conflict of universalism against particularism has lost some relevance since the advent of globalization, manifesting largely as the hegemony of Anglo-American liberalism and its emphasis on universal human rights as a tacit co-factor in market relations.

Amitai Etzioni

German–Jewish-born American philosopher Amitai Etzioni argued a form of communitarianism that is more politically focused. He argued that communitarian societies have two key elements—a balance between liberty and the common good, and a balance between individual rights and social responsibilities. Social institutions and policies reflect and embody the values within a community, which are internalized by the individual members. Unlike Bell, Etzioni was critical of the communitarianism of societies like Singapore, contrasting its suppression of individual autonomy through coercive social engineering and Draconian laws, with the traditional emphasis of filial bonds over individual interests in Japanese society.[33] Etzioni's form of communitarianism sought to balance particular individual needs with communal ones, within the context of a liberal democracy. Like MacIntyre, he points out that the historical–social conditions of specific societies affect this balance. As such, he saw that the balance may have tipped slightly away from liberal autonomy in the aftermath of 9/11.[34]

Communitarianism and Psychiatric Ethics

Communitarianism appears to offer some means by which a normative theory of psychiatric ethics can be better integrated into a social and cultural context. The substance of MacIntyre's critique of Enlightenment moral theories was that they lack historical context,[11] whereas Taylor saw the main problem with liberal moral theories as that they atomized the process of morality[7] and neglected the social constitution of the self.[6]

American bioethicist Daniel Callahan has been instrumental in clarifying what a communitarian approach to bioethics and, by extension, psychiatric ethics might be. Callahan saw communitarian bioethics as arising from the insinuation of liberal ideology into the bioethical discourse as a set of political and social values, which serve as a background to bioethical debate.[35] He defined communitarianism as meaning to

> characterize a way of thinking about ethical problems, not to provide any formulas or rigid criteria for dealing with them. It assumes that human beings are social animals, not under any circumstances isolated individuals, and whose lives are lived.[36]

Callahan's communitarianism used an ecology metaphor of bioethics—with the introduction of a species into an ecosystem, one needs to consider the effects of this action on the other species and the ecosystem in general. In this metaphor, liberal individualism focuses on the effect of the action on the introduced species.

To restate, the key issues in communitarianism are first that human beings exist in a network of other people and within the social institutions and culture of their society. Second, no sharp distinction can be drawn between the public and private spheres of moral life. Third, communitarianism begins with the welfare of a society as a whole. Finally, the historical context of moral systems is important.

Despite this position, there is a need to reflect upon human rights, without which consideration there is potential for individuals, particularly those who are vulnerable such as those suffering mental illness, to suffer at the hands of community interests. In the biomedical context, theoretical or applied ethical problems (such as the implications of stem cell research) will affect the community as a whole, including posing challenges to its traditional values. This necessitates a community-focused discourse of the human good, in which every member of the community ought to have a voice.

American bioethicist Ezekiel Emanuel[37](brother of former Obama Chief of Staff Raum Emanuel) has applied communitarian principles to bioethics. Emmanuel argues that, as with all social institutions, medicine is underpinned by public laws and values within a framework of shared views of what constitutes the good life. Emmanuel's communitarian bioethics are pluralist and, like Etzioni's, make some concessions to individual rights, requiring democratic processes to formalize communitarian ideas into laws. Emmanuel argued that biomedical ethical issues need to be debated by all citizens not merely the professionals involved.

Social factors underpin how psychiatric disorders are constructed and treated, making communitarianism a potentially useful theoretical approach to understanding psychiatric ethics. The emergence of potential communitarian themes in professional psychiatric ethics also relates to the highly contextual nature of the psychiatric profession. As discussed previously, American psychiatrist Allen Dyer attempted to contextualize the psychiatrist as moral agent in both psychodynamic terms and in a broader sociocultural setting. Dyer argued:

> a potentially destructive aspect of the field of medical ethics is that it has been operating in a cultural and psychological void as if there were no such thing as virtue or a moral agent.[38]

In a wide-ranging paper, two British psychiatrists, Julian Hughes and Bill Fulford, took the view that psychiatric ethics assumes the psychiatrist as embedded in a social and cultural context, in which different values, including religion and spirituality,[39] are relevant to the process of diagnosis and treatment of psychiatric disorder. As such, psychiatric ethics must be discussed in the light of philosophical concerns about the personhood. To Hughes and Fulford, psychiatric ethics are unique in their influence of values within both the community and the profession upon clinical practice, particularly in regard to diagnosis.

Conclusion: Communitarianism as a Moral Prism

The survey of the main ideas in communitarianism reveals both a form of political philosophy and the recognition that moral agents are socially constituted and cannot be atomized in the light of this social constitution. Questions of ontology, values, or public policy are all enlightened by the communitarian position. To restate the relevant tenets of communitarianism as one of the theoretical foundations of our methodology of psychiatric ethics, the following hold:

1. It acknowledges the sociocultural and historical context of values and moral dilemmas.
2. It acknowledges the social constitution of the psychiatrists as moral agents.
3. This social constitution informs the process of how values and knowledge are created by the group.
4. It acknowledges the competing perspectives of individual and collective good.
5. It permits a plurality of views including a sophisticated form of moral relativism.
6. It facilitates an approach to psychiatric ethics that is dynamic or organic.

As an ethical prism, communitarianism appears to necessitate consideration of the values constructed by psychiatrists, the factors that determine these values, as well as the multiple relationships the profession has in different contexts within its community.

The communitarian position informs the approach to psychiatric ethics by indicating that any prospective consideration of quandaries in psychiatric practice ought to consider both the values that can be identified as well as the influence of history, societal values, the law, and culture.

References

1. Etzioni A. Communitariansim. In: Kreiger J, ed. *The Oxford Companion to Politics of the World*. Oxford: Oxford University Press; 2001:221–223.

2. Beauchamp T, Childress J. *Principles of Biomedical Ethics, 5th Edition*. New York: Oxford University Press; 2001.

3. Rawls J. *A Theory of Justice*. Cambridge, MA: The Bellknap Press; 1971.

4. Rawls J. *Political Liberalism*. New York: Columbia University Press; 1993.

5. Gutman A. Communitarian critics of liberalism. *Philosophy and Public Affairs*. 1985;14:308–322.

6. Taylor C. *Sources of the Self: The Making of Modern Identity*. Cambridge, MA: Harvard University Press; 1989.

7. Taylor C. *Philosophy and the Human Sciences: Philosophical Papers 2*. Cambridge: Cambridge University Press; 1985.

8. Taylor C. Readings in forensic psychiatry. *British Medical Journal*. 1988;153:271–278.

9. Sandel M. *Public Philosophy: Essays on Morality in Politics*. New York: Harvard University Press; 2006.

10. Sandel M. *Liberalism and the Limits of Justice*. Cambridge: Cambridge University Press; 1981.

11. MacIntyre A. *After Virtue*. Notre Dame, IN: University of Notre Dame Press; 1984.

12. MacIntyre A. *Whose Justice? Which Rationality?* Notre Dame, IN: University of Notre Dame Press; 1988.

13. MacIntyre A. *Three Rival Versions of Moral Enquiry: Encyclopaedia, Geneology and Tradition*. Notre Dame, IN: University of Notre Dame Press; 1990.

14. Bell D. *Communitarianism*. 2004; http://plato.stanford.edu/entries/communitarianism/ (accessed April 25, 2006).

15. Engelhardt H. *The Foundations of Bioethics 2nd Edition*. New York: Oxford University Press; 1996.

16. Kymlicka W. *Contemporary Political Philosophy*. New York: Oxford University Press; 2002.

17. Sandel M. The procedural republic and the unencumbered self. *Political Theory* 1980;12:81–96.

18. Aristotle. Politics. Keyt D, trans. *The Clarendon Aristotle Series* Oxford: Oxford University Press; 1995.

19. MacIntyre A. Notes from the moral wilderness II. In: Knight K, ed. *The MacIntyre Reader*. Notre Dame, IN: University of Notre Dame Press; 1998:41–49.

20. Benhabib S. Taking ideas seriously can we distinguish political choices from philosophical truths? *Boston Review*. 2002/2003;27: http://bostonreview.net/BR27.26/benhabib.html (accessed December 22, 2006).

21. Hegel G. *Philosophy of Right*. Oxford: Clarendon Press; 1952.

22. Arendt H. *Eichmann in Jerusalem: A Report on the Banality of Evil*. London: Faber & Faber; 1963.

23. Knowles D. *Hegel and the Philosophy of Right*. London: Routledge; 2002.

24. Kant I. *Groundwork of the Metaphysic of Morals*. New York: Harper and Row; 1964.

25. Sullivan R. *An Introduction to Kant's Ethics*. Cambridge: Cambridge University Press; 1994.

26. Turner L. Medical facilities as moral worlds. *Journal of Medical Ethics: Medical Humanities*. 2002;28:19–22.

27. Taylor C. *Hegel and Modern Society*. Cambridge: Cambridge University Press; 1975.

28. Taylor C. Atomism. *Philosophy and the Human Sciences. Philosophical Papers 2*. Cambridge: Cambridge University Press; 1985:187–211.

29. Taylor C. *The Malaise of Modernity*. Concord, ON: Anansi Press; 1997.

30. Bell D. *Communitarianism and Its Critics*. Oxford: Clarendon Press; 1993.

31. Bell D. The East Asian challenge to human rights: reflections on an East West dialogue. *Human Rights Quarterly*. 1996;18:641–667.

32. Bell D. *East Meets West: Human Rights and Democracy in East Asia*. Princeton: Princeton University Press; 2000.

33. Etzioni A. Communitarianism. In: Turner B, ed. *The Cambridge Dictionary of Sociology*. Cambridge: Cambridge University Press; 2006:81–83.

34. Etzioni A. Public health law: a communitarian perspective. *Health Affairs: Perspective*. 2002;21:102–104.

35. Callahan D. Individual good and common good. *Perspectives in Biology and Medicine*. 2003;46:496–507.

36. Callahan D. Principlism and communitarianism. *Journal of Medical Ethics*. 2003;29:287–291.

37. Emmanuel E. *The Ends of Human Life: Medical Ethics in a Liberal Polity*. Cambridge, MA: Harvard University Press; 1991.

38. Dyer A. *Ethics and Psychiatry: Toward a Professional Definition*. New York: American Psychiatric Press; 1988.

39. Hughes J, Fulford K. Hurly-burly of psychiatric ethics. *Australian and New Zealand Journal of Psychiatry*. 2005;39:1001–1007.

4

Moral Agency in Psychiatry

Introduction

We have argued so far that the social constitution of psychiatrists as moral agents necessitates integration of different ideas including professional and Rawlsian notions of the social contract, virtue, and communitarianism. Our position regarding the ontology of psychiatrists as moral agents combined with the community's perspective on values provides an approach to ethics that allows for multiple contextual influences, such as the law, professional standards, and conceptions of the good from personal, community, and social perspectives.

Recall that our conceptualization of moral agency in psychiatry was based upon the notion of the noumenal self, influenced by context and therefore acting morally in a socially constituted way. The moral acts and deliberation existed at the *exo* level (social context); the *meso* and *endo* levels integrate values at professional, institutional, familial, and individual levels. We will explore the *exo* more broadly in Section II. In this chapter we will outline a method of moral deliberation for psychiatrists.

Psychiatrist as Socially Constituted Moral Agent

Hegel had argued that the ethical agent conceptualized the good as part of the life of an ethical community. Such a good is pursued in the light of the rules and conventions of social institutions, which exist in the context of a particular history.[1] This amounts to rejecting a grand overarching model of values in favor of more local ones. Alisdair MacIntyre concluded his most significant work, *After Virtue,*[2] by giving an account of the period in Imperial Roman history where small communities turned away from the requirements of maintaining a decaying empire to create settings that could sustain some forms of moral life in the face of external threats. MacIntyre argued that this was the case in Western moral philosophy:

> What matters at this stage is the construction of local forms of community within which civility and the intellectual and moral life can be sustained through the new dark ages which are already upon us. (p. 263)[2]

As described in a previous chapter, the American ethicist H. Tristram Engelhardt argued that it was impossible to have meaningful universal views of values that extended across cultures and across time.[3] Even allowing for the aftermath of the Nuremberg war crime trials in 1945 and the elaboration of the West's notions of universal notions of human rights, Engelhardt contended that large groups of "moral strangers" can only share a negotiated form of "procedural morality." This, in essence, is the notion of the social contract. This distinction is best articulated by the contrast of universalism and particularism in moral philosophy.[4] In the light of this, Engelhardt posited that the communitarian approach to ethics is the only means of achieving a substantive moral system among "moral friends."

There are, however, two contexts for such moral relationships. Within the kind of diverse, multicultural democratic society envisioned by Rawls, there would be secular approaches to values that were embodied in laws addressing basic tenets of liberty; this would usually reflect the perspective of common morality in terms of promise keeping, honesty in commercial transactions, and abiding safe and respectful conduct among the citizenry.

In contrast, small moral communities possess substantive ethics among moral friends. The essential nature of these small groups is best defined by notions of communities of memory and psychological communities, defined by shared values or historical linkages.[5] Medical facilities or professional groups possess the quality of small moral communities, where *ethics* are less oriented to rules and dilemmas and more attuned to practical matters of everyday social experience.[6] In considering the moral agency of physicians, Engelhardt highlighted that small groups of healthcare professionals have "double lives."[3] These double lives speak to the postmodern approach to ethics argued by Australian philosopher Richard Hugman,[7] who asserted that "caring professionals" experience tension between their responsibilities to patients in a particular setting and their broader social responsibilities.

In considering the moral constitution and agency of psychiatrists, our position is that the source of "the good" in psychiatry is in small groups of psychiatrists as moral friends who practice in relation to the broader psychiatric profession and the community.[8] The tension described by Engelhardt as "double lives" finds its manifestation in the theme in the dual-role dilemma, which is so prevalent in the literature in psychiatric ethics.[9]

Psychiatrist as Moral Agent

Values

The term *value* refers to a degree of importance of an entity. There are multiple discourses on the concept of value, such as in financial or commercial settings. In ethics, values are those entities that relate to a good life. These are habits or dispositions that are important to motivating or shaping attitudes or actions that are part of such a life.[10]

Aristotle distinguished between *intrinsic* and *instrumental* values.[11] The former are values that are an ultimate good—to Aristotle this was, ultimately, human reason. To Aristotle rational capacity was at the basis of human flourishing. In contrast, instrumental values are those that assist in approaching the good life. Values such as honesty, integrity, and agreeableness appear to contribute to human flourishing and are therefore valuable in their contribution toward this good life. In the same way, values can be relative or absolute. The former exist within individuals or groups, but may not generalize across cultures or history. Despite the seeming lack of universality to many values, the Scottish philosopher Alisdair MacIntyre posits that there have to be human qualities such as love or agreeableness that are absolutely valuable across times and cultures.[12]

Values are conceptually prior to ethics in that they help determine what a group regards as the good. To behave ethically is to behave in regard to such a conception of the good. American pragmatist philosopher John Dewey saw the definition of the good as the outcome of a process of valuation, an iterative continuous balancing of personal or cultural values. For Dewey, there was a constant flow between valuing and evaluation.[13]

Extending from the general concept of values is Values Based Medicine (VBM). This movement has been in large measure due to the work of Bill Fulford.[14] Fulford co-opted a description of values from the evidence-based medicine literature integrating the preferences, concerns, and expectations each patient brings to a clinical encounter. These must be integrated into clinical decisions based upon evidence-based medicine. This acknowledges the distinction of the practice of medicine as a moral and scientific enterprise rather than the mere application of science to disease states.[15]

Fulford described "values complex" issues in healthcare, including aspects of health management such as clinical governance, audit, quality assurance, cost-effectiveness, and proper evaluation of preventive and public health medicine. In addressing values-based practice, VBM employs a dialogic interaction with the patient integrating the patient's expectations, desires, and fears about the application of evidence-based medicine. Fulford argues that there are four components in engendering VBM during the professional development of junior doctors, particularly those training in psychiatry. The first is awareness of values evidenced in current practice. This is particularly the case in the diagnostic act. Fulford has emphasized the Fact–Value distinction in psychiatric diagnosis. This acknowledges that a psychiatric disorder contains factual and evaluative components. In the example of schizophrenia, demonstrable or factual elements comprise the demonstrable pathological or physiological disturbances associated with the illness in addition to the negative valuing of symptoms or functional changes seen.[16,17]

Fulford argues that VBM requires physicians to evolve sophisticated skills in moral reasoning and communication. The final evolution in VBM is the place of research into values and their essential role in medical practice. This is the area of inquiry that has been dubbed *empirical ethics.*

Empirical Ethics

There has been some enthusiasm at the prospect of the empirical turn in bioethics discourse.[18] This is not a new idea—Aristotle's moral philosophy emerged from his observations and descriptions of the habits of great men. Research methods used in social sciences such as anthropology, epidemiology, psychology, and sociology[19] now make an important contribution to the field of medical ethics.[20] Empirical methods aim at a descriptive rather than a normative account of ethics—they define the *what is* rather than the *what ought to be.* Empirical methods can inform the different phases of ethical reasoning—the description and assessment of moral questions, and the evaluation of the decision making around such questions.[21] Such approaches work in an iterative manner between theory and observation.[22] Empirical approaches to medical ethics can describe how physicians interact within a moral framework or better define the nature of a phenomenon such as a value system or the nature of an ethical dilemma.[23] Despite the promise of empirical ethics, there has been little research effort using empirical methods in psychiatric ethics,[24] and application of empirical ethics in psychiatry is a relatively new line of inquiry.[25]

The prospect of empirical ethics in psychiatry aims to reconcile how theoretical and empirical approaches to ethics inform each other in a cyclical manner. Two Dutch researchers, Wiidershoven and Van der Scheer, argued that the aspiration of empirical approaches to medical ethics is a process of describing how experienced clinicians generate solutions to real-life problems and the investigation of the validity of such views. By examining how experienced and caring psychiatrists approach ethical quandaries in their practice, normative theories or methods of reasoning in ethics can perhaps emerge.[26] Such empirical analysis also enables context-sensitive consideration or what is termed *idiographic accounts* of ethical issues in psychiatry.[27]

Several methods of empirical research in psychiatric ethics have been attempted, including ethnography, grounded theory, mixed methods (involving qualitative and quantitative approaches),[28] and case-history approaches. One enlightening ethnographic study of mental health workers in a long-term care setting used a participant–observer approach to observe caring acts and then conduct interviews with the relevant clinicians after them.[29] Another study of carers of dementia sufferers used a modified grounded theory approach. The investigators in this study were sufficiently concerned about theoretical sensitization that they modified the traditional grounded theory approach in a pilot study and the subsequent[30] main study.[31,32] The study gathered data using two interviews—the first, open ended; the second, a form of respondent validation through a structured interview with the same subjects, based upon the analysis of the original interviews.

We undertook a study seeking to identify the values underpinning Australian psychiatrists in their clinical work in an effort to empirically validate the *Code of Ethics* of the Royal Australian and New Zealand College of Psychiatrists (RANZCP).[33] This study used a methodology called *ethnomethodology*, which looks at how subjects deal with different dilemmas in their work setting. In this study we interviewed psychiatrists practicing in different settings about their work, after which we analyzed the content of the interviews using qualitative methods. Through a process of coding we identified four themes that represented values held by this specific group of psychiatrists—the value of the patient, the value of sophisticated understanding, the value of reflexivity, and the value of advocacy. We then considered the specific ethical principles and annotations of the RANZCP *Code of Ethics* to establish how well they reflected the values we identified in our study. Our conclusion was that the two perspectives seemed to reflect very similar values, although our research indicated some possible modifications for annotations of the code.

While our research offered a retrospective validation of the RANZCP *Code of Ethics*, what this work indicates is that future codes of ethics for different organizations can be both constructed and later modified in the light of changing circumstances using empirical research methods.

Ontology and Epistemology

Psychiatry sits at the intersection of multiple discourses. This speaks of the centrality of philosophy in psychiatry, a notion lost in its current biological paradigm. The philosopher and psychiatrist Karl Jaspers argued that philosophical studies exercised a restraining influence on the thought of psychiatrists, preventing them from pursuing lines of thought that were irrelevant or deployed prejudices.[34] Thus the ontology or existence of psychiatry, and perhaps medicine generally, cannot be reduced to a specific theme or discourse. As the tenets of VBM imply, psychiatrists in particular abide with a complex approach to knowledge and practice that integrates perspectives from science, sociology, ethics, phenomenology, anthropology, and epistemology. It is not merely a question of applying the knowledge derived from the scientific evidence base to a specific disease or syndrome, but reflection upon the more complex social and humanistic aspects of this activity. This represents the true challenges and rewards of a career in psychiatry.

American psychiatrist Nassir Ghaemi has written extensively in this area. Ghaemi sees psychiatry as a fundamentally pluralist enterprise. Pluralism in social and natural science is the position that some phenomena observed in science and social science require multiple methods to account for their nature. The essence of pluralism is that different epistemic positions (approaches to knowledge) are equally valid. In understanding depression in a particular patient, the physics of neurotransmitters is an equivalent, not superior, means of knowledge of the phenomenon as the intrapsychic, cognitive, or existential realms of the person. Each discourse is equally valued and retained in an attempt to know. To Ghaemi, the biopsychosocial model of Engel is eclectic, and an inferior epistemic approach to pluralism.[35]

Resolving the Dual-Role Dilemma

In the final analysis, the dual-role quandary is best resolved by negotiating a course of moral and practical action that reconciles both obligations. Like many quandaries in moral philosophy, the most practical means of doing this is abiding with the doctrine of the *golden mean*. Finding the mean between extremes of behavior extends to the origins of Western and Eastern philosophies. In Greek mythology, Icarus ignored his father, Daedalus's, warning to fly the middle course between the sun and the sea, only to meet disaster by flying too close to the sun. Socrates' injunction that men "must know how to choose the mean and avoid the extremes on either side, as far as possible" also places the golden mean at the core of practical wisdom. In the Confucian tradition, the "way of Zhongyong" advocated the mean between extremes of behavior.

The philosopher most associated with a doctrine of the golden mean was Aristotle. In the *Eudemian Ethics*[36] and throughout his other works, Aristotle refers to "the Middle state between." In Aristotle's moral philosophy, virtue is the trained habit of finding the mean between the extremes. A simple example of this is the cardinal virtue of courage. To rush recklessly into danger leads to disaster; to cravenly hide from confrontation usually results in harms to self and others. The middle ground is to define a course of action that permits an acceptable level of risk yet does resile from a successful response.

In the Aristotelian tradition, Thomas Aquinas argued in Question LXIV of his *Summa Theologica*:

> And therefore it is clear that the good of moral virtue consists in being up to the level of the measure of reason: which condition of being up to the level, or of conformity to rule, evidently lies in the mean between excess and defect.[37]

The cardinal virtues of Aquinas, justice, temperance, fortitude, and prudence—along with faith, hope, and charity—compose the seven theological virtues. While the first three cardinal virtues represent the core of a virtuous person, the last is the most significant in practical moral agency.

Prudence is often associated with Aristotle's work, where in the *Nichomachean Ethics*, he termed it *phronesis*. *Phronesis* (practical wisdom) contrasts with *sophia* (theoretical wisdom), and in Aristotle's view comes only from life experience. As we discussed in previously, *phronesis* is at the core of this practical wisdom and, combined with the method of casuistry, forms the basis of our proposed methodology for reasoning in psychiatric ethics.

Moral Reasoning in Psychiatry

Many decisions are based upon previous experience. Prior experience of the perceived consequences of an act or course of action forms the basis of the form of knowledge applied to similar circumstances. This form of inductive reasoning underlies most formulations of action. A salient example is clinical decision making in regard to choice of antidepressant agent. Scientific forms of knowledge do not readily offer the subtlety needed for sound decisions of which agent to use, at which dose, and in what circumstances.

What is evident from considering the various merits of many normative theories is that their application in psychiatric ethics usually requires combinations of reflective and instrumental theories. The proposed methods of R. M. Hare[38] required a reflective process prior to the application of a utilitarian framework to a problem. In 2006, Australian psychiatric ethicist Sid Bloch and Georgetown University academic psychiatrist Stephen Green proposed a combination of the ethics of care and principles-based ethics in moral deliberation in the setting of quandaries in psychiatric practice.[39]

Our model for approaching ethical dilemmas in psychiatry is shown in Figures 4.1 and 4.2. This approach to moral reasoning in psychiatric ethics involves two phases—a reflective phase and a deliberative phase.

Reflective Phase

In Figure 4.1, the first phase of moral deliberation, the reflective phase is shown. This process is an application of the principle of "reflective equilibrium" described by John Rawls. Reflective equilibrium is an iterative process of considering different judgments, maxims, and beliefs in relation to a particular issue. This is a form of "coherentist" epistemic justification, whereby a belief is justified if it coheres with other beliefs a person or group holds. The core of this form of epistemic justification is that individuals and groups "test" various parts of their system of beliefs against the other beliefs they hold.

The first focus of reflection is the clinical aspects of a particular quandary. This initially takes in perspectives from the patient, the patient's family, and carers. The moral agent appraises the clinical aspects of the situation, including questions of how well the illness or

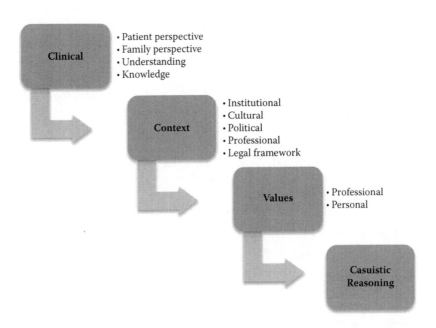

Figure 4.1 The reflective phase of moral deliberation.

crisis is understood, its effect upon the patient's autonomous capacity, and the requirements of management that emerge from this. The moral agent then questions the soundness of what is known about the clinical situation, particularly questions of how justifiable the knowledge of the patient is, the situation, and the scientific evidence of the different possible clinical interventions.

The next focus of reflection is the contextual aspects of the situation. Psychiatrists often work within institutional settings, such as hospitals or health service institutions, and within a professional framework embodied in organizations such as the Royal College of Psychiatrists or the American Psychiatric Association. These institutions and professional bodies characteristically assert codes of ethics and conduct, in addition to public positions and guidelines for clinical practice. Many aspects of culture affect psychiatric moral agency, including risk appetite and stigma, which may affect how psychiatrists respond to challenges. This is also the case with public policy and the indirect intercession of ministers or secretaries in specific clinical situations. In many circumstances, specific laws exist in relation to vexed ethical questions in psychiatry, particularly in regard to criminal procedures, statutory obligations to breach confidence, and mental health law.

The last focus of reflection is upon the area of values. Personal and professional values form the basis for maxims or rules of action. To function within specific moral quandaries, the psychiatrist will frequently revert to value systems as a point of reflection. Foundational values such as respect for patient autonomy, beneficence, truth telling, or the Hippocratic injunction often loom in the background of moral deliberation.

Deliberative Phase

The deliberative phase of moral agency begins with the process of casuistic reasoning, outlined in the Chapter 3 (Figure 4.2).

The first step requires identification of the paradigm case. Paradigm cases may be unique to specific settings or professional groups. Commonly, clinicians identify a particular instance of a similar dilemma where the course of action was considered ethical, desirable, or successful. This determination is often achieved in a process of collegiate or peer discussion. The next step is to identify similar cases and, through the process of normative analogy, establish a hierarchy or taxonomy of such cases in relation to the paradigm case. The proximity of a particular case to the paradigm case is usually a function of the similarities

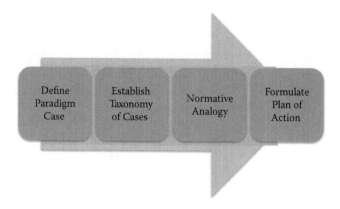

Figure 4.2 Casuistic reasoning—the first component of the deliberative phase of moral reasoning.

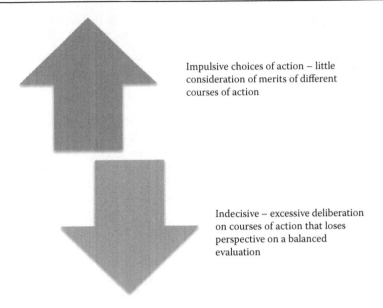

Impulsive choices of action – little consideration of merits of different courses of action

Indecisive – excessive deliberation on courses of action that loses perspective on a balanced evaluation

Figure 4.3 The doctrine of the golden mean—the second component of the deliberative phase of moral reasoning.

and relevant negative differences. When the place of the case under consideration is established, its proximity to the paradigm case enables the moral agent to identify the extent to which different courses of action are justifiable.

The second component of the deliberative phase is to formulate how the plan of action emerging from the casuistic paradigm fits within the dual-role dilemma rubric and where the mean between the extremes is located (Figure 4.3). This involves establishing both extremes, such as excessive caution or reckless indifference to safety. The process of *phronesis* requires iteration between the casuistic and golden mean phases, as the casuistic paradigm often illuminates the pathway to the mean.

We will now apply our methodology to a specific case example that highlights a common dilemma in psychiatric practice.

Case Example: A Dangerous Patient

A 45-year-old unemployed single man suffered recurrent episodes of paranoid psychosis occurring in the context of abuse of alcohol. When affected by alcohol, the man experienced a florid paranoid psychosis. When abstinent from alcohol, the man's mental state was free of any psychotic symptoms, and he regained full insight without antipsychotic treatment. He displayed, clinically, some level of impaired judgment and mental inflexibility, but was able to manage his finances and maintain a reasonable level of self-care. He could also comprehend the consequences of choosing to drink. There was no evidence of an "organic" cause to his mental-state disturbances. There had been marked deterioration in his psychosocial functioning, and he had estranged himself from his family, who had requested no contact from him due to his alcohol-related violent behavior.

During one episode of alcohol-related psychosis, the man developed the delusional belief that his neighbor was spying on him while he was in the shower. As a result, he attempted to stab his neighbor. He was arrested and subsequently convicted of malicious damage and assault. While he was found to be mentally ill by the court, he was released on a good behavior bond rather than referred to care as a mentally disordered offender. One condition of his release was that he was to abstain from drinking alcohol and attend counseling. The court's liaison officer contacted a local mental health service and stated that, as part of his release, the patient was to be randomly breathalyzed by the mental health service and that any breaches of his release conditions were to be reported to the probation and parole service. There had been a series of well-publicized homicides perpetrated by people with mental illness in the previous few months, with much media commentary on the perceived failures of mental health services. The relevant government authority had responded to these events by requiring different health services to report how they were managing risk. This specific health service had been the subject of civil legal action following several suicides. Each service director had been tasked with providing his or her superiors with detailed reports of the management of patients whose illness posed a risk of harm, including details of how that risk was being managed specifically in each case.

In light of the patient's history of violent offending and the clear risk that his illness posed, the psychiatrist in charge of the service opted to treat the patient with regular depot antipsychotic medication.

The patient attended an appointment in an intoxicated state with a psychiatrist working for the mental health service and admitted he had not attended alcohol counseling sessions. He demonstrated evidence of recent physical trauma and admitted that he had been involved in a number of fights. Although he was not floridly psychotic, probably due to the regular administration of depot antipsychotic medication, the patient was clearly in breach of his bond conditions.

Should the psychiatrist breach a confidence and notify the probation and parole service?

To apply the methodology to this specific case example—

Reflective Phase

Clinical Perspectives—The patient clearly desires not to go to prison and is distressed by both his symptoms and their consequences (Figure 4.4). His family is interested in his posing less of a threat to their safety and well-being. He has cognitive limitations, presumably due to alcohol, and this may be impairing his ability to engage with treatment approaches to his alcohol abuse. His motivation to reduce or cease alcohol use may be diminished by the nature of his clinical contact with the psychiatrist and health service, and it is likely that there

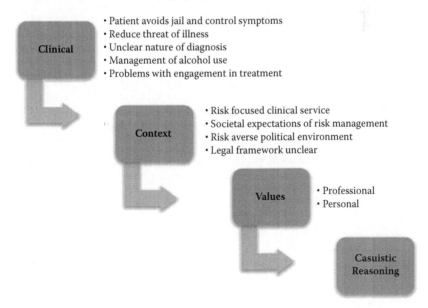

Figure 4.4 The reflective phase of moral deliberation in the case example.

has been limited therapeutic engagement given the context of the relationship—he has been coerced under threat of imprisonment to attend the clinical service. His diagnosis is not entirely clear: the presentation suggests the likelihood of alcoholic hallucinosis; however, the duration and nature of his psychotic symptoms suggest that a schizophrenic illness may be the likely problem.

Context—The psychiatrist worked in a public sector mental health service tasked with managing patients with high levels of clinical acuity and social disadvantage. As with most services, there is a consistent focus on risk management and risk mitigation. Any decisions regarding a patient with a constellation of problems such as in this situation would be influenced by this imperative. Moreover, there had been several, well-publicized incidents in the community involving people with mental illness perpetrating violent offences. While an aberration, it has clearly led to a widespread community concern about the risks posed by people suffering mental illness. The mental health service has been buffeted by several legal actions and clearly has a limited tolerance to any risk posed by patients' illnesses. In the light of recent events, the health authority or relevant government department has also communicated the expectation that risk become a focus of the various mental health services. The psychiatrist is required to report on how risk is being managed in the clinical care of each patient.

The dual-role dilemma in this case is the requirement of the psychiatrist to abide with the expectations of the community and superiors at institutional and governmental levels. This is crystallized in the issue of whether to breach a confidence in regard to the patient's defaulting on treatment. This is complicated by several factors. In the first instance, the notification of the patient's behavior will lead to the patient facing more time in prison. This will do little for the relationship between the patient and the service; it is likely that any further custodial sentence would be brief and the patient would return to the area, presumably still suffering the same problems. Further time in prison will likely be a traumatic experience, likely to escalate the patient's future substance misuse and mental illness. In essence, the psychiatrist and the risk-averse community and institutions in which he or she practices will face managing an even more difficult clinical situation with a patient who is likely to be deeply at odds with the people who were instrumental in his returning to prison.

Values—Few psychiatrists are entirely at ease with their presumed agency of "social control." Psychiatry has a troubling history of the use of their power in service of a greater good which has had little regard for the welfare of patients. A number of international and local professional declarations of ethics and conduct by psychiatrists assert specific injunctions against such utilization of power by psychiatrists. The Hippocratic tradition is clearly at odds with any act likely to harm a patient. A psychiatrist's personal value system is also affronted by the prospect of functioning as a proxy for a parole service; the psychiatrist may also be troubled by the idea of such a patient presenting a public menace in their community.

Deliberative Phase

The initial phase of deliberation involves the application of a casuistic paradigm to the dilemma. The initial step of this process is establishing the *paradigm case* (Figure 4.5). In most jurisdictions, there are provisions for the care of mentally disordered offenders within the criminal justice system. These provisions usually involve the detention of patients in a hospital, rather than in prisons, and their subsequent well-supervised conditional release into

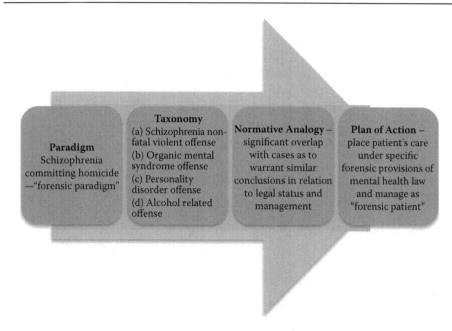

Figure 4.5 The first component of the deliberative phase of moral deliberation in the case example—casuistic reasoning.

the community. In such circumstances, the level of supervision and allocation of resources within a health service is usually higher than for other patients. Within the clinical service, it is probable that there would be consensus that the management of a patient suffering from schizophrenia who has committed a homicide or other violent offense presents a "gold standard" of care.

The next step is to construct a *taxonomy* of cases in regard to the paradigm case. Clinical scenarios encountered by the service include patients with schizophrenia who have committed nonfatal violent and nonviolent offenses, patients with organic mental syndromes or intellectual disability who have offended, patients with severe personality disorder who have offended, and patients with alcohol or other drug use problems who have offended (Figure 4.5). In the taxonomy of cases, the case under question appears to sit nearer the paradigm case than the case of a patient whose offense was in the context of drug or alcohol abuse.

Having placed the case in a close proximity to the paradigm case, the next step is the process of *normative analogy*. In this case, both the paradigm and the specific case have violent offending occurring against the background of paranoid psychosis. The optimal management of this situation addresses the risk variables that increase the likelihood of recidivism. Such management would involve a period of inpatient observation; considered use of antipsychotic medication; engaging the patient in care, addressing alcohol use and its complications; addressing the patient's social isolation, unemployment, and homelessness, and engaging his family in his care. While the nature of the patient's illness is unclear, the pragmatic option in this instance seems to err toward a diagnosis of more severe mental illness, particularly in regard to management. Moreover, many circumstances of violent offending perpetrated by people suffering schizophrenia are associated with use of alcohol

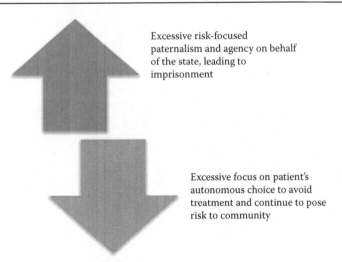

Excessive risk-focused paternalism and agency on behalf of the state, leading to imprisonment

Excessive focus on patient's autonomous choice to avoid treatment and continue to pose risk to community

Figure 4.6 The second component of deliberative phase of moral deliberation in the case example— the golden mean.

or psychoactive substances. Questions of his mild cognitive impairment do not seem to diminish the analogous relationship with the paradigm case.

The *plan of action* would therefore seem to be akin to the management of the paradigm case. The clinical service would therefore seek to have the patient's case transferred from the criminal law to the forensic provisions of the mental health laws. The patient would therefore be directed to a secure hospital setting and his case considered by the appropriate judicial body. This would seem to correct an error made in the original criminal proceedings, which saw the patient deemed guilty and responsible for a crime and released into the community with unrealistic expectations of good behavior.

In this setting, the patient's and community's interests are best served. This is also clearly a sound resolution of the dual-role dilemma in the light of the doctrine of the golden mean (Figure 4.6).

Conclusion

In this chapter we have expanded the notions of the noumenal self as moral agent, particularly in relation to values, to define a method of moral reasoning and deliberation for psychiatrists. In Section II we will outline the most significant contemporary contextual influences, relevant to the *exo* level.

References

1. Hegel G. *Philosophy of Right*. Oxford: Clarendon Press; 1952.
2. MacIntyre A. *After Virtue*. Notre Dame, IN: University of Notre Dame Press; 1984.
3. Engelhardt H. *The Foundations of Bioethics, 2nd Edition*. New York: Oxford University Press; 1996.

4. Bell D. *Communitarianism*. 2004; http://plato.stanford.edu/entries/communitarianism/ (accessed April 25, 2006).

5. Bell D. *Communitarianism and Its Critics*. Oxford: Clarendon Press; 1993.

6. Rubin S. Ethical dilemmas, good intentions, and the road to hell: a clinical-ethical perspective on yalom's depiction of Trotter's therapy. *Psychiatry*. 2001;61(2):146–157.

7. Hugman R. *New Approaches in Ethics for the Caring Professions*. Basingstoke: Palgrave Macmillan; 2005.

8. Robertson M., Walter G. Overview of psychiatric ethics VI: newer approaches to the field. *Australasian Psychiatry*. 2007;15:411–416.

9. Robertson M, Walter G. The many faces of the dual-role dilemma in psychiatric ethics. *Australian and New Zealand Journal of Psychiatry*. 2008;42:228–235.

10. Hare R. *The Language of Morals*. Oxford: Oxford University Press; 1952.

11. Aristotle. *The Nicomachean Ethics*. Oxford: Oxford University Press; 1998.

12. MacIntyre A. *A Short History of Ethics*. Milton Park: Routledge; 1998.

13. Dewey J. *Theory of Valuation*. Chicago: University of Chicago Press; 1939.

14. Fulford K. Values-based practice: a new partner to evidence-based practice and a first for psychiatry? *Mens Sana Monographs*. 2008;6:10–21.

15. Pellegrino E. *Humanism and the Physician*. Knoxville: University of Tennessee Press; 1979.

16. Fulford K. Analytic philosophy, brain science, and the concept of disorder. In: Bloch S, Green S, Chodoff P, eds. *Psychiatric Ethics*. 3rd Edition. New York: Oxford University Press; 1999:161–191.

17. Fulford K. The concept of disease. In: Bloch S, Chodoff P, eds. *Psychiatric Ethics*. 3rd Edition. Oxford: Oxford University Press; 1991:77–99.

18. Borry P, Schotsmans P, Dierickx K. The birth of the empirical turn in bioethics. *Bioethics*. 2005;19:49–71.

19. Sugarman J. The future of empirical research in bioethics. *Journal of Law, Medicine & Ethics*. 2004;32:226–231.

20. Hedhecoe A. Critical bioethics: beyond the social science critique of applied ethics. *Bioethics*. 2004;18:120–143.

21. Borry P, Schotsmans P, Dierickx K. What is the role of empirical research in bioethical reflection and decision-making? An ethical analysis. *Medicine, Healthcare and Philosophy*. 2004; 7(1):41–53.

22. Haimes E. What can the social sciences contribute to the study of ethics? Theoretical, empirical and substantive considerations. *Bioethics*. 2002;16:89–113.

23. Eastman N, Starling B. Mental disorder ethics: theory and empirical investigation. *Journal of Medical Ethics*. 2006;32:94–99.

24. McMillan J, Hope A. The possibility of empirical psychiatric ethics. In: Widdershoven G, Hope A, McMillan J, et al., eds. *Empirical Ethics in Psychiatry*. London: Oxford University Press; 2008:9–23.

25. Widdershoven G, McMillan J, Hope T, et al., eds. *Empirical Ethics in Psychiatry*. Oxford: Oxford University Press; 2008.

26. Widdershoven G, Van der Scheer L. Theory and methodology of empirical ethics: a pragmatic hermeneutic perspective. In: Widdershoven G, McMillan J, Hope T, et al., eds. *Empirical Ethics in Psychiatry*. Oxford: Oxford University Press; 2008:23–36.

27. Borry P, Schotsmans P, Dierickx K. The origin and emergence of empirical ethics. In: Widdershoven G, McMillan J, et al., eds. *Empirical Ethics in Psychiatry*. Oxford: Oxford University Press; 2008:37–50.

28. van Hoorren R, Widdershoven G, Van den Borne H, et al. Autonomy and intellectual disability: the case of prevention of obesity in Prader-Willi syndrome. *Journal of Intellectual Disability Research*. 2002;46:560–568.

29. Pols J. Which empirical research, whose ethics? Articulating ideals in long-term health care. In: Widdershoven G, McMillan J, Hope T, et al., eds. *Empirical Ethics in Psychiatry*. Oxford: Oxford University Press; 2008:51–67.

30. Hughes JC, Hope T, Reader S, et al. Dementia and ethics: the views of informal carers. *Journal of the Royal Society of Medicine*. 2002;95:242–246.

31. Baldwin C, Hughes J, Hope T, et al. Ethics and dementia: the experience of family carers. *Progress in Neurology and Psychiatry*. 2004;8:24–28.

32. Baldwin C. Family carers, ethics and dementia. In: Widdershoven G, McMillan J, Hope T, et al., eds. *Empirical Ethics in Psychiatry*. Oxford: Oxford University Press; 2008:105–121.

33. Robertson M, Kerridge I, Walter G. Ethnomethodological study of the values of Australian psychiatrists: towards an empirically derived RANZCP Code of Ethics. *Australian and New Zealand Journal of Psychiatry*. 2009;43:409–419.

34. Jaspers K. *General Psychopathology*. Hoenig J, Hamilton MW, trans. Chicago: University of Chicago Press; 1963.

35. Ghaemi N. *The Concepts of Psychiatry: A Pluralistic Approach to Mind and Mental Illness*. Baltimore: Johns Hopkins University Press; 2003.

36. Aristotle. *Aristotle's Eudemian Ethics: Books I, II, and VIII*. London: Clarendon Press; 1982.

37. Aquinas T. *Aquinas Ethicus: or, the Moral Teaching of St. Thomas. A Translation of the Principal Portions of the Second Part of the Summa Theologica*. London: Burns and Oates; 1892.

38. Hare R. *The Philosophical Basis of Psychiatric Ethics*. New York: Oxford University Press; 1993.

39. Bloch S, Green S. An ethical framework for psychiatry. *British Journal of Psychiatry*. 2006;188:7–12.

Section II

Contextual Influences

5

Involuntary Psychiatric Treatment

Introduction

Apart from preemptive detention in the case of national security in the post-9/11 world, only psychiatrists have the distinct power of both restricting the liberty of citizens and enforcing medical treatment. This is the most dramatic manifestation of the relationship between the psychiatric profession and the community. Prior to the nineteenth century, involuntary psychiatric commitment was an arbitrary process enacted by physicians, often in collusion with families. The mentally ill of that era were the object of fear and ridicule; in the eighteenth and nineteenth centuries, one could pay to visit (and taunt) the inmates of Bedlam hospital, rather like animals in the zoo. The use and abuse of this unique form of power underlies many of the distinct ethical dilemmas faced by psychiatrists. It is evident that with the endowment of such power, societal expectations of the psychiatric profession are immense, in aspects of both public safety and patient welfare.

In this chapter we will review the history of involuntary psychiatric treatment and consider the notion of *psychiatric power* and its operation in societies. We will then review the moral justifications of psychiatric treatments in contemporary societies.

Scope of Involuntary Psychiatric Treatment

Involuntary psychiatric treatment, or civil commitment as it is sometimes referred to in the United States, is the enforced hospitalization and psychiatric treatment of an individual citizen. In a growing number of societies, enforced psychiatric treatment also occurs for extended periods in the community.[1] The right of the state to coerce such treatment, as manifest in the empowerment of psychiatrists, is usually based upon the demonstrable or perceived risk posed by a person's mental illness. Although there is usually some form of judicial oversight, this process of restriction of liberty does not appear to have the same burden of proof as other forms of detention in most jurisdictions.

Prior to the 1960s, this process of civil commitment was based upon the physicianly value of the relief of suffering. In the light of the civil rights movement of the 1960s and '70s, the issue of psychiatric and state power came under question, falling under the same kind of scrutiny as race- or gender-based power imbalances. The current debate over involuntary psychiatric treatment is the coalescence of values from perspectives of medicine, the law, government, and community. Issues at play stream along the lines of public safety, motivation to social good, and budgetary responsibility.[2]

In most jurisdictions, there are essentially three criteria in the process of civil commitment—being a danger to self, being a danger to others, or being gravely disabled. Many see this as manifestly inadequate as it has forced many obviously mentally ill patients to have suffered deterioration in their mental state to the point where they are dangerous to their own or other's welfare, have offended and face criminal sanction, or have lost much of their social support.[3]

In the 1970s, several legal decisions in U.S. jurisdictions added the complexity of constitutional rights to the dilemma of civil commitment. In 1956, Kenneth Donaldson traveled from Philadelphia to visit his parents in Florida. Donaldson, who suffered paranoid schizophrenia, told his father of some persecutory beliefs relating to his neighbors in Philadelphia. Consequently, Donaldson's father sought civil commitment for Kenneth, who was then directed to the Florida State Hospital at Chattahoochee. At Chattahoochee, he shared a medical officer with 1,000 other patients, many of whom were violent offenders. For the next 15 years, Donaldson refused to accept that he was mentally ill and refused antipsychotic medication or other treatment. Donaldson filed a successful lawsuit against his detention. In *O'Connor v. Donaldson* (422 U.S. 563 (1975)), the U.S. Supreme Court deemed:

> while the State may arguably confine a person to save him from harm, incarceration is rarely if ever a necessary condition for raising the living standards of those capable of surviving safely in freedom, on their own or with the help of family or friends.

In essence, *O'Connor v. Donaldson* undermined any argument that the state could utilize involuntary psychiatric treatment in circumstances where the person's illness was not an acute threat of danger.

In April 1975, seven patients in the Boston State Hospital sucessfully filed suit to stop their enforced treatment with psychotropic drugs, with additional claims of malpractice. The plaintiffs contended that their rights under the First, Fourth, Fifth, Ninth, Fourteenth, and Eighteenth Amendments of the U.S. Constitution were violated by enforced psychotropic treatment.[4] Writing in the light of the Boston Hospital case, psychiatrists Paul Appelbaum and Thomas Guthiel[5] argued the ruling of Judge Tauro was based on a misunderstanding of psychotropic treatment and its benefits. They argued further that prolonging the period of untreated psychosis would lead to worsened prognosis. The ruling and its potential consequences would allow patients to "rot with their rights on."[6]

While both of these rulings occurred in the milieu of the civil rights movement in the United States, they illustrate the dilemma posed by the empowerment of psychiatrists by communities in mental health laws. On the one hand, there is expectation that this power will be used to serve the common good, invariably considered in terms of public safety. Yet on the other there is both a counterargument based on concern for the potential abuse of civil rights in the exercise of this power and an undermining of the process of mitigating risk through laws that arguably delay treatment and ironically heighten the risk associated with these illnesses.

Prior to considering the moral justifications of involuntary psychiatric treatment in the light of community and psychiatric professional values, we will briefly examine the nature of psychiatric power in Western societies.

Psychiatric Power

As actors in the social system, psychiatrists have considerable power. This power resides not only in the capacity to deprive liberty or enforce treatment, but also in terms of the causative properties of psychiatric diagnosis and its implications in multiple settings such as the courts, the workplace, and the family. Until the 1960s, this power resided specifically in psychiatric hospitals, or as they are termed in the literature, *the asylum*.

Psychiatric Power through the Eyes of the Antipsychiatry Movement

Michel Foucault argued in *Birth of the Clinic* that the "medical gaze" was constitutive of medical knowledge. By observing the patient, the doctor assessed symptoms and signs toward a diagnosis and treatment. The disciplinary power of medicine resided within the knowledge that emerged from the clinical gaze. The gaze of the psychiatrist occurred within a power relationship characterized by the imposition of some form of order upon the patient's illness.[7] From the period of the European Enlightenment, the notion of madness was one of "unreason." Foucault defined psychiatric power as the exercise of unbalanced or asymmetrical force acting within a "rational controlled game."[8] Foucault argued that psychiatric practice occurs within a profound imbalance of power. From the seventeenth century, in what Foucault described as the "Great Confinement," "unreasonable" members of the population were systematically locked away and institutionalized.[9] Rather than lepers, the insane became the excluded. While this was originally due to the pre-Enlightenment conceptualization of madness as demonic possession, the modern conceptualization of madness due to a loss of reason was just as stigmatizing.

In a lecture at the College de France on November 7, 1973, Foucault argued that in the setting of the psychiatric hospital or asylum, there is a "general regulative system" endowed with unlimited power "without symmetry or reciprocity." Foucault sees psychiatric cure being effected by the submission of the patient to the power of the asylum and the doctor. Psychiatric treatment is a battle of wills.

On November 14, 1973, Foucault gave another lecture in which he described the scene of the English King George III, psychotic amid an attack of porphyria, being subdued by his own guards on the orders of his physician, Dr. Willis. Foucault described this process as the replacement of the sovereign power of the king with disciplinary power, a power that is "anonymous, multiple, pale, and colourless." Foucault argued that this disciplinary power was invisible and existed in distributed networks and was only evident in "the obedience of and submission of those on whom it is silently exercised" (p. 22).[8] Foucault's grand metaphor demonstrated the medical usurpation of a man's sovereignty over himself by the disciplinary power of psychiatry. Surprisingly, Foucault argued that the exercise of disciplinary power by psychiatrists was an extension of the power of the patient's family, not of the state. This is also the view of the prominent antipsychiatrist Thomas Szasz.[10] Indeed, much civil commitment prior to more formal mental health legislation in the latter part of the twentieth century was at the behest of the family, not the state. Daniel Defoe, author of *Robinson Crusoe*, had argued in the late seventeenth century that psychiatric asylums had been used by husbands to control their errant wives.[11]

Erving Goffman's book *Asylum* (1961) lists psychiatric hospitals along with the military and prisons as "total institutions" where every aspect of the patient's life is controlled. This engendered a process Goffman termed "mortification," in which the patient's identity or "civilian self" was undermined and usurped, much like Foucault's metaphor of the mad King George III.

In *Stigma*,[12] Goffman outlined further the basis of psychiatric power through the process of labeling. Within the social system are the "discredited," who are obviously deviant, and the "discreditable," whose deviance is uncovered by the process of labeling—in this case, through the process of psychiatric diagnosis. The labeling process impacts the patient in the asylum setting, and then downstream in the experience of social disadvantage.

The specious nature of psychiatric labeling within the asylum was tested by the infamous study completed by David Rosenhan in 1973.[13] Rosenhan's study involved researchers presenting themselves to psychiatric hospitals with the sole complaint of hearing voices. Having analyzed the experience of his researchers, Rosenhan found that once a person was labeled mentally ill, he or she could no longer demonstrate his or her sanity. Moreover, Rosenhan's researchers experienced a profound sense of disempowerment, depersonalization, and isolation within the psychiatric hospital.

According to the views of those loosely conglomerated in the antipsychiatry movement (although Szasz would later reject his views being numbered among the antipsychiatrists[14]), psychiatric power very much resided within the confines of the asylum, with the family as much the benefactor as the community of the removal of the so-called insane.

Psychiatric power also arises from the direct empowerment of psychiatrists by governments or regimes, often for nefarious purposes as in the suppression of dissent. As such, no discussion of psychiatric power would be complete without considering the abuses of psychiatry in the Soviet Union. In our consideration, we will attempt to contextualize the discussion to our approach to psychiatric ethics.

Psychiatric Power in the Soviet Union

The Soviets believed mental illness, like crime, was a product of the capitalist system and would decline under communism.[15] From the period of the last years of Stalin's dictatorship until Gorbachev's *Glasnost*, psychiatrists loyal to the Communist party used diagnostic labels for political ends. According to one author, psychiatric hospitalization offered a gentler face to dealing with political dissent and offered the advantage of discrediting the dissidents and their causes as crazy.[16] The Soviet psychiatrists "genuinely believed the diagnosis they were making."[17,18]

Soviet psychiatrists championed numerous diagnoses such as *schizophrenia forme fruste* and *paranoia with delusions of reform*. The most infamous of diagnoses used by Soviet psychiatrists was *sluggish schizophrenia*. Sluggish schizophrenia, and indeed the whole specter of Soviet-era psychiatric abuses, is linked with the career of the prominent Soviet psychiatrist Andrei Snezhnevsky. Snezhnevsky was the director of the Institute of Psychiatry of the USSR Academy of Medical Sciences and was an esteemed corresponding fellow of the UK Royal College of Psychiatrists, a role he later relinquished in the face of criticism of his practice.[19] Considered the head of the Moscow School of Psychiatry, Snezhnevsky had a long-standing interest in schizophrenia and was one of the first to outline the now-accepted paradigm of positive and negative symptoms in schizophrenia.[20] The core assumption underlying the dominant Soviet paradigm of schizophrenia was that there was no plausible explanation for rejection of the Soviet model of society other than insanity.[21]

Unlike the requirement of specific symptoms of psychosis and disorganization in the *Diagnostic and Statistical Manual of Mental Disorders* or the International Classification of Diseases, the conceptualization of schizophrenia championed by Snezhnevsky defined schizophrenia purely by the clinical course of malignant, sluggish, or *schubweise* (episodic).[22] Given the lax requirements for specific psychotic symptoms, any form of psychopathology, from antisocial behavior to panic attacks, could attract a diagnosis of schizophrenia.[21]

Symptoms such as reformist delusions, litigation mania, or reformerism were apt to appear in the diagnosis of sluggish schizophrenia in particular.

The Soviet Union had two networks of psychiatric hospitals. One was an ostensibly mainstream network administered by the Ministry of Health; another comprised a network of *psikushka* (forensic psychiatric hospitals) administered by the Ministry of the Interior under the auspices of the KGB. Patients were sent to forensic hospitals following orders by Soviet courts and psychiatric tribunals. Many were admitted to the Serbsky Institute in Moscow, a facility that continues to operate as a secure psychiatric hospital.

The neurophysiologist Vladimir Bukovsky was a dissident who faced imprisonment in labor camps, prisons, and *psikushka* for a total of 12 years. During his persecution, Bukovsky chronicled his suffering at the hands of the Soviets and in 1971 smuggled his account to the West. Bukovsky's book *To Build a Castle*[23] provides a window into the experience of a *psikushka*. Bukovsky was first arrested in 1963 and charged with being in possession of *samizdat* (anti-Soviet literature). He was proclaimed insane and interned in a special psychiatric hospital for 14 months. In 1965 he was arrested again for his involvement in a demonstration on behalf of other dissident writers and sent to a series of *psikushka* until 1966. In 1967 he was again arrested after a demonstration but was sent to a labor camp for three years. Bukovsky spent 1971–1976 in prison and was then exiled.

Bukovsky's account of his treatment in various *psikushka* is disturbing. In the early 1960s, psychiatric prisoners were subjected to insulin coma therapy, excessive doses of antipsychotic or barbiturate tranquilizers, and unanesthetized electroconvulsive therapy. One particular form of restraint used was the so-called roll-up, in which a wet canvas strip was wrapped around an inmate and the strip shrank as it dried, effectively strangling the victim. Bukovsky noted that the orderlies in these facilities were in fact criminals who had been co-opted into the role. Bukovsky told an interviewer of the broken spirit of inmates in these facilities, whose torment continued after they were ultimately released:

> If you're just out of psychiatric hospital it's twice as bad because of the psychological tension there. You're constantly wondering if you're normal. Even though you know you were diagnosed for political reasons you still watch yourself. Perhaps I am mad? Those big nobs in white coats with diplomas and professorial status decided I was. There must be something wrong. You keep analysing yourself, comparing yourself with others. It's an additional burden.[39]

While the Soviet-era abuses in psychiatry are well documented, there remains some disputation of both the extent and malicious intent of these practices. Paul Calloway, an English psychiatrist who lived in the USSR during the latter part of the Soviet era, disputes the extent of persecution. Calloway contends that there were around 360,000 *refuseniks* (dissenters) yet only 4,000 were subject to the kind of psychiatric abuses documented. Moreover, Calloway argues that many of these patients were, in fact, mentally ill. Having been a participant–observer in Soviet psychiatry, Calloway avers that there is a considerable difference between Soviet psychiatry and Western psychiatry, particularly in terms of the classification of psychiatric disorder.[24]

Can the malfeasance of the practices of a number of psychiatrists in the Soviet Union be understood in terms of our methodology? As with the criminal acts of Irmfried Eberl and his fellow Nazis, we do not seek to justify or defend such behavior, but rather to understand it in terms of the current era. Despite the persistence of an apologist culture in some older Russian psychiatrists,[21] the psychiatric profession in Russia has sought to return to the prestige brought by such figures as Sergei Korskaoff.[25,26]

The social construction of schizophrenia in Soviet-era psychiatry emerged from a legitimate study of the disorder, although it is clear that the field of academic psychiatry was influenced by the regime.[21] Accounts such as that of Bukovsky indicate a propensity for sadism and criminality in some parts of the psychiatric profession, particularly in the *psikushka* system. It may be that some of the dissidents passing out *samizdat* in Red Square or Gorky Park may have been psychotic, although it would appear that a troublesome minority of dissenters were subjected to abuses by psychiatrists. It is impossible to generalize the intentions of the psychiatrists who abused human rights in the Soviet Union, but it would appear that the vague nature of the construct of schizophrenia facilitated the use of psychiatric power as a means of protecting the state. If one were to take a moral relativist position on this, then the provocative arguments of writers such as Paul Calloway come into sharper focus. In virtually all societies, psychiatric power is deployed on the grounds of public safety. In the eyes of the leaders of the Soviet Union, public safety was best served by the repression of dissents. Once the West learned of the excesses of Soviet psychiatrists described by men such as Vladimir Bukovsky, then this defense crumbled.

The question is begged as to whether any form of moral relativism is defensible in questions such as the Soviet abuses of psychiatry. David Wong has evolved a philosophy of sophisticated moral relativism.[27] In Wong's philosophy, the evaluation of the morality of a group or community cannot be made in terms of the means to an end, but rather how effectively the end is achieved. In the context of a community or society, the efficacy with which social cohesion, public safety, just distribution of resources, and other desirable attributes of well-ordered societies are the measure of the ethics of a community's or group's acts. Applying Wong's methodology to the question of Soviet psychiatry requires an evaluation of the good of the Soviet Union as a society. If it can be argued that the Soviet Union provided the kind of well-ordered society any citizen would desire, then the use of psychiatric power in service of this goal is defensible—this of course puts aside the problematic notion of abandoning the Hippocratic injunction. The main argument in defense of the contribution of Soviet psychiatry to political repression is somewhat of a *tu quoque* argument that psychiatric power serves a similar role in the West. In Chapter 13, we consider whether this is a credible argument in the light of the dangerous severe personality disorder legislation in the UK.

Regardless of any morally relativist position on this issue, the use of psychiatric power in the Soviet Union, through the discrediting process of the diagnostic act and the use of coercive powers of the state to deprive liberty, illustrate that the underlying notions are at the core of our methodology—the psychiatrist as moral agent and the construction of psychiatric disorder and treatment are utterly contextual to the particular social, historical, and cultural context in which they occur.

Moral Justification of Involuntary Psychiatric Treatment

In any enlightened, well-ordered society, coercion of a citizen or group of citizens in any form is the gravest of matters. In traditional notions of the social contract outlined by Hobbes,[28] the sovereign is empowered to enforce the obligations of citizens who benefit from the order and stability such a society offers, in addition to addressing the problem of the moral free rider, who seeks to benefit from society without obliging his or her part in the social contract.

As to the question of the state enforcing psychiatric treatment through detention, administration of treatment, or imposition of obligations in community care, these situations occur ostensibly under the rubric of *parens patriae*, or literally "parent of the nation." This originally referred to the power of the sovereign to intervene against an abusive or negligent parent, legal guardian, or informal caretaker and to act therefore as the parent of any child or individual who is in need of protection. This notion appeared in the sixteenth century within the King's Bench, the predecessor of modern-day supreme or high courts. The original invocation of *parens patriae* referred to safeguarding the interests of incompetent adults. The *parens patriae* doctrine should be distinguished from the *in loco parentis* doctrine, in that the latter involves care that is "temporary in character and not to be likened to [the permanent situation of] adoption."[29]

In the light of the doctrine of *parens patriae* are two broad moral justifications for involuntary psychiatric treatment. The first is the right to protect other citizens from harm, predicated on the harm principle of John Stuart Mill. The second we term "the duty of beneficence," which in essence represents the state providing a correction for the "natural lottery." This argument turns upon the notion of diminished or impaired autonomy in mental illness and reflects a fundamentally liberal notion of justice.

Mill and the Harm Principle

John Stuart Mill was arguably one of the most famous survivors of an abusive childhood. His father, James, was a Scottish philosopher and sought to condition his son John to be worthy of the family's proud intellectual heritage and in particular the very English philosophy of utilitarianism. Mill was isolated from his peers and tutored by Jeremy Bentham, the father of utilitarian thought.[30] By age 3 he was reading Greek; Latin by age 8. Not surprisingly, Mill's micromanaged childhood and restricted interpersonal experience caught up with him at age 20, at which time he likely suffered a severe depressive illness. Whether this experience influenced his notions of liberty is not clear; however, Mill's *On Liberty*[31] remains the text upon which much of the modern liberal state is based.

In the first instance, Mill argued

> that the only purpose for which power can be rightfully exercised over any member of a civilised community, against his will, is to prevent harm to others.

This is commonly known as the harm principle. On *prima facie* consideration, the state is justified in its intervention in the lives of its citizens if their actions, whatever their origin, are likely to be harmful to others. In the tradition of Hobbes, this is the exercise of the *Leviathan* in order to enforce the social contract.[28] Perhaps in light of his own experience, Mill made some attempt to qualify mental illness from his harm principle:

> And even … if the consequences of misconduct could be confined to the vicious or thoughtless individual, ought society to abandon to their own guidance those who are manifestly unfit for it? If protection against themselves is confessedly due to children and persons under age, is not society equally bound to afford it to persons of mature years who are equally incapable of self-government?

While Mill is clear that dangerous activity is at the core of the argument, he nominates that incompetent individuals are at risk from their own actions. In essence, the incompetent individual should be protected from the harm arising from his or her behavior. The harm principle has been used as an argument for involuntary psychiatric treatment of suicidal patients, in that the suicidal patient him- or herself is an individual who can be harmed by his or her actions.[32] This is akin to Kant's argument against suicide in that the death of the individual as the means to relieve that individual's distress thus violates the Categorical Imperative.[33] Another argument applies Locke's idea of the "transitive" nature of self,[34] i.e., that the same person may be a series of different people inhabiting the same embodiment, with different values or desires. In this approach the future "sane" individual must be protected against the dangerous acts of the "insane" individual.[35] To borrow a literary analogy, Jekyll must be protected from Hyde.

In applying Mill's philosophy to justify involuntary psychiatric treatment, it has been argued that the preconditions to paternalistic acts are that the individual in question is not responsible for his or her own actions, the individual's incompetence is about to cause harm, the act will ultimately enhance the individual's competence and/or prevent further deterioration, and the act takes place in the least restrictive manner. As such, Mill would have supported involuntary psychiatric treatment as an exception to the harm principle.[36]

Later, Mill seems to hedge a little when he writes,

> No person is an entirely isolated being; it is impossible for a person to do anything seriously or permanently hurtful to himself, without mischief reaching at least to his near connexions, and often far beyond them. If he injures his property, he does harm to those who directly or indirectly derived support from it, and usually diminishes, by a greater or less amount, the general resources of the community. If he deteriorates his bodily or mental faculties, he not only brings evil upon all who depended on him for any portion of their happiness, but disqualifies himself for rendering the services which he owes to his fellow-creatures generally; perhaps becomes a burthen on their affection or benevolence; and if such conduct were very frequent, hardly any offence that is committed would detract more from the general sum of good. Finally, if by his vices or follies a person does no direct harm to others, he is nevertheless (it may be said) injurious by his example; and ought to be compelled to control himself, for the sake of those whom the sight or knowledge of his conduct might corrupt or mislead.

So instead of an overtly dangerous psychotic patient, Mill seems to be extending the notion of harm beyond immediate physical or emotional danger to other violations of the social contract in family or community contexts. Harm occurs through either setting a poor example or presumably causing distress to others through the emotional affront of distressing self-neglect. No one feels the better for encountering a homeless mentally ill vagrant or an incontinent alcoholic. Harm would now seem to be a function of the overall downside of a person, for whatever reason, defaulting on his or her obligations in the social contract. Mill continues to argue

> If gambling, or drunkenness, or incontinence, or idleness, or uncleanliness, are as injurious to happiness, and as great a hindrance to improvement, as many or most of the acts prohibited by law, why (it may be asked) should not law, so far as is consistent with practicability and social convenience, endeavour to repress these also? And as a supplement to the unavoidable imperfections of law, ought not opinion at least to organize a powerful police against these vices, and visit rigidly with social penalties those who are known to practise them?

It would seem that Mill is arguing for greater scope of state intervention in the lives of citizens, brought about by the clear difficulty he has in delimiting the notion of harm. In expanding the notion of the harm principle, the starting point for Mill is the apparently simple notion of preventing harm to others. When Mill explores the downstream implications of the libertarian approach he advocates, the true polysemy of the term *harm* undermines his arguments to the point where the harm principle's apparent utility has declined.

Putting aside Mill's inherent contradictions, it seems he accepted the need for involuntary psychiatric treatment. Other moral philosophies such as utilitarianism, communitarianism, and the principle of beneficence all arguably support the use of involuntary psychiatric treatment;[9,37] although as American psychiatrist Paul Chodoff has argued in the light of human rights abuses perpetrated under the guise of psychiatric treatment in the Soviet Union, there is a need for a "self critical and chastened" paternalism.[38] Australian psychiatrist Stephen Rosenman has argued a potentially "self-chastening" method to resolve this dilemma.[39] He argues for the definition of psychiatric disorder along a continuum of social definition or biomedical definition of mental illness and a continuum of "harmfulness" to self or others. In Rosenman's model, he argues that coercive treatment of socially defined disorders occasioning harm to self is the most problematic pretext of involuntary psychiatric treatment.

Arguments against the Risk Basis of Mental Health Legislation

In mental health legislation, the harm principle is usually defined in terms of the construct of risk. *Risk* is a term that has multiple meanings in different disciplinary contexts, although all approaches to risk attempt to apply knowledge to an area of uncertainty.[40] The notion of risk assessment is usually considered the process of estimating the likelihood of dangerousness, such as completed suicide or harm to others. In the insurance industry, actuarial assessment is a mathematical discipline aimed at computing a probability of adversity, based upon a broad consideration of variables. Such an approach has been applied in criminology in the prediction of recidivism in sexual offences.[41] As a form of knowledge, the discourses of risk speak to an evaluative process that estimates the probability of a negative event. The estimation of risk is subject to "bounded rationality," i.e., the effect of particular biases influencing how such information is handled. In a culture that is averse to risk, bounded rationality is clearly more likely to favor an overestimation of risk.[40] Applying actuarial approaches to risk in mental health is a process of passively predicting the likelihood of harmful or dangerous behavior,[42] which is a profoundly inaccurate process, with only a quarter of all dangerous acts being predictable by psychiatrists.[43] Moreover, psychiatrists are usually inaccurate in overestimating risk.[44]

In addition to the imprecision of prediction of risk and the likelihood that the tendency to overestimate risk may subject many to coercive psychiatric treatment unnecessarily, mental health laws based upon risk often delay the access to treatment until the patient's illness is so severe that risk of harm becomes the focus of clinical attention.[45] In addition to the consequences of self-neglect and damage to reputation, finances, career, and relationships, delays in treatment lead to poorer prognosis after treatment. In the light of the inaccuracy of predicting dangerousness, many patients who may never satisfy the legal test of dangerousness may be denied access to treatment as their illnesses do not lead to such concerns.[46] By promoting risk of dangerousness as a feature of mental illness within the community, such laws promote stigma in relation to psychiatric disorders.[47]

Alternatively, risk-based mental health legislation may promote unrealistic expectations within the community in regard to a psychiatrist's capacity to mitigate risk. In cases of severe mental illness such as schizophrenia, dangerousness can be prevented in almost

70 percent of cases,[43] whereas in circumstances of violent or dangerous behavior occurring in the setting of personality disorders or drug abuse, the picture is less positive. Psychiatrists and the community are then posed the dilemma of detaining people whose psychiatric underpinnings of criminal or dangerous behavior are not amenable to intervention,[48] with the concomitant problem of containment being the only intervention possible. In the context of such laws, prisons have become de facto psychiatric hospitals and vice versa.

Beneficence Argument for Involuntary Psychiatric Treatment

People with mental illness tend to conceptualize the risk their illness poses more in terms of what happens to them rather than what they might do to others in the midst of a severe episode.[49] Vulnerability, poverty, unemployment, homelessness, and other forms of social disadvantage are very much in the minds of those suffering mental illness and those who care for them.

The beneficence argument for involuntary psychiatric treatment is based on the notion that mental illness impairs the sufferer from seeking treatment through the effects of the disorder. Impairments of reason, insight, or judgment are the presumed impairments to be compensated for by such legislation. Unlike other pretexts for the application of *parens patriae*, the beneficence argument is limited to enforcing intervention to ameliorate the specific impairments of mental illness that preclude the sufferer from seeking or accepting treatment. The supposition is that the person has a right to treatment and the effects of the mental illness deny that right to the sufferer.

A precondition of this argument is accepting the premise that the fundamental impairment of mental illness is the impairment of autonomy. If the most succinct definition of autonomy is the capacity for rational self-governance, this presupposes the capacity to understand and decide on questions affecting welfare and preferences. Arguably, this is not a full account of autonomy. "Dispositional autonomy" refers to the manner in which a person's life is lived, perhaps best considered the theme or recurrent motif of the person's individual narrative. This is more consistent with Kant's concept of *menscheit*[50]—a respect for the human capacity for practical reason or moral self-governance. In contrast, the concept of "occurrent autonomy" refers to the person's immediate capacity for rational decisions.

What is the nature of impairment of autonomy in mental illness? Megone argues that mental illness is the impairment of Aristotelian reason,[51] whereas Wakefield sees it as a "harmful dysfunction" of mental capacity, ultimately defined as an impairment of mental function, which leads to inability to enjoy "species normative function."[52,53] Such arguments do help in questions of the definition and classification of mental disorders but do not in themselves help with providing a basis of understanding the nature of the impairment of autonomy in mental illness.

The philosopher Jennifer Radden defined the impairment in autonomy of mental illness in terms of dispositional autonomy.[54] Radden has argued that mental illness disrupts the synchronic (or cross-sectional) component of identity. This presents the basis of a complex argument about the moral justification of involuntary treatment. The complexity of this argument resides in the notion of identity or selfhood.

Apart from rational capacity, humans are storytelling creatures, and their personhood is made up of a story comprising many factors. As French philosopher Paul Ricouer has argued, such narratives have *ipse* (the stable experience of self over time) and *idem* (the experience of self at a particular point) components.[55] Mental illness, whether the loss of reality in psychosis or the distortion of thinking in mania or profound depression, disrupts the *idem* (synchronic) or cross-sectional component of selfhood. This means that dispositional autonomy and therefore the capacity to make decisions consistent with the person's life plan are impaired. The *ipse* form of narrative is then imperiled by the deranged *idem*. In other words, the rational sane person (assuming recovery) ought be protected from the irrational insane person. The argument has returned to the harm principle, but perhaps more contextualized. Based upon the notion of impaired dispositional autonomy, we have a better account of what mental illness does to the autonomy of the sufferer.

Our beneficence argument emerges in the spirit of liberal egalitarianism, the philosophy first advanced by John Rawls[56] and further developed by Norman Daniels[57] and Martha Nussbaum.[58] As we described previously, Rawls argued that there is a natural lottery that distributes both good fortune and bad. The successful in life are no more responsible for their success than the failed are for their failure. This is because the attributes that lead to success—health, opportunity, and personal qualities—are the result of accidents of birth. Similarly, those attributes that lead to failure in life are equally arbitrary in their occurrence. Rawls adopts Kant's idea that humans aspire to lives of practical reason or autonomy and that social goods are instrumental to this. For Rawls, the well-ordered society enables all to be equal competitors for social goods in pursuit of such a life. In Rawls's society, we are all rational choosers in a social contract that facilitates the just distribution of goods that benefit the least well-off.

This is all very well, but in Rawls's imagined society, no one becomes psychotic. Norman Daniels tried to address this by defining healthcare as a distinct form of social good that specifically corrects for the vicissitudes of the natural lottery. To Daniels, healthcare exists to level the playing field for the sick and should be distributed or rationed differently from social goods. This underlies the position taken by many postindustrial Western societies who opt to provide universal healthcare. Daniels's argument is undermined in the face of the notion that much mental illness is chronic and leads to lifelong disability. The life of fulfillment aspired to in Rawls's philosophy is beyond the reach of many of those struggling with chronic mental illness. In the light of Daniels, the state is justified in allocating limited healthcare resources and enforcing treatment in order to correct for the disruption.

In advancing our argument we will now revisit how Martha Nussbaum addressed this problem in *Frontiers of Justice*.[58] Rather than Rawls's life of autonomous fulfillment, Nussbaum suggests that the natural lottery should be corrected for incapacities that prevent the experience of a "life of dignity." Nussbaum's approach to distributive justice focuses on human capabilities, that is, what people are actually able to do and be, and a threshold level of capabilities beneath which truly human functioning is not possible. In her book *Women and Human Development: The Capabilities Approach,*[59] she lists central human capabilities, ten of which she identifies as essential to human dignity. The list includes bodily health, freedom of movement, personal safety, the use of emotion, the ability to live a normal life span, to play, to seek a safe environment, and to participate in economic and political functioning. In *Frontiers of Justice* Nussbaum applied these ideas to the problem of those left behind in Rawls's philosophy—nonhumans, citizens of other states, and most relevant to this discussion, those with disabilities. Rather than rational choosers in a highly regulated game of competing for social resources to live a fulfilled autonomous life, the just society aims to provide those most vulnerable with a hierarchy of goods to enable them to live lives of dignity. In severe mental illness, this involves mitigation of the effects of disease, mitigation of the deleterious consequences of its treatment, and freedom from the socially imposed limitations of stigma and the status of second-class citizens.

How then do mental health laws fit with such a scheme? The problem remains of delimiting mental illness from other forms of human imperfection, the central problem we argue in Mill's philosophy. For the purposes of this discussion, we suggest that the focus of mental health laws be those people whose illnesses deprive them of the capacity to make decisions about their lives consistent with their dispositional autonomy. The aspirations of these laws is to intercede when mental illness precludes these people from exercising their right to access healthcare to ameliorate their bad luck in the natural lottery. Apart from the relief of distress or the preservation of life, the main aspiration of such laws is to allow the person to access social goods in order to achieve the good of a life of dignity. One review of the ethical justification of involuntary psychiatric treatment justifies the process as enabling "revolving door" sufferers of mental illness with their capacity to realize their "positive liberty."[60]

This argument relies on a suppressed premise that treatment can sufficiently ameliorate the effects of mental illness to allow this to happen. In the first instance, this necessitates the state to have legal capacity to impose such treatment beyond the circumstances of acute, severe episodes of mental illness. In many jurisdictions, this exists as the provision of continuing involuntary treatment in the community, or what is often termed "community treatment orders."[1,61,62] It is curious to note that the available evidence indicates that such orders do not decrease service usage but appear to protect against criminal exploitation of the subject of the order.[63] The extent of such laws would need to encompass "treatment" beyond enforced medication or containment, to include proxy decisions about the allocation of social goods such as housing, welfare, and access to healthcare for medical disorders. Such a usurpation of the patient's autonomy, no matter how minimal, presents an ethical challenge to a community, as it would seem to enforce a highly value-laden notion of a good life, at least as that particular community determines what that might be. Our argument is that this moral justification of involuntary psychiatric treatment is not related to engineering model citizens capable of abiding in a social contract, but correcting for the specific effect of mental illness on the dispositional autonomy of the patient and facilitating access to healthcare in pursuit of a life of dignity.

One might argue that the notion of isolating mental illness from other foci of guardianship or proxy decision making, such as intellectual disability or dementia, ought be abandoned. Is there really a difference between a person with intellectual impairment and a person with chronic psychosis in terms of their life journeys and their desires for dignity? If a society were to abandon specific laws for mentally ill citizens in favor of a more general notion of *parens patriae,* then this should be based upon a fundamental aspiration of that society for a life of dignity for its citizens.

We argue that the specific impairment of autonomy requires a specific law focusing intervention on the derangement of autonomous function unique to mental illness. This rests upon an expanded conceptualization of *risk* to encompass all pathways to an undignified existence. Within this expanded notion of risk is an expanded notion of intervention, to include healthcare in a broader definition. As Daniels argues, healthcare is not merely access to medical treatment but equal access to the social determinants of health such as education, housing, and freedom from poverty.[57]

The question is begged as to where the psychiatrist fits within this socially determined notion of harm and healthcare. Many aspects of intervention in mental health, such as welfare or housing, are beyond the biomedical framework in which psychiatrists practice.

This necessitates either an expanded scope of psychiatry or, preferentially in our view, an expanded social process of civil commitment and the process of a community engineering a just social system. Moving beyond the clearly problematic dangerousness or harm principle to the beneficence principle invites psychiatry to cede a large part of the power invested in it by communities in the process of civil commitment and coercive psychiatric treatment. In doing this, psychiatrists become a component of a just process of correcting for the natural lottery, rather than the empowered agents of social control so critiqued in the social movements of the 1960s and 1970s. This would liberate psychiatrists from the countertherapeutic quasilegal roles they are forced to play in the exclusively medical mode of civil commitment.[64] The de-emphasis of risk in this approach to involuntary psychiatric treatment also reduces the scope for the politicized nature of debate over mental health, which characterized legislative reform in the United Kingdom in the first decade of the twenty-first century.[65,66]

Moral Obligations of Involuntary Psychiatric Treatment

One aspect of the ethical implications of involuntary treatment is the obligation of the state to provide a reasonable standard of care. Beyond simple issues of fairness or the state's duty of care, there are specific ethical dilemmas for psychiatrists in the form of obligations to the patient subject to involuntary treatment. It is well established that chronic exposure to first-generation antipsychotic medications carries the risk of drug-induced movement disorder.[67] More recent concerns about the propensity for second-generation antipsychotics to lead to the development of obesity, dyslipidaemia, diabetes, and cardiovascular disease create a moral obligation to ameliorate such consequences of enforced treatment.[68]

Some might argue that the iatrogenic harm arising from enforced treatment with antipsychotic treatment is a manifestation of Aquinas's doctrine of double effect.[69] The doctrine of double effect is invoked to justify a well-intentioned or ostensibly beneficent action that causes a serious harm, although later writers have suggested additional conditions of the act being intentionally good[70] and being subject to proper evaluation of the balance between risk and benefit.[71] In general medicine, this might be a serious complication of an operation or a side-effect of medication. Patients giving informed consent to medication would be apprised of potential benefits and risks of that decision.

In contrast, putting aside concerns about capacity for autonomous choice, the patient subject to involuntary psychiatric treatment is not able to refuse treatment. This arguably heightens the need for the treating psychiatrist to exercise greater care in the use of such treatments. In the first instance, this represents a more specific consideration of the patient's best interests in terms of the risk–benefit analysis underlying treatment decisions.[72] In many such situations, the risk of untreated mental illness is considered against the high likelihood of iatrogenic harm coming from the enforced use of antipsychotic treatment.

In applying the double-effect doctrine to such a dilemma, what are the implications for enforced administration of psychotropic treatment in the community? In the first instance, such decisions require closer scrutiny or peer evaluation in terms of risks and benefits and, where possible, as much contribution to the decision by the patients or their carers. In the second, the choice of treatment should be justified in terms of what constitutes best practice, whether this is in relation to the scientific literature or the tenets of best practice within a professional organization. Third, the risk–benefit evaluation of the treatment choices should be transparent and clinical review of this a priority in management. Finally, the state must avail the patient of measures to mitigate or correct the adverse consequences of enforced psychiatric treatment. Such measures might include access to means to rectify metabolic disturbance, such as opportunities for physical activity, access to clinical management of diabetic or dyslipidemic states, or measures to support lifestyle modifications. As with decisions in relation to treatment of mental illness, the intrinsic impairments of the person with such problems may also impair choices in this area. Whether enforcement of these kinds of interventions is justified by the arguments made in favor of the treatment of the mental illness in the first place depends upon the particular circumstance. Our argument is that the state has a moral obligation to correct barriers to the patient's accessing social goods to remedy the adverse consequences of enforced psychiatric treatment.

Case Example 5.1: The Bag Lady

Edith was a 52-year-old homeless woman. She had lived rough in a local park for as long as any of the local residents could remember. Seemingly harmless, Edith came to the attention of the police when she yelled at a schoolboy as he crossed the park. Police took her into custody and when it became apparent that she was "mentally unstable," they took her to a psychiatric assessment center. After examination it was clear that Edith was grossly thought disordered, had delusional ideas of a persecutory nature, and was experiencing auditory hallucinations. She was disorganized in her behavior and appeared to be malnourished in addition to having lice and scabetic infestations. In the light of her yelling at the boy, the hospital resolved to initiate the process of civil commitment.

Edith could not provide any sense of her background. Hospital staff could not identify any relatives, and local charities and health services had no knowledge of who she was. Edith's various health problems were treated and she was started on an injectable form of antipsychotic medication. The treating psychiatrist had considered it unlikely that Edith would take tablets.

Edith was discharged to interim accommodation on a community treatment order. She was to allow community mental health staff to visit her and to receive regular injections of her medication. Edith abandoned her accommodation and defaulted on her treatment. Police found her in her usual location, in an alcove in the park she had inhabited for years. Edith was taken back to the hospital, where she remained for the next three months. It was clear that antipsychotic medication made Edith more communicative and less disorganized in her behavior; however, she remained thought disordered and chronically psychotic. Over the time of her hospital admission, Edith adhered to antipsychotic treatment and gained 25kg in weight. Her fasting glucose was elevated to the diabetic range, and her triglycerides and low-density lipoprotein (LDL) cholesterol levels were elevated.

Edith was once again discharged to more supervised accommodation. Her antipsychotic was administered by injection by the community mental health team, and the manager of the accommodation supervised her antidiabetic and cholesterol-lowering medication. Over time, Edith would balk at receiving her injection, but the threat of rehospitalization usually led her to acquiesce.

Over the next few years, Edith remained in her boarding house accommodation. She had begun smoking in the hospital and spent most of her time sitting in the yard of the house, smoking or watching television.

* * *

This vignette would be sadly familiar to most clinicians working in the community mental health setting. Edith was clearly mentally ill, and her illness had led her to homelessness and its attendant problems. Edith's disability was of little consequence to the community until her behavior, albeit trivial, implied a risk of dangerousness. In the final analysis, there was little likelihood that she would have harmed anyone, and she had been capable of protecting herself against predation, exposure, and hunger. Enforced treatment with antipsychotic medication caused iatrogenic harm and the transinstitutionalization of hospital and then the ersatz clinical setting of a boardinghouse with a cooperative manager did little to improve Edith's quality of life.

Several questions emerge from Edith's case. First, would mental health laws that did not require dangerousness as a pretext to involuntary treatment have led to Edith's coming to care earlier in her illness? Would this earlier intervention have improved her prognosis? The second question is, did the agents of the state in its *parens patriae* role exercise the appropriate caution in the double-effect doctrine in terms of foreseeability, adequate provision to avert negative consequences, or even the intention of treatment? Was the supervision of medication for serious metabolic derangements by a nonmedical person adequate care for the iatrogenic harm caused by enforced psychiatric treatment? Indeed, was Edith coerced into treatment because of the theoretical risk, no matter how marginal, her illness posed, or was her treatment motivated by compassion and the desire for her to lead a more dignified life?

Ultimately, the intention to help Edith derived from the inherent sense of justice of the community of which she lived on the margins. The manner of her care may have been less than ideal, and the manifest lack of resources for citizens like Edith raises questions of the just allocation of resources within that community. What is clear is that the state seems to have attempted in an imperfect fashion to compensate for Edith's illness upon her ability to seek treatment for it. The ultimate consequence of this process of intervention raises more questions for the community than merely for psychiatry. What is clear is that as long as communities consign involuntary psychiatric treatment to be a purely clinical enterprise based upon the expectation of the mitigation of risk, the manifest injustice of stories like Edith's will continue.

References

1. Dawson J. *Community Treatment Orders: International Comparisons.* Otago: Otago University Press 2005.

2. Peele R, Chodoff P. Involuntary hospitalization and deinstitutionalization. In: Bloch S, Greene P, eds. *Psychiatric Ethics, 4th Edition.* New York: Oxford; 2009:211–228.

3. Treffert D. The obviously ill patient in need of treatment: a fourth standard for civil commitment. *Hosp Community Psychiatry.* 1985;36:259–264.

4. Guerwitz H. Tarasoff: protective privilege versus public peril. *American Journal of Psychiatry.* 1977;134:289–292.

5. Appelbaum P, Gutheil T. The Boston State Hospital case: "Involuntary mind control," the Constitution, and the "right to rot." *Am J Psychiatry.* 1980;137:720–723.

6. Appelbaum P, Gutheil T. "Rotting with their rights on": constitutional theory and clinical reality in drug refusal by psychiatric inpatients. *Bull Am Acad Psychiatry Law.* 1979;7:308–317.

7. Foucault M. *The Birth of the Clinic: An Archaeology of Medical Perception.* Sheridan Smith A, trans. New York: Vintage Books; 1975

8. Foucault M. *Psychiatric Power: Lectures at the College de France 1973–74.* Houndmills: Palgrave Macmillan; 2006.

9. Foucault M. *Madness and Civilization*. Howard R, trans. New York: Pantheon; 1965.

10. Szasz T. The myth of mental illness. *American Psychologist*. 1960;15:113–118.

11. Defoe D. *An Essay upon Projects*. London: Cockerill; 1697.

12. Goffman E. *Stigma*. Harmondsworth: Penguin Books; 1961.

13. Rosenhan D. On being sane in insane places. *Science*. 1973;179:250–258.

14. Szasz T. *Antipsychiatry: Quackery Squared*. New York: Syracuse University Press; 2009.

15. Fry J. *Medicine in Three Societies: A Comparison of Medical Care in the USSR, USA and UK*. Aylesbury: MTP; 1969.

16. Smith T, Oleszczuk T. *No Asylum: State Psychiatric Repression in the Former USSR*. London: MacMillan; 1996.

17. Bloch S, Reddaway P. *Russia's Political Hospitals*. London: Gollancz; 1997.

18. Bloch S. Abuses in psychiatry. In: Reich W, ed. *Encyclopaedia of Bioethics*. New York: Macmillan; 1995:2126–2132.

19. Levine S. The Special Committee on the Political Abuse of Psychiatry. *Psychiatric Bulletin* 1981;5:94–95.

20. Tandon R, Greden J. *Negative Schizophrenic Symptoms: Pathophysiology and Clinical Implications*. Washington DC: American Psychiatric Press; 1991.

21. van Voren R. Political abuse of psychiatry: an historical overview. *Schizophrenia Bulletin*. 2010;36:33–35.

22. Lavretsky H. The Russian concept of schizophrenia: a review of the literature. *Schizophrenia Bulletin*. 1998;24:537–557.

23. Bukovsky V. *To Build a Castle: My Life as a Dissenter*. London: Viking; 1979.

24. Calloway P. *Soviet and Western Psychiatry*. Keighley: The Moor Press; 1992.

25. Polubinskaya S, Bonnie R. The code of professional ethics of the Russian Society of Psychiatrists. Text and commentary. *Int J Law Psychiatry*. 1996;19:143–172.

26. Polubinskaya SV. Reform in psychiatry in post Soviet countries. *Acta Psychiatrica Scandinavica*. 2000;101(399):106–108.

27. Wong D. Relativism. In: Singer P, ed. *A Companion to Ethics*. Oxford: Blackwell; 1991:442–449.

28. Hobbes T, ed. *Leviathan*. London: Penguin; 1985.

29. Quaqua Society. *Parens Patriae*. http://www.quaqua.org/parenspatriae.htm (accessed January 11, 2012).

30. Capaldi N. *John Stuart Mill: A Biography*. London: Cambridge University Press; 2004.

31. Mill J. *On Liberty*. New York: WW Norton; 1859/1975.

32. Levenson J. Psychiatric commitment and involuntary hospitalisation: an ethical perspective. *Psychiatric Quarterly*. 1986;58:106–112.

33. Kant I. *The Metaphysics of Morals*. Gregor M, trans. Cambridge: Cambridge University Press; 1797/1996

34. Locke J. An essay concerning human understanding. In: Thomas S, ed. Adelaide: University of Adelaide. 2004: http://ebooks.adelaide.edu.au/l/locke/john/l81u/ (accessed January 21, 2012).

35. Robertson M. Mad or bad, have we been had? A response to Patfield (Letter). *Australasian Psychiatry*. 2007;15:77–79.

36. Waithe M. Why Mill was for paternalism. *International Journal of Law and Psychiatry*. 1983;6:101–111.

37. Munetz M, Galon P, Frese F. The ethics of mandatory community treatment. *Journal of the American Academy of Psychiatry and the Law*. 2003;31:173–183.

38. Chodoff P. Involuntary hospitalization of the mentally ill as a moral issue. *American Journal of Psychiatry*. 1984;141:384–389.

39. Rosenman S. Psychiatrists and compulsion: a map of ethics. *Australian and New Zealand Journal of Psychiatry*. 1998;32(6):785–793.

40. Althaus CE. A disciplinary perspective on the epistemological status of risk. *Risk Analysis*. 2005;25(3):567–688.

41. Silver E, Chow-Martin L. A multiple models approach to assessing recidivism: Implications for judicial decision making. *Criminal Justice and Behavior*. 2002;29:538–568.

42. Hart S. The role of psychopathy in assessing risk for violence: conceptual and methodological issues. *Legal and Criminological Psychology*. 1998;3:121–137.

43. Douglas K, Kropp P. A prevention-based paradigm for violence risk assessment: clinical and research applications. *Criminal Justice and Behavior*. 2002;29:617–658.

44. Levinson R, Ramsay G. Dangerousness, stress, and mental health evaluations. *Journal of Health and Social Behavior*. 1979;20:178–187.

45. Large M, Nielssen O, Ryan C, et al. Mental health laws that require dangerousness for involuntary admission may delay the initial treatment of schizophrenia. *Soc Psychiatry Psychiatr Epidemiol*. 2008;43:251–256.

46. Large M, Ryan C, Nielssen O, et al. The danger of dangerousness: why we must remove the dangerousness criterion from our mental health acts. *J Med Ethics*. 2008;34:877–881.

47. Allan A. The past, present and future of mental health law: a therapeutic jurisprudence analysis. *Law Context*. 2003;20:24–53.

48. Brouillette M, Paris J. The dangerousness criterion for civil commitment: the problem and a possible solution. *Can J Psychiatry*. 1991;36:285–289.

49. Ryan T. Perceived risks associated with mental illness: beyond homicide and suicide. *Social Science and Medicine*. 1998;46(2):287–297.

50. Kant I. *Critique of Practical Reason*. Gregor M, trans. Cambridge: Cambridge University Press; 1787/1997.

51. Megone C. Aristotle's function argument and the concept of mental illness. *Philosophy, Psychiatry and Psychology*. 1998;5:187–201.

52. Wakefield J. The concept of mental disorder: on the boundary between biological facts and social values. *American Psychologist*. 1992;47:373–388.

53. Wakefield J. Disorder as harmful dysfunction: a conceptual critique of *DSM-III-R*'s definition of mental disorder. *Psychological Review.* 1992;99:23–39.

54. Radden J. Personal identity, characterization identity, and mental disorder. In: Radden J, ed. *The Philosophy of Psychiatry.* New York: Oxford University Press; 2004:133–146.

55. Ricouer P. *Oneself as Another.* Chicago: University of Chicago Press; 1992.

56. Rawls J. *A Theory of Justice.* Cambridge, MA: The Bellknap Press; 1971.

57. Daniels N. *Just Health Care.* Cambridge: Cambridge University Press; 1995.

58. Nussbaum M. *Frontiers of Justice.* Cambridge, MA: Bellknap; 2006.

59. Nussbaum M. *Women and Human Development: The Capabilities Approach.* New York: Cambridge University Press; 2000.

60. Dale E. Is supervised community treatment ethically justifiable? *Journal of Medical Ethics.* 2010;36(5):271–274.

61. O'Brien A-M, Farrell SJ, Faulkner S. Community treatment orders: beyond hospital utilization rates examining the Association of Community Treatment Orders with Community Engagement and Supportive Housing. *Community Mental Health Journal.* 2009;45(6):415–419.

62. Dawson J. Community treatment orders and human rights. *Law in Context* 2008;26(2):148–159.

63. Kisely S, Campbell L, Preston N. Compulsory community and involuntary outpatient treatment for people with severe mental disorders. *Cochrane Database of Systematic Reviews.* 2011;Art No: CD004408(2).

64. Sarkar S, Adshead G. Black robes and white coats: who will win the new mental health tribunals? *British Journal of Psychiatry.* 2005;186:96–98.

65. Welsh S, Deahl M. Modern psychiatric ethics. *The Lancet.* 2002;359:253–255.

66. Adshead G. Care or custody? Ethical dilemmas in forensic psychiatry. *Journal of Medical Ethics.* 2000;26:302–304.

67. Fernandez H, Friedman J. Classification and treatment of tardive syndromes. *Neurologist.* 2003;9:16–27.

68. Lieberman JA, Stroup TS, McEvoy JP, et al. Effectiveness of antipsychotic drugs in patients with chronic schizophrenia. *New England Journal of Medicine.* 2005;353:1209–1223.

69. Aquinas T. *Summa Theologica.* 1947; http://www.sacred-texts.com/chr/aquinas/summa/index.htm.

70. Mangan J. An historical analysis of the principle of double effect. *Theological Studies.* 1949;10:41–61.

71. Walzer M. *Just and Unjust Wars.* New York: Basic Books; 1977.

72. Wettstein R. Ethics and involuntary treatment. *Administration in Mental Health.* 1987;15:110–119.

6

Psychiatry across Cultures

Introduction

Many postindustrial societies have become multicultural. In most large Western cities many ethnicities both blend into the community and form distinct cultural enclaves. Many cities thrive upon this. Moreover, many developed economies are dependent upon immigrant labor, leading to large shifts in population makeup.

Assuming social equality and equity, and this is not a given in many communities, a polyglot society will flourish and be enriched by ongoing migration and the effect of different cultural influences. Beyond this, however, lies the challenge to psychiatry to provide an equivalent quality of care to all members of society. Because one of the most influential contexts in the craft of psychiatry is that of culture, this is at times a formidable challenge.

In this chapter, we will review the concept of *alienism*, how psychiatric disorders are constructed in particular social contexts, and the history of postcolonial Western psychiatry.

Alienism

Within a culture, society, or community are normative expectations of belief, language, or conventions that help to define the group. This sense of identity exists within narratives, popular culture, rituals, customs, and language. Such collectives also define themselves by what they are not; that is to say, they see themselves relative to others. This concept of the Other was discussed in Chapter 1; however, within the context of this consideration, we use the concept of the Other, or *alien*, to refer to members of a community who differ from the mainstream.

Foucault had identified this prototypic other as being the leper.[1] In Chapter 13 of *The Book of Leviticus*, those with a defiling skin disease are to be excluded from the community[45]:

Anyone with such a defiling disease must wear torn clothes, let their hair be unkempt, cover the lower part of their face and cry out, "Unclean! Unclean!"[46] As long as they have the disease they remain unclean. They must live alone; they must live outside the camp.

According to Foucault, by the time of the Enlightenment, quotation was the new leprosy. Apart from assuming the role of the Other through irrationality, insanity was also linked to criminality. In this way, alienism as a form of otherness within a community or society comprised both dangerous irrationality and criminality. The analogous existence of the prison and the asylum bore testimony to this formulation of madness as the post-Enlightenment form of alienism. In this way, the fledgling nineteenth century enterprise of psychiatry earned the additional appellation of *alienist* in that it played the role of "intermediary between the social world and the world of the mentally ill" (p. 33).[2] Like the job description for priests in *Leviticus 13*, alienists were tasked with identifying and containing aliens. Indeed, following advances in public health in containment of disease vectors, alienism served a public health role in containing madness and criminality.

The insane/criminal form of otherness was particularly potent in the context of immigration. In the late nineteenth and early twentieth centuries, diasporas of peoples from many parts of the globe descended on new world societies such as North America, Argentina, and Australia. Such societies faced the dilemma of diseases borne by migrants, both infectious and hereditary. In the United States, legislation prevented immigration of mentally ill, antisocial, or intellectually disabled individuals. There had been assumptions of excess mental illness in immigrants, particularly paranoid disorders;[3] one 1930s study highlighted a particularly high incidence of schizophrenia in Norwegian migrants to the United States.[4]

Social Construction of Mental Disorder

As part of our argument, we take the perspective that mental disorders are in large part social constructs. A social construct is an idea that may appear to be natural and obvious to those who accept it, but in reality is an invention or artifact of a particular culture or society. The implication is that social constructs are in some sense human choices rather than laws resulting from divine will or nature.[5] Such a process is historically and social contextualized and links knowledge and social action.[6]

Foucault's *Madness and Civilisation*[1] furthered this argument by tracing the development of "madness" through various eras. Madness is not a natural static phenomenon but dependent upon the society in which it occurs. In the eighteenth century, madness came to be seen as the reverse of reason. Various discourses in society, e.g., medicine and law, determine how madness is known and experienced. In the *Archaeology of Knowledge*[7] Foucault described the creation of "discursive formations," which organize concepts and generate "objects of knowledge" at both local (discipline) and general (cultural) level. Applied to medicine, this is the possession of the "medical gaze." The present dominant discourse in psychiatry is along the notion that all mental illnesses are the result of pathology in the brain. In *Birth of the Clinic*,[8] Foucault argued that the gaze of the physician in modernity could penetrate illusions of sickness to see through to the underlying reality of disease. All sickness, physical or mental, is reduced to diseases of the tissues, and the language of the discourse in medicine is the language of disease:

> Hence the appearance that pathological anatomy assumed at the outset: that of an objective, real, and at last unquestionable foundation for the description of diseases: A nosography based on the affection of the organs will be invariable. (p. 129)[8]

The physician thus replaced the clergyman of pre-Enlightenment as the protector of humanity, possessing the power of science and reason to see the hidden truth.

A more contemporary social constructionist view of psychiatric disorder was defined by American sociologist Allan Horwitz,[9] who defined the constructionist position in regard to psychiatric disorder as being constituted by social systems of meaning, not naturalistic phenomena. Psychiatric disorders are defined by cultural rules evident in language such as *unreasonable* or *dysfunctional*. The limits of this constructionist position of psychiatric disorder are, first, that it pays no heed to the observation that many psychiatric disorders have underlying brain pathology. Moreover, the constructionist position is undermined by its incapacity to provide an account of comparisons of psychiatric disorders between cultures and therefore it does not provide a coherent system for critiquing mental illnesses. According to Horwitz, "Constructing some kinds of disturbed human behaviour as diseases fits some conditions better than others," and the use of diagnosis should only be in situations "when people have internal dysfunctions" (p. 229).[9] In essence, Horwitz's thesis is that there is a core of psychiatric diagnosis, evident in conditions with some credible evidence of internal dysfunction. The constructionist position has more validity in conditions where it seems there are deviant responses to difficult situations.

Horwitz and American sociologist Jerome Wakefield applied their respective positions to depression in *The Loss of Sadness*.[10] Their core thesis is that normal sorrow is a nonpathological state that has been conflated with clinically significant depression. *The Loss of Sadness* argues that sadness is "responses that arise after losses of attachment, defeats in status contests, or the collapse of meaning systems or goal strivings" (p. 51). This is an elaboration of the Bowlby's typology of infant responses to separation. Sadness serves some adaptive functions such as the attraction of social support and other forms of secondary gain. Despite the obvious social advantages of sadness, Horwitz and Wakefield do not see it as a process that provides the species with an evolutionary advantage.

Borrowing from the ideas of evolutionary biologists Stephen Jay Gould and Richard Lewontin,[11] Horwitz and Wakefield define sadness, medicalized inappropriately into *depression*, as a "spandrel." A spandrel is the adornment of an otherwise redundant phenomenon with some form of significance. The original metaphor referred to the angular spaces beneath a cathedral dome, which are structural. Those who appointed cathedrals with art of religious significance adorned spandrels with artwork, rather than having them bare and thus inconsistent with the rest of the interior. The essence of the metaphor is that it is a category to conclude that spandrels were placed in cathedrals for artwork, rather than artwork masking an otherwise unsightly structural feature. Like a spandrel with an exquisite Raphael painting or a Michelangelo relief, Horwitz and Wakefield see the otherwise redundant phenomenon of normal sadness as being adorned with the concept of disorder. They aver that the phenomenon of sadness is a by-product of infant attachment drives in adulthood and, like the spaces below cathedral arches, has been adorned with the iconography of depression. This is not to say that the intense distress of grief or loss of a relationship is not true emotional pain; it is just not a disorder. Horwitz and Wakefield avoid charges of mean spiritedness by equating the psychiatric treatment of sadness with analgesia in childbirth—real pain, just not arising from a medical disorder. Indeed, Horwitz and Wakefield argue that this blurring of the boundaries has arisen in large part because of the neo-Kraepelinian approach of the *Diagnostic and Statistical Manual of Mental Disorders* (*DSM*) in utilizing symptoms as the basis of defining a psychiatric disorder.

The most controversial arguments made in *The Loss of Sadness* relate to the so-called "constituencies" that keep the distinction between depression and sadness deliberately blurred. Academics perpetuate the process so that their research will accord with the published literature. Psychiatry and the pharmaceutical industry adhere to the view to continue their influence and viability. Even those who suffer depression benefit from the existential comfort of having life's painful moments attributable to a treatable illness. Horwitz and Wakefield do not dispute the existence of the disorder of clinical depression— just the blurred boundaries. As they conclude:

It is now generally accepted that there are genuine medical disorders of the mind;
the problem is to understand the limits of the concept of disorder so that it does
not engulf all the problems that life poses. (p. 225)[10]

This view of psychiatry is provocative, but one is left questioning the instrumental value
of such arguments. Sad people do exist and, granted, are not necessarily sick. They still
suffer, however, and they sometimes commit suicide as a consequence of that suffering or the
deranged interpretations of the world that such distress creates. Physicians seek to alleviate
suffering and save lives. Moreover, sad people benefit from some intervention. Perhaps
the distinction of depression and sadness will avoid inappropriate use of antidepressant
medication—not a bad outcome. The real anxiety is that some people who seem sad are in fact
in the early phases of depression. To banish their suffering to the same status of evolutionary
irrelevance as the human appendix risks all the problems of untreated mental illness.

Construct of Mental Disorder

The origin of modern diagnostic systems in psychiatry was that of German psychiatrist
Emil Kraepelin, whose attempts to define *psychiatric disorder* on the basis of pathological
disturbance ultimately defaulted into an observation-based taxonomy.[12] Kraepelin classified at
least 15 disorders according to symptoms and, to a lesser degree, clinical course or progress.
Kraepelin's approach remains the dominant paradigm in psychiatric diagnosis. In the latter
twentieth century, disparate views of the nature of mental disorder have followed certain
philosophical assumptions. A reductionist view of medicine avers that mental and physical
disorders are in the same category. This view is associated with the work of American
bioethicist Leon Kass[13] and psychiatrist Robert Kendell.[14] American philosopher Christopher
Boorse[15] expands on this idea in defining an organism as healthy if it is not diseased, disease
being conceptualized as interference with normative species function. For Boorse a disease
becomes an illness if it is undesirable, is entitled to treatment, and provides a valid excuse to
otherwise abnormal behavior on the part of the sufferer.

Psychiatric disorder presents a different category of disturbance. Bill Fulford[16] argues
that psychiatric diagnosis is "situated between medicine and morality." He sees the process
of defining mental as a dialectic between the view of Thomas Szasz[17] and that of Kendell or
Kass. Fulford introduced the notion of health and illness as value-laden concepts in medicine
and proposed a fact-plus-value model in which certain conditions are value-laden or fact
laden. Some psychiatric diagnoses have more solid factual bases than others, whereas some
psychiatric diagnoses are more value laden.

Subsequently, Wakefield attempted to define mental disorders as "harmful dysfunctions."
This involved the failure of a mechanism in the person to perform a natural function for
which it was designed by natural selection, and a value judgment that the dysfunction
is undesirable.[18,19] Even this definition is limited in that it invites a problematic kind of
relativism.[20] In trying to define dysfunction in a more universal, naturalistic sense, much of
the discussion of this is along the Aristotelian notion of reason being the species-normative
function for humans.[22]

Other critiques of psychiatric diagnoses run along existential lines. This area is most
recognizable in the work of the so-called "antipsychiatrists," who saw mental disorder as
little more than a relativistic value judgment based on normative expectations of social and
interpersonal functioning. Szasz saw mental disorder as a construct to marginalize "problems

in living" and the process being beholden to social agency.[17] Scottish psychiatrist and philosopher R. D. Laing saw the flaw in mental disorder as a construct being more in terms of ontology.[23] As with the philosophers Dilthey and Husserl,[23,24] Laing saw that the application of the natural sciences to human experience could not define unique individual engagement in the world, and as such, a mental disorder was more a process of adapting to circumstance. It has been argued that much of Wittgenstein's work could be labeled schizophrenic.[25]

The sociological conceptualizations of mental disorder, particularly those orientated around stigma and labeling of deviant behavior, are usually attributable to sociologists Erving Goffman[26] and Thomas Scheff.[27] Scheff in particular argues that mental illness is defined by the violation of social norms taken as givens and not made explicit in laws or codes of conduct. In Scheff's view there are two key assumptions in the diagnosis of mental disorder: The first is that most chronic mental illness is at least in part a social role. The second is that the reaction of society usually determines who enters into that role, as well as how and when.

DSM and Psychiatric Diagnosis

The Association of Medical Superintendents of American Institutions for the Insane was founded 1844. In 1921, it became the American Psychiatric Association (APA). In the latter part of the nineteenth century, the U.S. government requested information about the prevalence of psychiatric disorders in the community. By 1880 there were seven disorders, based largely upon European diagnostic conventions. A definitive American psychiatric nosology did not emerge until 1952, with the publication of the First Edition of the *Diagnostic and Statistical Manual of Mental Disorders* (*DSM-I*). The *DSM-I* listed 106 psychiatric diagnoses. In 1968, the *DSM-II* added a further 76 disorders. In 1974, Dr. Robert L. Spitzer was tasked with the challenge of coordinating 13 research committees and examining myriad psychiatric disorders in pursuit of *DSM-III*, which appeared in 1980. The *DSM-III* listed 265 diagnoses. The *DSM-III-R* (1987) listed 292 diagnoses, and the *DSM-IV* (1994), 297 diagnoses.

The *DSM-III* represented a major shift in the way in which psychiatric disorders were classified in that it opted for an empirically based reliable diagnostic system, which appeared to represent a revisitation of the Kraepelinian approach to psychiatric diagnosis.[28] Psychiatric diagnosis was, to Spitzer and his colleagues, "a technical difficulty requiring technical solutions"[29] (p. 35). The benchmark for the legitimacy of a psychiatric disorder in the *DSM* was its reliability, defined as a kappa value (κ) > 0.7. Such a rigorous approach aspired to universalizability of psychiatric diagnosis.[20] This approach would transcend the influence of culture on diagnostic inferences[30] although the *DSM-IV* made some attempt to contextualize so-called culture-bound syndromes.[31] These have been criticized as racist and pejorative.[32]

Despite widespread misgivings, the *DSM* project has been remarkably successful.[33] Gerald Klerman proclaimed that the *DSM-III* had "already been declared a victory. There is not a textbook of psychology or psychiatry that does not use *DSM-III* as the organizing principle for its table of contents and for classification of psychopathology"[29] (p. 6).

There have been a variety of narratives surrounding how the *DSM* represents political, financial, and guild interests of the APA. More significantly, some critiques have argued that the *DSM* represents a controlling strategy in the face of diminishing health and academic resources.[34]

Apart from the critiques of the process of diagnosis in psychiatry, Sadler[35] has articulated the aesthetic value of psychiatric diagnosis in that it provides a simpler characterization of a complex phenomena, which penetrates beneath surface appearances and is receptive to multiple contexts balanced with reducing illness complexity. In addition it forges knowledge and moral purpose into action in a way that respects the patient in diagnostic practices and is rigorous, accountable, thorough, and consistent. Despite these qualities, many diagnoses emerge out of what the patients do, not what happens to them, which creates ambiguities about moral responsibility. Moreover, the process of diagnosis pathologizes some experiences the patient either values, such as the creativity of mania, or sees as a normal experience.[36]

Construction of Mental Disorder Using the Fact–Value Distinction

As we discussed earlier, the core of psychiatric disorder is difficult to define. All disorder requires elements of some sort of undesirable state, whether impairment of reason or deviation from normative expectations of social and interpersonal functioning. Even the notion of dysfunction being harmful is moot, as the notion of what species-normative functioning (as defined by Wakefield[18]) rests on the suppressed premise that the ultimate goal or *telos* of human function lies in reductionist ideas of species advancement and propagation of genes.

Fulford has evolved a model of mental disorder based upon the concepts of facts and values.[16] The Fact–Value distinction takes the position that phenomena considered disorders or diseases are based first on empirical observation of deviation from normative or desirable parameters, and second on negative evaluation of the effects of this phenomenon. Facts can be independently verified and form the basis of testable hypotheses. In contrast, values require subjective evaluation and are more qualitative in nature. Fulford highlights the problem of this in contrasting the difference between individuals' evaluation of a strawberry as opposed to a work of art. It is arguably easier to achieve consensus on what constitutes the quality of a good strawberry, whereas a work of art is much more subjective in its value. Similar distinctions could be made of aspects of life, such as the difference between suffering from distressing psychotic or anxiety symptoms and suffering from certain social or interpersonal difficulties. In the example of a disorder such as hypertension, the factual component of the disorder is the observation of elevated blood pressure readings and structural observations of the alterations of blood vessels. The evaluative component is the association of the condition with heightened risk of stroke or heart disease.

We have previously adapted Fulford's approach in considering the nature of psychiatric disorders[37] (Figure 6.1). If one considers both facts and values as dimensional constructs, a quadrantic model develops. In one quadrant, a diagnosis is heavily factually based and only minimally value laden. Acute delirium is a pathological state that emerges as a consequence of physical illness, such as sepsis, which has distinct laboratory and neurophysiological demonstrable facts at its core. In contrast, the diagnosis of personality disorder, at least in the present state of knowledge in psychiatry, lacks significant factual basis, and the diagnosis is predicated on consistent patterns of behaviors that deviate from social norms. Grief lacks any factual basis as a disorder. Moreover, few if any value judgments are applied to a grieving person, despite distress and dysfunction, albeit time limited.

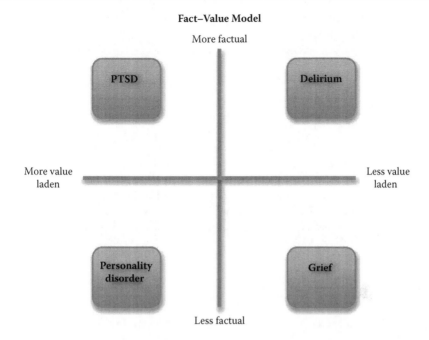

Figure 6.1 Fulford's Fact–Value model applied to some psychiatric disorders. (After Robertson, M.D. and Walter, G., *Psychiatric Annals*, 37, 2007, 793–797.)

By way of example, we will consider posttraumatic stress disorder (PTSD). Most people who experience a traumatic event develop some intrusive symptoms such as flashbacks or vivid dreams, although only about 8 percent develop the full syndrome of PTSD, including hyperarousal, cognitive impairment, dissociative symptoms, and phobic avoidant behavior.[38] Interpersonal violence, either physical or sexual assault, is the most likely traumatic event to lead to the survivor's developing PTSD,[39] although the most common traumatic event defined by the *DSM-IV-TR* criteria A1 for PTSD is "unexpected bereavement."[40] Community studies indicate approximately 1–2 percent of the general U.S. population meet criteria for PTSD at any given time.[41]

In this model PTSD sits in a quadrant of being both factual and value laden. There is ample evidence for pathophysiological dysregulation in PTSD,[42–46] i.e., a factual basis. Mindful of the notion that symptoms persisting well beyond the time of a traumatic event, Wakefield argued:

> The fact that in PTSD the person's coping mechanisms often fail to bring the person back to functional equilibrium months and even years after the danger is gone, and that PTSD reactions are dramatically out of proportion to the actual post-traumatic danger, suggests that the response is indeed independent of any environmental maintaining cause and therefore is a dysfunction.[19]

Such an assertion begs the question, is it in fact desirable to restore a state of psychological or physical equilibrium in all circumstances? PTSD may well represent an adaptive set of behaviors that have survival advantage. In a situation where there is constant threat of harm, a state of perpetual physiological arousal, hypervigilance to threat in the environment, and phobic avoidance has arguably an atavistic and adaptive function. PTSD has been argued to represent, in ethological terms, either an over learnt survival response[47] or a behavioral adaptation to avoid predation.[48] Indeed, socially contracted, stable societies (as opposed to the Hobbesian state of human nature[49]) are only a relatively recent phenomenon in human history.

No human society in history has provided indefinite periods of geopolitical stability, let alone freedom from calamity or interpersonal threat. As such, the value component of PTSD in Fulford's model rests on the suppressed premise that societies and communities are perpetually safe.

To return to the construction of PTSD as a psychiatric disorder, there is an ample factual basis to justify the contention that it represents a nonphysiological, aberrant state. Now under debate is whether the evaluation of the disturbance as being undesirable can be justified. Granted, no reasonable person desires to be traumatized and suffer psychopathology as a consequence, yet it is possible that the psychological changes inherent in PTSD are undesirable only in settings where there is little prospect of danger. As such, a disorder has been socially constructed.

Transcultural Psychiatry

In the late 1970s an American psychiatrist, Arthur Kleinman, made an examination of a series of patients in a clinic in Hunan Province in China. Kleinman observed that while many of these patients described symptoms that would fall under the rubric in Western psychiatry of somatization, a large majority also met criteria for *DSM-III* major depressive disorder.[50] Kleinman concluded that while the two clinical presentations may have emerged from the same underlying pathophysiological disturbance, the *illness* differed from the *pathology*. This seminal observation provided the foundation for much of Kleinman's subsequent work.[51] Throughout his career, Kleinman has been at pains to highlight that the physician must move beyond a process of applied science at the bedside to a more holistic understanding of the narrative or experience of illness of the patient. Applied to traumatic stress, Kleinman has dubbed this process as "social suffering," i.e., placing the experience of traumatic stress in social, cultural, and political contexts.[52] This form of narrative ethic has become central to the craft of psychiatry practiced within and between cultures and may inform the clinician's approach to fundamental ethical dilemmas such as the place of the patient's family in consent and decision making.[53]

Returning to the issue of psychiatric diagnosis, anthropological perspectives indicate that this always occurs in a specific cultural context. The cultural background of the psychiatrist and the patient influence how specific observations are interpreted. This is not a new observation, as in the late nineteenth century, Karl Jaspers wrote of the hermeneutic (interpretation) process, in which the context of the observer was critical to his or her interpretation of the phenomenon under observation.[23,54] Under Jaspers's rules, all empirical understanding is interpretation, and such understanding occurs in a hermeneutic circle (*kriese*). In Jaspers's hermeneutic approach, things that appear inconsistent are part of the process of understanding, which by its nature does not reach closure, and therefore there is endless interpretation. Jaspers borrowed from Heidegger's concept of understanding as a form of illumination or unmasking of a phenomenon; Heidegger had used the term *lichtung*, loosely interpreted as "a clearing," much like a clearing in a forest.[55]

Jaspers and Kleinman implore the psychiatrist to engage in a process of continual reflection of their interpretation of the patient's experience. In the discipline of sociology, the concept of *cultural relativism* is frequently discussed in relation to psychiatric diagnosis and treatment. Cultural relativism is the view that the normative mores, customs, and practices of particular cultures can be truly known only within the culture in which they are occurring. In other words, the alien observer cannot know or understand the norms of a culture. Applied to the concept of mental disorder, cultural relativism takes the position that mental disorders are social constructs.

Anthropologist Ruth Benedict's book *Patterns of Culture*[56] provided an anthropological foundation of the process of social constructionism and cultural relativism in defining psychiatric disorder. Benedict observed that each culture chooses a few characteristics that become normative. From the position of cultural relativism, each culture thus creates its own moral imperatives that can be understood only if one studies that culture as a whole. Normality is relative to the values of the culture. A person whose behavior or views are deviant from the rest of the culture (or a "normal" member of that culture placed in another) would be deemed mentally ill in the view of cultural relativism. This explains the position that delusions, for example, must be beliefs inconsistent with the person's culture. In clinical practice, such a perspective requires that the clinician be aware of the need to see the patient's experience in the context of his or her particular culture. Put simply, the question must be, How would a typical member of this group view this situation?

In mainstream Western psychiatry, the clearest instances of this phenomenon are the so-called culture-bound syndromes described in *DSM-IV* and *DSM-IV-TR*, including such diagnoses as *amok* found in the Malay culture, and *uqamairineq* among the Yupik Eskimos. Culture-bound syndromes are seen as "folk illnesses" in which changes of behavior figure prominently.[57] The phenomenon of *amok,* found in Malaysia and Indonesia, involves a person (usually male) exhibiting a deranged state of agitation and hostile aggression, often leading to destruction of property. From the perspective of the person's culture, such behavior may be viewed as being within the bounds of normal behavior. In the era of British and Dutch colonial rule, and its associated psychiatric institutions, such behavior represented grounds for involuntary psychiatric treatment of patients in Malaya and the East Indies (present-day Malaysia and Indonesia).[58] Thus a Western pathologizing of a normative behavior represented an example of the use of psychiatry as a process of exerting social control. The argued limitations of the *DSM-IV-TR* in non-Western patients is apropos of the concept of cultural relativism.[59] American psychiatrist and anthropologist Horacio Fabrega argues that psychiatry reflects a cultural interpretation about personal experience, responsibility, social behavior, and the requirements for social order.[59] The argument that unusual behavior that might be normative in one setting is grounds for a psychiatric diagnosis in a Western setting represents a quandary. Indeed, one author has argued that the existence of culture-bound syndromes in the *DSM-IV* evokes notions of the "crazy native" of colonial times.[32]

The other significant theme in the field of transcultural psychiatry concerns the presence of a possible latent racism in psychiatric diagnosis.[2,32,60] This extends from the alienist era. Non-Western patients are more likely to be diagnosed with psychotic disorders, receive higher doses of antipsychotic medication, and are more likely to be secluded while on inpatient wards in Western societies.[32] Non-Western patients are viewed as being more likely to be dangerous or unpredictable and are therefore subject to greater levels of coercive psychiatric treatment. Whether this represents the comparative mental ill-health of non-Western patients or the peril of evaluating mental disturbance and, in particular, estimating the risk or threat it poses is not clear. Clearly, the challenge to psychiatrists who care for patients from different cultures is the apparent poorness of fit between patients of non-Western backgrounds and what has been and is currently offered by Western psychiatry.

Colonial and Postcolonial Psychiatry

In light of the notion of psychiatric power evident in involuntary psychiatric treatment discussed in Chapter 5, we will now consider the manifestation of psychiatric power in a transcultural setting. Historically, coercive power between dominant and submissive cultures has appeared in the process of colonization. The specter of psychiatric power lies within the power imbalance between colonizer and colonized. Moreover, the trauma of displacement and dispossession are part of the legacy of colonization and are critical in conceptualizing the mental health of indigenous populations in postcolonial settings.

Frantz Fanon applied the prism of psychiatry to the violent exercise of power manifest in colonization. Born on the Caribbean island of Martinique, Fanon experienced racism perpetrated against the population of the island by Vichy French soldiers garrisoned there after the fall of France in 1940. Fanon joined the Free French army in response and fought in Europe with Allied forces in 1945, before being wounded. He studied medicine and later psychiatry in France. He completed his training in Algeria in 1953 and became chief psychiatrist at the Blida-Joinville hospital in Algiers.

Fanon, like Che Guevara, was a medical practitioner and revolutionary. In addition to his revolutionary politics, Fanon pursued a project of reform in the psychiatric profession in Algeria.[61] Fanon's double life as a colonial-era psychiatrist and as an Algerian Front de Liberation Nationale (FLN) activist has invited much criticism in revisionist views of his life. His most recent biographer refers to his reputation as a "talented hater."[62] Other critics cannot look past his complicity in FLN atrocities, such as bombings and sabotage.[63] His activities as a terrorist led to his deportation from Algeria in 1957. He died at age 31 from complications of acute myeloid leukemia.

Fanon ran his clinical service with the emphasis on his patients remaining connected with their social worlds rather than in confinement and isolation within the European-style asylum. Therapeutic programs were run on a day-stay basis, a form of outpatient, community-focused psychiatry that preceded such approaches in the West by several decades.[64] Fanon viewed "madness" as being sociogenic, and so psychiatric treatment took place in psychiatric hospitals that functioned as institutions of social change. Fanon's approach to psychiatric treatment required the psychiatrist and patient to develop a "common culture."[65] Fanon has been described as a "social psychiatrist driven by humanism to unmask inhumanity."[61]

While many of Fanon's writings are associated with revolutionary struggle, his writings add important insights into psychiatric power as it existed in colonial times as well as postcolonial and neocolonial times. Fanon saw psychiatry and psychiatric institutions as being extensions of the power of the colonizer. The process of colonization requires the negation of the indigenous population in terms of their link to the land, their identity, and their culture (p. 9).[66] Fanon's most important work in this regard, *The Wretched of the Earth,*[60] highlighted how European psychiatry functioned in a colonial setting to alienate the colonized population from their society by forcing a questioning of identity through the European psychiatric prism. Fanon identified colonial psychiatry in Algeria as Eurocentric and as exerting a hegemonic cultural influence upon the population as a perpetuation of the colonizer–colonized dynamic. The cultural estrangement and institutionalized racism brought about by Eurocentric psychiatry creates a sense of the Other in the colonized population, forcing them to constantly question, who am I?

While much of the psychiatric material in *The Wretched of the Earth*[60] and Fanon's other famous work *Black Skin, White Mask*[67] was co-written and possibly anecdotal,[68] it provides a critical appraisal of the disempowering effects of psychiatric power in colonized peoples. Fanon reformulated Jacques Lacan's notion of *meconnaissance*[69] in relation to this process. The translation of the term is to "misconstrue" or "misinterpret"; Lacan considered that throughout life the ego sustained its sense of itself through a repeated process of misidentification. Applied to the colonizer–colonized dynamic, *meconnaissance* represents the process of psychiatric diagnosis, confinement, and treatment as effecting the alienation of the colonized from their cultural, social, and political elements. Fanon saw this ultimately as a process of the subjugated colonized as internalizing the injustice inherent in colonization.[64] European psychiatric power engendered a form of otherness by enforcing a psychology of the colonized.

Later Fanonian scholars have expanded this through the passing mentions Fanon made to petrification[70]—Fanon had used the term *thingified* in his writing. Recall *petrification* was a term used by Goffman to refer to the process of eroding the individual identity or selfhood of inmates in the psychiatric asylum.[71] In European psychiatric institutions in colonial settings, petrification denudes the identity of the colonized, and through the imposition of Western notions of normative behavior and the good life. The colonizer ultimately alienates the colonized from his or her land, enforcing a sense of self as loyal subjects of the colonizing power.

European powers were divested of colonial possessions after both World Wars, either through brutal conflict, civil disobedience, or in the case of many former British colonies, the gradual assumptions of office within colonial institutions by the local population. Postcolonial societies struggled with national identity, internecine conflicts between groups, and economic instability. Many retained colonial-era institutions such as Westminster system of government. Psychiatric institutions, whether asylums, professional bodies, or mental health laws, also remained redolent of colonial-era forms.[72]

Since the advent of neoliberalism, there has been a process of economic and cultural colonization, particularly through international institutions such as the World Bank and the International Monetary Fund. Again, scholarship, which applies a Fanonian lens to current circumstances, places psychiatry within this process of putative neocolonization. Rather than the violence and coercion of nineteenth and twentieth century colonization and the equally repressive psychiatric institutions that accompanied it, neocolonial psychiatry assumes a softer form. One Fanonian scholar sees this evident in the insidious influence of the export of the Western construct of PTSD to non-Western populations.[73] English psychiatrist Derek Summerfield argues that PTSD is the product of the imposition of Western scientific ideas on other cultures[74] and that the Western tendency to isolate the individual and his or her own experience of calamity (as opposed to that of the group or community) is not the norm in other cultures.[75-77] Summerfield argues that the Western Cartesian tradition fails to identify the broader, "lived" context of traumatic events and that it is a form of irresponsible social agency in the face of mass calamity.[78] He contends that the PTSD construct fails to acknowledge the way in which the experience of trauma is contextualized within a society and culture[75] and that treatment models based upon such assumptions are limited in their scope.[79] As a result of this approach, Summerfield has been highly critical of the approaches many Western nongovernment organizations have taken to the relief efforts in non-Western countries affected by mass disaster or war.[79] This issue is more vividly demonstrated in the novel *Masking Terror*,[80] which highlights the destructive effects of the imposition of individually focused psychological interventions in a Sri Lankan village, a process that ultimately denies the victims their culturally determined, collective coping strategies.

The ongoing situation of injustice faced by indigenous people in Australia manifests as physical and mental illness and social discord.[81] These social processes emerge as substance misuse, risk-taking, violence, and social discord.[81,82] It also indicates that for indigenous populations, physical health, mental health, and social deprivation are inseparable. While it is evident that indigenous people suffer common *DSM* psychiatric disorders,[83] these are often experienced in the context of factors such as guilt or self-reproach arising from the experience of such injustice and social failure. This profoundly influences help-seeking among indigenous people, whose relationship with healthcare professionals from nonindigenous society is often characterized by problematic power relationships.[84] There are frequent breakdowns of order in indigenous communities, leading to demoralization and anomie.[85] As representatives of a more powerful group in society, nonindigenous healthcare workers find themselves in a difficult situation. This has created a discourse in indigenous mental health, which has realized the need for culturally respectful and sensitive mental health services.[86] Aboriginal communities are based upon kinship and linkages with the natural world granting an "ontologic legitimation,"[87] poorly grasped by traditional Western models of mind and mental illness. Experience in this area indicates that workable approaches to indigenous mental health require empowerment of their community and, in particular, their healthcare workers in a process described as deep listening to the community[88] and more extensive consultation.[89]

Case Example: Ms. P

Ms. P was a 42-year-old married Australian Aboriginal woman of mixed race background who had five children. She had not worked consistently since her 20s. Ms. P was made a ward of the state as a young child in the 1970s. She was removed from her biological mother by social services, who had deemed the mother unfit. Ms. P was subsequently placed with a white family and raised with several step-siblings.

Ms. P became aware of her Aboriginal background in her early teens and became profoundly distressed. From that point, she felt "lost" within her family, and when her racial background became known among her peers, she was teased and marginalized. Her academic performance declined, and throughout her later adolescence she developed a pattern of antisocial and disruptive behavior, including oppositional behavior, substance misuse, petty theft, and truancy. After completing three years of high school, she dropped out and fell in with a bad crowd.

In her late adolescence Ms. P was able to meet her biological mother and visit the township where her mother's family lived. She recalls this as being a somewhat sterile affair of a visit supervised by social services and a tour of the Aboriginal community, which made her "feel like a tourist."

Regardless, Ms. P relocated to the township in her early adulthood but was never made to feel welcome by the community. Her first marriage saw her relocate to be with her husband's "mob." The marriage was violent and characterized by alcohol abuse and severe physical beatings, often with weapons. She escaped this relationship and later married a man with whom she felt "at home." Ms. P tried to make contact with members of the "Stolen Generation,"* but she was told that because her removal was not under the same legislation, she was not legitimately a member of this group, despite her having a similar sense of dislocation and alienation from her racial background.

---

* The term "Stolen Generation" refers to survivors of an Australian government policy to remove Aboriginal children of mixed race background from their families to be raised in institutions. The policy ended in the 1970s and was the subject of a formal government apology in 2008.

In the community in which she lived, she continued to feel traumatized by the ongoing removal of children by social services from "at-risk" Aboriginal households. She had become highly dependent upon her husband for day-to-day care, and her family lived in impecunious circumstances. She felt like a gypsy and had no sense of stability in the current community. She worried constantly that her younger children would be removed as a consequence of the social instability.

Ms. P had suffered psychopathology since her early adolescence. She had been plagued by chronic depressive symptoms and emotional lability. Her self-esteem was chronically low. She isolated herself from most social situations. She had broken and unrefreshing sleep, periods of fatigue, amotivation, and cognitive impairment. Throughout adult life she had made several suicide attempts, usually by overdose of medication. She had previously abused alcohol habitually, likely suffering alcohol dependence, although she had since modified this to a pattern of binge drinking on a fortnightly basis. Her alcohol use had led to numerous social and legal consequences. She had a brief custodial sentence for an assault perpetrated while intoxicated.

Ms. P consulted a doctor through an Aboriginal medical service and had been taking an antidepressant medication. She had rejected any attempts at psychological therapy, claiming "talking don't do much good."

Ms. P described symptoms that were consistent with a diagnosis of dysthymic disorder and alcohol abuse disorder. As such, she had sustained a psychological injury emerging in the course of her experience of cultural dislocation.

* * *

Perhaps most relevant to Ms. P was the affront presented by her alienation from both her Aboriginal origins and the white family and culture in which she was raised. In essence, Ms. P was displaced ontologically. She had been rejected by both white society as being Aboriginal and by Aboriginal society as being white. Even the survivors of the Stolen Generation rejected her, albeit on technical grounds. It is evident that in a critical point of her development, i.e., latency years and early adolescence, Ms. P's self-concept was fractured by the revelation that she was not a part of the white family she had assumed she was throughout the early part of her development. When she sought to reconcile with her biological family, her culture and community rejected her as being the Other, leading to a profound sense of dislocation that could be conceptualized in terms of disordered attachment, traumatic stress, or other clinical constructs.

In the final analysis, Ms. P experienced a catastrophic decline in her psychosocial functioning from her early to midadolescence, which led to a trajectory of antisocial behavior, substance misuse, chronic depression, and a propensity to victimization. She met criteria for a variety of *DSM-IV* disorders, but this in no way captured the meaning of her suffering to her, nor did it provide a pretext to treatment. Ms. P sought little more than security—financial and social. As such, Western models of mental healthcare, strictly applied, had little to offer her.

Conclusion

Regardless of the presumed universal assumptions of biological psychiatry, psychiatric practice occurs in a specific cultural context. Psychiatrists conceptualize illness, its treatment, and recovery in terms of cultural norms. There is a cultural chauvinism inherent in this process, and the questions of universal assumptions about psychiatry in terms of history and culture, such as whether one culture's depression is another's normative response, remain problematic. Psychiatric power has been a proxy for other forms of coercive power in recent history, and this vexed issue may be taking new forms of commercial and economic power in a global market for healthcare as a commodity. These questions will intensify as societies become more diverse and populations disperse across increasingly porous national boundaries.

References

1. Foucault M. *Madness and Civilization.* Howard R, trans. New York: Pantheon; 1965.

2. Littlewood R, Lipsedge M. *Aliens and Alienists, 3rd edition.* London: Routledge; 1997.

3. Kino F. Refugee psychosis in Britain: Alien's paranoid reaction. *Journal of Mental Sciences.* 1951;97:589–594.

4. Odegaard O. Emigration and insanity. *Acta Psychiatrica et Neurologica.* 1932(Supp 4).

5. Berger P, Luckman T. *The Social Construction of Reality.* London: Penguin; 1966.

6. Burr V. *An Introduction to Social Construction.* London: Routledge; 1995.

7. Foucault M. *The Archaeology of Knowledge.* New York: Pantheon Books; 1969.

8. Foucault M. *The Birth of the Clinic: An Archaeology of Medical Perception.* Sheridan Smith A, trans. New York: Vintage Books; 1975.

9. Horwitz A. *Creating Mental Illness.* Chicago: University of Chicago Press; 2002.

10. Horwitz A, Wakefield J. *The Loss of Sadness: How Psychiatry Transformed Normal Sorrow into Depressive Disorder.* New York: Oxford University Press; 2007.

11. Gould S, Lewontin R. The Spandrels of San Marco and the Panglossian Paradigm: A Critique of the Adaptationist Programme. *Proceedings of the Royal Society of London.* 1979;205:581–598.

12. Kraepelin E. *Psychiatrie.* Leipzig: Elibron; 1927/2006.

13. Kass L. Regarding the end of medicine and the pursuit of health. *Public Interest.* 1975;40:11–24.

14. Kendell R. The concept of disease and its implication for psychiatry. *British Journal of Psychiatry.* 1975;127:305–315.

15. Boorse C. What a theory of mental health should be. *Journal for the Theory of Social Behaviour.* 1976;6:61–84.

16. Fulford K. Analytic philosophy, brain science, and the concept of disorder. In: Bloch S, Green S, Chodoff P, eds. *Psychiatric Ethics.* New York: Oxford University Press; 1999:161–191.

17. Szasz T. The myth of mental illness. *American Psychologist.* 1960;15:113–118.

18. Wakefield J. The concept of mental disorder: on the boundary between biological facts and social values. *American Psychologist.* 1992;47:373–388.

19. Wakefield J. Disorder as harmful dysfunction: a conceptual critique of *DSM-III-R*'s definition of mental disorder. *Psychological Review.* 1992;99:23–39.

20. Gert B, Culver CM. Defining mental disorder. In: Radden J, ed. *The Philosophy of Psychiatry.* New York: Oxford University Press; 2004:415–425.

21. Megone C. Aristotle's function argument and the concept of mental illness. *Philosophy, Psychiatry and Psychology.* 1998;5:187–201.

22. Laing R. *The Divided Self: An Existential Study in Sanity and Madness.* Harmondsworth: Penguin; 1960.

23. Schwartz M, Wiggins O. Phenomenological and hermeneutical models: understanding and interpretation in psychiatry. In: Radden J, ed. *The Philosophy of Psychiatry.* New York: Oxford University Press; 2004:351–363.

24. Phillips J. Understanding/explanation. In: Radden J, ed. *The Philosophy of Psychiatry*. New York: Oxford University Press; 2004:180–190.

25. Sass L. *Madness and Modernism: Insanity in the Light of Modern Art, Literature, and Thought*. New York: Harvard University Press; 1992.

26. Goffman E. *Stigma*. Harmondsworth: Penguin Books; 1961.

27. Scheff T. *Being Mentally Ill: The Sociological Theory*. Chicago: Aldine Press; 1999.

28. Sharfstein S. *Descriptions and Prescriptions: Values, Mental Disorders and the DSMs*. Baltimore: Johns Hopkins University Press; 2002.

29. Kirk S, Kutchins H. *The Selling of the* DSM: *The Rhetoric of Science in Psychiatry*. New York: Aldine de Gruyer; 1992.

30. Spitzer M. The basis of psychiatric diagnosis. In: Sadler J, Wiggins O, Schwartz M, eds. *Philosophical Perspectives on Psychiatric Diagnostic Classification*. Baltimore: Johns Hopkins University Press; 1994:163–177.

31. Fabrega H. Culture and history in psychiatric diagnosis and practice. *Psychiatric Clinics of North America*. 2001;24:391–405.

32. Bhugra D, Bhui K. Racism in psychiatry: paradigm lost—paradigm regained. *International Review of Psychiatry*. 1999;11:236–243.

33. First M, Spitzer R. The *DSM*: not perfect, but better than the alternative. *Psychiatric Times*. 2003.

34. Schacht T. *DSM* and the politics of truth. *American Psychologist*. 1985;40:513–521.

35. Sadler J. *Values and Psychiatric Diagnosis*. New York: Oxford University Press; 2005.

36. Sadler J. Diagnosis/antidiagnosis. In: Radden J, ed. *The Philosophy of Psychiatry*. New York: Oxford University Press; 2004.

37. Robertson M, Walter G. The ethics of psychiatric diagnosis. *Psychiatric Annals*. 2007;37:793–797.

38. Kessler R, Bromet E, Nelson CA, et al. Posttraumatic stress disorder in the National Comorbidity Survey. *Archives of General Psychiatry*. 1995;52:1048–1060.

39. Breslau N, Kessler R. The stressor criterion in *DSM-IV* posttraumatic stress disorder: an empirical investigation. *Biological Psychiatry*. 2001;50:699–704.

40. Breslau N, Kessler R, Chilcoat H, et al. Trauma and posttraumatic stress disorder in the community: the 1996 Detroit Area Survey of Trauma. *Archives of General Psychiatry*. 1998;55:626–632.

41. Helzer J, Robins L, McEvoy L. Posttraumatic stress disorder in the general population. *New England Journal of Medicine*. 1987;317:1630–1634.

42. Pittman R, Orr S, Shalev A, et al. Psychophysiological alterations in posttraumatic stress disorder. *Seminars in Clinical Neurosychiatry*. 1999;4:234–241.

43. McFarlane A, Yehuda R, Clark R. Biologic models of traumatic memories and post-traumatic stress disorder: the role of neural networks. *Psychiatric Clinics of North America*. 2002;25:253–270.

44. van der Kolk B. The body keeps the score: memory and the evolving psychobiology of post traumatic stress. *Harvard Review of Psychiatry*. 1994;1:253–265.

45. van der Kolk B. The trauma spectrum: the interaction of biological and social events in the genesis of the trauma response. *Journal of Traumatic Stress*. 1988;1:273–290.

46. Southwick S, Krystal J, Johnson D, et al. Neurobiology of post-traumatic stress disorder. In: Tasman A, ed. *Annual Review of Psychiatry (Vol. 11)*. Washington DC: American Psychiatric Press; 1992.

47. Silove D. Is posttraumatic stress disorder an overlearnt response? An evolutionary-learning hypothesis. *Psychiatry: Interpersonal & Biological Processes*. 1998;61:181–190.

48. Cantor C. *Evolution and Posttraumatic Stress: Disorders of Vigilance and Defence*. London: Routledge; 2005.

49. Hobbes T, ed. *Leviathan*. London: Penguin; 1985.

50. Kleinman A. *Social Origins of Distress and Disease: Depression, Neurasthenia, and Pain in Modern China*. New York: Yale University Press; 1986.

51. Kleinman A. *The Illness Narratives: Suffering, Healing and the Human Condition*. New York: Perseus; 1988.

52. Kleinman A, Kleinman J. The appeal of experience; the dismay of images: cultural appropriations of suffering in our times. In: Kleinman A, Das V, Lock M, eds. *Social Suffering*. Berkeley: University of California Press; 1997:1–24.

53. Kleinman A. Culture, Illness, and care: clinical lessons from anthropologic and cross-cultural research. *Annals of Internal Medicine*. 1978;88:251–258.

54. Jaspers K. *General Psychopathology*. Hoenig J, Hamilton MW, trans. Chicago: University of Chicago Press; 1963.

55. Heidegger M. *Being and Time*. Macquarrie J, Robinson E, trans. San Francisco: Harper; 1962.

56. Benedict R. *Patterns of Culture*. New York: Houghton Mifflin; 1934.

57. Simons R, Hughes C. *The Culture-Bound Syndromes: Folk Illnesses of Psychiatric and Anthropological Interest*. Boston: Reidel; 1986.

58. Pols H. The development of psychiatry in Indonesia: from colonial to modern times. *International Review of Psychiatry*. 2006;18:363–370.

59. Fabrega H. Culture and history in psychiatric diagnosis and practice. *Psychiatric Clinics of North America*. 2001 24:391–405.

60. Fanon F. *The Wretched of the Earth*. New York: Grove; 1963.

61. Adams P. The social psychiatry of Frantz Fanon. *American Journal of Psychiatry*. 1970;127:809–814.

62. Macey D. *Frantz Fanon: A Life*. London: Granta; 2001.

63. Fulford R. Frantz Fanon: a poisonous thinker who refuses to die. *The National Post*. 2002; http://www.robertfulford.com/FrantzFanon.html (accessed June 21, 2008).

64. Fanon F, Geronimi C. L'hospitalisation de jour en psychiatrie, valeur et limites. *La Tunisie Medicale* 1959;37:713–732.

65. Verges F. To cure and free: The Fanonian project of decolonized psychiatry. In: Gordon L, Sharpely-Whiting T, White R, eds. *Fanon: A Critical Reader*. London: Blackwell; 1996:85–99.

66. Gibson N. Preface: Living Fanon. In: Gibson N, ed. *Living Fanon*. New York: Palgrave; 2011:1–10.

67. Fanon F. *Black Skin, White Masks*. Markmann C, trans. New York: Grove Press; 1952.

68. Hopton J. The application of the ideas of Frantz Fanon to the practice of mental health nursing. *Journal of Advanced Nursing*. 1995;21:723–728.

69. Lacan J. *Écrits: The First Complete Edition in English*. Fink B, trans. New York: W.W. Norton & Co; 2006.

70. Ficek D. Reflections on Fanon and petrification. In: Gibson N, ed. *Living Fanon*. New York: Palgrave; 2011:75–84.

71. Goffman E. *Asylums: Essays on the Social Situation of Mental Patients and Other Inmates*. New York: Doubleday; 1961.

72. Higginbotham N, Marsella A. International consultation and the homogenization of psychiatry in South East Asia. *Social Science and Medicine*. 1988;27:553–561.

73. Cherki A. Fanon, fifty years later: Resisting the air of our present time. In: Gibson N, ed. *Living Fanon*. New York: Palgrave; 2011:131–138.

74. Summerfield D. Cross-cultural perspectives on the medicalization of human suffering. In: Rosen G, ed. *Post-traumatic Stress Disorder: Issues and Current Controversies*. Chichester: John Wiley and Sons; 2002:233–245.

75. Bracken P, Giller J, Summerfield D. Psychological responses to war and atrocity: the limitations of current concepts. *Social Science and Medicine*. 1995;40:1073–1082.

76. Summerfield D. The effects of war: "trauma," moral knowledge, revenge, reconciliation and medicalised notions of "recovery." *Rivista Sperimentale di Freniatria: La Rivista della Salute Mentale*. 2005;129:17–26.

77. Summerfield D. The psychological legacy of war and atrocity: the question of long-term and transgenerational effects and the need for a broad view. *Journal of Nervous and Mental Disease*. 1996;184:375–377.

78. Summerfield D. War, exile, moral knowledge and the limits of psychiatric understanding: a clinical case study of a Bosnian refugee in London. *International Journal of Soical Psychiatry*. 2003;49:264–268.

79. Summerfield D. A critique of seven assumptions behind psychological trauma programmes in war-affected areas. *Social Science and Medicine*. 1999;48:1449–1462.

80. Aregnti-Pillen A. *Masking Terror: How Women Contain Violence in Southern Sri Lanka*. Philadelphia: University of Pennsylvania Press; 2002.

81. Wilkinson R. *The Impact of Inequality: How to Make Sick Societies Healthier*. New York: The New Press; 2005.

82. Marmot M. Health in an unequal world: social circumstances, biology and disease. *Clinical Medicine*. 2006;6:559–572.

83. Westermeyer J. Alcoholism and co-morbid psychiatric disorders among American Indians. *American Indian and Alaska Native MentalHealth Research*. 2001;10:47–51.

84. Baskin C. Conceptualizing, framing and politicizing Aboriginal ethics. *Journal of Ethics in Mental Health*. 2007;2(2).

85. Spencer D. Anomie and demoralization in traditional cultures: the Australian model. *Transcultural Psychiatry*. 2000;37:5–10.

86. Eley D, Young L, Hunter K, et al. Perceptions of mental health service delivery among staff and Indigenous consumers: it's still about communication. *Australasian Psychiatry*. 2007;15:130–134.

87. Petchkovsky L, San Roque C. *Tjunguwiyanytja,* attacks on linking: forced separation and its psychiatric sequelae in Australia's "Stolen Generations". *Transcultural Psychiatry.* 2002;39:345–366.

88. Norris G, Parker R, Beaver C, et al. Addressing Aboriginal mental health issues on the Tiwi Islands. *Australasian Psychiatry.* 2007;15:310–314.

89. http://www.earlychildhoodaustralia.org.au/early_childhood_news august_2007_government_intervention_in_indigenous_communities_responses_continue.html 2008 (accessed June 10, 2008).

7

Neoliberalism

Introduction

Since the Enlightenment, the notion of personal, economic, and political freedom has been paramount in Western societies. The modern state is founded on such principles, particularly evident in the work of John Stuart Mill, whose *On Liberty*[1] outlined the relationship between the liberal state and the individual.

The Scottish philosopher Adam Smith, regarded as the father of the modern market economy so dominant in the postindustrial West, published *The Wealth of Nations*[2] in 1776, the same year as the revolt in the American colonies. Smith argued that free trade was the best means of economic development, and he called for the abolition of government intervention in economic matters and the liberalization of trade across nations. This evolved into the nineteenth century mode of capitalism known as *laissez-faire*, loosely translating as "let do." This was the dominant mode of trade until the Great Depression in 1929. The spectacular failure of the capitalist system in the 1930s saw the distinctly ill-liberal ideas of British economist John Maynard Keynes implemented in depressed economies. Under Keynesian ideas, the social democratic state flooded the economy with funds in a highly regulated program of government spending, epitomized in the New Deal of President Roosevelt in the United States. As economic liberalism lay dormant through the Depression and postwar years, Keynesian ideas and a philosophy of semiplanned capitalist economies remained the dominant paradigm. It was not until the 1980s that liberal ideas would replace the social democratic basis of Western governments and become a dominant influence on society and culture.

What Is Neoliberalism?

Neoliberalism is often referred to as *supply-side economics* in the United States or *economic rationalism* in Australia, although the latter was a milder version than its northern hemisphere counterpart. The emergence of a new form of liberalism in economics, neoliberalism, is usually associated with the governments of Margaret Thatcher in the UK and Ronald Reagan in the United States. With the collapse of communism and the discrediting of the political left in the late 1980s, neoliberal ideology was effectively unopposed. This prompted the American political scientist Francis Fukuyama to proclaim "the end of history" with the triumph of capitalism.[3] It would later come to pass that there was a little more to come in the history of capitalism.

The neoliberal state morphed into the globalized economy throughout the remainder of the twentieth century, and neoliberal ideas dominated political and economic discourses until 2008, when a series of economic crises engulfed the global economy.

Broad Principles of Neoliberalism

Neoliberalism encompasses a program of public policies that impose the rule of the market, or what Adam Smith famously quipped as the "invisible hand" of the market. This occurs through the removal of trade barriers; deunionization of the workforce, leading to myriad contracts between employers and employees; the removal of price controls and barriers to trade; and the reduction of public expenditure on social goods, such as health and welfare. Indeed, neoliberals see that the market is the best place to resolve the seemingly intractable problem of effective and affordable health and welfare, through the sale or privatization of health and welfare services. The redistribution of wealth through taxation is an anathema to neoliberal governments, other than for the provision of a safety net for the least fortunate members of society. Neoliberals seek the removal of all forms of regulation in the economy and see the government as providing little more than a means of intervention in breaches of trade, such as in cases of corruption or fraud.

Most significant in neoliberalism is the assumption of personal responsibility in all matters relating to the individual. In 1987, Margaret Thatcher stated:

I think we've been through a period where too many people have been given to understand that if they have a problem, it's the government's job to cope with it. "I have a problem, I'll get a grant." "I'm homeless, the government must house me." They're casting their problem on society. And, you know, there is no such thing as society. There are individual men and women, and there are families. And no government can do anything except through people, and people must look to themselves first. It's our duty to look after ourselves and then, also to look after our neighbour. People have got the entitlements too much in mind, without the obligations. There's no such thing as entitlement, unless someone has first met an obligation.[4]

In the universe of neoliberals, the state had no business interfering in the lives of citizens or resolving their problems. All citizens could and should be responsible for their own flourishing. Previous state responsibilities such as health, welfare, should not be enshrined within government but be the responsibility of each individual. Already, there is a problem here in relation to the plight of the mentally ill in neoliberal societies.

In nineteenth century capitalism, manufacturing and the accumulation of capital were characteristic of such economies. Under neoliberalism, intricate networks of contracts and service provision replaced manufacturing as the economic trademark. In the UK the economic center of gravity moved from manufacturing textiles in Manchester in the 1800s to financial services in London in the period from the 1990s onward.

In neoliberal economies, contracts for labor between individuals and employers or institutions replaced the notions of substantive employment with the protections brought about by generations of struggle by trade unions.

Neoliberalism had four main pillars: (1) the privatization and commodification of public goods; (2) financialization, in which the contract related to any kind of good or service can be turned into an instrument of economic speculation; (3) the management and manipulation of crises; and (4) state redistribution, in which the state becomes an agent of the upward redistribution of wealth.[5] The implication of the first two was the transformation of the role of the state to merely refereeing the multitude of trades and contracts for goods and services. The second two have far more sinister overtones, which we will explore later in the chapter.

Critical in the ascendancy of neoliberalism are the International Monetary Fund and the World Bank. Both of these organizations intervene in national economies in times of crisis, invariably insisting on major restructure toward the neoliberal tenets or reduced public debt, liberalization of trade, and promotion of free-market solutions to economic problems.

Chicago School and the Neoliberal Economy-State

Beyond the notions of Smith and Mill, Vienna-born economist Friedrich von Hayek is considered the father of neoliberalism. A distant cousin of the philosopher Ludwig Wittgenstein, Hayek was among the most influential European thinkers of the twentieth century. At university, Hayek was something of a polymath, with a deep interest in philosophy, neurology, and psychology. He was profoundly influenced by the work of his equally famous cousin. Hayek served with the Austrian army on the Italian front in World War I. As a result of his experiences, Hayek realized that the carnage and destruction of war, in the final analysis, was the consequence of bad government leading to the collapse of geopolitical order. Initially sympathetic to social democracy, Hayek became progressively disaffected and drawn toward more classical liberalism, particularly in the light of economic turmoil in Great Britain and Weimar Germany.

Hayek left Austria for Great Britain and joined the London School of Economics in 1931. In 1943, he published his most famous work, *The Road to Serfdom*.[6] Hayek's core thesis was that the abandonment of liberal principles in economic affairs had done little to promote prosperity, and centralized planning had paved the way for totalitarian regimes. According to Hayek, in centralized planned economies, "the individual would more than ever become a mere means, to be used by the authority in the service of such abstractions as the 'social welfare' or the 'good of the community.'" Hayek had been profoundly affected by the fate of Europe under the tyranny of Nazism, and he viewed weak, centrally planned social democracies as culpable in the flourishing of fascism and its disastrous consequences.[7]

After World War II, Hayek emigrated to the United States, where he took up a post at the University of Chicago in 1950. Despite the association of neoliberalism with the Chicago School of Economics, Hayek himself was not a member of that faculty. In 1974 Hayek shared the Nobel Prize in economics, ironically, with the Swedish socialist economist Gunnar Myrda. Within a year, the Nobel Laureate economist found himself in audience with the newly elected leader of the British Conservatives, Margaret Thatcher. So convinced was Thatcher of the rectitude of Hayek's ideas that at a Conservative Party meeting in 1975 she produced a copy of Hayek's *The Constitution of Liberty* and proclaimed, "This is what we believe," and banged the book down onto a table.[8]

Apart from Hayek, the other name associated with the neoliberal project was Milton Freidman. Freidman was born in Brooklyn, the son of Jewish emmigrants from what is present-day Ukraine. Friedman had graduated from Rutgers University majoring in mathematics; however, he was drawn to the "dismal science" in the context of the Great Depression. Friedman found a role in Roosevelt's New Deal, the apotheosis of the ideas of British economist John Maynard Keynes, the intellectual nemesis of neoliberals. Keynes had always argued for government intervention in economies, and Western governments, desperate to clamber out of the Great Depression, embraced Keynes's advocacy of government spending programs, wage and price controls, and regulation. Throughout his time in Washington, Freidman became disenchanted with Keynesianism, although he never fully rejected the need to help the unemployed or stimulate struggling economies.[9]

In 1946, Freidman accepted a role at University of Chicago and over the next decades helped build the Chicago School of Economics. Freidman's main idea was the concept of monetarism—that the quantity of money in economies determined price and employment levels in the short term. Freidman became a Nobel Laureate in 1976, and his primary intellectual legacy is seen in the role of central banks in developed economies in setting monetary policy—the regulation of the supply of money in an economy through the setting of official interest rates.[10] Like many neoliberals, Freidman saw the need for government in the provision of some public goods but regarded these as better provided by private enterprise.

Neoliberalism in its current form also has its genealogy in the philosophy of objectivism, propagated by the Russian-born novelist and philosopher Ayn Rand. Under Rand's objectivism, the greatest good for humans was the happiness brought about by enlightened self-interest, or *rational egoism*.[11] In this worldview, only the most laissez-faire of capitalist systems were moral, and no state involvement could be abided. As with many philosophies, Rand's objectivism was corrupted in its implementation. In the setting of economic history, some have laid this squarely at the feet of the former chairman of the U.S. Federal Reserve Alan Greenspan, whose social Darwinist approach to economics is seen as the basic fault beneath the economic crisis arising in 2008 known as the *Global Financial Crisis* (GFC).[12] It is also curious to note that the young Greenspan's radicalism alienated him from Rand, who later excluded him from her social circle.[13]

Neoliberalism has its critics, some of whom are apostates. The British philosopher John Gray was initially an advocate of neoliberalism, only to abandon it, well prior to the GFC. In one of his later works, *Black Mass*, Gray revised his view of neoliberalism and, much like communism, confined it to the status of one of many failed utopian dreams in Western history.[14] The eminent historian Eric Hobswam was highly critical of the cultural contradictions and economic instability of neoliberalism. Hobswam wrote in the final tome of his magnum opus, *The Age of Extremes*:[15]

Those of us who lived through the years of the Great Slump still find it almost impossible to understand how the orthodoxies of the pure free market, then so obviously discredited, once again came to preside over a global period of depression in the late 1980s and 1990s, which once again, they were equally unable to understand or to deal with. (p. 103)

In essence, the critics of neoliberalism see it as little more than another of history's "isms." Some have gone so far as to proclaim the end of neoliberalism. Former Australian Prime Minister Kevin Rudd wrote that in the aftermath of the GFC, the great neoliberal experiment had failed, and it now fell to social democracy to salvage the world economy. Far from the continuation of the Keynes–Hayek roundabout, neoliberalism had destroyed itself:

The time has come, off the back of the current crisis, to proclaim that the great neo-liberal experiment of the past 30 years has failed, that the emperor has no clothes. Neo-liberalism, and the free-market fundamentalism it has produced, has been revealed as little more than personal greed dressed up as an economic philosophy. And, ironically, it now falls to social democracy to prevent liberal capitalism from cannibalising itself.[16]

The Chilean Miracle

The traumatic and divisive experience of dictatorship in Chile has served as the quintessential laboratory for the neoliberal project. The Chilean story also provides an insight into the impact of neoliberalism on the development and operation of health systems, particularly in regard to the plight of the most disadvantaged within the community.

The Canadian author and social activist Naomi Klein has provided a critique of neoliberalism as a predatory phenomenon, coining the term *disaster capitalism*. To Klein, neoliberalism emerges and prospers most in times of crisis or war rather than in processes of democratic change. In Klein's *Shock Doctrine*,[17] Chile serves as the most illustrative example of this process.

In one of the great ironies of modern history, the overthrow of the popularly elected socialist government of Salvador Allende in a U.S.-backed coup d'état took place on September 11, 1973. The leader of the coup, General Augusto Pinochet, was appointed president of Chile in December 1974 and presided over the imposition of the Chicago School's ideal form of neoliberalism in a process referred to by Milton Freidman, in his weekly *Newsweek* column on January 25, 1982, as the "Chilean miracle."[18]

Augusto José Ramón Pinochet Ugarte was born in the world-heritage town of Valparaíso. Educated by the Catholic order of Marist Brothers, Pinochet entered the Chilean military academy in 1931. Pinochet rose through the staff ranks of the Chilean army through a variety of postings in mainly training and educational roles and was appointed commander-in-chief of the armed forces by Allende just weeks before the coup. Apart from being the leader of a murderous regime, Pinochet was part of a kleptocracy. As a warrior of neoliberalism, he enjoyed the patronage of many Western leaders, most conspicuously Margaret Thatcher. Chile provided valuable support to the UK during the Falklands War, and Pinochet enjoyed the hospitality of the Tory government in the UK. In 1998, soon after the election of a Labour government in the UK, Pinochet was indicted by the Spanish magistrate Baltasar Garzón for human rights violations under a new concept of "universal jurisdiction," formulated by the International Court of Justice (later named the International Criminal Court). Pinochet remained under house arrest but fought extradition on grounds of ill health. The British government finally released him in March 2000. Pinochet soon returned to Chile and in 2004, Chilean judge Juan Guzmán ordered Pinochet be placed under house arrest. Again Pinochet resisted trial on medical grounds, and by the time of his death in December 2006, he faced over 300 criminal charges.[19]

After the coup, a military junta (composed of representatives of army, navy, air force, and national police) exercised both executive and legislative functions of the government. The junta suspended the constitution and the congress, imposed strict censorship and curfews, banned the activities of all political parties, and halted all political activities. After the appointment of Pinochet as president in December 1974, the junta remained strictly a legislative body. Pinochet agreed to free elections in Chile in 1987, following the visit of Pope John Paul II.

Apart from the outrage of overthrowing a sovereign, popularly elected government, the junta in Chile is associated with a period of brutal repression, torture, and extrajudicial executions. According to the "Rettig Report"[20] (the official "National Commission for Truth and Reconciliation Report"), 2,279 people "disappeared" during the junta and approximately 31,947 were tortured.

In the light of these human rights outrages, what could any reasonable person hold as miraculous about the junta in Chile? In 1972, the Chilean economy was floundering under a national hyperinflation rate of 150 percent. This was due to many structural problems within the economy and the fact that the Chilean central bank printed more and more money to prop up the economy. As far back as 1950, the U.S. State Department had funded the so-called *Chilean project*, which sought to influence economic development in the country. In this paradigmatic instance of postwar U.S. foreign policy, the establishment of Chile as an economically flourishing state, imbued with the U.S. system of market capitalism, would influence other South and Central American nations to follow suit and halt the existential threat of communist expansion in the region. Over time, many Chileans studied either in Chicago directly under Friedman and his colleague Arnold Harberger or at the Catholic University of Chile, where the economics program was effectively a proxy for the Chicago School. As an aggregate, these dissenting Chilean economists were dubbed the "Chicago boys." The Chicago boys formulated a 500-or-so-page economic plan for Chile, which due to the thickness of the printed version became known as *El Ladrillo* (the brick). The basic tenet of the plan implemented by the brutality of Pinochet's regime was the assumption that the only possible framework for economic development in Chile was the unfettered operation of the private sector and the market. Influenced by Freidman's main idea, the crippling inflation in Chile necessitated the dramatic alteration of monetary policy through a drastic government austerity program. The implementation of *El Ladrillo* was not immediately successful in realizing the neoliberal ideal. By 1976, government austerity had done little for inflation but had impoverished many through wage stagnation and increased unemployment.[21]

Chile now has an enviable economic situation, one of the best in South America. It is true that Allende's government was ruinous for the economy. Part of Chile's recovery was related to abandoning many of Allende's policies, and it is likely that some of Pinochet's reforms were instrumental. It is also likely that the surge in demand for copper was, in large measure, instrumental in Chile's economic recovery.[22] By the time of free elections, Chile continued to have a mixture of government spending and free-market forces, despite the proclamations of neoliberalism. The broader moral question remains, does any form of economic progress absolve such unspeakable human rights violations?

Under the enforced neoliberalism of Pinochet, the Chilean health system underwent radical reform. With the return of democratic government to Chile there has been some moderation of the market reforms within that system, which allow for analysis of their effect on healthcare and the plight of the most vulnerable in the community.

The basic thrust of Pinochet's reforms in the health sector was the introduction of competition, initially between the state-funded public health sector and a new private sector.[23] The junta introduced a private health insurance scheme, Isapres, to compete against the national health fund, Fonasa. The national health system in Chile was devolved into 26 territorial health authorities, and primary healthcare further devolved to different municipalities. The budgets for both were curtailed severely. Membership of Isapres peaked in 1995 at 26 percent of the population, only to decline to 16 percent in 2006; Isapres consumed a disproportionate amount of GDP, and provided care to less than the relatively more efficient Fonasa and public health systems.[24] Regardless of Isapres' inefficiency, it turned a 20 percent profit for its shareholders.[25]

Within the neoliberal reform, public infrastructure crumbled and disparate primary healthcare services lacked any coordination.[26] Mental healthcare comprised a mixture of public and private systems, although the burden fell predominantly upon the floundering public system. Under the auspices of the Fonasa/public system, access to specialist services to the poor, indigent, rural, and other disadvantaged was delayed for up to four years in some circumstances.[27] By the time of further reform under successive democratic governments, inequity and inequality were marked in Chile's health system, particularly with regard to the mentally ill.[24]

Chileans now enjoy some of the best health indicators compared with similar countries.[28] Much of this is attributable to economic development, although the basic model of Chile's health system under Pinochet remains. In the final analysis, it has been argued that Chile's health system has functioned well in spite of, rather than due to, neoliberal reforms. Those reliant on the Fonasa/public health system still face inequities and inequalities. Despite this, mental health in Chile has flourished under the reform process that began in 2004, the Regime of Explicit Health Guarantees (AUGE).[29] Under this reform, services for severe and high-prevalence disorders have improved in terms of both quality and quantity, despite financial pressures forcing many psychiatrists into the private sector.[30] The Chilean healthcare experience in the 1970s and '80s provided a portent of neoliberal influence on healthcare.

Neoliberalism and Health Systems

Healthcare, previously considered by many as a unique form of social good,[31] has been profoundly affected by neoliberal principles. The concept of medical neoliberalism is predicated upon the commodification of health and wellness and the transformation of physicians from carers to providers of services. In the first instance, neoliberal healthcare introduces the influence of market forces within healthcare by transferring responsibility for service provision to the private sector. Moreover, in the context of healthcare, neoliberalism seeks to redefine relationships between the patient and various health service providers as one of individual choices, converting patients into consumers.[32]

Since the nineteenth century, the medical profession has had a complex relationship to the state. Traditionally, the medical profession has been subject to statutory regulation, primarily in regard to competence and professional conduct. Neoliberalism has since become another regulatory paradigm. Physicians now are tasked as economic managers who help facilitate the individual responsibility of the patient implicit in the basic assumptions of neoliberalism.[33]

Having considered the Chilean neoliberal healthcare experiment, it is now useful to compare and contrast the effects of unconstrained neoliberal health economics in the United States and a more moderate manifestation of neoliberal health economics in the United Kingdom.

In our consideration of the U.S. healthcare system, we will take as our starting point the introduction of Medicare in 1965. Medicare was signed into law as part of the federal Social Security Act (1935). Medicare existed to provide health insurance to citizens over age 65 as well as younger people with disabilities. In the United States, Medicare approximated a single-payer system (i.e., healthcare funded by the state from a central pool) but still involved some out-of-pocket expenses. For other U.S. citizens, health was tied to private insurance obtained either as part of employment or out of pocket.

In the U.S. healthcare system, the other extant entity has been the health maintenance organization (HMO). The role of an HMO is to broker cost-effective healthcare services on behalf of insurers. The first formal HMO was the Southern California–based Ross-Loos Medical Group, established in 1929. In 1973, the Health Maintenance Organization Act

(Public Law 93-222) mandated that any company with more than 25 employees utilize HMOs as part of any health insurance condition of employment. Following from this, Medicare too utilized HMOs in its provision of health services.

This market-based system appeared to work well; however, by the 1990s, various HMOs faced accusations of "cherry picking" and providing worse outcomes with higher costs. There have been several instances of corporate malfeasance involving HMOs. One of the most notable involved the HMO Tenet Healthcare (formerly National Medical Enterprises), which was found to have effectively bribed psychiatrists for referrals of patients to their hospitals and, more alarming, to have improperly detained patients in psychiatric hospitals for longer periods to boost profits.[34]

The U.S. healthcare system is seen by many as the illustration of the inefficiency of neoliberalism in this area. In 2009, the United States spent $2.5 trillion on healthcare, 17.3 percent of its GDP.[35] The World Health Organization (WHO) in 2000 ranked the U.S. healthcare system as the highest in cost, first in responsiveness, 37th in overall performance, and 72nd by overall level of health. In 2007, 46 million Americans were uninsured.[36] Around 45,000 U.S. citizens die annually due to lack of health insurance.[37] The one exception to this abysmal state of affairs is the single-payer Veteran's Administration (VA) system, which provides effective and affordable healthcare.[38] In 2011, President Obama signed into law the Patient Protection and Affordable Care Act (PPACA), which sought to address many of the inequities and inequalities in the U.S. healthcare system. The reforms are broad based but retain the neoliberal idea of patient responsibility in the notion of the "individual mandate," effectively coercing uninsured citizens to purchase health insurance via government subsidy through newly established "health insurance exchanges." The other significant component of what has been dubbed "Obamacare" is the elimination of exclusions for coverage of patients of preexisting conditions.

In stark contrast to the situation in the United States, the National Health Service (NHS) in the UK represented the diametrically opposite system of universal healthcare, independent of market forces. In 1946, the Labour government passed into law the National Health Service Act. This law replaced a complex system of arcane arrangements, such traditional fee-for-service, local government healthcare provision, "poor laws," and charitable institutions with a universal form of health insurance. The task of dealing with the resistive British Medical Association in the sweeping health reform fell to Aneurin Bevan, the son of a Welsh coal miner. As Minister of Health in Atlee's postwar Labour government, Bevan was able to placate the obstinacy of the British medical profession in the face of the NHS reforms by agreeing to generous employment conditions for consultants appointed to NHS hospitals. In a quote never properly referenced, Bevan was attributed with the concession that he had stuffed the mouths of the British medical profession with gold.

The NHS originally comprised a three-part system of hospitals, primary care practices, and community services. Over time, the system grew and the London-controlled health system devolved into a network of regional health authorities. As Britain faced the challenge of all developed postwar health systems—escalating costs of healthcare and an aging population—the neoliberal agenda insinuated into the NHS.

In 1990 the Thatcher government imposed two of the hallmarks of neoliberalism on the NHS under the National Health Service and Community Care Act. In a process termed the *internal market*, the Conservative government reforms of the NHS saw the adoption of a managerialist culture and the introduction of a purchaser–provider split. In the former reform, the health system developed a bureaucratic structure that was identical to any bureaucracy in the economy. NHS entities were run like any other medium-sized corporations, complete with the bureaucratese that has come to characterize modern management culture. In the second reform, the local health authorities evolved into "strategic health authorities" and were effectively run as a not-for-profit business, purchasing health services from the employees of the local hospital, or other sector, depending upon the market. In this somewhat sinister way, the original aspirations of the NHS as free healthcare for all provided by excellent institutions operating in the light of value systems evolved into another neoliberal system of multiple contracts for service by an atomized series of providers. This became the dominant paradigm in what was originally intended to be a just system of equal access to healthcare determined by need, not means. Even the social democratic professions of Prime Minister Tony Blair were no foil for the neoliberal reforms. By his second term, Blair renounced his promise to eradicate the internal market and actually strengthened it—closing redundant facilities, outsourcing services to the private sector, and establishing public–private partnerships have all been features of the ostensibly social-democratic agenda of New Labour.

By 2011, the minority Conservative government in the UK sought to devolve government involvement through further private sector competition, placing more responsibility for economic management to fund-holding general practitioners and effectively shifting the emphasis of healthcare to one of personal responsibility.[39] In essence, the patient journey envisioned by Aneurin Bevan had been replaced as one of a savvy consumer having services brokered on their behalf by family doctors now tasked with economic management.

As we have demonstrated, neoliberalism is a philosophy that has both moral and economic dimensions. In healthcare this combines the assumptions of personal responsibility in consumer choices around health services and the recasting of healthcare as yet another service commodity traded in an open market. Paradoxically, neoliberal freedom has been characterized by the emergence of complex, self-perpetuating bureaucracies whose role is to supervise the invisible hand of market forces. Far from the literal applications of the prescriptions of Hayek, the neoliberal era has seen more expansion of both the size and expenditure of governments than in the Great Depression. Indeed, when posed with the question as to which of the rival economic theories, Hayek or Keynes, triumphed, the answer could be either both or neither.[40]

The neoliberalism of the 30 years to 2008 has seen the evolution of health systems with complex bureaucracies, clinical governance structures, and other administrative components, all nonclinical functions. Such managerialism has both strengths and weaknesses. On the one hand, the existence of a management culture appears necessary to the function of a large, multibillion-dollar industry, but on the other, the focus of healthcare has moved from a moral, values-based enterprise to one focused on outcomes. The nineteenth century sociologist Max Weber distinguished between bureaucracies that were either goal or value rational. This distinction has become all the more critical as healthcare has evolved from an essential role of government to a for-profit enterprise in most postindustrial democracies.[41]

Neoliberalism and Mental Health

In the light of the effect of the neoliberal project on healthcare, the specifics of mental healthcare under the tenets of neoliberalism require consideration.

In the first place the question is begged, Does the neoliberal health system pose particular challenges for psychiatric ethics?

Psychiatrists, like all health professionals, face some form of obligation to financially responsible practice. This invariably involves reconciling the needs of the patient, abiding by best clinical practice, and the responsibility to equitable allocation of finite health resources. As we have argued, this is a particularly vexed manifestation of the dual-role dilemma.[42]

Psychiatric treatment is costly. Taking the example of Australia, where neoliberal ideas have been implemented with some moderation in healthcare, mental health presents a considerable cost burden. In terms of expenditure on pharmaceuticals, in the 12 months prior to June 2010, of the top 20 medications by cost, 5 were psychotropic medications.[43] Psychiatric hospitalizations consumed 66 percent of the mental health budget.[44] These costs are one of a number of impositions on the public purse—enabling access to welfare, housing, and other social goods is also part of mental healthcare. In the face of the costs of psychotropic treatments and hospitalizations (not to mention outpatient psychotherapy or other consultations), how can such expenditure be justified?

In the health marketplace, the preferred methodology to demonstrate the burden of disease has been the use of Daily Adjusted Life Year (DALY) and Quality Adjusted Life Year (QALY).[45] DALY and QALY are the standard means of quantifying cost-effectiveness of interventions in terms of prolonging and improving the quality of life. In the case of chronic (as opposed to high prevalence) psychiatric disorders, where the economic benefits of treatment are less distinct, the QALY and DALY methodologies have led to mental health services usually losing out in utilitarian calculations for the health budget.[46,47] In the neoliberal health system, psychiatrists face formidable challenges in mounting arguments for a piece of the pie for their more severely ill patients.

The second domain of challenge for psychiatrists in the neoliberal health system is the notion of consumerism in mental health. The trend toward empowerment and a greater contribution by those suffering mental illness toward decisions about their care is characteristic of a number of reforms in mental health and in general is considered a positive. In the UK, the advent of *userism* has been a prominent theme of the reform of mental health services in the NHS.[48] Even in legal discourses, mental health law in its various forms has become a form of "enforced partnership of medicine and the law" in the joint venture of ensuring mental healthcare as a commodity moves toward liberal autonomy as a consumer outcome.[49] Even though the state reserves the right to *parens patriae*, in the neoliberal world, this is yet another consumer–provider contract of service.

In the neoliberalism-influenced health system, the notion of the consumer–provider interaction would seem to completely change the nature of the therapeutic relationship. Traditionally the sufferer–healer dyad, predicated on the Hippocratic injunction, existed as the basis of the relationship between physician and patient. Today there exists a contract for services, policed by various statutes or other forms of professional regulation. In this interaction, the patient remains the vulnerable party, despite the apparent inversion of the power differential within the relationship engendered by its quasi-commercial nature.

The critical issue here is the loss or, perhaps, denial of "patienthood." The subtle shift in language creates a shift in the status of patient, from one who suffers and seeks to assume a sick role or pattern of illness behavior to a consumer of services negotiating a system of contracts for service. This demands the negotiation of relationships between a particular bureaucracy and a provider of clinical service. The philosopher of medicine Edmund Pellegrino described the experience of patienthood as a state of "wounded humanity."[50] In this state of patienthood, the sufferer assumes an existential compromise in submitting to a power relationship with a physician or other healthcare professional. This state of vulnerability allows the assumption of the sick role and allows for the process of intervention and recovery. The very submission necessitated by patienthood is at odds with the neoliberal conception of individual responsibility.

In mental healthcare, this presents a more significant challenge. Given the premise that there is a distinct vulnerability to the psychiatric patient, the assumption of rational or autonomous choice requires closer consideration. The distinct nature of psychiatric ethics speaks to the distinct nature of mental healthcare. The diminished autonomy of the mentally ill person, the uniqueness of the psychiatric enterprise, the distinct stigma of mental illness, and the specter of coercive psychiatric treatment factor to place mental health in a distinct category.[51] This is not to argue, by any measure, that notions of individual choice have no place in mental healthcare. Indeed, the most enlightened mental health services valorize the exercise of patient choice in the provision of care for their mental health difficulties. As with all manifestations of the dual-role dilemma, the neoliberal mental health system requires the reconciliation of the dual role of provider of efficacious and responsible healthcare with that of healer in the therapeutic relationship characterized by the profound existential compromise of mental illness.

Commodification of the Body

The commodification of healthcare within the neoliberal health system has also led to the commodification of body systems. Rather than a holistic focus on the patient, neoliberal healthcare has led to a situation of what has been deemed *technoluxe*—this is a transhumanist model of medicine in which the focus is no longer on healthcare but on the enhancement or optimum functioning of a body part or system.[52] In one example, a patient who seeks help after discovering a breast lump and attends a breast center may receive on-site clinical, radiographic, and histopathological assessment of the lump, and leave the service either reassured or referred for further specialized care. Rather than a distressed patient with a concerned family seeking help, the consumer is provided with specific, focused service provision after which the diseased or dysfunctional body part is remedied.

Applied to a mental illness such as depression, the technoluxe effect of neoliberal healthcare sees the problem defined as a nervous system dysfunction rather than the result of the kind of complex formulations upon which psychiatry is based. The increase in the use of antidepressants would arguably be an extension of this process. This pharmaceuticalization of health[53] is distinctly neoliberal, as it involves the interaction of large multinational companies. In the context of depression, antidepressants play a role in the technoluxe of psychiatry as being a part of the solution to the dysfunctional brain. Rather than potentially life-saving treatment, Prozac and its competitors have become consumer goods that aid the failing brain. The shift is from treatment to enhancement.

The commodification of depression and antidepressants has become the stuff of popular culture. Antidepressants are depicted as consumer goods that have as much an enhancing effect on the underperforming nervous system as the relief of distress from depression. The prospect of "cosmetic psychopharmacology"[54] was popularized in the book *Listening to Prozac*, which observed that Prozac was touted as giving social confidence to the habitually timid and lending the introvert better social skills.[55] Moreover, in the commoditized neoliberal world of mental healthcare, disorder is increasingly defined by treatment. In her semibiographical work, *Prozac Nation*,[56] Elizabeth Wurtzel has it that the suffering wrought by her depression finds meaning in her recovering through taking Prozac. In Wurtzel's experience, the consumer good Prozac brings her to depression, not vice versa.

This process has also led to hypertrophy in the criticism of antidepressants and the apparent relationship between psychiatry and the pharmaceutical industry. Not only is the issue of antidepressants questioned, but the entire validity of the construct of depression or anxiety is now fair game for critique.[57] The delegitimizing effect of the criticisms of depression and its treatment merely confuses, rather than enlightens, the discourse on the area.

Beyond the cultural manifestations of this process, the commodification of mental healthcare also allows large corporations, either pharmaceutical companies or larger healthcare provider conglomerates, to insinuate into territory such as education for physicians and consumers and influence how diseases are both conceptualized and treated.

The commercialization of mental healthcare, particularly through pharmaceuticals, finds its most explicit manifestation in the phenomenon of direct-to-consumer advertising by pharmaceutical companies. Direct-to-consumer advertising is the beneficiary of a favorable 1997 U.S. Food and Drug Administration ruling and has been most notable in the marketing of antidepressants.[58] Since the legitimation of this advertising, psychotropic medications such as antidepressants, hypnosedatives, and anxiolytics have appeared in television and print media advertising in the United States, imploring patients to approach physicians for prescriptions. Akin to this process is the specter of what has been dubbed either *medicalization*[59] or the more provocative term *disease mongering*.[60] The philosopher of medicine Ivan Illich defined medicalization, or *iatrogenesis*, as occurring in both clinical and social/structural domains. Within the clinical domain, medicalization is manifest as iatrogenic harm from excess medical intervention, increasing the level of pathology. The social/structural domain, perhaps most akin to the current neoliberal paradigm, sees biomedical discourses and instrumental approaches to life's problems as being accepted within a society as the best approach to their resolution.

In contrast, disease mongering is considered as the process by which the manufacturers of various pharmaceuticals promote awareness of a particular disorder in order to pique the curiosity of the potential sufferer, or indeed physician, who may be susceptible to such marketing.

One celebrated instance in the process of direct-to-consumer advertising involved the pharmaceutical company Smith Kline Beecham (SKB), which marketed the antidepressant medication Paxil (paroxetine).[61] In 1999, SKB retained the New York–based public relations firm Cohn & Wolfe to promote awareness for a condition called social anxiety disorder. Unlike the *DSM-III-R* disorder social phobia, social anxiety disorder referred to an expanded domain of social anxiety, reframing shyness as a milder variant of severe, disabling social phobia. Cohn & Wolfe generated an advertising slogan, "Imagine Being Allergic to People." Television advertising of social anxiety disorder appeared in the United States, imploring people who felt awkward or shy in unfamiliar social settings to seek treatment with Paxil. There were academic precedents to this; in the *DSM-IV*, avoidant personality disorder and social phobia could co-exist to create a more vaguely defined generalized social phobia. In the U.S. National Comorbidity Survey, the lifetime prevalence of social anxiety disorder was 7.4 percent,[62] whereas an Australian epidemiological study, conducted using identical methodology, found a prevalence of 2 percent for the condition.[63] Whether this difference is explicable in terms of diagnostic practice is conjectural. What is clear, however, is the proximity of the pharmaceutical industry to a process in which a comparatively uncommon disorder was both reconceptualized as a dimensional construct and the source of a marketing campaign, promoting a disorder as well as a commodity, Paxil, to deal with it. It is arguable that the social construction of a psychiatric disorder makes it more likely to be a focus of such commodification. This emphasizes the nature of the challenge this aspect of neoliberal mental healthcare poses to psychiatrists. There is significant tension between resisting the commercially motivated promotion of a disorder and its treatment and recognizing that expanded forms of a disorder represent progress in the field.

Ethical Psychiatrist and Neoliberal Healthcare System

In this chapter, we have sought to integrate a number of ideas derived from economic history, sociology, and philosophy of medicine. In essence, the neoliberal healthcare system is based on a philosophy that has moral, structural, and economic dimensions. As far as implementing Hayek's vision of an economy free of constraint, the neoliberal-influenced healthcare system is a highly bureaucratized and regulated system that is almost entirely outcome focused. In its extreme form in the United States, the neoliberal healthcare system has seen inequities, inequalities, and inefficiencies unparalleled in history. In societies such as the United Kingdom or Australia, neoliberal ideas have profoundly altered initially noble aspirations of universal healthcare. In the neoliberal healthcare system, patients have to either abandon or profoundly modify their experience of patienthood and seek healthcare services as rational choosers in a complex system. This necessitates their establishing relationships not only with the physician but with the system as well. In a sense, it is the patient's own dual-role dilemma.

The commodification of healthcare in the neoliberal system has led to the conceptualization of disease as a malfunction of an organ or tissue system for which a service or good, such as a pharmaceutical, can provide rectification. This atomized view of the individual consumer calls into question our assumptions of illness as a social role assumed in the context of the effects of a pathological dysfunction.

For the psychiatrist, the moral agency within this system creates a number of challenges. In the first instance, the distinct vulnerability of the psychiatric patient, particularly where insight or judgment has been impaired, calls into question the assumption of rational choice as a consumer. As a component of a process of service provision, the psychiatrist assumes a dual role with the patient as both healer and provider of services. Where there are third-party interests such as insurance companies or funding bodies, both of these roles have accountabilities to that third party. Where the existing methodologies to demonstrate economic outcomes are insensitive to change in mental illness, or where the focus of treatment is not disease eradication or restoration of normal social functioning but rather incremental improvements in dignity, symptom relief, or more autonomy, the psychiatrist faces a particularly difficult challenge in reconciling the valued role of advocacy versus the responsibility to the market-based system.

In practicing a craft where much of disorder is predicated upon values-based assumptions of normative experience or functioning, the psychiatrist finds him- or herself working within a culture of diagnosis or construction of disorder influenced by market forces as much as scientific ones. If mental illness and its treatment are as much cultural as medical phenomena, particularly in the light of notions of cosmetic psychopharmacology, psychiatry has ceded ground in its professional domain of the detection and treatment of mental illness.

This raises the question, Where does the psychiatrist contribute to public discourse over public health issues such as depression? We will try to address this in the third section of the book.

References

1. Mill JS. *On Liberty*. New York: WW Norton; 1859/1975.

2. Smith A. *The Wealth of Nations*. New York: Random House; 1994.

3. Fukuyama F. *The End of History and the Last Man*. New York: Free Press; 1992.

4. Keay D. Interview with Margaret Thatcher. *Woman's Own*. 1987:8–10.

5. Harvey D. *A Brief History of Neoliberalism*. London: Oxford University Press; 2005.

6. Hayek F. *The Road to Serfdom*. Chicago: University of Chicago Press; 1994.

7. Judt A. *Ill Fares the Land*. New York: Penguin Press; 2010.

8. Ranelagh J. *Thatcher's People: An Insider's Account of the Politics, the Power, and the Personalities*. London: Fonatana; 1994.

9. Skousen M. *The Making of Modern Economics: The Lives and Ideas of the Great Thinkers*. Armonk, NY: ME Sharpe Inc; 2009.

10. Freidman M. *Studies in the Quantity Theory of Money*. Chicago: University of Chicago Press; 1956.

11. Peikoff L. *Objectivism: The Philosophy of Ayn Rand*. New York: E. P. Dutton; 1991.

12. Steverman B, Bogoslaw D. The financial crisis blame game. 2008 (October 18); http://www.businessweek.com/investor/content/oct2008/pi20081017_950382. htm?chan=top+news_top+news+index+-+temp_top+story.

13. Taibbi M. *Griftopia: Bubble Machines, Vampire Squids, and the Long Con That Is Breaking America*. New York: Random House; 2010.

14. Gray J. *Black Mass: Apocalyptic Religion and the Death of Utopia*. London: Penguin; 2007.

15. Hobswam E. *The Age of Extremes: The Short Twentieth Century 1914–1991*. London: Abacus; 2002.

16. Rudd K. The global financial crisis. *The Monthly*. Melbourne: Black Inc; 2009.

17. Klein N. *The Shock Doctrine: The Rise of Disaster Capitalism*. New York: Picador; 2007.

18. Freidman M. Weekly Column. *Newsweek*. Jan 25. New York: Washington Post Company; 1982.

19. Dinges J. *The Condor Years How Pinochet and His Allies Brought Terrorism to Three Continents*. New York: New Press; 2004.

20. The Rettig Report. *National Commission for Truth and Reconciliation*. Santiago 1991; http://www.usip.org/publications/truth-commission-chile-90 (accessed November 29, 2011).

21. Letelier O. The Chicago boys in Chile: economic freedom's awful toll. *The Nation*. Aug 28, 1976.

22. Winn P, ed. *Victims of the Chilean Miracle: Workers and Neoliberalism in the Pinochet Era, 1973–2002.* Durham, NC: Duke University Press; 2004.

23. Reichard S. Ideology drives health care reforms in Chile. *J Public Health Policy.* 1996;17:83–98.

24. Unger J, De Paepe P, Cantuarias G, et al. Chile's neoliberal health reform: an assessment and a critique. *PLoS Medicine.* 2008;5:e79.

25. Homedes N, Ugalde A. Privatización de los servicios de salud: las experiencias de Chile y Costa Rica. *Gaceta Sanitaria.* 2002;16:54–62.

26. Annick M. The Chilean health system: 20 years of reforms. *Salud Publica.* 2002;44:60–68.

27. Pan American Health Organization. *Información para la equidad en salud en Chile* 2001.

28. Hiscock J, Hojman D. Social policy in a fast-growing economy: the case of Chile. *Soc Pol Adm.* 1997;31:345–370.

29. World Bank. Realizing rights through social guarantees: an analysis of new approaches to social policy in Latin America and South Africa. 2008; http://siteresources.worldbank.org/EXTSOCIALDEVELOPMENT/Resources/244362-1164107274725/3182370-1164107324437/Realizing_Rights_through_Social_Guarantees-web1.pd.

30. Araya R, Alvarado R, Minoletti A. Chile: an ongoing mental health revolution. *The Lancet.* 2009;374:597–598.

31. Daniels N. *Just Health Care.* Cambridge: Cambridge University Press; 1995.

32. Henderson S, Petersen A. *Consuming Health: The Commodification of Health Care.* New York: Routledge; 2002.

33. Osborne T. On liberalism, neo-liberalism and the "liberal profession" of medicine. *Economy and Society.* 1993;22:345–356.

34. Woolhandler S, Himmelstein D. Competition in a publicly funded healthcare system. *BMJ.* 2007;335:1126–1129.

35. Norman J. Washington health policy week in review national health expenditures now grab 17.3 percent of GDP, study projects 2010. http://www.commonwealthfund.org/Newsletters/Washington-Health-Policy-in-Review/2010/Feb/February-8-2010/National-Health-Expenditures-Now-Grab-173-Percent-of-GDP-Study-Projects.aspx.

36. US Census Bureau. Income, poverty, and health insurance coverage in the United States. 2007. http://www.census.gov/prod/2008pubs/p60-235. pdf (accessed December 8, 2011).

37. Wilper A, Woolhandler S, Lasser E, et al. Health insurance and mortality in U.S. adults. *Am J Public Health.* 2009;99:1–7.

38. Oliver A. The Veteran's Health Administration: an American success story? *Millbank Q.* 2007;85:5–35.

39. Black N. Liberating the NHS: another attempt to implement market forces in English health care. *NEJM.* 2011;363:1103–1105.

40. Wapshott N. *Keynes/Hayek: The Clash That Defined Modern Economics.* Melbourne: Scribe; 2011.

41. Weber M. *The Theory of Social and Economic Organization.* New York: Oxford; 1947.

42. Robertson M, Walter G. The many faces of the dual-role dilemma in psychiatric ethics. *Australian and New Zealand Journal of Psychiatry.* 2008;42:228–235.

43. Australian Government—Department of Health and Ageing. Pharmaceutical Benefits Scheme (PBS)—Expenditure and prescriptions twelve months to June 30, 2010. 2011; http://www.health.gov.au/internet/main/publishing.nsf/Content/pbs-stats-pbexp-jun10 (accessed December 22, 2011).

44. Parliament of Australia—Senate. Report of Senate Select Committee on Mental Health. 2006; http://www.aph.gov.au/senate/committee/mentalhealth_ctte/report/c04.htm (accessed December 21, 2011).

45. NHS. National Institute of Clinical Excellence. Measuring effectiveness and cost effectiveness: the QALY. 2010; http://www.nice.org.uk/newsroom/features/ measuringeffectivenessandcosteffectivenesstheqaly.jsp (accessed December 21, 2011.

46. Evers S, Van Wijk A, Ament A. Economic evaluation of mental health care interventions. A review. *Health Economics.* 1997;6:161–177.

47. Ayuso-Mateos J, Salvador-Carulla L, Chisholm D. Use of quality of life measures in mental health economics and care planning. *Actas Espanol Psiquitra.* 2006;34:1–6.

48. Ramon S. Neoliberalism and its implications for mental health in the UK. *International Journal of Law and Psychiatry.* 2008;31:116–125.

49. Carney T. The mental health service crisis of neoliberalism: an antipodean perspective. *International Journal of Law and Psychiatry.* 2008;31:101–115.

50. Pellegrino E. *Humanism and the Physician.* Knoxville: University of Tennessee Press; 1979.

51. Radden J. Psychiatric ethics. *Bioethics.* 2002;16(5):397–411.

52. Frank A. Emily's scars: surgical shapings, technoluxe and bioethics. *Hastings Centre Report.* 2004;34:18–29.

53. van der Geest S, Whyte S, Hardon A. The anthropology of pharmaceuticals: a biographical approach. *Annual Review of Anthropology.* 1996;25:153–178.

54. Klerman G. Psychotropic hedonism vs. pharmacological Calvinism. *Hastings Center Report.* 1972;2:1–3.

55. Kramer P. *Listening to Prozac.* London: Fourth Estate; 1994.

56. Wurtzel E. *Prozac Nation.* New York: Penguin; 1994.

57. Horwitz A, Wakefield J. *The Loss of Sadness: How Psychiatry Transformed Normal Sorrow into Depressive Disorder.* New York: Oxford University Press; 2007.

58. Healy D. *Let Them Eat Prozac: The Unhealthy Relationship between the Pharmaceutical Industry and Depression.* New York: New York University Press; 2004.

59. Illich I. *Limits to Medicine.* London: Penguin; 1976.

60. Moynihan R, Cassels A. *Selling Sickness: How the World's Biggest Pharmaceutical Companies Are Turning Us All into Patients.* New York: Norton; 2005.

61. Koerner B. Disorders made to order. *Mother Jones Magazine.* Sep/Oct 2002.

62. Kessler R, Berglund P, Demler O, et al. Lifetime prevalence and age-of-onset distributions of *DSM-IV* disorders in the National Comorbidity Survey Replication. *Arch Gen Psych.* 2005;62:593–602.

63. Lampe L, Slade T, Issakidis C, et al. Social phobia in the Australian National Survey of Mental Health and Well-Being (NSMHWB). *Psychological Medicine.* 2003;33:637–646.

8

Psychiatry and Popular Culture

Introduction

The most salient conceptualization of culture to our consideration is the notion of it as a set of shared attitudes, values, goals, and practices that characterizes an institution, organization, or group. Stories, language, and custom provide insights into how a community sees itself, its environment, and the challenges it faces. Scholarship of previous societies has focused upon art, literature, music, architecture, and design as windows to culture. In the postindustrial period, particularly the vertiginous pace of technological development that has characterized the period from the 1990s to the present, culture has become a consumer commodity, and the mind of contemporary society is routinely infused with media content.

Given our thesis that psychiatrists act and think in a social context, culture is a critical influence on their moral agency. Contemporary culture provides an insight into the values of a society; these values influence the psychiatric profession and its relationship with the society. In this chapter, we will consider four domains of contemporary culture—cinema, literature, the media, and Web 2.0.

Cinema

The majority of films depicting psychiatry and mental illness have been made in the United States. In the postwar period, Hollywood films depicting psychiatry and mental illness tended to depict female patient characters and male psychiatrists. The mental illnesses of the female psychiatric patients in Hollywood films have been associated with menace. One of the original films addressing this theme was *The Snake Pit* (1948). The film's protagonist, Virginia Cunningham, has a psychotic illness, which causes her to abandon her marriage to her very sane husband. She is institutionalized and placed under the care of Dr. Kik. Virginia is given electroconvulsive therapy, psychotherapy, and hypnotherapy. Following a fairly hackneyed Freudian paradigm, Dr. Kik sees Virginia's problems along the classic analytic formula of childhood difficulties leading to adult dysfunction. This Freudian theme also underlies the film *The Three Faces of Eve* (1957), in which the film's protagonist, Eve White, suffers dissociative identity disorder, a condition later popularized in the television series *The United States of Tara*. Eve's multiple identities are ascribed by her psychiatrist, Dr. Luther, as related to the trauma of the 6-year-old Eve having to kiss her dead grandmother. While such clichéd Freudian nostrums are a source of bemusement to the contemporary viewer, they provided filmmakers with tidy, aesthetically pleasing denouements to these stories.

A more sinister and traumatic narrative underlies the equally famous film *Sybil* (1976), which ironically features Joanne Woodward, who had played Eve in the 1957 film, as the psychiatrist. Sybil's propensity to dissociate identities was the consequence of horrendous cruelty perpetrated on her by her sadistic, and likely psychotic, mother. Several of Alfred Hitchcock's films depict the potentially dangerous nature of dissociation, particularly in women. While the focus of the 1960 classic *Psycho* was not female, the derangement of the film's main character relates to a bizarrely sexualized relationship with his disturbed mother. The main character in the film *Marnie* (1964) is disabled by phobias caused by sexual assault and her witnessing a murder perpetrated by her prostitute mother.

The dangerousness of the mentally ill female character in Hollywood films is represented in numerous examples. *Whatever Happened to Baby Jane?* (1962) features a tour de force of Bette Davis's depiction of a highly disturbed and menacing female protagonist. More malign disturbed female characters appear as stalkers in *Play Misty for Me* (1971), *Fatal Attraction* (1987), *Misery* (1990), and *Single White Female* (1992). Less dangerous but equally disturbed are the female protagonists of *Breaking the Waves* (1996), *Girl Interrupted* (1999), and *Black Swan* (2010).

In contrast, mentally ill male characters in Hollywood films have more psychopathic than borderline personality styles. The male protagonist in Hitchcock's *Frenzy* (1972) is more evil than mad. The apparent insanity of the character of Travis Bickle in *Taxi Driver* (1976) inspired a copy-cat assassination attempt of then U.S. President Ronald Reagan in 1980. The male protagonists in *Apocalypse Now* (1979), *The Shining* (1980), and later *The Silence of the Lambs* (1991) and *Hannibal* (2001) all have murderous or violent behavior emerging as a consequence of their madness. One slight deviation from this theme is the male protagonist Melvin Udall in *As Good as It Gets* (1997). Udall provides the more sophisticated viewer of the film with the opportunity to speculate that his misfortunes relate more to personality flaws than his apparent obsessive-compulsive disorder:

Carol: *OK, we all have these terrible stories to get over, and you …*

Melvin: *It's not true. Some of us have great stories, pretty stories that take place at lakes with boats and friends and noodle salad. Just no one in this car. But, a lot of people, that's their story. Good times, noodle salad. What makes it so hard is not that you had it bad, but that you're that pissed that so many others had it good.*

The other theme in Hollywood's depiction of mental illness in males is the undercurrent of a more noble form of trauma, such as war or violent crime, as opposed to the squalid nature of the childhood abuse suffered by many of Hollywood's female characters. *The Deer Hunter* (1979) is the first major Hollywood film to engage with the Vietnam War experience. In the period since the Vietnam War, the trauma of combat underlies the stories of male characters in *Birdy* (1984), *Platoon* (1985), *Jacob's Ladder* (1990), and *Born on the Fourth of July* (1989), all of which relate to the Vietnam War experience. The anomic emotional disconnection of the main character in *The Hurt Locker* (2010) related to the trauma of the Iraq War. In *Ordinary People* (1980) the protagonist is tortured by the drowning death of his brother. In *The Fisher King* (1991) the two male characters are traumatized by a murder. In *Memento* (2000) the male character suffers the consequences of a head injury experienced in a violent robbery.

Beyond the clearly dichotomous view of gender stereotypes within the culture, Hollywood has also depicted psychiatry's at times conflicted relationship with society. Indeed, many films to emerge from the period around the social liberation movement reflected the quasimalfeasant nature of the empowered psychiatrist as social agent.

The first clear inkling of this appeared prior to the social liberation movement. In *Suddenly Last Summer* (1959) the female lead character, Catherine Holly, is institutionalized after her cousin Sebastian dies in suspicious circumstances during a holiday in Europe. Catherine's family seeks to bury the scandal by having her institutionalized and discredited. Not obviously insane, Catherine is evidently being subdued by the psychiatric power residing within the asylum, with the ever-present threat of lobotomy looming. By the time the psychiatrist involved sees beyond this process and engages Catherine in a therapeutic process leading to the inexorable trauma denouement, the damage is arguably done to psychiatry's credibility. While much of the patient journey of Frances Farmer depicted in the film *Frances* (1982) is arguably apocryphal, the implied brutality of psychiatric institutions and psychiatric treatments remains with the audience.

The most cited of this genre of antipsychiatry cinema is *One Flew Over the Cuckoo's Nest* (1975). The male protagonist, Randal McMurphy, is odious in that he seeks the relative ease of a psychiatric hospital by confecting the signs of madness rather than serving a prison sentence for the statutory rape of an adolescent girl. Unable to resist the misogyny of the culture, the evil in the story lies not with the child rapist McMurphy but with the female character of Nurse Ratched. The struggle between McMurphy's fomented resistance within the asylum and the psychiatric power wielded by Nurse Ratched is straight out of the pages of Foucault. The overwhelming power of the asylum is symbolized by McMurphy's lobotomy scar at the end of the film. Such stories, if indeed true, would not have been out of place in the Soviet Union.

For better or worse, Hollywood's treatment of mental illness in recent years has moved to an ostensibly more sympathetic portrayal. Indeed, virtuoso performances of mental illness on the screen seem a precondition to success in a Hollywood career, as this exchange between two characters (who are meant to be famous Hollywood actors) from the film *Tropic Thunder* (2008) implies:

Kirk Lazarus: *Everybody knows you never go full retard.*

Tugg Speedman: *What do you mean?*

Kirk Lazarus: *Check it out. Dustin Hoffman, "Rain Man," look retarded, act retarded, not retarded. Counted toothpicks, cheated cards. Autistic, sho'. Not retarded. You know Tom Hanks, "Forrest Gump." Slow, yes. Retarded, maybe. Braces on his legs. But he charmed the pants off Nixon and won a ping-pong competition. That ain't retarded. Peter Sellers, "Being There." Infantile, yes. Retarded, no. You went full retard, man. Never go full retard. You don't buy that? Ask Sean Penn, 2001, "I Am Sam." Remember? Went full retard, went home empty handed....*

Since the 1990s, audiences have been enlightened by sympathetic or responsible depictions of conditions such as schizophrenia, e.g., *Shine* (1996), *A Beautiful Mind* (2001), *The Soloist* (2009); autism, e.g., *Rain Man* (1988), *Forrest Gump* (1994) *The Black Balloon* (2007); or mania, e.g., *The Madness of King George* (1993), *Mr. Jones* (1993), *The Beaver* (2010).

Literature

In 1774 Johan Wolfgang von Goethe penned *The Sorrows of Young Werther.* Very much the polymath, Goethe's work was, *inter alia*, part of the Sturm und Drang movement of the mid-to-late eighteenth century, in which literature and art engaged in works of emotional extremes as a reaction to the constraints of reason emerging from the European Enlightenment. Goethe's book is a series of letters from young Werther to his friend Wilhelm. Young Werther, an artist of independent means, meets and falls in love with Lotte, a woman engaged to be married to Albert. As the date of Lotte's wedding approaches, Werther leaves and attempts to forget Lotte. He returns to the home of Lotte and Albert. His obsession with Lotte antagonizes his friends, and Werther finds himself further on the outer of his social circle. He writes what ultimately becomes a suicide note to Wilhelm. Following this he borrows Albert's pistol and shoots himself.

While *Werther* was the origin of his success as a novelist, Goethe evolved an intense dislike for his literary masterpiece Werther as much for the self-inflicted invasion of his privacy (Werther was semiautobiographical) as for the so-called Werther-Fieber (Werther fever). This saw young European men dressing as Werther make pilgrimages to Goethe's home in Weimar, and also a spate of copy-cat suicides in a phenomenon later dubbed "the Werther effect."

As one of the first examples of "emo chic" in modernity, Goethe's literary problem child illustrates the capacity for art to provide a window into the relationship between a social system and phenomena within it. Whether or not the prism of the artistic form provides such perspectives "through a glass darkly," the influence of the relationship is significant.

In recent times, cinema and high-production-value television has overtaken literature as the dominant artistic media. Even critically acclaimed or commercially successful fiction tends to find greater audiences in cinema than in print. Regardless, like Goethe's *Werther*, there exist works of literary fiction that echo the culture as much as present-day cinema, television, and increasingly, Web 2.0.

Many psychopathologies are evident in literature in modernity. Examples are the malignant narcissism of Raskolnikov, the main character in Dostoyevsky's *Crime and Punishment* (1866); the joyous anxiety neurosis found in Proust's writings; and the cyclic insanity of Stevenson's *Strange Case of Dr. Jekyll and Mr. Hyde* (1886). In the twentieth century, psychosis is evident in Dwayne Hoover, the protagonist of Vonnegut's *Breakfast of Champions* (1973); Deborah Blau in Greenwood's *I Never Promised You a Rose Garden* (1964); and Nicole Diver in F. Scott Fitzgerald's *Tender Is the Night* (1934). Severe depression is given its most vivid and compelling portrait in the experiences of Esther Greenwood in Sylvia Plath's *The Bell Jar* (1963). The commodification of depression and its treatment is at the core of Wurtzel's *Prozac Nation* (1994).

As a mirror to culture, the best literary example of this from the nineteenth century is the misogyny of mid-nineteenth century France depicted in the promiscuity and emotional excesses of the female protagonist Emma in Flaubert's *Madame Bovary* (1856). It is clear that uncharitable treatment of mental illness in women in a culture is not unique to postwar America.

Salinger's *Catcher in the Rye* (1951) is regarded as one of the great American novels. Its protagonist, Holden Caufield, endures a form of alienation or anomie. This appears to reflect a counterculture reaction to the sensibilities of the industrialized, highly regulated postwar U.S. society. The book is larded with references to sexuality; homosexual predation upon children is a recurrent theme. The novel makes constant contrasts between the virtues of childhood and the vices of adulthood. Indeed the symbolism inherent in the book's title—children in a rye field coming close to falling into the evils of adulthood—speaks to the dark theme of children suffering at the hands of adults. Holden alludes to spending time in a psychiatric hospital and his lack of change or maturation at the end of the novel implies that something more serious, such as a mental illness or substance abuse problem, has occurred. Whether a critical theorist can interpret *Catcher in the Rye* from a psychiatric perspective as being at one level about child abuse, Salinger constantly alludes to something sinister within society that serves as a toxin to children. If the reader is to intuit that Holden

Caufield has endured sexual abuse, this speaks to a darkness in the society that is not evident in the popular consciousness at the time. Indeed, the book was both reviled and celebrated throughout the decade following its publication. As a work of young adult fiction, it is a masterpiece; as a mirror to an unacknowledged evil within society, it is a discomfiting portrait of a young adult damaged by older adults.

Psychiatry and the Fourth Estate

Most of us spend some part of our day ingesting news or reports of current affairs. Granted, much of the celebrity culture consumed in lieu of politics or geopolitical affairs is redolent of the ancient Roman emperor Augustus's tactic of *panem et circenses* (bread and circuses); most members of a community engage in some form of discourse over the day's events.

As regards psychiatry's relationship with the fourth estate, what we will henceforth refer to as *the media*, there are two dimensions. The first is the role psychiatrists play directly within the media. The second is the role psychiatrist's play in moderating or responding to how the media reports on psychiatry and mental illness. Historically, the focus of the latter has been in the realm of the role the media plays in stigmatizing or destigmatizing mental illness and its treatment.

Reporting Mental Illness in the Media

The overwhelming conclusion from the literature in the field is that mental illness is portrayed negatively in the mass media. One UK study looking at media content in 1996 found almost half of the content was negative in regard to mental illness.[1] Violence is a prominent theme in media accounts of mental illness.[2] It is also evident that media exert a significant influence upon attitudes toward mental illness and its treatment.[3,4] Given most of the population develop their views about mental illness from the media rather than from direct experience, these are important observations. Stigma presents a considerable burden for those suffering mental illness and for their families. One might mount an argument that there is a public health implication of negative portrayals in the media of mental illness; these poison community views toward people suffering mental illness, leading to an array of social disadvantage that ultimately impacts upon their welfare.

It is also clear from the literature that mental health promotional activities in the media have the potential to positively influence community attitudes toward mental illness.[5] In light of this, the question is begged—What role for psychiatrists is necessitated by such observations? If it were an issue such as the apparent protective effect of maternal education and literacy in improving the mental health of a community, few would argue against the legitimacy of psychiatry positioning itself in the relevant public policy debate in this regard. Yet, in terms of what appears in newspapers or television, it is clear that the media appears to keep their own counsel—if the apparent malfeasance of News Corporation journalists in the UK in 2011 is any indication, such self-regulation is in a primitive state of affairs. Several jurisdictions have attempted to impose professional standards on reporting matters surrounding mental illness, such as the Australian Press Council (APC), which in 2011 issued guidelines for the reporting of suicide.[6] In this instance, psychiatrists and other interested parties provided consultation and advice to the APC. This would seem to represent an appropriate level or degree of advocacy and social activism by psychiatrists—informing public discourse of the implications of particular laws, policies, or statutes from a particular disciplinary perspective. As far as advising Hollywood to modify its depiction of mental illness or its treatment, there is a precedent. In 2000, Twentieth Century Fox released the film *Me, Myself, and Irene,* which depicted schizophrenia in both an inaccurate and misleading way. Mental health advocacy groups and psychiatrists in Canada and Australia both condemned the film in the popular press, in addition to making representations to the film's distributors that it was stigmatizing to people suffering mental illness.[7]

Psychiatrists Commenting in the Media

The hawkish Arizona Senator Barry Goldwater was a divisive figure in U.S. politics. His militant political conservatism earned him the Republican nomination for the 1964 presidential election. One month after Goldwater received the nomination, a questionnaire sent by *Fact* magazine to more than 12,000 psychiatrists asked if he was psychologically fit to be president. Only 20 percent of psychiatrists responded, the vast majority of whom said Goldwater was psychiatrically unsuitable to be president.[8] This was seen as "political bias ... wrapped up in pseudo-technical flagellation of Senator Goldwater."[9] Goldwater later sued *Fact*, obtaining a large damage settlement. Ironically, it was Goldwater who had helped modify the controversial Alaska Mental Health Enabling Act of 1956, ensuring that civil rights of people with mental illness were preserved by the legislation.* Following the furor, the American Psychiatric Association (APA) added Rule 7.3 to its *Principles of Medical Ethics: With Annotations Especially Applicable to Psychiatry*:

> On occasion psychiatrists are asked for an opinion about an individual who is in the light of public attention or who has disclosed information about himself/herself through public media. In such circumstances, a psychiatrist may share with the public his or her expertise about psychiatric issues in general. However, it is unethical for a psychiatrist to offer a professional opinion unless he or she has conducted an examination and has been granted proper authorization for such a statement.[10]

This injunction is now referred to as the "Goldwater rule." It sought in essence to set the tone for psychiatrists providing commentary in the media. The Goldwater rule sought to remove the ad hominem component of public statements by psychiatrist *qua* members of the profession. The Goldwater rule serves as a foil to psychiatrists' misusing their power for personal or political ends; however, the rule assumes the persisting sanity of all political figures, raising concerns about free speech. Moreover, mental illnesses suffered by celebrities or public figures often provide opportunities to address the issue in the mainstream media in a way that moves away from the stigmatic stereotypes usually provided to the public. Assuming the celebrity patient gives consent to public statements made on his or her behalf by his or her treating psychiatrist, then there would be no violation of confidentiality. In the United Kingdom, this issue was manifest in the controversial but popular TV show *In the Psychiatrist's Chair*, where a psychiatrist used his interviewing skills to provide insights into celebrities or public figures.

There is, however, a broader issue. The question is begged as to whether the psychiatrist giving consented commentary about a famous patient in the mainstream media is the beneficiary of the vicarious celebrity that comes with this exposure. In other words, is the

---

* This legislation transferred federal resources and jurisdictions, allowing Alaska to build large psychiatric institutions in the wilderness. The bill's most contentious element was the capacity for the other 48 states to transfer psychiatric patients to Alaska for treatment, thus dubbing it "The Siberia Bill". Goldwater had this removed from the bill, allowing its passage through the Senate.

commentary more for the benefit of the psychiatrist than the patient, or for the broader discourse over mental illness. There is also the potential for excessive, ill-informed commentary by psychiatrists to diminish the profession or its status within the scientific community. Indeed a former president of the APA lamented the capacity for "psychobabble" in the media to undermine the status of psychiatry.[11]

As to the broader issue of psychobabble, there is ample scope to reflect upon the appropriate scope of psychiatrists' commentary in the media on areas other than mental illness and its related issues. Psychiatrists who identify themselves as members of the profession and presumably use this as a pretext to have their views worthy of print or airtime (as opposed to any other views) do potentially diminish the profession in commenting beyond their expertise in areas such as popular culture, politics, or sport.

Social Media: Web 2.0

Few would argue that widespread ownership of home computers and the relative ease of access to the Internet has transformed life in the postindustrial West. Browsing or "surfing" the World Wide Web availed the average citizen of a surfeit of information that was easily accessible. The capacity to send and receive email both simplified communication and broadened the reach of an individual.

By the early twenty-first century, access to the Internet had become so widespread as to make slow or inefficient Internet access at home or in the workplace the source of grievance. In the first decade of the new millennium, the nature of the Internet and its use changed dramatically.

This change was the process of the Internet evolving from a source of passive receipt of information, and increasingly the venue of consumerism, to a virtual space in which participants changed and developed the content of what existed on the Web. This change was dubbed Web 2.0 and is "a group of Internet-based applications that build on the ideological and technological foundations of Web 2.0, and that allow the creation and exchange of user-generated content."[12] Beyond simple emails, there now exist within the rubric of Web 2.0, so-called social media, including sites such as Twitter, MySpace, Facebook, Linkedin, Instagram, and YouTube as well as web logs (blogs), bulletin boards, and chat rooms. Social media now accounts for nearly a quarter of all Internet use.[13]

Through social media, the interpersonal world of many, predominantly younger, people has changed significantly. Many relationships begin or are conducted online, and much communication occurs on social media. In lieu of the face-to-face contact of life prior to Web 2.0, the social media phenomenon provides many with a means of social interaction that is unique in history. With the advent of smartphones and mobile tablet computers such as iPads, which make social media a literally constant presence in the lives of many, through enabling continual access to the Web, the intensity of this phenomenon has escalated.

The French sociologist Jean Baudrillard foresaw the effects of information overload on society. Baudrillard argues that through their attempts to understand the world, people have become *seduced* into thinking that total knowledge of the world is possible. In light of the ease of disseminating and acquiring information and the scope of communication, this seduction is quite profound in the age of Web 2.0. As Baudrillard warns, a complete understanding of the complexity of the natural world and indeed of human life is impossible. When people are deluded into thinking otherwise, they become drawn toward a "simulated" version of reality, which he termed *hyperreality*.[14] Baudrillard's prototypic example of this was the first Gulf War, where remotely launched missiles and "surgical strikes" based on satellite-gathered intelligence saw the war conducted with minimal human contact. While not disputing the brutality of the impact of such ordnance on Iraqi soldiers and civilians, Baudrillard argues that as the Anglo-American experience of the war was in front of a screen, this was not really a war in the sense that face-to-face carnage of World War I had been war. Symbols replaced reality to create a hyperreality of a television war.

In the state of hyperreality, the rapid exchange of symbols replaced the reality that it is meant to signify. Much of contemporary culture exists as bombarding the individual with multiple symbols in rapid succession—consumerism is predicated on this immersion of the consumer in symbols of brands. Self-concept is thus trapped in a web of symbols, information, and signs. This distinctly postmodern concept of the self sees the individual dominated by media and technological experience.[15] Unlike the example of the steam engine being a reflection of industrialization, rather than a determinant of industrial society (a moot point), the technological progress reflected in social media does seem to have been profoundly influential on human interaction to the point where the self arguably exists in a completely postmodern way—where the experience of the technologically determined world overrides the individual self.[15]

Psychiatry in the World of Web 2.0

If one accepts the premise of the postmodern self, contextualized to social media (at least for some), there are immediate implications for psychiatrists. First, the experience of self becomes intimately linked with cyberspace and its varied permutations. Second, patients will seek to morph their relationships with psychiatrists into forms similar to their other social media relationships. Third, there are clearly mental health implications for improved clinical services through the wide and easy reach of social media. Finally, there are likely to be potential mental health consequences to the experience of the self in the unpoliced and unknown cyberworld.

Psychiatrists appear to have been resistive to the uptake of such technologies. While videoconferencing and telemedicine have become mainstream in many settings; there appears to have been professional resistance to the concept of "e-psychiatry." Even the comparatively Luddite technology of email communication between psychiatrists and their patients has not been taken up, as only 16 percent of psychiatrists have any form of regular email contact with their patients.[16] This has been explained in terms of concerns about blurred clinical boundaries, the conflation of the doctor–patient relationship with other forms of online relationships, and the creation of expectations of rapid response to communication, which might compromise care as work email accounts may not be checked regularly enough to provide reliable clinical contact.[17]

Many patients now Google their psychiatrists, and several websites that rate clinicians and their performance have become mainstream. This has changed the dynamics of patient–therapist boundaries and also raises the need for psychiatrists to consider what information is available on the Internet or on social media. In the converse, psychiatrists have the capacity to obtain similar information about patients. Does this represent a violation of patients' rights? Presumably, if a person provides information about him- or herself in these settings, he or she does so aware of the likelihood that it will be viewed. The question is begged as to whether the therapeutic relationship and its boundaries makes seeking such information about a patient, no matter how well intentioned, unethical. Granted, information about a patient may be legitimately sought from other informants, this is generally provided in the context of building understanding of the patient and his or her problems. Indeed, obtaining information from social media about a patient unconsented is much akin to eavesdropping on a conversation the patient is having.[18] In light of this, one author has proposed some general ethical principles surrounding the interaction between psychiatrists and patients using social media or the Internet generally.[19] These include the principles of confidentiality and consent, in addition to addressing problems surrounding boundaries and the possibility of a dual relationship in addition to avoiding soliciting favorable testimonials from patients in such a public forum.

While concerns about the impact of such modes of interaction on the therapeutic relationship are not misplaced, the potential for social media or online communication in providing mental health services challenges the legitimacy of psychiatrists' resistance to their adoption in practice.[20] Social media and online interactions have been successfully adopted in enterprises such as networking among self-help groups, outreach programs (particularly in younger people's mental health), working to reduce stigma, and education. For clinicians, online resources providing updated clinical and other scientific information are available at any point with the advent of smartphones.[21] Social media allows for interaction with colleagues, which had previously been possible only for psychiatrists able to travel to international meetings.[22]

There is emerging evidence that Internet-based therapies may be effective for panic[23] or obsessive-compulsive disorder.[24] Assuming patients have access to adequate Internet services, online therapy presents a potential means of increasing access to psychiatric care by reducing costs of therapy or the practical demands of making it to appointments.[25] With such approaches to clinical interaction come problems with data security, confidentiality, and control of quality. Given the proliferation of online content, online therapy resources that are not properly supervised or moderated may harm unwary patients.[26]

Psychopathology in the World of Web 2.0

While Web 2.0 offers much opportunity, there is a danger that too much Internet use corresponds with worsening depression.[27] Patients suffering from schizophrenia may also fare badly from routine use of the Internet. Such patients are vulnerable to stimulus overflow, are often overwhelmed by the abundance of information, suffer difficulties with concentration, and may find that too much engagement with online resources exerts a deleterious effect on their mental states.[28]

Beyond the potential problems of Web 2.0 on established mental illness, the prominence of social media in the cultural framework of younger people raises many questions. Social media seems to have led to a lower threshold of sharing personal information or self-disclosure, particularly among younger people. This is most troubling in the phenomenon of "sexting"—the broadcast of sexually provocative material via social media. Beyond this, the potentially adverse impacts on mental health of engagement in the unregulated social media universe are now being recognized.

The suicide of Megan Meier, a 13-year-old girl from O'Fallon, Missouri, has become the cause célèbre of the phenomenon of cyberbullying. Meier had befriended the daughter of 49-year-old Lori Drew. Meier had experienced long-standing difficulties with her mood, having been treated for depression the year before her death. When the friendship between Meier and Drew's daughter ended acrimoniously, Drew grew concerned that Meier was spreading rumors about her daughter. Drew created a fake MySpace profile under the pseudonym Josh Evans, depicted as a 16-year-old boy. Through this fiction, Drew lured Meier into a flirtatious relationship with "Josh." In mid-October 2006 Drew told Meier via the Josh Evans avatar that the world would be better off with her dead. Other MySpace "friends" of the fictional Evans further besieged Meier, who then hanged herself in her bedroom. In 2008 Drew was indicted on several counts of vague misdemeanors over unauthorized use of computers;[29] her conviction was later overturned on appeal. The evidence argued at the Drew trial highlighted the truly frontier nature of Internet law and how difficult it would be to properly regulate cyberspace and the social media world.

Cyberbullying has been defined as "the use of information and communication technologies to support deliberate, repeated, and hostile behavior by an individual or group, that is intended to harm others."[30] About one-third of adolescent and young adult users of social media report being victimized or bullied online, with the bullying mostly in the form of ridicule or name calling. More concerning, around 10 percent of this group reported being threatened with actual harm.[31] Apart from the acute distress of experiencing cyberbullying, the hyperreal nature of social relationships in this setting appears to amplify the distress of negative feedback. Some have dubbed this "Facebook depression," where psychological distress correlates with a paucity of friends and the experience of social rejection in social media.[32] As the Megan Meier tragedy demonstrated, adverse experiences on social media can worsen the course of established psychiatric disorders.[33]

Social media appears to also provide a window on the mental state of many users. About a quarter of Facebook users exhibit psychopathology; some 10 percent of those appear to be suffering a major depressive illness.[34] More concerning is the use of social media as a venue to communicate suicidal intent. Given the predatory nature of some interactions, communicating suicidal thoughts in that venue might lead to negative responses, which increase the likelihood of completed suicide.

When 42-year-old Simone Back, a charity worker from Brighton in the UK, announced her intention to commit suicide in a status update on Facebook, over 1,000 Facebook "friends" responded by ridiculing her. The following posts outline the reception Back's announcement received:

10:53 p.m., *Back posted: Took all my pills be dead soon bye bye everyone*

11:01 p.m., *Friend A: She ODs all the time and she lies.*

11:02 p.m., *Friend B: I hope that she is lying about this or you're going to feel guilty tomorrow.*

12:56 a.m., *Friend A: She does it all the time, takes all of her pills. She's not a kid anymore.*

12:01 p.m., *Friend D: She has a choice and taking pills over a relationship is not a good enough reason*

Back committed suicide on Christmas Day and wrote in her Facebook status, "Took all my pills be dead soon bye bye everyone."[35]

Such public acts of suicidal behavior may raise concerns about the possibility of copy-cat behavior. Copy cat suicides have previously been attributed to publicity surrounding suicides in a culture, usually in the media.[36] In the 1970s, sociologist David Philips dubbed this the "Werther effect"[37]—named after the character in Goethe's novel. While there remains uncertainty over the degree of propensity for media reporting to increase the incidence of suicides,[38] it certainly appears that publicity around suicides leads to emulation of suicidal methods.[39] So far, evidence suggests that suicide announcements on Facebook do not exert a Werther effect.[40]

Akin to the problematic nature of many interactions in social media is the apparent narcissism of much of the user-generated content on the Internet. Twitter invites "tweeters" to share all manner of personal information and musings in a moment-by-moment fashion—the social utility of this remains unclear. Moreover, the status of opinion in this setting is not always a function of the validity or intrinsic worth of postings. In the 1990s the "cypherpunk" movement emerged in California. The most prominent cypherpunk, Tim May, a former chief scientist in the Intel company, was notorious in his online posts proposing "assassination markets" for politicians and making numerous contemptuous remarks about his fellow citizens.[41] The two perpetrators of the 1999 Columbine shootings posted hateful messages on their personal web pages or in chat rooms. Indeed, as author Andrew Keen argued that there is now a profound "digital narcissism," in which those who shout loudest online become the most authoritative.[42] Writing in *The Weekly Standard* in 2006, Keen averred that this narcissism was a malign influence on the culture:

> Another word for narcissism is "personalization." Web 2.0 technology personalizes culture so that it reflects ourselves rather than the world around us. Blogs personalize media content so that all we read are our own thoughts. Online stores personalize our preferences, thus feeding back to us our own taste. Google personalizes searches so that all we see are advertisements for products and services we already use. Instead of Mozart, Van Gogh, or Hitchcock, all we get with the Web 2.0 revolution is more of ourselves.[43]

In essence, the broad canvas of Web 2.0 appears to encourage a breakdown in interpersonal boundaries and a radical alteration of both self-concept and the individual's sense of his or her place in the world.

In light of such a profound cultural process, what should psychiatrists make of Web 2.0? In the first place, there is an irresistible process of the Internet transforming many aspects of culture. The craft of medicine is now transacted in cyberspace as well as at the bedside. There are clearly benefits and risks to this process, and it would appear that psychiatrists in particular have resisted engaging in the changes. Enhancements to practice and clinical care have to be weighed against the effect of Web 2.0 on the psychiatric profession and its relationship with patients. These are as much questions of individual value as they are of professional values. Web 2.0 poses potential challenges to public health, particularly concerning the effects of interpersonal failure in such public forums, given the apparently hyperreal nature of many interactions in this setting. People with established mental illness or vulnerability to mental illness face particular affronts in Web 2.0, with potentially fatal consequences. Is such a potentially damaging influence a focus of public health? In drawing an analogy with bullying in schools or the workplace, clearly this is the case, and therefore psychiatrists in each community have to consider whether there are appropriate grounds to speak out or advise on questions of public policy that will inevitably consider how the Web 2.0 environment is regulated. The inability to prosecute the virtual murderer of Megan Meier highlights the need for such questions to be carefully considered by communities and societies.

Conclusion

What is clear from our consideration of this area is that psychiatry has engaged with the culture and will continue to do so. Mental illness and its treatment is the focus of many cultural outputs, from the novels of Goethe to the unrestrained opinions of the blogosphere. These cultural entities speak of the values of the society that produced them, and psychiatrists can and indeed should maintain awareness of this cultural milieu and the relevance for the ethical practice of their craft.

References

1. Ward G. *Making Headlines. Mental Health and the National Press.* London: Health Education Authority; 1997.

2. Philo G, McLaughlin G, Henderson L. Media content. In: Philo G, ed. *Media and Mental Distress.* Essex: Addison Wesley Longman; 1996.

3. Granello D, Pauley P, Carmichael A. Relationship of the media to attitudes toward people with mental illness. *Journal of Humanistic Counseling Education & Development.* 1999;38:98–103.

4. Benkert O, Graf-Morgenstern M, Hillert A, et al. Public opinion on psychotropic drugs: an analysis of the factors influencing acceptance or rejection. *Journal of Nervous & Mental Disease.* 1997;185:151–158.

5. Medvene L, Bridge R. Using television to create a more favorable attitudes toward community facilities for deinstitutionalised psychiatric patients. *Journal of Applied Social Psychology.* 1990;20:1863–1878.

6. Australian Press Council. Standards: suicide reporting. 2011; http://www.presscouncil. org.au/document-search/standard-suicide-reporting/.

7. Byrne P. Schizophrenia in the cinema: *Me, Myself and Irene. The Psychiatrist.* 2000;24:364–365.

8. Romano J. Reminiscences: 1938 and since. *Am J Psychiatry.* 1990;147:785–792.

9. Gorman M. Psychiatry and public policy. *Am J Psychiatry.* 1965;122:56–60.

10. American Psychiatric Association. *The Principles of Medical Ethics: With Annotations Especially Applicable to Psychiatry.* Arlington, VA; 2008.

11. Brainard C. Covering "crazy." *Columbia Journalism Review.* 2011; http://www.cjr.org/ the_observatory/covering-crazy.php?page=all (accessed February 22, 2012).

12. Kaplan A, Haenlein M. Users of the world, unite! The challenges and opportunities of Social Media. *Business Horizons.* 2010;53:59–68.

13. Nielson Wire. Social networks/blogs now account for one in every four and a half minutes online. 2010; http://blog.nielsen.com/nielsenwire/global/ social-media-accounts-for-22-percent-of-time-online/.

14. Baudrillard J. *The Gulf War Did Not Take Place.* Bloomington: Indiana University Press; 1995.

15. McLuhan M. *Understanding Media.* London: Abacus; 1974.

16. Brooks R, Menachemi N. Physicians' use of email with patients: factors influencing electronic communication and adherence to best practices. *J Med Internet Res.* 2006;8:e2.

17. Seeman M, Seeman M, Seeman N. E-psychiatry. *Psychiatric Times.* 2010;22:18–29.

18. Wingerson L. Internet social media present new quandaries for psychiatrists. *Psychiatric Times* 2009. http://www.psychiatrictimes.com/conference-reports/apa2009/display/article/10168/1414489.

19. Kolmes K. iTransference: mental healthcare & social media policy. *Psychiatry Weekly*. 2011;6(27). http://www.psychweekly.com/aspx/article/articledetail.aspx?articleid=1379 (accessed February 1, 2012).

20. Seeman M, Seeman B. E-psychiatry: the patient–psychiatrist relationship in the electronic age. *CMAJ*. 1999;161:1147–1149.

21. Luo J. Health information technologies for practicing psychiatrists. *Psychiatric Times* 2010;27:16–18.

22. Luo J. Social networking: now professionally ready. *Primary Psychiatry*. 2007;14:21–24.

23. Bergström J, Andersson G, Karlsson A, et al. An open study of the effectiveness of Internet treatment for panic disorder delivered in a psychiatric setting. *Nord J Psychiatry*. 2009;63:44–50.

24. Andersson E, Ljótsson B, Hedman E, et al. Internet-based cognitive behavior therapy for obsessive compulsive disorder: a pilot study. *BMC Psychiatry*. 2011(11):125.

25. Katz S, Moyer C. The emerging role of online communication between patients and their providers. *J Gen Intern Med*. 2004;19:978–983.

26. Bessière K, Pressman S, Kiesler S, et al. Effects of Internet use on health and depression: a longitudinal study. *J Med Internet Res*. 2010;12:e6.

27. Morrison C, Gore H. The relationship between excessive Internet use and depression: a questionnaire-based study of 1,319 young people and adults. *Psychopathology*. 2010;43:121–126.

28. Schrank B, Sibitz I, Unger A, et al. How patients with schizophrenia use the Internet: qualitative study. *J Med Internet Res*. 2010;12:e70.

29. *U.S. v. Lori Drew 259 F.R.D. 449,* (C.D. Cal 2009).

30. Belsey B. Cyberbullying. http://www.cyberbullying.org/ (accessed February 1, 2012).

31. Hinduja S, Patchin J. Cyberbullying: an exploratory analysis of factors related to offending and victimization. *Deviant Behavior*. 2008;29:129–156.

32. Kim J, Lee J. The Facebook paths to happiness: effects of the number of Facebook friends and self-presentation on subjective well-being. *Cyberpsychol Behav Soc Netw*. 2011;14:359–364.

33. Takahashi Y, Uchida C, K M, Sakai M, et al. Potential benefits and harms of a peer support social network service on the Internet for people with depressive tendencies: qualitative content analysis and social network analysis. *J Med Internet Res*. 2009;23(e29).

34. Moreno M, Jelenchick L, Egan K, et al. Feeling bad on Facebook: depression disclosures by college students on a social networking site. *Depress Anxiety*. 2011;28:447–455.

35. "Took all my pills, bye bye": Woman commits suicide on Facebook … and none of her 1,082 online friends help. *Daily Mail*. January 6, 2011.

36. Phillips D, Carstensen L. Clustering of teenage suicides after television news stories about suicide. *New England Journal of Medicine*. 1986;315:685–689.

37. Phillips D. The influence of suggestion on suicide: substantive and theoretical implications of the Werther effect. *American Sociological Review.* 1974;39:340–354.

38. Sullivan G. *Should Suicide Be Reported in the Media? A Critique of Research.* New York: Routledge; 2007.

39. Berman A. Fictional depiction of suicide in television films and imitation effects. *Am J Psychiatry.* 1988;145:982–986.

40. Ruder T, Hatch G, Ampanozi G, et al. Suicide announcement on Facebook. *Crisis.* 2011;32:280–282.

41. Manne R. The Cypherpunk Revolutionary: Julian Assange. *The Monthly.* 2011. http://www.themonthly.com.au/julian-assange-cypherpunk-revolutionary-robert-manne-3081 (accessed February 6, 2012).

42. Keen A. TCotARH. *The Cult of the Amateur.* New York: Random House; 2007.

43. Keen A. Web 2.0. *The Weekly Standard.* February 14, 2006.

9

Psychiatric Ethics in the Light of Neuroscience

Introduction

On July 17, 1990, U.S. Presidential Proclamation 6158 decreed—

> … the decade beginning January 1, 1990, [shall be known] as the Decade of the Brain. I call upon all public officials and the people of the United States to observe that decade with appropriate programs, ceremonies, and activities.[1]

Expectations were high that the anticipated progress in neuroscience would reveal the cause and cure of mental and neurological illness. There was to be a massive investment in research and development in public and private sectors. By the end of the first decade of the twenty-first century, it was clear that much of the promise of George H. W. Bush's proclamation remained unfulfilled. Indeed, Akil and colleagues have argued,

> … there have been no major breakthroughs in the treatment of schizophrenia in the past 50 years and no major breakthroughs in the treatment of depression in the past 20 years.[2]

Large-scale studies of the state of treatment of schizophrenia, most notably the Clinical Antipsychotic Trials of Intervention Effectiveness (CATIE),[3] indicate that the lot of a person suffering from schizophrenia has changed little since the advent of chlorpromazine in the 1950s. More to the point, the level of untreated medical illness in this group of people is alarmingly high, the product of iatrogenic harm and the gross social disadvantage they face. The management of depression, at the heart of mental healthcare, has equally disappointed in the aftermath of the decade of the brain. Far from merely confirming 1990s-era assumptions about treatment efficacy of antidepressants, the Sequenced Treatment Alternatives to Relieve Depression (STAR*D)[4] findings paint an even bleaker picture of the actual benefit of these drugs.

Regardless of the poor return on investment in neuroscience in the two decades from the presidential proclamation, the ongoing expectations of neuroscience progress has created a novel discourse in bioethics, the field of neuroethics.[5] It is unclear when the term *neuroethics* appeared or to whom it can be attributed. As with most interdisciplinary fields, neuroethics has evolved through a number of disciplines including neurology, cognitive neuroscience, computer science, neuroimaging, neurophysiology, and psychiatry. The most simple definition of the field of neuroethics is that it is the neuroscience of ethics and the ethics of neuroscience.

If one surveys the literature in the field of neuroethics, a number of themes emerge, highlighting different questions from different disciplinary perspectives:

1. How do putative neurological models of human experience such as emotion, selfhood, agency, and intentionality refine understanding of common ethical dilemmas, such as responsibility, in clinical and medicolegal settings?
2. What are the implications for the Self of observations of the alteration of brain structure and function after treatment of mental illness?
3. What are the dilemmas raised by progress in neuroimaging and genetics, particularly in the realm of the diagnosis and classification of psychiatric disorders?
4. What are the implications of establishing a neurological basis for moral deliberation and action?
5. What are the ethical dilemmas raised by cognitive enhancement or "cosmetic psychopharmacology"?

This list is by no means exhaustive, and the field of neuroethics remains largely speculative. Regardless, there are questions raised by the incremental progress in neuroscience, subsumed under the rubric *neuroethics*, that help make up the context of moral agency by psychiatrists.

Discussion of the ethical challenges raised by the advances in neuroimaging, in particular incidental findings in both structural and functional neuroimaging, was one the primary discourses in neuroethics.[6]

Much of the discourse in neuroethics relates to speculative, rather than actual, dilemmas. Regardless, the mere existence of such dilemmas appears to be influencing the field of mental healthcare. A qualitative study of 32 semistructured interviews with mental health professionals indicated that the subjects had begun to reconceptualize mental illness and mental healthcare with a neuroscience gaze. In the particular example of neuroimaging, they demonstrated "an epistemic commitment to the value of a brain scan to provide a meaningful explanation of mental illness for their clients."[7]

Our aim in this chapter is to survey some of the neuroethics dilemmas that are salient to psychiatry. Many of these seem to be a process of revisiting old conundrums through the lens of neuroscience. In keeping with our methodology, we will integrate the individual and communal perspectives on these dilemmas with our conceptualization of the moral agency of psychiatrists.

Moral Agency and Neuroscience

Free Will and Responsibility

Perhaps the core philosophical dilemma facing those who deal with the construct of mind is that of free will. This is a question that was first engaged in antiquity, although several millennia later it remains unresolved. In the *Nichomachean Ethics*,[8] Aristotle distinguished "voluntary" (*ekousion*) from "unwilling" (*akousion*) acts. Put simply, *akousion* acts might include those where there is ignorance of the consequences of the act or where the act was performed under irresistible force or compulsion. In contrast, Aquinas argued human nature was determined by the need to find an end with the greatest good and that free will emerged in the choice of means. Numerous other philosophers have grappled with this philosophical dilemma, the nature of which is entangled in similar debates over the Cartesian (mind) or materialist (brain) positions on the nature of conscious awareness.

The work of neurophysiologist Benjamin Libet at University of California–San Francisco is an apt starting point for the neuroethics perspective on this question.[9] Libet's experimental design sought to identify a relationship between brain activity and the experience of volitional acts. Libet's experimental method had the participant seated in front of an oscilloscope timer, with continuous scalp electroencephalogram (EEG) monitoring. The participant would then be told to execute a simple motor activity, such as pressing a button. The subject noted the position of the dot on the oscilloscope timer when he or she became aware of the intention to act, and the button action would record the approximate moment of execution of the motor act. In comparing the oscilloscope dots, approximately 200 milliseconds elapsed between the first appearance of conscious will to press the button and the act. After analysis of the EEG recordings for each trial, Libet's team noted that that brain activity involved in the motor cortex occurred 500 milliseconds *before* the subject pushed the button. In essence, the neurological activity associated with an intentional act occurred 300 milliseconds *prior* to the participants' first awareness of conscious will to act. Libet termed the brain electrical activity preceding the awareness of the will to act the *bereitschaftspotential* or "readiness potential."

The literal interpretation of Libet's work was to support the determinist position. Brain activity associated with an action occurs prior to the conscious awareness of the intent to act. The brain, determined by the physical universe, determines behavior. There are numerous possible criticisms of Libet's methodology and the simplistic nature of the interpretations; however, the fact remains that there is evidence that intelligent behavior originates from physical activity of the brain outside of the awareness of the person.

Perhaps the most balanced view of the work of Libet and similar researchers is the notion that behavior has its origins in the physical universe, but this does not vitiate the individual's free choice to act on behavior. Libet's experimental subjects became aware of the intention to act but arguably retained the capacity to freely choose not to act. In essence, the corollary of Libet's work is not that there is a "free will" but rather a "free won't."

The Neurological Basis of Moral Agency

One of the more popular utilitarian thought experiments is the so-called trolley problem.[10,11] In its first form, the switch variant, the moral agent places him- or herself as the driver of a runaway trolley car that cannot be stopped but can only be steered from one rail track onto another. The trolley approaches a fork—there are five workmen on one track and one workman on the other. The choice is to crash into and kill either one man or five. In the second form of the problem, the trolley is hurtling down a track toward five people. The moral agent is standing next to a very fat man on a bridge, under which the trolley will pass. The moral agent has the option of doing nothing and seeing five people get killed, or stopping the trolley by pushing the fat man onto the track, killing him to save five.

At the Massachusetts Institute of Technology, Joshua Greene and colleagues posed the trolley problem to research participants and analyzed functional magnetic resonance imaging (fMRI) scans performed as they grappled with both variants of the dilemma.[12] Greene's hypothesis suggested that encountering such conflicts evokes antagonistic emotional and rational cognitive responses. In Greene's analysis, the "fat man" variant of the trolley problem resulted in significantly higher activity in brain regions associated with response to conflict, such as in the limbic system. In the "switch" variant, fMRI scans indicated more activity in brain regions associated with executive functioning. As such, Greene proposes a dual-process theory of moral judgment. The dual process sees either reason or emotion recruited to moral deliberation and action, depending on the situation. He uses the metaphor of the "moral brain" as a camera with manual presets, such as landscape, and manual adjustments. Greene sees emotional responses as the presets and rationale as the manual adjustment.

Psychologist Michael Gazzaniga proposes another theory of the neural basis of moral action. In his book *The Ethical Brain*[13] Gazzaniga describes altruism as emerging from a neurological basis akin to mirror neurons.[14] A mirror neuron is a neuron that fires both when an animal acts and when it observes the same action performed by another. This clearly has a survival value for behaviors that are adaptive. In an analogous process described by Gazzaniga as "simulation theory," the witnessing of the travails of another activates the limbic system in the observer's brain. In other words, the limbic system of an observer of another's distress activates in the same pattern as if it were happening to him or her. In Gazzaniga's theory, moral agency can be redefined in terms of self-interest—moral action arises as the need to abolish the pain of the mirrored activation of the moral agent's limbic system.

The Problem of Psychopathy

The concept of psychopathy is at the core of a specific dilemma raised by neuroethics. Character traits such as gross lack of empathy or remorse, impulsivity, deceitfulness, interpersonal exploitativeness, and irresponsibility are recognized as the hallmarks of the psychopathic individual. In 1941, Cleckley outlined the problem of psychopathy (previously termed *moral insanity*) in his classic work *The Mask of Sanity*.[15] More contemporary notions of psychopathy are attributed to the work of Canadian psychiatrist Robert Hare.[16]

While psychopathy is reified as a mental disorder in the *Diagnostic and Statistical Manual of Mental Disorders (DSM)* as *antisocial personality disorder*, most do not consider it a psychiatric disorder in the same category of schizophrenia. Contemporary conceptualizations of schizophrenia are its being a neurodevelopmental disorder with demonstrable psychopathological processes originating in the brain. Such notions invite special consideration of criminal responsibility, reflected in the precedents from the so-called M'Naghten case[17] in legal systems of English lineage. In particular, psychopaths are thought responsible for their behavior, particularly in the settings of criminal justice systems.

Progress in neuroscience has challenged the notion that psychopathy is not a disorder in the same category as schizophrenia. Numerous studies have identified structural and functional impairments in the orbitofrontal, dorsolateral frontal, and anterior cingulate cortex in individuals with antisocial behavior.[18] Antisocial behavior correlates with low levels of serotonin in the central nervous system.[19] A study based on the Dunedin cohort concluded that maltreated children with a low-activity polymorphism in the promoter region of the MAO-A gene were more likely to develop antisocial conduct disorders than controls.[20]

Such observations would indicate that individuals labeled psychopaths in most likelihood are possessed of specific disorders of brain structure and function, which would suggest that their behavior originates from neurological dysfunction. As such, it is not fanciful to imaging circumstances where such factors become the basis of legal defense of criminal behavior. Is it reasonable for genetic or fMRI profiles to be offered as evidence of diminished responsibility for behavior?

Again, Gazzaniga provides one of the clearest perspectives of this clear dilemma in neuroethics.[13] In essence, Gazzaniga argues that a person should be considered responsible for an act if he or she had the ability to do otherwise. Gazzaniga seeks to resolve the matter in arguing that responsibility is a social, not a neurological, concern. Neuroscience cannot resolve the dilemmas around criminal responsibility.

To a psychiatrist practicing within a particular societal setting, specific statutes or legal precedents often void discretion over the issue of criminal responsibility. What is unclear is the value courts can place upon neuroscience data and its interpretation in the context of criminal behavior and what role psychiatrists play in this.

Psychiatric Genetics

Introduction

American psychiatrist Kenneth Kendler[21] outlined four paradigms in the field of psychiatric genetics:

1. Basic genetic epidemiology
2. Advanced genetic epidemiology
3. Identification of specific genetic loci associated with disorder
4. Molecular genetics

The last category has been of most interest in recent research efforts, in that the expression of genes as part of a pathological process offers some hope of establishing the molecular basis of psychiatric disorder, paving the way for newer treatments. Establishing the molecular basis of psychiatric disorder also invites the prospect of molecular diagnosis of psychiatric disorder.

Genetic Diagnosis in Psychiatry

John Sadler at the University of Texas Southwestern has written extensively in the area of psychiatric diagnosis. In Sadler's view, diagnosis of psychiatric disorders has been hitherto based on descriptions of phenotypes and integration of specific values in demarcating these from normative or desirable forms. In the face of the prospect of molecular diagnosis, Sadler sees a problem in how putative genotypic or molecular-based diagnosis of mental disorder can be integrated with the psychological, cultural, and social values that are the basis of psychiatric diagnosis.[22] Sadler is also critical of the ongoing level of funding of research in psychiatric genetics given the clear lack of progress in establishing a molecular basis of the etiology or treatment of psychiatric disorder.[23]

In schizophrenia, particular complexes of symptoms and signs are considered in association with the level of distress and psychosocial impairment in order to establish a categorical case. One possible genetic basis of schizophrenia is variants of the enzyme cathechol-O-methyl-transferase (COMT). In individuals with the Val158Met variant of the COMT enzyme, there is an increased risk of onset of schizophrenia.[24] If an individual is possessed of this presumed molecular pathology, as opposed to symptoms and signs of schizophrenia, and exhibits a deviant pattern of social or interpersonal functioning, then a diagnosis of schizophrenia is an entirely different proposition.

Serotonin Transporter Gene and Its Implications

One of the actual manifestations of the possible molecular diagnosis of psychiatric disorder involves the serotonin transporter protein (SERT). The gene encoding the SERT is the 5HTTLPR, with a promoter region the SLC6A4, found on chromosome 17 on location 17q11.1–q12. This gene has polymorphisms with short and long repeats. The short repeat variant leads to less synthesis of a form of the SERT that may lead to anxiety and vulnerable personality.[25] The original study in this area identified that possession of the short form of SERT seemed to moderate the influence of stressful life events on depression[26]—individuals with one or two copies of the short allele of the 5-HTT promoter exhibited more depressive symptoms, diagnosable depression, and suicidality in relation to stressful life events than individuals homozygous for the long allele. Moreover, having this particular polymorphism contributes to anxious and depressive cognitive schema.[27] Subsequent meta-analysis of similar studies has not supported such relationship.[28]

Regardless of the confusion surrounding the actual findings of the study and our previous arguments about the problems of molecular diagnosis of psychiatric disorders, the potential for screening for this genetic variant in the population raises specific concerns. On the one hand, identification of this putative genetic diathesis for psychiatric disorder presents an opportunity for potential intervention and the possibility of primary or secondary intervention, such as the use of serotonergic antidepressants.[29] On the other hand, screening for this particular genetic variation may present significant problems to the individual involved, as well as to family members. The prospect of an increased likelihood of an episode of psychopathology may well diminish the quality of life for the individual and create disadvantage in securing employment, advancing career opportunities, or securing health or life insurance.

In the light of the capacity to identify a putative genetic diathesis to depression or other states of psychopathology, the question is begged as to how such information should be handled by the community. Should there be a mass screening program for this genetic vulnerability to depression, or should it be confined to specific cases where there is extensive consideration of the results of such assays and the measures taken by the patient?

Perhaps this could be resolved by analogous argument—is screening for the short variant of the 5HTTLPR akin to screening newborns for metabolic disorder, or akin to testing for Huntington's disease?

The original newborn screening for the phenylketonuria was developed by Robert Guthrie.[30] Over time, testing for other reversible conditions such as hyperthyroidism was added to the panel, although contemporary newborn screening protocols now include nonreversible conditions such as cystic fibrosis. For the point of this argument by analogy, the simple Guthrie test is one of the analogous situations. If a newborn is identified as having the mutant gene for phenylalanine hydroxylase, he or she will develop phenylketonuria. Lifelong restriction of the intake of the amino acid phenylalanine is effectively preventive in the development of intellectual disability and seizures. In this case, identification of the specific gene has value for the patient and the community.

Huntington's disease is an invariably fatal degenerative neurological disorder that tends to appear in early midlife. As an autosomal dominant condition, the presence of a proband with the disease in a family conveys enormous implications. The molecular basis of Huntington's disease is the possession of particular alleles of the huntingtin (HTT) gene. If a person has more than 36 repeats of cytosine-adenine-guanine (CAG) on this gene, this is indicative of the disease.[31] Given the catastrophic nature of this molecular diagnosis, a person undergoing this test participates in an extensive counseling program, which addresses education about the disease, the significance of a positive test and the person's concerns surrounding anxiety, survivor guilt, discrimination, and estate planning. The structure of the counseling program in Huntington's screening has become the paradigm for counseling for other heritable disorders, such as breast cancer.[32] Not surprisingly, more than 95 percent of people at risk decline to undergo screening.[31]

In using a normative analogy method for ethical reasoning, the first step is to identify the question at issue—in this case, how should genetic testing for the short arm 5HTTLPR be handled by a community? The next task is to consider the implications of a positive test. An increased risk for depression is an undesirable state, and the opportunity to prevent depression is arguably desirable for both the community and the individual. By analogy, it is uncontested that preventing as far as possible the onset of depression, phenylketonuria, or Huntington's disease is a desirable goal for a community.

The next task is to identify the negative relevant differences between the different dilemmas. In the case of the mutant phenylalanine hydroxylase gene or more than 36 trinucleotide repeats on the huntingtin gene, the proband will develop the relevant diseases. Possession of one or two short-arm alleles of the 5HTTLPR increases the vulnerability for depression and certain maladaptive personality styles but is not a molecular diagnosis as the two analogs are. Both phenylketonuria and Huntington's disease conform to classical Mendelian patterns of inheritance and do not involve gene-environment interactions the way it appears that 5HTTLPR polymorphism does. This returns us to the dilemma of molecular as opposed to clinical diagnosis.

As regards the instrumental value of the information provided by both tests, in phenylketonuria, the disorder can be prevented, whereas the opposite holds for Huntington's disease. Serotonin reuptake inhibitors may be more efficacious in treating depression in patients with the short-arm 5HTTLPR variant, but there is no credible argument for prophylactic antidepressant therapy for asymptomatic probands with the pathological variant of the gene, the way there would be for providing thyroid hormone replacement for children with congenital hypothyroidism. More important is the question of the imperative to prevent depression in the light of identifying the 5HTTLPR short-arm genotype. Here a slight detour might help clarify this reasoning. In breast cancer and perhaps other gynecological cancers, possession of the BRCA1 or BRCA2 genes significantly increases the risk of the disease.[33] Such is the risk that preventive mastectomy is a credible strategy in the case of this molecular diagnosis.[34] What is the analog in the case of the short-arm variant of the 5HTTLPR? Given that the genotype is not itself causative of depression but rather its interaction with negative life events, then does this necessitate controling the environment of the person who tests positive for the genetic variant? The logic of preventive mastectomy seems to be that the removal of one variable is a primary prevention. In the same way, is taking all measures to guarantee certain styles of parenting, education, and control of interpersonal environment analogous to preventive mastectomy? It may well help reduce the extent of the problem, much in the way that this type of early intervention helps children with developmental disorders in terms of cost–benefit and individual benefit,[35] but the implications for individual autonomy, resources, and the individual in question are immense. Here lie particular problems of stigma and disadvantage. The baby born with the short-arm allele of the 5HTTLPR may well be wrapped in cotton wool in childhood but will also be disadvantaged by insurance actuaries and future employers aware of a duty of care to prevent workplace-related psychiatric disorders.

In the final analysis, the case of the 5HTTLPR polymorphism is not akin to any of the comparative medical conditions. What we have is a genetic test that neither confirms a diagnosis nor indicates a particular intervention, either preventive or remedial. Granted, research in the area is in its infancy, and it is possible that a closer genotype–phenotype relationship may be established or a more definitive mode of intervention may emerge. In the interim, there remains much interest in the area, and bedside testing using polymerase chain reaction is commercially available. Over time, associations between this particular genetic entity and psychiatric disorder will likely strengthen. There appears no real clinical benefit to the test, although the emerging field of individualized medicine may use the test as a means of guiding the use of different classes of antidepressant.[36] There appears to be no benefit to the community in mass screening for the gene at the present state of knowledge and there is limited utility in the case of the individual patient. There is ample potential for misuse of this information akin to the dystopian images of the 1997 film *Gattaca*, where genetically inferior members of the community become second-class citizens, denied many opportunities. As with so many aspects of neuroethics, this particular dilemma in psychiatric genetics represents more a case of psychiatrists needing to temper any social or community expectations of the technology. There is no credible precedent for handling the form of knowledge created by this technology, and so at this point, the challenge is to find middle ground between the potential benefits of further research in the field and restraining the urge to form laws or practices within the community that may represent a source of disadvantage to members of the community who have the trait.

Psychosurgery

The Problem of Definition

Apart from electroconvulsive therapy (ECT), the most emotive issue in the history of psychiatry is undoubtedly the practice of psychosurgery, or lobotomy in the mid-twentieth century. Cinematic depictions of lobotomy in films such as *One Flew over the Cuckoo's Nest, Suddenly Last Summer,* and *Frances* did much to outrage audiences and poison the communities' attitudes toward psychosurgery, or indeed the psychiatric profession.

In the 1880s the Swiss psychiatrist Gottlieb Burckhardt noted the potential therapeutic effects of surgical alteration of the central nervous system of patients suffering from mental illness.[37] The practice of psychosurgery then evolved through to its heyday in the mid-twentieth century.

One of the problems in contemporary debate over psychosurgery is that of an adequate definition of the procedure.[38] The World Health Organization defines psychosurgery as the selective surgical removal or destruction of normal brain tissue with a view to influencing behavior. An alternate definition is simply neurosurgery for psychiatric disorders. What is common to these definitions is the concept of operative alteration of brain structure to achieve a desired change in emotional or other psychopathological state.

The neurosurgeon and philosopher Grant Gillett offered the following syllogism in defining psychosurgery:[39]

- All behavior, thoughts, and moods result from brain activity;
- psychological problems reflect abnormal instances of such brain activity;
- psychological problems can be addressed by altering the underlying brain activity;
- the most direct way to alter brain activity is neurointervention (psychosurgery); and therefore,
- the most direct way to affect a psychological problem is neurointervention (psychosurgery).

Assuming that altering underlying brain activity is the critical issue in the definition of psychosurgery, there is a problem. Psychotropic treatments such as antidepressants have similar effects. Hippocampal atrophy is a frequent observation in patients with depression.[40] Recovery from depression through antidepressants,[41,42] electroconvulsive therapy,[43] and psychotherapy[44] is associated with reversal of this atrophy. This is likely mediated by the effects of these treatments on the activity of the peptide hormone brain-derived neurotrophic factor (BDNF).[45] It would seem that if one were to take issue with psychosurgery, one must take issue with all forms of psychiatric treatment.

Lobotomy

Following on from the work of Burckhardt, Portuguese psychiatrist Egas Moniz developed the procedure of leucotomy, performing his first procedure in 1918. Despite surviving one attempted murder by an aggrieved former patient, Moniz considered the procedure in general quite helpful. Although Moniz may have been the creator of the modern practice of psychosurgery, and indeed shared the Nobel Prize for medicine in 1949 for this work, the name that is most associated with psychosurgery, in particular lobotomy, is Walter Freeman.

Walter Freeman was born to privilege in Philadelphia. Freeman attended Yale and completed his medical training at University of Pennsylvania Medical School. After graduating, Freeman became head of neurology at George Washington University. Freeman was inspired by Moniz's work, and as he lacked surgical training, he enlisted the assistance of neurosurgeon James Watts. In 1936, Watts and Freeman performed modified lobotomy on 63-year-old Alice Hammat.[46] Hammat had been plagued by depression and suicidal episodes, and despite her lack of actual consent to the procedure, she was restrained and underwent lobotomy in September 1936. Postoperatively, she exhibited apathy and avolition, effectively a frontal lobe syndrome, although in the years before her death in 1941, her family was well pleased by the apparent reduction in her suicidal behavior.

Patricia Moen, an Oregon senior, underwent lobotomy performed by Dr. Freeman in 1962. She recalled being told by Freeman of the procedure, "You can come out a vegetable, or you can come out dead," although added that the operation had the effect of making her "a more free person after I'd had it. Just not to be so concerned about things … I just, I went home and started living, I guess is the best I can say—just started living again."[47]

Freeman's practice grew and he gained national prominence for his lobotomy "cures." One of the more distasteful aspects of Freeman's national profile was his gold-plated leucotome and his driving around the United States in his self-dubbed "lobotomobile."[48] By the time of his retirement in the 1960s, Freeman had performed more than 3,000 lobotomies, claiming benefit in up to 40 percent of cases.[46]

The most confronting aspect of Freeman's practice was his use of the "ice-pick method" of lobotomy. The original procedure for lobotomy utilized burr holes in both frontal bones. An Italian neurosurgeon, Amarro Fiamberti, pioneered a new method of lobotomy using a transorbital approach to the orbito-medial frontal cortex. Apart from reduction of operative trauma to the skull, the benefit of the transorbital approach was that the patient did not require anesthesia and the procedure could be performed outside of operating rooms. Freeman modified Fiamberti's procedure and developed the leucotome, the instrument akin to an ice pick used in the transorbital approach. Freeman's lobotomy patients were given unmodified, unanesthetised ECT prior to the procedure to induce seizure and effectively stun the patient. Following this, Freeman effectively tapped the leucotome into frontal cortex through the patient's lacrimal duct.

Apart from the development of frontal lobe syndromes, lobotomies were complicated by hemorrhage, infection, or stroke. One of Freeman's more famous patients, Rosemary Kennedy—the sister of Senator and later President John F. Kennedy—suffered significant postoperative complications after lobotomy.

While much of this seems grotesque to the lay reader, or even some within mental health professions, it would seem unreasonable to characterise Walter Freeman as an evil figure. Although some parts of his story are at worst ill-savory or crass, Freeman's greatest flaw was that he was clearly self-promoting and ambitious—hardly qualities unique to him. What is clear on closer analysis of Freeman's life and his work was his zeal to remedy the suffering of chronically and severely distressed and disabled patients in asylums or in the community.[49]

The decline in the use of lobotomy followed primarily from the advent of chlorpromazine in the 1950s. Other factors such as the frequency of neurological complications, lack of clarity in the evidence supporting its efficacy, and the association of the procedure with the questionable work of many charlatans also contributed to the rejection of lobotomy.[50] The advent of stereotactic techniques and the elucidation of the role of the limbic system and its functional connections transformed the crude lobotomy practice of psychosurgery to more accurate, effective, and safer procedures.

The contemporary relevance of the debate over psychosurgery, at least in terms of neuroethics, is the issue of equivalence between lobotomy and the current practice of stereotactic procedures, predominantly for obsessive-compulsive disorder[51] and the new therapeutic technique of deep brain stimulation (DBS).

Is Deep Brain Stimulation Latter-Day Psychosurgery?

DBS involves the implantation of a "brain pacemaker" into a region of the brain to stimulate certain structures or neural circuits to achieve a therapeutic benefit.[52] DBS was first approved in the United States for treatment of essential tremor in 1997 and later for Parkinson's disease. More recent work has indicated that continuous stimulation of the subgenual cingulate gyrus (Brodmann Area 25) may produce a significant antidepressant benefit.[53] An open-label study of 21 patients with treatment-resistant depression demonstrated that DBS targeting the subcallosal cingulate gyrus and showed a 40 percent reduction in depressive symptoms in the majority of the study participants.[54]

DBS is clearly distinct from the ice-pick leucotomies of Walter Freeman and his contemporaries. The technological sophistication of DBS places it in closer proximity to stereotactic psychosurgery. Distinguishing DBS from the ethical problems of lobotomy highlights problems in the definition of psychosurgery. If the definition of psychosurgery relates to the physical destruction of brain tissue in order to effect a change in mood or behavior, then DBS is distinct in that it stimulates, rather than destroys, a brain area (this of course allowing for any minor, incidental damage caused by the placement of the hair-width electrodes to Brodmann Area 25). If the definition of psychosurgery is predicated upon the notion of alteration of brain structure or function to achieve an emotional or behavioral change, then this invites comparison with all forms of psychiatric treatment. As Grant Gillett quips:

> Burn, heat, poke, freeze, shock, cut, stimulate or otherwise shake (but not stir) the brain and you will affect the psyche. You may affect it in ways that call to mind language dealing with the soul, and thereby pose questions of identity, responsibility, personality, character, spirit, relationship, integrity, and human flourishing.[39]

Any argument that psychosurgery should be rejected due to the potential for iatrogenic harm is diminished by the alarming evidence of physical illness consequent upon contemporary psychotropic treatment.[3]

As an ethical dilemma, the relationship between DBS and lobotomy has manifest in the Australian state of New South Wales (NSW), where DBS, used for neurological disorders, has been specifically outlawed in the treatment of psychiatric disorders.[55] This would seem an overreaction to the Chelmsford Hospital scandal in the 1980s in Sydney, where numerous patients died from complications of deep sleep therapy implemented by a psychiatrist who had been a strong advocate of psychosurgery.[56] In this instance, it is arguable that the outlawing of DBS was an overreaction to the malfeasance of one psychiatrist. In particular, it would appear that the moral justification of the ban on DBS in NSW is not based on a reasoned comparison with lobotomy, but rather a wholesale rejection of any psychiatric treatment in any way reminiscent of the now discredited lobotomy procedures.

Cosmetic Psychopharmacology

In a 1972 edition of the *Hastings Center Report*[57] an academic debate distinguished "psychotropic hedonism" and "pharmacologic Calvinism." Psychotropic hedonism held the position that medications should relieve all distress. In contrast, the Calvinist view held that psychotropic medications should be restricted to use in severe illness. This debate seems to have occurred well before its time, as the advent of Prozac, and the cultural shift that followed, was more than a decade away.

One of the crucial issues in this area is the distinction between therapy and enhancement.[58,59] As with the Calvinist–hedonist dichotomy, this distinction is between the use of medical science to alleviate pathological states and improving the capabilities of an otherwise well person. The advent of cosmetic neurology arguably sees three general categories: improvement of motor systems, attention, learning, and memory; mood; and affect.[60] The latter two would be most aptly seen as the purview of psychiatry.

Prozac and Beyond

The Food and Drug Administration approved the marketing of fluoxetine (Prozac) in 1987. Prior to its patent expiry in 2001, Prozac was a commercial success for Eli Lilly. Prozac also became a cultural phenomenon, evidenced in the book and later film *Prozac Nation*.[61]

In 1994, Peter Kramer published the book *Listening to Prozac*.[62] This book revisited the Calvinist–hedonist debate, coining the term *cosmetic psychopharmacology*. Before acquiring the celebrity from the book's success, Kramer was a psychiatrist on faculty at Brown University. Kramer was a mood disorder specialist and had a dim view of the trivialization of depression in popular culture, and in particular the apparent misuse of antidepressants.

It is evident that serotonin-boosting antidepressants reduce negative affect and increase levels of affiliative behavior[63] in otherwise normal individuals. They also make humans and primates less submissive in social settings.[64] In addition to their social benefits, serotonergic antidepressants appear to dull emotional distress, even in the absence of actual depression. This phenomenon has been dubbed by the serotonergic antidepressant critic David Healy as "psych-analgesia."[65]

Kramer's core thesis was that using antidepressants to engender an enhanced social and interpersonal self in an otherwise psychologically healthy individual was illegitimate. In a consumer culture, the kind of technology evidenced in antidepressants represented a way of enhancing the self in the "social mirror."[66]

If antidepressants represent both an anodyne and a social leg up, there is one other group of psychotropic agents that add to the picture of cosmetic psychopharmacology.

Cognitive Enhancement

Drugs used to treat hyperactivity disorders have been abused for their euphoriant, alertness, and cognitive benefits by nonaffected people, particularly college students, for many years.[67] In fact, many college students regularly use stimulants such as methylphenidate or atomoxetine for both recreational and academic purposes.[68]

Enhanced cognitive function is also possible through agents used to treat dementia, such as cholinesterase inhibitors. Otherwise healthy pilots performed better on flight simulator tasks when given donepezil, a cholinesterase inhibitor usually used in the treatment of Alzheimer-type dementia.[69] The glutamate neurotransmitter system appears to be critical in new learning, particularly in the hippocampus. Indirect stimulation of glutamatergic neurotransmission through the AMPA receptor is one means of enhancing learning.[70] The antituberculosis drug D-cylcoserine (DCS) is an AMPA-receptor agonist and appears to enhance new learning in patients undergoing cognitive therapy for obsessive-compulsive disorder[71] or social anxiety disorder.[72] In light of this, DCS may enhance new learning in otherwise normal individuals.[73]

There is ample evidence that psychotropic agents enhance social functioning and cognitive performance. This would place these medications in a particular category, akin to anabolic steroids, human growth hormone, or erythropoietin in competitive sports. It is clear that a college student taking a stimulant medication to improve performance in an exam is not akin to an athlete taking digoxin with the expectation of a faster time in the 400 meter foot race. These agents appear to have a social utility, much like caffeine, and this requires a specific consideration of their place in nonclinical settings.

The ethical implications of using antidepressants or cognitive enhancers to assist euthymic and cognitively normal individuals present two contrasting dilemmas. If these drugs do help gain a competitive advantage in business, why should they be considered any different from caffeine or alcohol? If an individual is aware of the risks, why should he or she be denied this opportunity? On the other hand, if the presumed off-label use of these drugs is not subsidized by the health system, is it reasonable to allow one group of better-resourced individuals within a community to have access to these compounds?

From a community perspective, are we better served by having our pilots, train drivers, or police force cognitively enhanced by stimulants or AMPA agonists? It was deemed reasonable to administer the stimulant benzedrine to flight crew in bomber command during World War II.[74] This also raises the dilemma of whether it is reasonable for employers to mandate cosmetic psychopharmacololgy as part of an employment contract or as a means of discrimination among employees.[75]

Cosmetic Psychopharmacology and the Self

The very nature of self is based upon experience. The experience of self is arguably a form of narrative linking a sequence of experiences, interpreted through the prism of temperament, cognitive style, and affective tone. Any measure that alters any of these variables, whether it be psychotherapy or medication, represents a potential means of alteration of the self. This is pronounced in the experience of psychological trauma.

Traumatic stress is a virtual human universal[76] and exerts a profound effect on the experience of the self and the world.[77] While traumatic events such as the Holocaust or the dispossession of indigenous populations from their traditional land may unite or define communities, individual experience of and response to traumatic stress is far more problematic. There is a significant psychopathological burden borne after traumatic stress exposure,[78–80] with tremendous cost to the community. The most recognizable and paradigmatic of consequences of trauma is posttraumatic stress disorder (PTSD). Efforts to prevent the onset of PTSD after traumatic stress, particularly the use of acute intervention strategies such as debriefing, are commonplace.[81]

One of the areas of research in the prevention of PTSD is the use of psychotropic medications to prevent the onset of PTSD. The rationale for this resides in the notion of iconic memory—that the onset of PTSD is based upon the laying down of an iconic, traumatic memory around which the psyche's response builds the symptom complex and characteristic impairments of PTSD.[82,83] In this vein, the amnestic effects of benzodiazepines have been explored as a means of blocking the encoding of traumatic memories after traumatic stress exposure.[84] Administering beta-blockers after traumatic events makes the experience of these events more emotionally neutral, presumably by dampening the sympathetic nervous system response associated with their encoding,[85] and may represent a means of preventing the onset of PTSD.[86]

A multitude of ethical dilemmas are presented by this area. On the one hand, reducing the burden of posttraumatic morbidity may be desirable to both the community and the individual, but are there potential abuses? PTSD has been a highly politicized issue, particularly in the Vietnam War era, when it was a means of discrediting the political views of veterans.[87,88] It has been argued that PTSD is overreported and represents a potential source of abuse of the welfare sector.[87,89,90] Traumatic stress is also a feminist issue, particularly given that the vast majority of trauma survivors are women.[91] In recent times, PTSD has been part of the public policy debate over asylum seekers and social policies toward them.[92,93] The question is begged—are these groups better off if they are administered, *en masse*, beta-blockers or benzodiazepines or whatever other agent is found to impair the encoding of traumatic memories? More relevant, is the suppression or minimization of traumatic memory a potential means of discrediting these groups and their claims for justice or social welfare? As with the notion of employer mandates for cognitive enhancement of certain groups of employees, the mandatory administration of psychotropic medication to suppress traumatic memory may emerge as a public health policy debate, particularly mindful of the cost of PTSD to the community.

A more subtle debate is the implications for the self over such policies. The experience of trauma, as much a dimensional as a categorical phenomenon, is a part of the experience of self. The existential aspects of trauma and its aftermath are profoundly influential in the development of the self, regardless of the implications for the community; social policies that seek to attenuate this would appear to represent the most militant forms of political communitarianism.

Conclusion

While not a domain unique to psychiatry, neuroscience has been profoundly influential on the profession. Many psychiatrists see the neuroscience underpinnings of their craft as both its core and the basis of its future flourishing. This is not without its challenges. Our survey of the field of neuroethics demonstrates that the contextual influences of the ethics of neuroscience raise as many dilemmas as they purports to solve. Areas such as cosmetic psychopharmacology, genetics, and molecular-level understandings of mental illness and its treatment imply a seismic paradigm shift in how psychiatrists practice their craft. If psychiatry evolves into a form of applied neuroscience, the influence of neuroscience progress and its associated quandaries will be profound.

References

1. Presidential Proclamation 6158, July 17, 1990. 1990; http://www.loc.gov/loc/brain/proclaim.html (accessed November 10, 2010).

2. Akil H, Brenner S, Kandel E, et al. The future of psychiatric research: genomes and neural circuits. *Science* 2010;327:1580–1581.

3. Lieberman JA, Stroup TS, McEvoy JP, et al. Effectiveness of antipsychotic drugs in patients with chronic schizophrenia. *New England Journal of Medicine.* 2005;353:1209–1223.

4. Gaynes B, Rush AJ, Trivedi M, et al. A direct comparison of presenting characteristics of depressed outpatients from primary vs. specialty care settings: preliminary findings from the STAR*D clinical trial. *Gen Hosp Psychiatry.* 2005;27:87–96.

5. Levy N, ed. *Neuroethics. Challenges for the 21st Century.* New York: Cambridge University Press; 2007.

6. Illes J. Neuroethics in a new era of neuroimaging. *Am J Neuroradiol.* 2003;24:1739–1741.

7. Borgelt E, Buchman D, Illes J. "This is why you've been suffering": reflections of providers on neuroimaging in mental healthcare. *Journal of Bioethical Inquiry.* 2011;8:15–25.

8. Aristotle. *The Nicomachean Ethics.* Oxford: Oxford University Press; 1998.

9. Libet B. Unconscious cerebral initiative and the role of conscious will in voluntary action. *Behavioral and Brain Sciences.* 1985;8:529–566.

10. Foot P. *The Problem of Abortion and the Doctrine of the Double Effect in Virtues and Vices.* Oxford: Blackwell; 1978.

11. Thomson J. Killing, letting die, and the trolley problem. *The Monist.* 1976;59:204–217.

12. Greene J. The secret joke of Kant's soul. In: Sinnott-Armstrong W, ed. *Moral Psychology—Vol. 3: The Neuroscience of Morality.* Cambridge, MA: MIT Press; 2008:35–79.

13. Gazzaniga M. *The Ethical Brain.* Dartmouth: Dana Press; 2005.

14. Rizzolatti G, Craighero L. The mirror-neuron system. *Annual Review of Neuroscience.* 2004;27:169–192.

15. Cleckley H. *The Mask of Sanity: An Attempt to Reinterpret the So-Called Psychopathic Personality.* St. Louis: Mosby; 1941.

16. Hare R. *Without Conscience: The Disturbing World of Psychopaths among Us.* New York: Pocket Books; 1993.

17. *M'Naghten's case.* 1843; http://www.bailii.org/uk/cases/UKHL/1843/J16.html (accessed November 15, 2007).

18. Yang Y, Raine A. Prefrontal structural and functional brain imaging findings in antisocial, violent, and psychopathic individuals: a meta-analysis. *Psychiatry Res.* 2009;174:81–88.

19. Brown S, Botsis A, Van Praag H. Serotonin and aggression. *Journal of Offender Rehabilitation.* 1994;3–4:27–39.

20. Caspi A, McClay J, Moffitt T, et al. Role of genotype in the cycle of violence in maltreated children. *Science.* 2002;5582:851–854.

21. Kendler KS. Psychiatric genetics: a methodologic critique. *The American Journal of Psychiatry.* 2005;162:3–11.

22. Sadler J. *Values and psychiatric diagnosis.* Oxford: Oxford University Press; 2004.

23. Sadler J. Psychiatric molecular genetics and the ethics of social promises. *Journal of Bioethical Inquiry.* 2011;8:27–34.

24. Caspi A, Moffitt T, Cannon M, et al. Moderation of the effect of adolescent-onset cannabis use on adult psychosis by a functional polymorphism in the catechol-O-methyltransferase gene: longitudinal evidence of a gene X environment interaction. *Biol. Psychiatry.* 2005;57:1117–1127.

25. Lesch K, Bengel D, Heils A, et al. Association of anxiety-related traits with a polymorphism in the serotonin transporter gene regulatory region. *Science.* 1996;274:1527–1531.

26. Caspi A, Sugden K, Moffitt TE, et al. Influence of life stress on depression: moderation by a polymorphism in the 5-HTT gene. *Science.* 2003(301):386–389.

27. Murphy D, Li Q, Engel S, et al. Genetic perspectives on the serotonin transporter. *Brain Research Bulletin.* 2001;56:487–494.

28. Risch N, Herrell R, Lehner T, et al. Interaction between the serotonin transporter gene (5-HTTLPR), stressful life events, and risk of depression: a meta-analysis. *JAMA.* 2009;301:2462–2471.

29. Hu X, Rush A, Charney D, et al. Association between a functional serotonin transporter promoter polymorphism and citalopram treatment in adult outpatients with major depression. *Arch Gen Psychiatry.* 2007;64:783–792.

30. Clague A, Thomas A. Neonatal biochemical screening for disease. *Clin. Chim. Acta.* 2002;315:99–110.

31. Walker F. Huntington's disease. *Lancet.* 2007;369:218–228.

32. Hayden M. Predictive testing for Huntington's disease: a universal model? *Lancet Neurol.* 2003;2:141–142.

33. Thompson D, Easton D. The Breast Cancer Linkage Consortium. Cancer incidence in BRCA1 mutation carriers. *Journal of the National Cancer Institute* 2002;94:1358–1365.

34. Taucher S, Gnant M, Jakesz R. Preventive mastectomy in patients at breast cancer risk due to genetic alterations in the BRCA1 and BRCA2 gene. *Langenbeck's Archives of Surgery.* 2003;388:3–8.

35. Guralnick M. *The Effectiveness of Early Intervention.* Baltimore: Brookes; 1997.

36. Smeraldi E, Zanardi R, Benedetti F, et al. Polymorphism within the promoter of the serotonin transporter gene and antidepressant efficacy of fluvoxamine. *Mol Psychiatry.* 1998;3:508–511.

37. Berrios G. The origins of psychosurgery. *History of Psychiatry.* 1997;8:61–82.

38. Gostin L. Ethical considerations of psychosurgery: the unhappy legacy of the pre-frontal lobotomy. *J Med Ethics.* 1980(6):149–154.

39. Gillett G. The gold-plated leucotomy standard and deep brain stimulation. *Journal of Bioethical Inquiry.* 2011;8:35–44.

40. Warner-Schmidt J, Duman R. Hippocampal neurogenesis: opposing effects of stress and antidepressant treatment. *Hippocampus.* 2006;16:239–249.

41. Russo-Neustadt A, Beard R, Huang Y, et al. Physical activity, and antidepressant treatment potentiate the expression of specific brain-derived neurotrophic factor transcripts in the rat hippocampus. *Neuroscience.* 2000;101:305–312.

42. Drzyzga Ł, Ukasz R, Marcinowska A, Obuchowicz E. Antiapoptotic and neurotrophic effects of antidepressants: a review of clinical and experimental studies. *Brain Research Bulletin.* 2009;79:248–257.

43. Taylor S. Electroconvulsive therapy, brain-derived neurotrophic factor, and possible neurorestorative benefit of the clinical application of electroconvulsive therapy. *The Journal of ECT.* 2008;24:160–165.

44. Martin S, Martin E, Rai S, et al. Brain blood flow changes in depressed patients treated with interpersonal psychotherapy or venlafaxine hydrochloride: preliminary findings. *Arch Gen Psychiatry.* 2001;58:641–648.

45. Binder D, Scharfman H. Brain-derived neurotrophic factor. *Growth Factors.* 2004;22:123–131.

46. Freeman W, Watts J. *Psychosurgery. Intelligence, Emotion and Social Behavior Following Prefrontal Lobotomy for Mental Disorders.* Springfield, IL: Charles C Thomas; 1942.

47. National Public Radio (NPR). Walter Freeman's Lobotomies: Oral Histories; 2005.

48. Rowland L. Walter Freeman's psychosurgery and biological psychiatry: a cautionary tale. *Neurology Today.* 2005;5:70–72.

49. El-Hai J. *The Lobotomist.* Hoboken, NJ: Wiley; 2005.

50. Mashour G, Walker E, Martuza R. Psychosurgery: past, present, and future. *Brain Research Reviews.* 2005;48:409–419.

51. Hodgkiss A, Malizia A, Bartlett R, et al. Outcomes after the psychosurgical operation of stereotactic subcaudate tractotomy. *J. Neuropsychiatry Clin. Neurosci.* 1995;7:230–234.

52. Gildenberg P. Evolution of neuromodulation. *Stereotact Funct Neurosurg.* 2005;83:71–77.

53. Mayberg H, Lozano A, Voon V, et al. Deep brain stimulation for treatment-resistant depression. *Neuron.* 2005;45:651–660.

54. Lozano A, Giacobbe P, Hamani P, et al. A multicenter pilot study of subcallosal cingulate area deep brain stimulation for treatment-resistant depression. *Journal of Neurosurgery.* 2011; Ahead of Print: Pages 1–8.

55. Ministry of Health NSW. Mental Health Act (2007). 2007; http://www.health.nsw.gov.au/policies/ib/2007/ib2007_053.html (accessed January 5, 2012).

56. Bromberger B, Fife-Yeomans J. *Deep Sleep: Harry Bailey and the Sandal of Chelmsford.* East Roseville, NSW: Simon & Schuster; 1991.

57. Klerman G. Psychotropic hedonism vs. pharmacological Calvinism. *Hastings Center Report.* 1972;2:1–3.

58. Wolpe P. Treatment, enhancement, and the ethics of neurotherapeutics. *Brain Cogn.* 2002;50:387–395.

59. Daniels N. Normal functioning and the treatment-enhancement distinction. *Cambridge Quarterly.* 2000;9:309–322.

60. Chatterjee A. Cosmetic neurology: the controversy over enhancing movement, mentation, and mood. *Neurology.* 2004;63:968–974.

61. Wurtzel E. *Prozac Nation.* New York: Penguin; 1994.

62. Kramer P. *Listening to Prozac.* London: Fourth Estate; 1994.

63. Knutson B, Wolkowitz O, Cole S, et al. Selective alteration of personality and social behavior by serotonergic intervention. *Am J Psychiatry.* 1998;155:333–339.

64. Tse W, Bond A. Serotonergic intervention affects both social dominance and affiliative behavior. *Psychopharmacology.* 2002;161:373–379.

65. Healy D. *The Antidepressant Era.* Cambridge, MA: Harvard University Press; 1997.

66. Elliott C. American bioscience meets the American dream. *The American Prospect.* 2003;14:38–42.

67. Teter C, Mc Cabe S, La Grange K, et al. Illicit use of specific prescription stimulants among college students: prevalence, motives, and routes of administration. *Pharmacotherapy.* 2006;26:1501–1510.

68. Babcock Q, Byrne T. Student perceptions of methylphenidate abuse at a public liberal arts college. *J Am College Health.* 2000;49:143–145.

69. Yesavage J, Mumenthaler M, Taylor J, et al. Donepezil and flight simulator performance: effects on retention of complex skills. *Neurology.* 2002;59:123–125.

70. Newcomer J, Krystal J. NMDA receptor regulation of memory and behavior in humans. *Hippocampus* 2001;11:529–542.

71. Kushner M, Kim S, Donahue C, et al. D-cycloserine augmented exposure therapy for obsessive-compulsive disorder. *Biol Psychiatry.* 2007;62:835–838.

72. Hofmann S, Meuret A, Smits J, et al. Augmentation of exposure therapy with D-cycloserine for social anxiety disorder. *Arch Gen Psychiatry.* 2006;63:298–304.

73. Davis M, Ressler K, Rothbaum B, et al. Effects of D-cycloserine on extinction: translation from preclinical to clinical work. *Biol Psychiatry.* 2006;60:369–375.

74. Rasmussen N. *On Speed: The Many Lives of Amphetamine.* New York: New York University Press; 2008.

75. Appel J. When the boss turns pusher: a proposal for employee protections in the age of cosmetic neurology. *J Med Ethics.* 2008;34:616–618.

76. McFarlane A, van der Kolk B. Trauma and its challenge to society. In: van der Kolk B, McFarlane A, Weisath L, eds. *Traumatic Stress.* New York: Guilford; 1996:24–46.

77. Janoff-Bulman R. *Shattered Assumptions: Towards a New Psychology of Trauma.* New York: Free Press; 1992.

78. Breslau N, Davis GC, Andreski P, et al. Traumatic events and posttraumatic stress disorder in an urban population of young adults.. *Archives of General Psychiatry.* 1991;48:216–222.

79. Cunningham M, Cunningham J. Patterns of symptomology and patterns of torture and trauma experiences in resettled refugees. *Australian and New Zealand Journal of Psychiatry.* 1997;31:555–565.

80. Galea S, Nandi A, Vlahov D. The epidemiology of post-traumatic stress disorder after disasters. *Epidemiological Reviews.* 2005;27:78–91.

81. Rose S, Bisson J, Wessely S. Psychological debriefing for preventing post traumatic stress disorder (PTSD) (Cochrane Review). *The Cochrane Library*, issue 4 (accessed January 17, 2007) 2001.

82. Young A. *The Harmony of Illusions: Inventing Post-Traumatic Stress Disorder.* Princeton: Princeton University Press; 1995.

83. Young A. When traumatic memory was a problem: On the historical antecedents of PTSD. In: Rosen G, ed. *Posttraumatic Stress Disorder: Issues and Controversies.* Chichester: John Wiley and Sons; 2004:127–146.

84. Mellman T, Bustamante V, David D, et al. Hypnotic medication in the aftermath of trauma. *Journal of Clinical Psychiatry.* 2002;63:1183–1184.

85. Cahill L, Prins B, Weber M, et al. Beta-adrenergic activation and memory for emotional events. *Nature.* 1994;371:702–704.

86. Pitman R, Sanders K, Zusman R, et al. Pilot study of secondary prevention of posttraumatic stress disorder with propranolol. *Biol Psychiatry.* 2002;51:189–192.

87. Burkett B, Whitley G. *Stolen Valor: How the Vietnam Generation Was Robbed of Its Heroes and Its History.* Dallas: Verity Press; 1998.

88. Shepherd. *A War of Nerves: Soldiers and Psychiatrists 1914–1994.* London: Pimlico; 2002.

89. Dohrenwend B, Turner J, Turse N, et al. The psychological risks of Vietnam for U.S. veterans: a revisit with new data and methods. *Science.* 2006;18:979–982.

90. Frueh B, Gold P, de Arellano M. Symptom overreporting in combat veterans evaluated for PTSD: differentiation on the basis of compensation seeking status. *Journal of Personality Assessment.* 1997;68:369–384.

91. Herman J. *Trauma and Recovery.* New York: Basic Books; 1992.

92. Iversen V, Morken G. Differences in acute psychiatric admissions between asylum seekers and refugees. *Nordic Journal of Psychiatry.* 2004;58:465–470.

93. Steel Z, Silove D. The mental health implications of detaining asylum seekers. *Medical Journal of Australia.* 2001;175:596–599.

Dr. Irmfried Eberl, the Aktion T4 psychiatrist who became the commandant of the Treblinka Death camp. Eberl committed suicide prior to facing trial for his crimes. (Picture courtesy of the Holocaust Education and Archive Research Team, http://www.holocaustresearchproject.org.)

Smoke billowing from the crematorium of the Hadamar euthanasia center in Hesse, Germany. More that 70,000 patients were murdered by the psychiatrists in Aktion T4. (Picture courtesy of the Holocaust Education and Archive Research Team, http://www.holocaustresearchproject.org.)

Aktion T4 staff unwinding off-duty from their euthanasia "duties" at Hadamar euthanasia center. (Picture courtesy of the Holocaust Education and Archive Research Team, http://www.holocaustresearchproject. org.)

Adolf Eichmann on trial in Israel in 1961. Eichmann, the architect of the "Final Solution," lived incognito in Argentina until his capture by Israeli agents in 1961. Eichmann's trial was observed by the philosopher Hannah Arendt, whose observation of the "banality of evil" is one of the most famous phrases in moral philosophy. (Picture courtesy of the Israeli National Photo Collection.)

Frantz Fanon, a Martinique-born psychiatrist whose clinical and revolutionary activities in Algeria have become the focus of intense study by scholars of post-colonial societies. Fanon's ideas, particularly those in *The Wretched of the Earth*, provide insights into the use of psychiatry as an exercise of oppressive power by colonial rulers. (Picture courtesy of Pacha J. Wilka.)

Friedrich von Hayek, along with Milton Friedman, is the main figure in the economic philosophy of neoliberalism, the tenets of which have dominated economics in post-industrial societies. (Picture courtesy of LSE Library.)

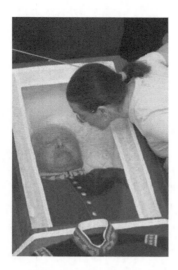

Augusto Pinochet lying in state. Pinochet led the 1973 coup in Chile, which saw the murder and torture of thousands of civilians and the imposition of free market ideas on the Chilean economy. Despite his complicity in crimes against humanity, Pinochet remained a polarizing figure by the time of his death in 2006. (Photo courtesy of En Todos Lados.)

The Serbsky Institute in Moscow. Now a secure psychiatric hospital in suburban Moscow, the Serbsky Institute was infamous as a site of imprisonment of political dissidents deemed "insane." (Picture courtesy of Michael Robertson.)

Senator Barry Goldwater, the hawkish Republican senator from Arizona, was the GOP nominee in the 1964 presidential election. Goldwater was defamed by a magazine article that quoted a number of psychiatrists who deemed him unsuitable to be president. Following the successful defamation case, the American Psychiatric Association evolved the Goldwater Rule, restraining psychiatric commentary in the popular media. (Photo courtesy of the United States Library of Congress.)

Bette Davis (Jane) and Joan Crawford (Blanche) in the 1962 Hollywood film *Whatever Happened to Baby Jane?* The depiction of madness in cinema, particularly in Hollywood films, has tended to depict mentally ill women as disturbing, often predatory characters. (From Warner Home Video.)

The Escuela de Suboficiales de Mecánica de la Armada (ESMA) or "Naval School" where many of the victims of the Dirty War were tortured and killed by the Argentine Junta. (From Wikimedia Commons.)

The town of Chillenden in Kent, England. In July 1996 the murder of Lin and Megan Russell by Michael Stone prompted the debate over the management of people with severe and dangerous personality disorders by psychiatrists. (Photo courtesy of Nick Smith via Wikimedia Commons.)

Falun Gong practitioners have been subject to persecution by Chinese authorities. Some Chinese psychiatrists have been implicated in Soviet-era style abuses of power relating to the practice of the *qigong*. (Photo courtesy of 明慧分类资料网.)

An asylum seeker protesting the conditions of his detention in the Villawood Immigration Center in Sydney. Australian psychiatrists have been advocates for the rights of asylum seekers despite the popular policy of mandatory detention of "unauthorized arrivals." (Photo courtesy of Adam JWC.)

Section III

Psychiatric Ethics

10

Reappraisals

Introduction

Throughout this book, we have argued that most dilemmas in psychiatric ethics are best conceptualized as manifestations of the dual-role dilemma. The essence of this dilemma is that the psychiatrist as moral agent acts within a tension between different, often competing expectations. This conceptualization of ethical dilemmas in psychiatry allows ready application of our reflective and deliberative phases of moral agency prior to elaborating a mean between the extremes.

In this chapter, we will apply the prism of the dual-role dilemma to some of the main themes addressed in the literature in psychiatric ethics, where we have not considered these elsewhere, e.g., involuntary psychiatric treatment in Chapter 5. Ethical dilemmas in psychiatry are regularly addressed by the approach of *quandary ethics*,[1] in which morally acceptable resolutions are sought to clear up problematic clinical situations. Virtually all of the quandaries psychiatrists face in their professional conduct relate to the potential for conflicting obligations toward an individual patient's interests and those of another party or group, usually an institution or the community.

Forensic Psychiatry and the Dual Role

The dual-role dilemma emerged within the ethical discourses of forensic psychiatry,[2-6] in which the obligation to serve the interests of justice comes into conflict with the Hippocratic principle of *primum non nocere*.[7] In this context, the dual role posits that there is a *prima facie* conflict between the duties of the psychiatrist as either treater or evaluator. This debate was explored in two classic papers in the psychiatric ethics literature. In the "The Ethics of Forensic Psychiatry: A View from the Ivory Tower,"[8] Harvard professor of psychiatry Alan Stone argued that the role of evaluator moved the forensic psychiatrist away from the role of physician and the fundamental notion of nonmaleficence. Taking a contrary view, Paul Appelbaum, then professor of psychiatry at the University of Massachusetts, argued in "The Parable of the Forensic Psychiatrist: Ethics and the Problem of Doing Harm"[9] that beneficence and nonmaleficence are not central ethical issues in forensic psychiatry. Consequently, Appelbaum suggested that forensic psychiatry has a distinct set of ethics. Indeed, a distinction can arguably be made between forensic psychiatry and clinical psychiatry in the notion of what English psychiatrists Sameer Sarkar and Gwen Adshead termed a "forensicist."[10] The ethics of the forensicist are directed toward the benefit of society, not the patient, and therefore the central responsibility of the forensicist is to justice, not the patient.[11]

In minor criminal or civil matters, this issue may seem comparatively benign compared with the role of psychiatrists in the administration of the death penalty. It has been argued that psychiatrists should not participate in any assessment process that may ultimately lead to execution.[12] An opposing stance is that the consequences, rendered by the state, of a psychiatric assessment cannot be the basis of consideration whether such assessments are ethical.[13] In other words, no distinction should be drawn between a psychiatric assessment that facilitates a financial penalty (or benefit), a custodial sentence, or the death penalty.

These dilemmas seem to be more relevant to the practice of psychiatry in the United States, where forensic psychiatry has a particular profile in relation to justice. In the British context, the "evaluator–treater" manifestation of the dual-role dilemma has historically been absent.[14] The ethical dilemmas faced by British forensic psychiatrists have been more related to their advocacy role in the clinical care of mentally disordered offenders[15] and political pressures impacting on the welfare of their patients.[16]

Beyond the criminal setting, the psychiatric evaluation of prospective employees raises another potential dual-role dilemma.[17] In either identifying possible risk factors for vocationally acquired psychiatric disorder or diagnosing established mental illness or personality disorder, the psychiatrist is using his or her skills for the benefit of the prospective employer or worker's compensation insurer, rather than the patient. Moreover, such psychiatric evaluations will potentially disadvantage the individual socially or financially, thus having a potentially harmful effect.

Psychotherapy and the Dual Role

Since the advent of neoliberalism as an influence in psychiatric practice, one particular theme in the psychotherapy ethics literature relates to the impact of market forces on the practice of psychotherapy. This has largely placed the psychiatrist in the dual role—advocating the best treatment for the patient versus exercising financial responsibility for the benefit of an organization, health insurer, or even the public purse.[18] As the English psychiatrist Jeremy Holmes asked, "is it ethically correct to [only] prescribe the most cost-effective [psychotherapies], thereby freeing resources for other potential beneficiaries" (p. 227)?[19] The intrusion of third-party payers, into the patient–therapist relationship has created new ethical dilemmas. These include breaches of patient confidentiality to financial stakeholders, or the use (or avoidance) of certain psychiatric diagnoses to attract insurance benefits on behalf of the patient—an issue that has appeared a number of times in this book.

Another, more subtle manifestation of the dual-role dilemma in psychotherapy relates to the notion of psychotherapy representing the imposition of certain values onto the patient. It has been argued that in creating the "talking cure," Freud had attempted to convert moral discourse to a scientific one.[20] As such, psychotherapy has been described as a masked form of moral discourse, with allusions to a quasireligious conception of the good,[21] "veering," as British psychoanalyst Bob Hinshelwood argues, "between being a scientific and a moral activity" (p. 195).[22] Indeed, psychotherapy has been conceptualized as the integration of a nonreligious but spiritual view in the pursuit of empathic understanding.[23] Moreover, psychotherapy often works best when the value systems of both patient and therapist approximate each other but do not necessarily converge.[21] As Jeremy Holmes has argued, through its advocacy for the inner world and self-reflection, "psychotherapy reflects and transmits the values of the prevailing culture" and "makes its own unique contribution to cultural and ethical development within our pluralistic societies" (p. 226).[24] By liberating patients from their suffering, psychotherapy can be considered as enabling patients to become moral agents[25] and enhancing autonomy by encouraging self-knowledge.[19] This necessitates an injunction for therapists to deliberate on how their own values affect their work,[24] but there is also a potential to see this area as a manifestation of the dual-role dilemma. Put simply, one view of the psychotherapeutic enterprise is that it represents a process of bringing the patient around to a worldview consistent with his or her fellow citizens. Whether this is via dialectic behavior therapy leading patients to experience their distress in less socially disruptive ways, or the radical reconstruction of the self into a more functional citizen, there is, perhaps, a tension between pseudosocial engineering and beneficence for the patient. In the disastrous circumstance of a colleague committing a serious boundary violation with a patient, the dual role manifests in the duty to the patient involved and the community balanced against the duty to the care and possible rehabilitation of a colleague in addition to the imperative to maintain the integrity of the profession.

Child Psychiatry and the Dual Role

Childhood is a recent social construction.[26] The conceptualization of childhood within the context of psychiatric ethics relates fundamentally to the distinction between children and competent adults as autonomous, self-legislating people. The idea of evolving or future autonomy of the child has existed both in terms of their cognitive development and the therapeutic setting.[27] Some of the literature in ethics and child psychiatry has considered the viability of the construct of informed consent in childhood and how this should reflect the wishes of the child.[28,29] Ultimately, the therapeutic relationship in child psychiatry is unique in that it frequently casts the therapist in the role of *de facto* parent or authority figure as well as that of advocate for the child.[30] There are parallels between the undeveloped autonomy of the child and the variably impaired autonomy of any psychiatric patient, the difference being the interests or desires of others, such as parents or social institutions, with significant influence over the child patient's situation. In some circumstances, such as enforced removal of a child from a family, the wishes of the child and his or her family may clash with a social institution's child protection interests. It is also clear that mentally ill children are potentially much more vulnerable than mentally ill adults. The tension is thus between a duty to a patient with variable capacity for autonomous choice and a duty to beneficence, which might be against the wishes of the child or his or her family. Moreover, there may be situations where the psychiatrist's position in support of parental wishes is at odds with that of the child. This comes to the fore in circumstances where there is a clinical indication for physical treatments such as medication, or rarely, ECT.

Confidentiality and the Dual Role

More than in any other field of medicine, confidentiality is instrumental to the therapeutic relationship in psychiatry.[31,32] Regardless of its clinical necessity, the maintenance of patient confidentiality has been the subject of much discussion, in light of both necessary breaches of confidence and also the potential implications for the extension of the therapeutic obligations of psychiatrists beyond the individual therapeutic relationship.[33] Indeed, as two professors of psychiatric ethics, Stephen Green and Sid Bloch, have argued, "Confidentiality can never be absolute, and therein lies its ethical intricacy" (p. 154). [34]

Prosenjit Poddar was a Bengali student who commenced postgraduate studies at the University of California–Berkeley in 1968. Poddar met Tatiana Tarasoff, a Brazilian-born student, at folk dancing classes at the International House on the campus. They had a friendly but not amorous acquaintance throughout 1968 until New Year's Eve. Tarasoff kissed Poddar as an innocent gesture at a party. In India, Poddar was of the "untouchable" caste, and so it is likely that Tarasoff's kindness had added significance. Poddar thus interpreted the kiss as a sign that Tarasoff sought a relationship. When Tarasoff indicated that this was not the case, he developed a depressive illness, which led him to evolve malevolent intent toward her.

Poddar sought counseling with a student health psychologist, Lawrence Moore. In the summer of 1969, Poddar communicated to Moore his intent to kill Tarasoff when she returned from Brazil following the summer break. Moore informed the campus police, who questioned Poddar about his statements. Poddar seems to have backpedaled, and the campus police took no further action. Following this, the staff at campus health were instructed by their clinical director to desist at attempts to force Poddar to be hospitalized. Presumably aggrieved by the breach of confidence, Poddar defaulted on therapy and his mental state deteriorated. On October 27, 1969, Poddar went to Tarasoff's home and stabbed her fatally with a kitchen knife. Poddar then notified police. Poddar was convicted of manslaughter and served 4 years in prison, although a court of appeal ordered a retrial on a technicality. Poddar agreed to leave the United States and avoid facing court. He subsequently married and now lives in India.

The now infamous "Tarasoff Case"[35] provides a canonical event in the discourse over confidentiality in psychiatry and the so-called duty to inform. The California supreme court heard the case twice, in 1974 and 1976. In the first hearing the court ruled that the campus police at Berkeley were liable for the wrongful death. This was not upheld in the subsequent hearing. In contrast, Moore was held liable because of the "special relation that arises between a patient and his doctor or psychotherapist." Despite various arguments that the predictive validity of psychiatric assessments of risk was low and there would be excessive amounts of inappropriate warnings of danger, the court concluded that a reasonable assessment of dangerousness warranted the need to take necessary measures, such as a duty to inform the prospective victim.

While the implementation of this Californian legal ruling has been variable across jurisdictions,[36] the ethical issues raised in the case have formed the basis of much ethical reasoning in this area[5] and have presented another clear manifestation of the dual-role dilemma.[37] In essence, there is a tension between the duty to manage the risk a patient poses to others through a breach of confidence and the role of therapeutic intervention. As with many ethical dilemmas in psychiatry, laws asserting statutory obligations to breach confidence, such as in the case of children at risk, have trumped the *prima facie* conflict within the dual role by effectively eliminating the obligations of one of the roles in tension with the other.

Psychiatric Research and Publication and the Dual Role

Concerns about the ethics of psychiatric research emerged following the revelations of human rights abuses in the Nazi era,[38] resulting in international declarations of ethical guidelines for research, such as the Declaration of Helsinki,[39] and the requirements of ethical approval of studies as part of the process of scientific publishing.[40] The main theme in this area has been a tension between the duty to protect vulnerable individuals and the duty to advance scientific knowledge. Issues of informed consent and competence to participate in psychiatric research[41,42] have tended to be the focus of the literature in the area. Clinical trials involving psychotropic medications are problematic given the enforced nature of much psychiatric treatment, particularly in the chronic mentally ill.[43] The use of children as subjects in psychiatric research has been discussed in similar terms.[44–46]

As a manifestation of the dual-role dilemma, the conflicting roles are between psychiatrist as advocate for the patient, whose potential for exploitation in clinical trials presents a concern, and psychiatrist as scientist, whose quest for knowledge may benefit the rest of the community.

Psychiatry of Old Age and the Dual Role

The core issue in ethics relating to the psychiatric care of older people has surrounded the nuances of managing permanent cognitive impairment arising from dementing illness. These have been traditionally assessed as concerns about patient competence and testamentary capacity, particularly in regard to financial estates and decisions about the patient's healthcare.[47] This discussion has extended to cognitively impaired patients' right to refuse disclosure diagnosis of dementia to themselves,[48] highlighting the complexity of breaching confidentiality in this clinical setting.[49] In each of these circumstances, the wishes of the patient and the wishes of the patient's family are at times in conflict, placing the psychiatrist in a dual-role quandary relating to the differing expectations of the patient and the family.

As with other areas in psychiatric ethics, autonomy has required its consideration as a dimensional rather than categorical process. One particular approach has been the use of *precedent autonomy*, in which proxy decisions are made on behalf of the patient based upon the patient's attitudes to life prior to the onset of dementia.[50] This and other forms of surrogate decision making in the face of cognitive impairment have been explored in detail elsewhere.[51] One particular approach to this process is the notion of the *situated embodied agent* view of people. This argues that the embodiment of the person links him or her with his or her culture and history, assisting his or her carers to estimate decisions on behalf of the person that assist in the notion of integrity with his or her life's philosophy.[52] Related to this area is the consideration of advance directives, or so-called "Ulysses contracts", made by older patients. Considerable efforts have been made to develop models of such decisions that are contextualized to the individual person.[52,53] Such approaches need to distinguish a patient's critical interests (higher-order aspects of one's life such as dignity and autonomy) and his or her experiential interests (those that bring stimulation and pleasure).[54] In addressing this, the psychiatrist faces a dual-role dilemma that virtually has a metaphysical dimension. In a sense, the psychiatrist may be compelled to act against the wishes of a patient with an advanced state of dementia to protect the interests of the nondemented person who expressed these prior to the onset of dementing illness.

Up to 25 percent of vulnerable older adults report abuse in the previous month, which equates with 6 percent of the general elderly population being subject to such treatment.[55] This problem has been dubbed "elder abuse." Despite these alarming statistics, very few cases of elder abuse are reported.[56] Elder abuse represents instances of harmful actions or omissions of actions occurring within any relationship involving older people where there is an expectation of trust. The problem is therefore one of the violation of trust on the part of carers of older people. As with the injunctions arising from Tarasoff, some jurisdictions have mandatory requirements to report elder abuse. Akin to the dilemma of a child at risk, there is a tension between breaching the patient's confidentiality and the clinician's obligation to beneficence.[57]

A growing problem in the psychiatry of old age is the use of psychotropic drugs in the care of patients in nursing homes suffering from dementia. Australian figures indicate that 47.2 percent of nursing home residents were being administered one or more psychotropic drugs regularly, with 3.5 percent given such medications *pro re nata*.[58] While many jurisdictions have guidelines relating to obtaining consent for such measures, a UK study highlighted that up to 15 percent of nursing home residents were not capable of consenting to either being in a nursing home or taking medications. This study showed that up to 6 percent of these patients were given psychotropic medications without consent.[59] The issue is made more problematic by the recent concerns that the efficacy of newer antipsychotic medications in behavioral disturbances arising from dementia is disputed, and more alarmingly, these medications appear to be associated with an increased risk of stroke or other cardiovascular complications.[60] The psychiatrist working in the field of psychiatry of old age is frequently confronted with the familiar dual role of the expectations and needs of the institution, fellow residents, and family as opposed to the best interests of the patient.

General Hospital Psychiatry and the Dual-Role Dilemma

One of the fundamental features of the role of a general hospital or consultation-liaison (C-L) psychiatrist is the ambiguous nature of the relationship with the patient. C-L consults are frequently sought by the treating team and not the patient, which creates a fundamentally social role in C-L psychiatry.[61] This social role focuses on the relationship between primary physician or nonmedical health professionals and consultant psychiatrist who works within an institutional setting.

A frequent pretext of the involvement of a C-L psychiatrist is to provide an intervention at the level of the system, such as where there is a problematic relationship between a difficult patient and a medical team. In such circumstances, the C-L psychiatrist is expected to be "all things to all people."[62] Indeed, it has been argued elsewhere that by virtue of its broad perspective, C-L psychiatry has a credible role providing ethical guidance in difficult clinical situations.[63,64] Such circumstances create a tension between the expectations of the patient and those of the referring physician or indeed the institution itself. In some instances, it has been argued that some interventions of the C-L psychiatrist are directed at the staff, rather than the patient, creating a "bipolarity of practice."[65] Interventions such as a reframing of a patient's challenging behavior on a medical ward serve to improve the functioning of the therapeutic relationship between the patient and other health professionals by engendering an attitudinal shift in the staff on a medical ward. This often makes use of what has been described as a "situational diagnosis,"[66] in which a diagnostic statement, integrating multiple perspectives of a situation regarding a patient, is made to help resolve a therapeutic impasse on a medical ward. An example is the frequent use of the diagnosis of *adjustment disorder* in C-L settings, in which the emphasis on the overwhelming stressor of a physical health crisis removes the focus from the patient's more difficult interpersonal behaviors.

C-L psychiatrists often encounter broader dilemmas in medical ethics in their liaison roles within medical units. C-L psychiatrists routinely assess patients for their suitability for transplantation. A particularly contentious instance of this is the assessment of patients for liver transplants, particularly following paracetamol (acetaminophen) overdose. This is a vexed area, as this frequently represents an end-of-life decision given the fulminant nature of paracetamol-induced hepatotoxicity. Herein lies the tension between the needs of a gravely ill patient and the limited resources available to a transplant service. While such evaluations are not the ultimate arbiter of the allocation of transplant resources, they are highly influential.

In other circumstances, C-L psychiatrists sometimes find themselves in the midst of controversial clinical situations such as the procurement of late-term termination of pregnancy. In these settings, the C-L psychiatrist is asked for a clinical opinion on the prospective psychological effects of the procedure's occurring or not. While this information is not, of itself, ethical, it may be highly influential in the final clinical decision. As such, psychiatric opinions require careful reflection upon the potential influences on their formation, including pressures on the part of the patient or other clinicians to obtain a speculative statement of psychological impact, which will facilitate a particular decision. Mindful of the socially constructed nature of moral agency, such decisions are influenced by personal and community values.

Discussion: Reappraisals

In each domain where the dual-role dilemma occurs, the psychiatrist finds him- or herself the servant of two masters—the patient and a third party. This third party—whether it be the courts, the family, employers, or society—is usually in a position of power over the patient. With the exception of some aspects of the literature in forensic psychiatry, the dual-role predicament, in its many faces, produces tension within the individual psychiatrist or the psychiatric profession.

Despite controversy about the current relevance of the Hippocratic tradition in medical ethics, there is still a fundamental obligation to the best interests of the patient. As this survey of the literature has indicated, the dual-role dilemma is protean in nature and represents a set of implied obligations outside the therapeutic relationship. It is clear that society endows the profession of psychiatry with powers beyond most other professional groups. Powers such as detention in secure hospitals, enforced treatment with psychotropic medication, and professional opinions that are highly influential in the justice system appear to come at the cost of serving society's interests over the patient's. While this notion segues into narratives of psychiatry as an agency of social control, the fact remains that the dual-role dilemma appears to arise out of the powers given to psychiatry. As discussed elsewhere, professional ethics in relation to psychiatry refer to the application of skills and knowledge for the collective good.[67] In light of our review, this frequently puts the patient's interests or preferences at odds with those of the rest of society.

In this context, the dual-role dilemma can be seen as reflecting the social constitution of the psychiatrist as moral agent. In other words, the ethical quandaries of psychiatry, and the values psychiatrists bring to these, integrate social and cultural issues as much as clinical ones.

Implicit here is the view that there is a moral equivalence between psychiatrists serving the collective good and serving the good of the patient. While this view may be uncontested in liberal democracies, this has only been a recent state of affairs. History is sadly replete with instances of psychiatrists exerting their socially apportioned powers for malfeasant ends in societies whose values were clearly in violation of any notion of human rights. The dual-role dilemma in Hitler's Germany or the Soviet Union is, ostensibly, a different proposition from the present-day liberal West. Given the ubiquity of the dual-role dilemma, the creeping influence of communitarianism, and the drift of societies away from civil rights in the post-9/11 geopolitical setting, this assumption requires regular reflection.

References

1. Pincoffs E. Quandary ethics. *Mind.* 1971;75:552–571.

2. Verdun-Jones SN. Forensic psychiatry, ethics and protective sentencing: what are the limits of psychiatric participation in the criminal justice process? *Acta Psychiatrica Scandinavica.* 2000;101(399):77–82.

3. Callahan D, Gaylin W. The psychiatrist as double agent. *Hastings Center Report.* 1974;4:12–14.

4. Strasburger L, Guthiel T, Brodsky A. On wearing two hats: role conflict in serving as both psychotherapist and expert witness. *American Journal of Psychiatry.* 1997;154:448–456.

5. Miller R. Ethical issues involved in the dual role of treater and evaluator. In: Rosner R, Weinstock R, eds. *Ethical Practice in Psychiatry and the Law.* New York: Plenum Press; 1990:129–150.

6. In the service of the state: the psychiatrist as double agent. *Hastings Center Report, Special Supplement.* April 1978:S1–23.

7. Guthiel T. *The Psychiatric Expert Witness.* Washington DC: American Psychiatric Press; 1998.

8. Stone A. The ethics of forensic psychiatry: a view from the ivory tower. *Law, Psychiatry and Morality.* Washington DC: American Psychiatric Press; 1984:57–75.

9. Appelbaum P. The parable of the forensic psychiatrist: ethics and the problem of doing harm. *International Journal of Law and Psychiatry.* 1990;13:249–259.

10. Sarkar S, Adshead G. Ethics in forensic psychiatry. *Current Opinion in Psychiatry.* 2002;15(5):527–531.

11. Appelbaum P. A theory of ethics in forensic psychiatry. *Journal of the American Academy of Psychiatry and the Law.* 1997;25:233–247.

12. Freedman A, Halpern A. Forum: Psychiatrists and the death penalty: some ethical dilemmas. A crisis in the ethical and moral behaviours of psychiatrists. *Current Opinion in Psychiatry.* 1998;11:1–2.

13. Bonnie R. Forum: Psychiatrists and the death penalty: some ethical dilemmas. A crisis in the ethical and moral behaviours of psychiatrists. Comments. *Current Opinion in Psychiatry.* 1998;11:5–7.

14. Gunn J. Future directions for treatment in forensic psychiatry. *British Journal of Psychiatry.* 2000;176:332–338.

15. Taylor P. Readings in forensic psychiatry. *British Medical Journal.* 1988;153:271–278.

16. Welsh S, Deahl M. Modern psychiatric ethics. *The Lancet.* 2002;359:253–255.

17. McCallum R. Ethics in occupational health. In: Gillon R, ed. *Priniciples of Health Care Ethics.* Chichester: John Wiley and Sons; 2004:933–945.

18. Choddoff P. The effect of third-party payment on the practice of psychotherapy. *American Journal of Psychiatry.* 1972;129:540–545.

19. Holmes J. Ethical aspects of the psychotherapies. In: Bloch S, Green S, Chodoff P, eds. *Psychiatric Ethics.* New York: Oxford University Press; 1999:225–243.

20. Reiff P. *Freud: The Mind of the Moralist.* Chicago: University of Chicago Press; 1959.

21. Bergin A. Psychotherapy and religious values. *Journal of Consulting and Clinical Psychology.* 1980;48:95–105.

22. Hinshelwood R. *Therapy or Coercion? Does Psychoanalysis Differ from Brainwashing?* London: Karnac; 1997.

23. Lomax J, Karff R, McKenny G. Ethical considerations in the integration of religion and psychotherapy: three perspectives. *Psychiatric Clinics of North America.* 2002;25(3):547–559.

24. Holmes J. Values in psychotherapy. *American Journal of Psychotherapy.* 1996;50:259–273.

25. Engelhardt H. Psychotherapy as meta-ethics. *Psychiatry.* 1973;36:440–445.

26. Green S, Bloch S. Special clinical populations. In: Green S, Bloch S, eds. *An Anthology of Psychiatric Ethics.* Oxford: Oxford University Press; 2006:282–289.

27. Green J, Stewart A. Ethical issues in child and adolescent psychiatry. *Journal of Medical Ethics.* 1987;13:5–11.

28. Dickenson D, Jones D. The philosophy and developmental psychology of children's informed consent. *Psychiatry, Psychology and Philosophy.* 1995;2:287–303.

29. Pearce J. Consent to treatment during childhood. *British Journal of Psychiatry.* 1994;165:713–716.

30. Koocher G. Ethical issues in psychotherapy with adolescents. *Journal of Clinical Psychology.* 2003;59:1247–1256.

31. Gabbard G. Disguise or consent. *International Journal of Psychoanalysis.* 2000;81:1071–1086.

32. Bok S. *Secrets.* Oxford: Oxford University Press; 1996.

33. Wexler D. Patients, therapist, and third parties: the victimological virtues of Tarasoff. *International Journal of Law and Psychiatry.* 1979;2:1–28.

34. Green S, Bloch S. Confidentiality. In: Green S, Bloch S, eds. *An Anthology of Psychiatric Ethics.* Oxford: Oxford University Press; 2006:151–155.

35. Lazarus J, Pollack D. Ethical aspects of public sector managed care. In: Minkoff K, Pollack D, eds. *Managed mental health care in the public sector: a survival manual.* Amsterdam: Harwood Academic Publishers; 1997.

36. Anfang S, Appelbaum P. Twenty years after Tarasoff: reviewing duty to protect. *Harvard Review of Psychiatry.* 1996;4:67–76.

37. Guerwitz H. Tarasoff: protective privilege versus public peril. *American Journal of Psychiatry.* 1977;134:289–292.

38. Lifton R. *The Nazi Doctors*. New York: Basic Books; 1986.

39. The Declaration of Helsinki. *British Medical Journal*. 1996;313:1448–1449.

40. Walter G, Bloch S. Publishing ethics in psychiatry. *Australian and New Zealand Journal of Psychiatry* 2001;35:28–35.

41. Roberts L, Roberts B. Psychiatric research ethics: an overview of evolving guidelines and current ethical dilemmas in the study of mental illness. *Biological Psychiatry*. 1999;46(8):1025–1038.

42. Wing J. Ethics and psychiatric research. In: Bloch S, Chodoff P, Green S, eds. *Psychiatric Ethics*. New York: Oxford University Press; 1999:461–478.

43. Roberts L. Evidence-based ethics and informed consent in mental illness research. *Archives of General Psychiatry*. 2000;57(6):533–538.

44. Munir K, Earls F. Ethical priniciples governing research in child and adolescent psychiatry. *Journal of the American Academy of Child and Adolescent Psychiatry*. 1992;31:408–414.

45. Roberts L. Ethics and mental health research. *Psychiatric Clinics of North America*. 2002;25(3):525–545.

46. Fisher C. Reporting and referring research participants: ethical challenges for investigators studying children and youth. *Ethics & Behaviour*. 1994;4:87–95.

47. Jacoby R, Bergmann K. Testamentary capacity. In: Jacoby R, Oppenheimer C, eds. *Psychiatry in the Elderly. 2nd edition*. Oxford: Oxford University Press; 1997.

48. Marzanski M. On telling the truth to patients with dementia. *West J Med*. Nov 2000;173(5):318–323.

49. Hughes JC, Louw SJ. Confidentiality and cognitive impairment: professional and philosophical ethics. *Age Ageing*. Mar 2002;31(2):147–150.

50. Dworkin R. Autonomy and the demented self. *Millbank Quarterly*. 1986;64:4–16.

51. Buchanan A, Brock D. *Deciding for Others: The Ethics of Surrogate Decision Making*. Cambridge, MA: Cambridge University Press; 1989.

52. Hughes J. Views of the person with dementia. *Journal of Medical Ethics*. 2001;27:86–91.

53. Halpern A, Szmukler G. Psychiatric advance directives: reconciling autonomy and non-consensual treatment. *Psychiatric Bulletin*. 1997;21:323–327.

54. Dresser R. Dworkin on dementia: elegant theory, questionable policy. *Hastings Center Report*. 1995;25:32–38.

55. Cooper C, Selwood A, Livingston G. The prevalence of elder abuse and neglect: a systematic review. *Age Ageing*. 2008;37:151–160.

56. Ahmad M, Lachs MS. Elder abuse and neglect: what physicians can and should do. *Cleve Clin J Med*. Oct 2002;69(10):801–808.

57. Gilbert DA. The ethics of mandatory elder abuse reporting statutes. *ANS Adv Nurs Sci*. Jan 1986;8(2):51–62.

58. Snowdon J, Day S, Baker W. Current use of psychotropic medication in nursing homes. *International Psychogeriatrics*. 2006;18:241–250.

59. MacDonald A, Roberts A, Carpenter L. De facto imprisonment and covert medication use in general nursing homes for older people in South East England. *Aging Clinical and Experimental Research.* 2004;16:326–330.

60. Sink K, Holden K, Yaffe K. Pharmacological treatment of neuropsychiatric symptoms of dementia. a review of the evidence. *JAMA.* 2005;293:596–608.

61. Agich G. Roles and responsibilities: theoretical issues in the definition of consultation liaison psychiatry. *Journal of Medicine and Philosophy.* 1985;10:105–126.

62. Ramchandani D. Ethical issues for the consultant in the general hospital. *Current Psychiatry Reports.* 2000;2:264–267.

63. Steinberg M. Psychiatry and bioethics: an exploration of the relationship. *Psychosomatics.* 1997;38:313–320.

64. Youngner S. Consultation-liaison psychiatry and clinical ethics: historical parallels and diversions. *Psychosomatics.* 1997;38:309–312.

65. Cottencin O, Versaevel C, Goudemand M. In favour of a systemic vision of liaison psychiatry. *Encephale.* 2006;32:305–314.

66. Lederberg M. Making a situational diagnosis: psychiatrists at the interface of psychiatry and ethics in the consultation-liaison setting. *Psychosomatics.* 1997;38:327–338.

67. Robertson M, Walter G. An overview of psychiatric ethics I: professional ethics and psychiatry. *Australasian Psychiatry.* 2007;15:201–206.

179

11

Power and Knowledge in Psychiatry

Introduction

Within any professional enterprise there is a specialized form of knowledge. Knowledge, as distinct from data, information, or fact, represents a complex process of contextualized understanding of sense experience, noumenal processes, and socially constructed methods of observation, quantification, or qualification and consensual validation of the methods of analysis.

The formal philosophical discipline of understanding of knowledge, or epistemology, dates to at least classical times and emerged in its most significant form in the writings of Plato. Plato's epistemology and metaphysics are indebted to Pythagoras, particularly the notion of the mathematical harmony of an ordered universe. Plato's ideas about the different levels of reality and knowledge are found in Books VII and X of *Republic*.[1]

Plato's ideas of knowledge and reality are best elaborated in the cave allegory. In this allegory there are prisoners, destitute of philosophy, bound to chairs in a dark cave. They are aware only of shadows of forms and their "contingent sensuous properties." As a prisoner breaks free of his chains and painfully ascends to "an upper world of Forms," he stares at the sun and discovers the multitude of forms do not comprise a harmonious and ordered universe. In the metaphoric tool of the prisoner staring at the sun, Plato forms a potent metaphor of a single divine unitary form "who gives the seasons and the years, and is the guardian of all that is in the visible world." The sun is the metaphoric "Good," the single normative principle, which brings harmony among the many forms. In this metaphor it is knowledge.

Plato clearly lays out his ideas of knowledge through "the divided line"—dividing the world of ideas (intelligible realm) and the world of objects (visible realm). He distinguishes between two categories of knowledge—*doxa* (opinion) and *episteme* (science). *Doxa* as a form of knowledge concerns itself with appearances and visible objects, which are known through *eikasia* (illusion) and *pisitis* (belief based upon perception). As with the deluded prisoners in the cave, knowledge through *doxa* is flawed and must be transcended through the method of dialectic into the higher levels of *episteme*. *Episteme* concerns itself with intelligible mathematical and hypothetical entities known through *dianoia* (hypothesis and analysis) and the ultimate level of knowledge, *noesis*, which exists independent of physical objects and approximates the Good. *Dianoia* relies predominantly on mathematics for its method—not the applied mathematics of counting sheep, but the mathematician's mathematics of theoretical constructs, particularly geometry. Through the dialectic process, the philosopher ascends from the world of illusion and objects, through the intelligible *dianoia*, to come to know the Good, through *noesis*.

In the early twenty-first century, knowledge derived from the physical sciences is deemed a higher form of knowledge. Scientific method, at least in its current form, is based on the generation of a testable hypothesis (sometimes mathematically modeled), which is then considered against observations made of phenomena in support or refutation of it. Empiricism—knowledge based on observation—is critical to this process. Plato's ideas are at odds with empiricism. English analytic philosopher Bertrand Russell[2] emphasized that to Plato there was "nothing worthy to be called knowledge to be derived from the senses ... the only real knowledge has to with concepts" (p. 63).

There is, arguably, a divided state of knowledge in psychiatry. In the discourse over psychiatric knowledge there appears to be a dichotomy concerning a scientific evidence-based medicine (EBM) approach and a form of narrative knowledge, or what would be regarded as clinical experience. Not only do psychiatrists experience this tension as a contextual influence, but profound moral questions arise from this epistemic quandary. In this chapter, we propose to survey a number of important epistemic ideas of relevance to this dichotomy and examine in detail how these manifest in an ethical dilemma in a famous and landmark case in American psychiatry, the Osheroff case.

Psychiatry and the Two Cultures

Psychiatrists see their discipline as both an art and a science. The art in psychiatry is the nuance, the subtle integrating of theory and experience and its application of these in the fundamentally moral enterprise of clinical practice. The discourse of psychiatry is currently dominated by the neurosciences. Amid this are the softer sciences of psychoanalysis, behaviorism, and sociology. Philosophical theories of mind, such as notions of Cartesian dualism, dwell as background concepts. The integration of the humanities with science is a source of both strength and weakness for psychiatry. Psychiatry is the quintessential third culture.

The coexistence of the different cultures of science and humanities, and the possibility of a third, middle-ground culture, extends to 1959 in which the novelist Sir Charles Percy Snow made a claim about the existence of two cultures, the scientific and the nonscientific. In a Rede Lecture at Cambridge University, Snow argued that there was a "gulf of mutual incomprehension" between scientists and what he termed "literary intellectuals." Snow's ideas were outlined in the book *The Two Cultures: A Second Look*, which was published in 1964.[5] In it, Snow introduced the notion of a third culture. Snow imagined a culture where literary intellectuals conversed directly with scientists as equals. Many now loosely consider Snow's third culture as including economics, political science, and indeed, psychiatry.

Evidence-Based Medicine and Psychiatry

Among of the most influential movements in modern medicine has been that of evidence-based medicine. In essence, EBM avers the principle that the only treatments that should be used in clinical practice are those for which there is robust evidence of efficacy. EBM originated largely at the instigation of a British researcher, Archie Cochrane, who proclaimed that nothing could be said of any treatment until the first patient had been randomized in a scientific study. In the eyes of EBM, the most robust scientific studies are randomized control trials (RCTs). RCTs are large, complex to conduct, and expensive, and the information they provide does not always reflect the realities of clinical practice. The limitations of RCTs, as applied to treatments for psychiatric disorders, are commonly criticized on many grounds, including selection bias, sample enrichment, arbitrary treatment end points, and unrepresentative definitions of states of illness.

In 2001, Israeli academic Leonard Leibovici published a somewhat tongue-in-cheek critique of RCTs in the *British Medical Journal*.[6] Leibovici considered the power of "remote, retroactive intercessory prayer" (having a cleric pray for the patient's recovery a year after the admission to hospital) in treating septicemia. Leibovici took the names of 3,393 adults who had been admitted to hospital with septicemia and randomized half to the prayer intervention. There was no difference in the number of deaths for either of the groups, but there were statistically significant differences in length of hospital stay and duration of fever. Leibovici was compelled to conclude, "Remote, retroactive intercessory prayer can improve outcomes in patients with a bloodstream infection. The intervention is cost effective and probably has no adverse effects, and should be considered for clinical practice." What Leibovici seems to have succeeded in demonstrating is that considering mathematical maneuvers of empirical observations, leading to a rejected null hypothesis as indicating a comprehensive, generalizable form of knowledge is a serious category error.

Despite the criticisms of EBM based upon the methodological shortcomings of RCTs, a source of significant concern in psychiatry is the gaps in knowledge being equated with the assumption that unproven treatments are inappropriate for clinical use. The aphorism that "deficiency of evidence is not evidence of deficiency" is particularly apposite in the field of psychotherapy, where the comparatively RCT-friendly manualized treatments such as cognitive behavior therapy enjoy distinct advantages over longer-term expressive psychotherapy treatments in terms of EBM. In the alternate, RCTs that generate observations with highly statistically significant rejections of the null hypothesis are often subject to a category error in which statistical significance is in some way equivalent to clinical significance. A 5 percent change in a measured phenomena with a $p < 0.0005$ may be a robust finding but does not warrant a generalizable statement of significant clinical benefit that should form an evidence base of practice that translates into treatments being approved or disapproved.

Philosophical Basis of Knowledge

Francis Bacon and the *Idola*

Francis Bacon's epistemological project identified many flaws in human knowledge. In Bacon's time, the ongoing influence of Aristotle meant that the dominant form of knowledge in Western culture was deductive syllogism. Like many of his fellow empiricists, Bacon believed that knowledge should actually proceed from observable fact to an axiom and thence to a natural law. Bacon argued, however, that human thought was corrupted by a multitude of factors that distort perception of truth. In his *Novum Organum*,[3] Bacon identified these distorting factors, which he dubbed *idola,* or idols. *Idola tribus* (idols of the tribe) are factors within a culture that affect the perception and interpretation of experience. *Idola specus* (idols of the cave) is a direct allusion to Plato and highlights distortions of thought that are unique to an individual. *Idola fori* (idols of the marketplace) arise from the vagaries and limits of language, and *idola theatri* (idols of the theater) result from the abuse of authority and the effect of power on knowledge, such as Galileo's persecution at the hands of the Vatican.

The *idola* seem to relate biases in our interpretation of experience. Idols of the tribe are clearly evident in history, from witch burnings to the current excesses of social media and Web 2.0. Idols of the marketplace and idols of the theater are more relevant to our inquiries of research in psychiatry. The emotive and causative properties of terms such as *efficacy*, *empirically validated*, and *cost-effective* are most evident in determining the form of knowledge in psychiatry.

The idols of the theater are the most significant of the *idola* in understanding the state of knowledge in psychiatry. This primarily speaks of the relationship between knowledge and power, advanced by the genealogical methods of Nietzsche and Focault. In modern times, the power structures of some parts of the academy, the pharmaceutical industry, and neoliberalism are the *idola fori* most relevant to knowledge in psychiatry.

Nietzsche's Suspicions of Science

Nineteenth century German philosopher Friedrich Nietzsche was concerned about the apparent excesses of science. Nietzsche was particularly aware of power structures in society that control the form that knowledge takes. At the core of Nietzsche's thoughts about knowledge was his concern that science merely represented a way in which man tried to make things comprehensible, rather than know them as they truly are. The notion of man embracing the harsh, unforgiving, and meaningless universe features in Nietzsche's earliest writings. In *The Birth of Tragedy,*[4] Nietzsche contrasted reality undifferentiated by forms as associated with the Greek god Dionysus with reality as differentiated by forms as represented by the god Apollo. The notion of an intelligible universe is contrasted with the notion of a chaotic, unintelligible universe. To Nietzsche, the tragedies of Aeschylus and Sophocles were the high point of art in that the Apollonian and Dionysian themes coexisted. The Apollonian view saw its apotheosis in the notion of a universe comprehensible through reason and scientific method. In the same way that man sheltered from the notion of a harsh and unforgiving universe by seeking refuge in the notions of a God, Nietzsche argued man also hubristically claimed to understand the world through science. Science showed the universe as we chose to see it, not as it truly is. This was Nietzsche's direct challenge to Platonism.[5]

Nietzsche did not wish to destroy science completely, in *Thus Spake Zarathustra,*[6] he argued that a scientific truth was of value not if it was proven or not, but rather if it had an instrumental value. In other words, to Nietzsche scientific truth should be judged on the merits of whether it is "species preserving" or "species enhancing." This kind of pragmatism can be found in the distinctly American pragmatic philosophies of John Dewey and William James.

Foucault and the Archaeology of Knowledge

French philosopher Michel Foucault's ideas on the nature of knowledge extend from those of Nietzsche and are particularly apposite to psychiatry. Nietzsche's bequest to Foucault's thought and later postmodernism was the notion that the composition of knowledge was indistinguishable from the powerful influences in social settings. Foucault described knowledge as taking the form of discursive formations—an ongoing interaction between insiders party to the discourse. Foucault also recognized that knowledge itself was not a constant, linear evolution of ideas. He wrote of an "archaeology of knowledge," where the discourse had taken different forms in different eras in history.[7] An era of knowledge was dubbed an "episteme." Episteme were discontinuous, and frequently appeared abruptly against the previous episteme. In Foucault's estimation, knowledge and power could not be distinguished; he frequently referred in his work to *savoir/pouvoir* (knowledge/power). In *Discipline and Punishment*[8] he wrote:

> Knowledge linked to power, not only assumes the authority of "the truth" but has the power to make itself true. All knowledge, once applied in the real world, has effects, and in that sense at least, "becomes true." Knowledge, once used to regulate the conduct of others, entails constraint, regulation and the disciplining of practice. Thus, there is no power relation without the correlative constitution of a field of knowledge, nor any knowledge that does not presuppose and constitute at the same time, power relations. (p. 27)

As a consequence of culture, social hierarchies, and other potent forces, certain forms of thought are privileged over others, being considered to have *cultural capital*. These ideas are hegemonic and exert firm control over the discourse. Foucault was particularly impressed with the cultural capital of psychoanalysis in determining the concept of madness in human societies. Foucault advanced this idea in describing prisons as microcosms of society—a "carcereal" society where power/knowledge made human sciences, such as psychiatry and sociology, possible. Knowledge and the state were one and the same.

Applying his archaeology of knowledge to medicine, in particular psychiatry, Foucault saw the Enlightenment as being the major watershed. In *Birth of the Clinic*,[9] Foucault described the Enlightenment period as producing the myth that the medical profession held a unique place of a wise and almost sacred order, burdened with the preservation of the health of humanity. Foucault also implied that doctors were the "carriers of cultural wisdom." Linked with this concept was the ability of doctors to see things that others cannot, dubbed the clinical or observing "gaze." Foucault's notion of the archaeology of knowledge in medicine and psychiatry was its abrupt shift from the episteme of bedside medicine to hospital medicine during the Enlightenment. The change was driven largely by the practice of postmortem examination of patients identifying diseased tissues or organ systems. In the previous episteme, the ancient and medieval theories of the four humors—blood, black and yellow bile, and phlegm—were the dominant discourse. With softening attitudes of the church toward dissection of corpses, the notion of the pathological basis of disease and illness emerged and fractured the connection with the previous episteme. The practice of clinical medicine has since evolved into a laboratory-based practice, where evidence of processes of pathological derangement of tissues or organ systems is required to establish a diagnosis—infections require the identification of pathogens; obstructed or failing viscera can be visualized using elaborate scans; inherited diseases are visible with specific genetic markers. In contrast, the practice of psychiatry is still at the bedside. While not at the level of the four humors, it has lacked the progression of other medical science. In *Madness and Civilisation*,[10] Foucault traced the evolution of the concept of insanity from the pre-Enlightenment notion of spiritual or demonic possession to the enlightened era of moral treatments that characterized the work of French psychiatrists such as Pinel.

In integrating the notions of madness, discursive formations, and archaeology of knowledge, Foucault's ideas about psychiatric knowledge could be interpreted as follows:

1. The current episteme of psychiatry remains at the bedside.
2. The discursive formation as to what psychiatric disorder is and how best to treat it is influenced by ideas with strong cultural capital, such as psychoanalysis and biology, in preference over other equally valid ideas.

3. Power/knowledge structures, such as government and academia, control the discourse and define madness along the lines of deviant or undesirable behavior, with a frame of reference to social norms.

4. Psychiatric disorder and its treatment is thus what those in positions of power define it to be.

Imbued with a relativist notion of madness, psychiatry becomes the agent of the state (and possibly other neoliberal patrons such as the pharmaceutical or insurance industries).

This process had its most recent manifestation in the formulation of the *Diagnostic and Statistical Manual of Mental Disorders, Fifth Edition (DSM-V)*. Allen Frances, the American psychiatrist who oversaw the formulation of the *DSM-IV* and *DSM-IV-TR*, has been highly critical of the secretive and nontransparent means in which the *DSM-V* has been fashioned by an elite and select group of psychiatrists.[11] In February 2012 he wrote in the online journal the *Huffington Post*:

> The public statements of the DSM 5 leadership consistently reveal just how insulated they are—far out of touch with the proper purpose of their task and unable to see serious risks that seem perfectly apparent to everyone else. DSM 5 is probably stuck on its disastrous course unless it can finally be restrained by outside forces—some combination of press shaming, public and professional opposition, and/or governmental intervention.[12]

The *DSM-V* threatened, through its dimensional, as opposed to categorical, constructs of disorder, to expand mental illness into normative states. As Frances's (and many others') public condemnation highlighted, the discursive formations of the *DSM-V* committee were restricted to a small number of academic psychiatrists, many with links to the pharmaceutical industry. This was the most apposite example in recent times of *savoir/pouvoir*, in that those few party to the discourse have participated in the genesis of psychiatric knowledge, which is profoundly powerful.

Jürgen Habermas and the Frankfurt School

A particularly enlightening epistemological perspective comes from the so-called Frankfurt school and the body of thought, dubbed "critical theory." Among the most influential thinkers of the Frankfurt school is Jürgen Habermas, whose 1968 classic *Knowledge and Human Interests*,[13] his main work on epistemology, is illuminating, particularly with reference to science.

Habermas wrote of "knowledge constitutive interests" that divide knowledge into three categories. *Technical empirical knowledge* arises out of the Enlightenment and is, in essence, scientific. Technical empirical modes of understanding involve developing a theory and then making sets of highly contrived observations that seek to either prove or disprove the theory. Applied to EBM, particularly in psychiatry, this mode of thought would place faith exclusively in scientific studies that were well constructed and adhered to certain methods of investigation, including complex statistical calculations.

Practical Interpretive knowledge, in contrast, seeks to study the world as it is lived in. Learning and knowledge evolve from observing the world as it presents to the subject, and then by a process of reflection upon the status of the observer, deeper understandings can emerge. This kind of knowledge is usually associated with qualitative research methods. At the core of these methods is language and reflective interpretation. In the psychiatric setting it would be the knowledge derived from having experienced numerous interactions and made consistent observations. To contrast this form of knowledge with technical empirical knowledge, consider the decisions made about antidepressants. EBM takes the position that the choice would be guided only by what robust findings from well-controlled studies would indicate. In the case of practical Interpretive knowledge, the decision would come down to what the particular clinician has seen and experienced working in the past.

Habermas then described *emancipatory knowledge*, which tends to integrate social influences and the power structures associated with knowledge. Habermas was critical of Foucault in this regard, as he saw him as being too extreme in his rejection of the Enlightenment and modernity. To Habermas, technical empirical knowledge poorly tolerates challenges to it as a basis of knowledge. Habermas, when referring to science, terms this dominance as being *scientism*—science's belief in its own supreme power. There is therefore hegemony of science over other forms of knowledge. The process of emancipatory knowledge is achieved through a process of critical reflection, in which we ponder the state of our knowledge and what has brought us to think in such ways. To emancipate one's thinking is to think about what we think, why we think it, and what has influenced us to think this way. Unlike Foucault, Habermas is not determined to destroy the notion of truth or meta-narrative, but rather to consider different pathways to knowledge.

Jean-Francois Lyotard and Postmodernism

The French postmodernist writer Jean-Francois Lyotard also distinguished between scientific and narrative knowledge. Along the same lines of demarcation as those of Habermas, Lyotard distinguished between technical empiricism and practical forms of knowledge.[14] Lyotard recognized in the 1970s that information and knowledge were as critical a resource as material wealth and that nation-states and social structures that possesed such information were in positions of profound influence. It therefore followed that powerful nation-states would accumulate knowledge in addition to material wealth. Apart from distinguishing between scientific and narrative forms of knowledge, Lyotard also emphasized that scientific knowledge had become so dominant in the postmodern world that it was erroneously assumed to be the only form of knowledge.

Philosophy of Science

Empiricism is at the core of the scientific method. Descartes and other rationalists argued that humans possessed *a priori* knowledge such as extension, mathematics, and geometry. Descartes further argued that perceptual experience could not be trusted as a basis of knowledge as our senses can be fooled by a metaphorical *malin génie* (evil demon). Empiricists such as English philosopher John Locke rejected this notion and argued that sense experience was the basis of knowledge. Our perceptions of the universe guide our knowledge of it. Our perceptions help us form ideas about the world, and our observations are made in support of or against a particular conceived notion of the universe. If we believe that there is a force called gravity that acts on objects, then a trolley rolling off a table and falling to the ground is seen to support this idea. The notion of scientific empiricism is that we are able to make sets of structured observations that are associated and infer that these are causally linked. If A happens and B happens in some form of temporal relationship, the assumption is that this A and B are causally rather than incidentally linked.

This view of causation is not universally accepted. The Scottish Enlightenment philosopher David Hume argued quite strongly that this reasoning was misleading, as our observations are dependent upon the vagaries of our perceptive capacities. All we can say of pairs of observations, such as described above, is that from our experience, we form expectations that when A happens, B follows. Hume believed that perhaps the human mind possessed a sense of causation to the point that we almost willed things to be true. Later exponents of Hume's thoughts, such as Bertrand Russell, dismissed causation as little more than magical thinking. Claims to causal relationships are therefore far more vulnerable to confirmation biases, external influences, and heuristics, such as our hopes, expectations, and manner of observing phenomena. To sceptical Humeans, causation arises from human psychology rather than any truth of the universe.

The scientific basis of psychiatry, whether it be the observation of a certain type of genetic composition associated with the onset of psychiatric disorder, or the observed benefits of treatment trials, is therefore assumptions about causation that can never be held to be fact. Scientific empiricism is based upon generalizations that are confirmed by the experience of witnessing phenomena that fit with a testable hypothesis. If one believes that tricyclic antidepressants improve melancholic depressive symptoms, observing the two events, i.e., the administration of a tricyclic antidepressant and the observation of improvement in melancholic symptoms, tests this hypothesis.

This argument is also illustrated in exchanges between John Stuart Mill[15] and William Whewell.[16] In simple terms, Whewell accepts that if an experimental hypothesis or theory seems to explain experimental observations, then that is sufficient grounds for knowledge. If an antidepressant seems to, time and time again, make depression better in treatment trials, then that is a sufficient basis of knowledge for Whewell. Whewell even conceded that even if one's theory might be wrong, it might at least lead one in the right direction.

Mill on the other hand did not accept such a proposition. He believed, as did Karl Popper in the next century,[17] that disproving false theories was the only way to approximate scientific truth. Popper took the view that a theory is only scientific if it is testable, i.e., open to the possibility to being *falsified*. In essence, scientific theories can only be disproved, not verified. In Popperian logic, if a theory is proven, it is likely that the hypothesis has been modified to fit with the experience of observations. For Popperians, however, to assert that a theory is unscientific is not to hold that it is meaningless, but rather that it does not allow itself to be tested and falsified. The context of a particular hypothesis may change, such as when advancement in technology makes it more feasible; this makes a hypothesis testable and therefore scientific.

Reductionism in Psychiatric Thought

In the fourteenth century, the Franciscan friar and scholastic philosopher William of Ockham proposed the view *Pluralitas non est ponenda sine neccesitate*, which translates as, "Entities should not be multiplied unnecessarily." Rather than merely "keep it simple," Ockham's razor suggests that when we are faced with two theories that have the same predictions and the available data cannot distinguish between them, we are compelled to study in depth the simplest of the theories, rather than take the more complex. This view is frequently applied in medicine and science as the parsimonious view that all symptoms and signs should be reduced to the one pathological process. By Ockham's razor, psychiatrists are better served considering the physics of neurotransmitters than the arcane and complex ideas of Klein or Kohut.

One idea that pervades within the medical model of psychiatry is the notion of reductionism. In essence, reductionism is the view that phenomena can be explained in terms of their more basic elements. Psychological states are considered naturalistic phenomena and are subsumed in physiological functions of the central nervous system; neurophysiological functions are seen in terms of biochemical processes; biochemical processes are reduced to the physics of molecules. The reductionist principle is that everything can be known and comprehended by reducing it to its fundamental elements.

Applying reductionism to psychiatry has tended to see it opt for biological explanations of psychiatric disorders and their treatment. In the case of schizophrenia, the reductionist view is that it is a brain disease enacted by processes of deranged information processing, disordered biochemical activity, and genetic variation. The simple forms of knowledge applied here are molecular genetics, neurochemistry, and neurophysiology. In the case of depression, the reductionist view sees it largely as a state of deranged brain biochemistry. Life events are defined as mere external influences on the internal milieu of the brain.

American philosopher Daniel Dennett's controversial book *Darwin's Dangerous Idea*[18] used the term "greedy reductionism" as a condemnation of those forms of reductionism that try to explain too much with too little. This is a process in which "in their eagerness for a bargain, in their zeal to explain too much too fast, scientists and philosophers … underestimate the complexities, trying to skip whole layers or levels of theory in their rush to fasten everything securely and neatly to the foundation" (p. 82). In Aristotelian tradition, Dennett argues for the "reasonable middle ground" between rejecting reductionism and greedy reductionism.

Pluralism in Psychiatry

The modern epistemological foundation of psychiatry is the biopsychosocial model of American psychiatrist George Engel,[19,20] which argues that human function and dysfunction arise from the interaction of biological, psychological, and social factors. As such, understanding psychiatric disorder and its treatment requires an understanding of the interaction of these three domains. In practice, this model has led to the development of multidisciplinary professional approaches to the patient and his or her problem.

The biopsychosocial model has attracted criticism from several angles. British psychiatrist David Pilgrim has argued that Engel's model merely forces several themes into coexistence rather than genuine theoretical integration.[21] American psychiatrist Nasser Ghaemi's critique of Engel's theory is more comprehensive in that it defines Engel's approach as "eclectic" and therefore not intellectually rigorous. Upon reflection on the philosophical underpinnings of science and psychiatry, Ghaemi urged psychiatrists to accept an approach of pluralism and integration in the way they think about their patients, rather than the eclecticism evident in Engel's approach.[22]

Pluralism in this sense is the assumption that phenomena observed empirically require multiple explanations to account for their nature, hence denying that there is one unified scientific method. The need for pluralism, as opposed to the eclecticism of Engel, is based on the assumptions that psychiatric disorders are disorders of the mind and not the body, that different classes of mental disorders require different explanatory approaches, and that different psychiatric disorders result in dysfunction of different aspects of a person's life. Ghaemi based his philosophy of psychiatry on the work of American pragmatist Charles Sanders Peirce and German philosophers Wilhelm Dilthey and Karl Jaspers. To Ghaemi, human life is characterized by existential situations, or crises, which become opportunities for authentic existence. He argues that psychiatry has failed to understand Jaspers's pluralism and in doing so has subscribed to a limited epistemological approach of Popperian scientific method.[23]

Case Example: Mrs. C

Mrs. C was a woman in her mid-40s who developed significant depressive illness as a consequence of difficulties at work. She was in receipt of benefits and treatment costs paid for by an insurance company. In the course of her depression, Mrs. C had made a number of serious suicide attempts. Mrs. C had trialed medications including citalopram, fluoxetine, escitalopram, mirtazapine, venlafaxine, nortriptyline, clomipramine, lithium, sodium valproate, and olanzapine. She had poorly tolerated all of these. Over a period of several years she underwent frequent hospitalizations, during which she underwent repetitive transcranial magnetic stimulation (rTMS). Several psychiatrists assessed her depressive symptoms as being treatment refractory.

A psychiatrist retained by the insurance company assessed Mrs. C and concluded that given she had not trialed electroconvulsive therapy (ECT) or tranylcypromine, a costly course of rTMS should not be reimbursed by the insurer. Based upon this opinion, the funding for further treatments ceased and Mrs. C was denied further access to rTMS.

The matter was taken to an arbitration process, where another psychiatrist was tasked with assessing Mrs. C's clinical situation and making a determination whether the insurer should continue to fund rTMS treatments. When the psychiatrist examined Mrs. C, she noted that her mood had deteriorated since the cessation of treatment, that she was significantly disabled by the depressive illness, and that suicidal thinking had re-emerged. Mrs. C reported that she felt considerable improvement for a week after a series of treatments with rTMS, but her mood would then decline. Mrs. C had experienced a traumatic general anesthetic for dental work several years before, and while an inpatient she had been quite disturbed by the confusion she witnessed in several fellow patients undergoing ECT. She did not exhibit psychotic symptoms or psychomotor change, which appeared to indicate that ECT may not have been as effective as indicated by the other independent psychiatric assessor. Given Mrs. C's sensitivity to medication side effects, it was also likely that she would not benefit from tranylcypromine.

The psychiatrist concluded that the clinical situation was exceptionally complex and that legal and medical discourses would not coalesce to a satisfactory resolution. She noted that rTMS was a comparatively new treatment for depression, and the evidence base supporting its use was controversial. She noted that there were a number of randomized control trials supporting its efficacy in treatment of major depression; however, a Cochrane database review found little evidence supporting its efficacy. Several meta-analyses indicated that rTMS has an efficacy approximating that of antidepressant medication.

The independent psychiatrist concluded that the issue relating to the ongoing provision of rTMS was not able to be resolved definitively with reference to the scientific literature or the body of clinical experience. While the evidence base was equivocal for rTMS, in the specific case of Mrs. C, she appeared to benefit from rTMS in a maintenance phase of treatment and therefore it should continue. She recommended that the treating clinician should be methodical in measuring the clinical benefit of further rTMS treatments.

* * *

In this example, the use and abuse of expert opinion as a form of knowledge that traversed the legal and medical discourses over the issue of Mrs. C's care presented moral dilemmas. The insurance company took the position that the significant cost of ongoing treatment was not justifiable given the novelty of the treatment and sought expert opinion to support this position. A psychiatrist averred that knowledge based on a rigid interpretation of scientific evidence, seemingly disregarding a nuanced understanding of Mrs. C's situation. In the alternate, the second psychiatrist had to reconcile the knowledge that emerged from the evidence base for rTMS with the knowledge derived from the direct experience of Mrs. C's clinical care. The moral dilemma was clearly one of the implications for Mrs. C's care and therefore her welfare. If the insurance company was ordered to fund ongoing treatment with rTMS, this posed a precedent that further requests would have to be heeded, threatening to bankrupt the system. The assertion of an opinion based on a literal interpretation of the literature was problematic in that the presentation of this opinion as being an authoritative, scientifically based form of knowledge did not acknowledge the limitations of the science. Conversely, to disregard the evidence base would be equally problematic, as there are broader responsibilities to the patient and funding systems to ensure that all can access the best care and that costly treatments that are idiosyncratic in benefit do not deplete the pot of funding schemes.

This case example, and the issues it raises, is redolent of another, more canonical clinical dilemma in American psychiatry, with equally broad implications for the field.

Knowledge, Power, and the Troubling Case of Dr. Osheroff

Raphael Osheroff, a middle-aged renal physician, had suffered long-standing complex psychological symptoms, ultimately deemed to be a vexed combination of bipolar disorder and pathological narcissism.[24] In 1979, Osheroff admitted himself to Chestnut Lodge, a prestigious psychiatric hospital in Maryland with a renowned reputation for psychoanalytic treatments. Osheroff had not derived benefit from an initial trial of antidepressant medication. At Chestnut Lodge, Osheroff was diagnosed with having a depressive illness borne of a narcissistic personality disorder. His psychiatrists noted the likelihood of bipolar depression although resolved that the primary issue was his pathological narcissism. Osheroff was prescribed intensive psychoanalytic psychotherapy, along the guidelines the hospital's treatment practice for such conditions. Osheroff was not offered psychotropic treatment at Chestnut Lodge.

Osheroff's problems did not resolve quickly in treatment at Chestnut Lodge. He became significantly depressed and agitated. He paced around the hospital up to 16 hours per day and developed ulcers on the soles of his feet. He lost a significant amount of weight and neglected his self-care. Osheroff's marriage ultimately fractured under the burden of his deranged psychological state; his medical career and finances evaporated.

After three months of Chestnut Lodge's treatment, Osheroff's family sought another medical opinion. He transferred his care to another psychiatric hospital, Silver Hill Foundation, where he was diagnosed with a severe psychotic depression, formulated as a part of a long-standing bipolar disorder. He was prescribed antidepressant medication and was said to have promptly recovered from his depressed state.

Aggrieved at the perceived negligence of Chestnut Lodge, Osheroff took legal action. In *Osheroff v. Chestnut Lodge*,[25] Osheroff's lawyers claimed that Chestnut Lodge was negligent in its misdiagnosis and its failure to provide or even offer the standard pharmacological treatment for depression. Osheroff also claimed that the institution's failure to adequately inform him of other treatment options was also in breach of their duty of care. Osheroff's lawyers argued that the standard of care to which Chestnut Lodge should be held was the adequate provision of those treatments that were evidence based.

Osheroff's team retained the expertise of Yale and Harvard professor Gerald Klerman, who argued that clinicians had an ethical duty to offer treatments of demonstrated efficacy. In an article later published in the *American Journal of Psychiatry*, Klerman wrote of the "proposed right of the patient to effective treatment."[26] Klerman called for widespread reform in psychiatric practice, in particular the adoption of standards of practice guided by scientific studies. In essence, only treatments that are shown to work in scientific studies should be practiced, and by implication, funded.

Chestnut Lodge retained expert testimony from Harvard professor of psychiatry Alan Stone. Chestnut Lodge's lawyers attempted to invoke the defense of the so-called respectable minority rule, pointing out that psychoanalytic treatment was widely used for depression, even though the research supporting its effectiveness was less robust than for antidepressant medication. Stone argued that, in the case of the evidence base for psychotherapy and depression, the lack of scientific evidence had been erroneously equated with the notion that psychotherapy was lacking as a treatment.

Stone argued that the clinical issues in Raphael Osheroff's case were far more complex and subtle than Klerman had argued. In a response to Klerman's assertions in *The American Journal of Psychiatry*, Stone wrote:

> Klerman's proposals could have serious consequences for the innovation, diversity, and independent thought essential to scientific progress in psychiatry.[24]

This was a polemic debate. Osheroff used his experience to advocate for evidence-based treatments.[27] Psychiatric researcher Myrna Weissman wrote that Alan Stone later recanted his position on Osheroff:

> In reference to the use of narratives as therapeutics he [Stone] stated that "based on the scientific evidence now available to us, the basic premises may all be incorrect." ... He stated that psychoanalysis is "an art form that belongs to the humanities and not to the sciences."[28]

The Osheroff case was settled out of court and no case law precedent was set. The case became a *cause célèbre* among the North American psychiatric profession. The debates over *Osheroff v. Chestnut Lodge* crystallized the state of knowledge in psychiatry. The Osheroff case saw the conflict between two forms of knowledge in psychiatry—evidence-based medicine and clinical experience. Klerman's view was that psychiatric knowledge as applied to Raphael Osheroff was based only upon those facts that stood up to the scientific scrutiny. At the time, antidepressants had a solid evidence base in support of their use. The only thing that could be truly known, according to Klerman, was that antidepressants effectively treated depression.

In the case of clinical experience, or what Habermas dubbed "practical interpretive knowledge," the wisdom of the Chestnut Lodge therapists held that Osheroff's problems could only resolve through the confrontation of the unconscious disturbances affecting his day-to-day life. Antidepressants were argued to have provided more rapid symptomatic relief to Osheroff, although the complexity of his problems suggested that outcomes other than reduction in depressive symptoms, such as improved insight or enhanced interpersonal efficacy, may have been equally desirable and necessary. Antidepressant medication has an advantage over psychoanalysis in more rapidly reducing depressive symptoms. Observations of the reduction in the intensity of depressive symptoms are relatively straightforward when compared to measurement of changes in intrapsychic functioning. Antidepressants, or structured forms of psychotherapy, have an advantage over psychoanalysis in that they are more amenable to measurement of outcome in RCTs. It is arguable that the aspirations of psychoanalysis and psychopharmacology are completely different—some patients want relief, and others want growth or internal change. Comparing the two is not comparing like with like.

A simple view of *Osheroff v. Chestnut Lodge* was that medication worked—Klerman was right and Stone was wrong. This view verged on becoming a powerful force that would dominate the state of knowledge in psychiatry. The discourse incorporated highly emotive issues such as right to treatment and the banishment of certain forms of knowledge as a basis of clinical practice.

What does Osheroff say about knowledge in psychiatry? In clinical terms, Dr. Osheroff had complex problems. He was depressed and his life was failing. He sought help from one arm of the psychiatric profession, who saw him as being a deeply disturbed narcissist whose personality vulnerabilities had led to repeated failures in relationships. He required long-term psychological therapy to contain these aspects of his problem and help him rebuild his life. This was inappropriate either because Osheroff had an endogenous depression or because, as with many disabled by narcissistic pathology, Osheroff was not prepared to tolerate his needs not being met in a manner he expected. He therefore decamped from treatment and sought another opinion.

It is not clear what kind of recovery Osheroff made with antidepressant medication, but there are many ways his clinical course could be interpreted. One might argue that his brain physiology was the simple issue. Others might say that his prompt recovery was a placebo effect, spiting the failure of Chestnut Lodge to meet his needs, much as the threatened litigation seemed to be.

What is known is that this case crystallized the issue of one form of knowledge dominating another in psychiatry. Klerman called for the banishment of treatments without RCT supporting their efficacy. Stone argued that the world was not so simple and that the import of Klerman's statements was misleading and potentially catastrophic to the psychiatric profession. Many patients with disturbed personalities derive benefit from psychological therapies. In a number of cases it is life saving. These patients often fail to benefit from biological psychiatry.

In the final analysis, neither of the parties could claim a definitive victory over the other. The troubling part of *Osheroff v. Chestnut Lodge* is the attempted annihilation of one form of knowledge by another. This issue seems to be continually revisited in psychiatry. Perhaps the ultimate lesson arsing from *Osheroff v. Chestnut Lodge* is the need for the psychiatric profession to be comfortable with pluralism and less driven by dogma.

Summary

Knowledge in psychiatry is a communal store of fact and theory, a form of discourse within the profession. Psychiatric knowledge is as much a cultural and social process as an academic one. In a sociocultural setting, knowledge is subject to power structures, such as the state, financial, and cultural factors, which largely determine what composes the discourse.

Since the Enlightenment, scientific empiricism has dominated Western thought, particularly medicine. Science is based on the process of making assumptions about the causation of sets of observations, yet this notion is flawed. Science has come to so dominate the discourse of knowledge in medicine, particularly psychiatry, that is has become an *idée fixe* that excludes many of the other equally valid sources of knowledge, such as that derived from the experience of the lived in world. This has led to a tendency to greedy reductionism in psychiatry, which seeks to explain all phenomena in predominantly biological terms.

The scientific hegemony in psychiatry has predominated over the last 20–30 years to the point that scientific knowledge has been assumed to be the only form of knowledge. The vanguard of scientific knowledge in psychiatry is the RCT, yet even the most methodologically complex RCTs do not provide information that can be applied literally in day-to-day practice. It is not the popularity of EBM in psychiatry that is the problem, but rather its perceived arrogance in invalidating the other sources of knowledge. As the case discussions have demonstrated, what is taken to be knowledge has significant impact on decisions made by clinicians, governments, and social institutions. Knowledge therefore has a moral dimension.

The moral aspects of this epistemic problem in psychiatry are not in the uncertainties, but rather the manner in which the profession advocates its certainties.

References

1. Plato. *Republic*. Oxford: Oxford World's Classics; 1994.

2. Russell B. *A History of Western Philosophy*. London: Routledge; 1993.

3. Bacon F. *Novum organum. The Works of Francis Bacon (Vol. VIII)*. Spedding J, Ellis R, Heath D, trans. Boston: Taggard and Thompson; 1863.

4. Nietzsche F. *The Birth of Tragedy and the Case of Wagner*. Kaufman W, trans. New York: Random House; 1967.

5. Nietzsche F. *Twilight of the Idols and the Anti-Christ*. Baltimore: Penguin; 1968.

6. Leibovici L. Effects of remote, retroactive intercessory prayer on the outcomes in patients with bloodstream infections: randomised controlled trial. *British Medical Journal*. 2001;323:1450.

7. Foucault M. *The Archaeology of Knowledge*. New York: Pantheon Books; 1969.

8. Foucault M. *Discipline and Punishment: The Birth of the Prison*. New York: Vintage; 1977.

9. Foucault M. *The Birth of the Clinic: An Archaeology of Medical Perception*. Sheridan Smith A, trans. New York: Vintage Books; 1975

10. Foucault M. *Madness and Civilization*. Howard R, trans. New York: Pantheon; 1965.

11. Frances A. A warning sign on the road to *DSM-V*: beware of its unintended consequences. *Psychiatric Times*. 2009;26(8).

12. Frances A. The *DSM 5* follies, as told in its own words. *Huff Post Science* 2012; http://www.huffingtonpost.com/allen-frances/dsm-5_b_1251448.html (accessed June 18, 2012).

13. Habermas J. *Knowledge and Human Interests*. Boston: Beacon Press; 1971.

14. Lyotard J-F. *The Postmodern Condition: A Report on Knowledge*. Manchester: Manchester University Press; 1984.

15. Walzer M. *Just and Unjust Wars*. New York: Basic Books; 1977.

16. Fernandez H, Friedman J. Classification and treatment of tardive syndromes. *Neurologist*. 2003;9:16–27.

17. Kaplan A, Haenlein M. Users of the world, unite! The challenges and opportunities of social media. *Business Horizons*. 2010;53:59–68.

18. Seeman M, Seeman M, Seeman N. E-psychiatry. *Psychiatric Times*. 2010;22:18–29.

19. Engel G. The need for a new medical model: a challenge for biomedicine. *Science*. 1977;196:129–136.

20. Engel G. The clinical application of the biopsychosocial model. *American Journal of Psychiatry.* 1980;137:535–544.

21. Beauchamp T, Childress J. *Principles of Biomedical Ethics.* New York: Oxford University Press; 2001.

22. Ghaemi N. *The Concepts of Psychiatry: A Pluralistic Approach to Mind and Mental Illness.* Baltimore: Johns Hopkins University Press; 2003.

23. Ghaemi N. Existence and pluralism: the rediscovery of Karl Jaspers. *Psychopathology.* 2007;40:75–82.

24. McLuhan M. *Understanding Media.* London: Abacus; 1974.

25. Baudrillard. *The Gulf War Did Not Take Place.* Bloomington: Indiana University Press; 1995.

26. Klerman G. The psychiatric patient's right to treatment: implications of *Osheroff v Chestnut Lodge. American Journal of Psychiatry.* 1990;147:419–427.

27. Seeman M, Seeman B. E-psychiatry: the patient–psychiatrist relationship in the electronic age. *CMAJ.* 1999;161:1147–1149.

28. Latour B. *Reassembling the Social: An Introduction to Actor-Network-Theory.* Oxford: Oxford University Press; 2005.

12

Salud Mental
Social Agency and Argentine Psychiatry

Introduction

Argentina is one of the most enigmatic countries in South America. Argentina is comprised of a highly urbanized population, many of whom regard themselves as a European enclave. Argentine literature displays narratives of disillusionment, isolation, and colonization from European cultures. José Hernández's poem *La Vuelta de Martín Fierro* (1879), considered to be somewhat of an Argentine foundation myth, depicts themes of a gaucho's hope for a better life in the face of Europeanization of Argentina, only to be bitterly disappointed. Manuel Puig's novel *Betrayed by Rita Hayworth*[1] tells of the virtual solipsism of Argentines locked into an insular perspective of their lives. One particular feature of the lives of *los porteños* (residents of Buenos Aires) is the national preoccupation with psychoanalysis. Argentina has 29 analysts per million people, one of the highest concentrations in the world.[2] The psychologist Sandra Baitia described the recent Argentine experience:

> I live in a country that has faced lots of societal tragedies in the last three decades. We've had military governments that spread terror and literally made thousands of persons disappear. We have had consecutive financial crises that dropped thousands of people into poverty, malnutrition and unemployment … We have lots of people who had to deal with the effects of several kinds of traumas, in which there was always a constant and deep sense of not being important to those who are supposed to care about you. (p. 2)[3]

Themes in Recent Argentine History

Perónism

During the late nineteenth and early twentieth centuries, Argentina's economy grew rapidly, supported by a high volume of exports and foreign investment. Consequently, Argentines identified themselves with Europe and North American rather than with Latin America. Unfortunately, for the remainder of the twentieth century, Argentine history has been characterized by instability, corruption, and coercive use of state power. Military coups occurred in 1930, 1943, 1955, 1962, and 1976.

Juan Perón, a prominent officer in the Argentine military, had distinguished himself as the head of the Department of Labor in the government that had assumed power following a coup in 1943. In this role Perón and his celebrity second wife, Eva (Evita), championed social justice. By June 1946 Perón had been elected president of Argentina on this reformist platform. Perón had met both Hitler and Mussolini earlier in his career and was influenced by the reforms they had achieved in the wake of the Great Depression. His political party, the *Partido Justicialista,* was similar in its platform to fascism. Indeed Perón had observed of European fascism

an organized state for a perfectly ordered community, for a perfectly ordered population as well: a community where the state was the tool of the nation, whose representation was, under my view, effective. (p. 28)[4]

While Argentina had welcomed many European Jewish refugees in the midst of the Second World War, it was also a haven for ex-Nazis such as Adolf Eichmann, Erik Priebke, and Josef Mengele.[5]

In the course of a five-year plan, Perón nationalized many industries, expanded government services, and established universal healthcare. Much of this was popularized by Evita through her celebrity and the social agency of her foundation. Evita's death from uterine cancer was experienced by many as a national tragedy; indeed the place of Evita in the Argentine psyche is as prominent as that of Princess Diana in the Anglosphere.

Perónism, while intellectually indebted to fascism, was very much the movement of workers, often disdainfully referred to as *descamisados* (shirtless) by middle- and upper-class Argentines. In his second term, much of Perón's social reforms put him at odds with the Catholic Church, leading Pius XII to take the extraordinary step of excommunicating him in June 1955. Civil unrest and political violence emerged in the face of divisive Perónism, and Juan Perón fled into exile in the face of a coup d'état backed by conservative and political Catholic forces. Free elections were held in 1973, and Héctor Cámpora, a Perónist candidate, won the presidency. Cámpora allowed Perón to return from exile that year, and he then resigned, allowing Perón to seek the presidency. Perón was reelected president, and his third wife, Isabel, became vice-president. Perón succumbed to coronary artery disease in 1974, and Isabel assumed the presidency.

A military coup d'état removed Isabel Perón from office in March 1976. A military junta followed, led consecutively by Generals Videla, Viola, Galtieri, and Bignone. Political persecution had predated the dictatorship, and it is possible that up to 1,000 Argentines disappeared under the rule of Isabel Perón, whose complicity with the military prior to the dictatorship led to her being indicted for crimes against humanity in January 2007.[6]

Dictatorship

The military dictatorship from 1974 to 1982 was the bloodiest in South American history. Up to 30,000 Argentines perished in what was described as a "mini Holocaust."[7] The military had seized power on the pretext of instability caused by insurgency within the population. As one author described,

In the years that preceded the coup d'etat of 1976, there were acts of terrorism that no civilized community could justify. Citing these deeds, the military dictatorship unleashed a terrorism infinitely worse. (p. 5)[8]

The Argentine military had a tradition of perpetrating pogroms. "Throat slashing squads" were in operation during the nineteenth century Pampas wars. After the end of the military junta in 1982, many of the perpetrators of human rights abuse exported expertise to other dictatorships in Guatemala and El Salvador.[9]

Following the assumption of power in 1976, the military embarked on the National Reorganization Process (*el Processo*)—promarket reforms and deregulation to attract foreign investment. As part of this, the military also prosecuted La Guerra Sucia (The Dirty War) against activist groups such as trade union members, academics, journalists, and students. Argentine citizens who suddenly vanished were dubbed *los desaparecidos,* meaning "the missing ones" or "vanishing ones." To be "disappeared" was a new verb in the Argentine lexicon. Tortured prisoners were either executed and buried in the outskirts of Buenos Aires or thrown from helicopters into the mouth of the Rio Plata in a process dubbed *vuelos de la muerte* (death flights).

Torture centers were established, the most notorious being the Escuela de Suboficiales de Mecánica de la Armada (ESMA) or "Naval School." In one of the most bizarre and dissonant moments in the history of sports since Nazi Germany hosted the 1936 Olympics, the Argentine junta hosted the FIFA World Cup in 1978. The final, in which the host nation defeated the Netherlands 3–1, was held at the River Plate Stadium, less than a mile from ESMA. There is little doubt the tortured prisoners of the dictatorship would have heard the cheers of their fellow countrymen during the tournament from their cells.

The Argentine press remained silent out of both self-interest and fear. Individual journalists and editors collaborated with members of the dictatorship.[7] Some medical practitioners assisted in the torture of prisoners; however, there is no credible evidence of systematic abuses of human rights by the psychiatric profession in the prosecution of La Guerra Sucia.[10]

After the Dictatorship

The military dictatorship ended after Argentina's defeat in the Malvinas (or Falklands) War in 1982. This cynical and most unnecessary of conflicts invigorated the failing neoliberal project of Thatcher's Tories in the UK, while ending the same economic moment in Argentina. It is little wonder the United States was lukewarm or even resistive to the UK in their hostility toward one of their disaster capitalism projects in South America. Subsequent Argentine governments faced the difficult task of maintaining social stability, appeasing the military, and leading efforts to come to terms with the nation's violent recent past.

One of the first attempts of the latter was the establishment of a truth commission, the National Commission on the Disappearance of Persons (Comisión Nacional sobre la Desaparición de Personas, or CONADEP), created by President Raúl Alfonsín. The results of its investigations were documented in the *Nunca Más* (Never Again) report, delivered to President Alfonsín on September 20, 1984.[11] During the activities of CONADEP, psychiatrists provided support to individuals who had suffered from the psychological effects of trauma.[12] Many survivors drifted into institutional psychiatric care.

A particular theme in the account of the national narrative over *el Proceso* was of denial or repression of the event.[13] Repression, dissociation, and denial are as much phenomena of collective social as well as individual consciousness.[14] As one writer observed concerning how Argentines dealt with such events, "The answer, perhaps for the majority of Argentines, was that you got over it by pretending it had never happened" (p. 64).[15] Argentine psychologist Sandra Baita has argued that this process of denial relates to the post-Perón influence of Lacanian thought in the Argentine culture.[16]

At a political level, such denial manifest ultimately as gross injustice in dealing with the perpetrators of human rights abuses. Following CONADEP, nine former junta members were tried for mundane violations of Argentine law, not for crimes against humanity. Attempted prosecutions of members of the military led to three abortive uprisings against Alfonsín. To safeguard his rule, Alfonsín then passed *Ley de Punto Final* (full stop law) in December 1986; this decreed that there would be no new prosecutions relating to the dictatorship after 60 days. Alfonsín also passed the *Ley de Obediencia Debida* (obedience law) that exempted low-ranking officers against prosecution, virtually enshrining in law the Nuremberg defense.

Financial Crisis

Carlos Menem was elected president of Argentina in 1989. Nominally a populist Perónist, Menem presided over the dismantling of the Perónist project in Argentina with the closure of nationalized industries, ending government centralism. Such policies led to rising unemployment, abrupt shifts in wealth, and the disruption of traditional social structures. Much of the Argentine population declined into poverty. Political discontent grew through the 1990s. By mid-2002, the Argentine peso, previously pegged to the U.S. dollar, was worth about US$0.25. Riots in mid-December 2001 led to 26 deaths, prompting President De la Rúa to declare a state of siege and the imposition of censorship of all news outlets from Buenos Aires. In 2002 Nestor Kirchner became president. Kirchner was less neoliberal, and his tenure aspired to a retreat from the complete laissez-faire approaches of his immediate predecessors.

Themes in the History of Psychiatry in Argentina

Origins

Argentina has been characterized as a conglomerate of psychoanalytic culture, a recent history of political violence, and an "unrealized project of social modernity" (p. 44).[17] In Argentina, psychiatry is on the margins of medicine. Contemporary psychiatry in Argentina comprises "a heterogenous set of practitioners—psychoanalysts, neuroscientific psychiatrists, drug marketers, patient activists and others" who "creatively assimilate multiple techniques into their work of expertise" (p. 177).[17]

Psychiatry was not defined as a separate discipline in Argentina until the late 1940s. Early twentieth century Argentine psychiatry was closely linked to criminology and was strongly influenced by alienism and mental hygiene. The *Liga de Higiene Mental* was founded in 1929. Crime and "degeneracy" were considered a consequence of immigration, and the large wave of migration to Argentine in the early twentieth century was considered responsible for the increase in crime. Psychiatry, predominantly based in large asylums (*manicomios*), became part of a larger medical apparatus set up by the state to control the new urban masses.[2,18] Argentine psychiatrists adopted German psychiatrist Ernst Kretschmer's concept of constitutional psychiatry. Kretschmer developed a classification system based on body types:

1. asthenic/leptosomic (thin, small, weak)
2. athletic (muscular, large boned; later combined into the category asthenic/leptosomic)
3. pyknic (stocky, fat)

Each body morphology displayed certain personality traits and associated psychopathologies.[19]

Psychiatric patients, mainly immigrants or residents of poor rural areas, fell victim to psychiatric admissions processes in which civil codes were largely ignored. A number of patients faced involuntary admission on the basis of pecuniary family interests.[18]

Psychoanalysis

In Argentina, psychoanalysis was considered initially to be a therapeutic tool, although it has since evolved to become part of the culture. As the Argentine historian Mariano Plotkin argues, psychoanalysis provided Argentine society with a filter of intelligibility to understand cultural, political, or social processes and developments in Argentina.[20] Articles published in *Psicoterapia*, Argentina's psychoanalytic journal, conceptualized psychoanalysis as a response to the problems of modernity. It advanced a progressive political agenda that comprised the complete renovation of society through psychoanalysis. In an attempt to integrate the ideas of Freud and Marx, it was argued that the psyche was merely a reflection of the social order. Argentine psychiatry evolved into a tradition of social action. The mental health community in Buenos Aires defined itself as *mundo-psi*. Poverty, social injustice, and sociopolitical tensions were considered in *mundo-psi* as contributory to mental illness and therefore of concern to psychiatry.[21]

Perón barred psychoanalysts from the public health system, which saw nonmedical psychoanalysts distance themselves from psychiatrists and adopt a more Lacanian view. Psychoanalysis then morphed from a medical intervention into a cultural response to Perónism.[22] As Plotkin argues "in the 1960s psychoanalysis was simultaneously used as a therapeutic method, a means to channel and legitimise social anxieties, and an item of consumption that provided status to a sector of the population obsessed with 'modernity'"[2] (p. 71).

Salud Mental

The *salud mental* (mental health) movement in Argentina derived from a similar movement in the postwar United States. *Salud mental* psychiatrists were motivated by the failure of the dilapidated and oppressive asylums (*manicominos*). In 1957, the Instituto Nacional de Salud Mental (INSM) was established. The INSM functioned as an agent of Perónism prosecuting a social welfare project of modernization focused upon the workers of Argentina, from whose ranks many of the mentally ill emerged. The *salud mental* practitioner emphasized the notion of social citizenship with rights of access to education, labor laws, and healthcare. *Salud mental* rejected the disease model of mental illness and sought the social reintegration of the mentally ill with their community. While developments in pharmacological management of mental illness such as the advent of chlorpromazine in the early to mid-1950s aided the *salud mental* project, their form of psychiatry placed such measures in the background of efforts at social justice.

In 1958, Mauricio Goldenburg, the president of the INSM, launched Plan Goldenburg as a project of replacing the system of *manicominos* with networks of general hospital outpatient clinics and community mental health programs. The INSM sought to broaden its social justice focus to entire communities, to facilitate the return of the mentally ill. Many of the INSM's activities therefore required the engagement of *salud mental* psychiatrists in a form of militant political agency as champions of Perónism. After the overthrow of Perón in 1955, when Argentina was effectively de-Perónized and Argentine psychiatry was further radicalized, many psychiatrists were persecuted for their social activism. To the junta leaders, psychiatry was an instrument of social and political struggle.

Following the end of the Perónism, the focus of *salud mental* psychiatrists shifted to the views of Swiss-born psychoanalyst Enrique Pichon-Rivière. Pichon had created the Argentine Psychoanalytic Association in 1942 and had attempted to integrate medicine and culture through the mainstream dissemination of psychoanalysis as a methodology for social activism. Indeed, so radical was Pichon's advocacy of psychoanalysis as a means of revolution that there was an acrimonious split within the Argentine Psychoanalytic Association, with conservative members denouncing mental health centers as centers of "subversive indoctrination" (p. 206).[22] During *el Proceso*, Freud was proclaimed an intellectual criminal. Psychiatrists and psychologists were persecuted. *Salud mental* practitioners were targets of kidnapping and torture during the dictatorship. However, some forms of psychoanalysis were encouraged by the dictatorship, because it believed that it encouraged introspection and discouraged attempts to change social and political conditions.[2] *Salud mental* practitioners returned to positions of influence after the dictatorship, but in a diminished capacity. The *salud mental* experience of the dictatorship possessed "historical consciousness."[17] Plotkin argued that the ultimate consequence of *el Proceso* was the uncoupling of psychoanalysis and the political left.

The economic and social crisis of late 2001 had a significant effect on Argentine psychiatry. Psychiatrists faced financial hardship—in some circumstances, cheap or free psychotherapy was offered as part of a barter system in *clubs de trueque* (exchange clubs). The widespread economic instability imperiled the bourgeois demand for psychoanalysis. The use of antidepressants and briefer psychotherapies increased significantly. As part of the new *proceso*, Argentine psychiatrists were forced to eschew their psychoanalytic and *salud mental* traditions and embrace psychiatric neoliberalism. This was most evident with the compulsion to adopt the system of psychiatry based on North American biomedical and *Diagnostic and Statistical Manual of Mental Disorders* (*DSM*) standards. Apart from yielding to the need to standardize psychiatric diagnosis, the colonization of Argentine psychiatry by its northern hemisphere colleagues saw the emergence of biological psychiatry as the dominant paradigm in the field. This effectively undid generations of thought within Argentine psychiatry and in particular the social reformist projects of the INSM.

The neoliberal colonization of Argentine psychiatry saw the increase of the power of pharmaceutical and biotech companies both in the psychiatric academy and in the conceptualization and treatment of mental illness. This was the focus of an excellent ethnographic study by American sociologist Andrew Lakoff.[17] Lakoff's study noted the implications of a French company, Genset, financially motivating the Hospital Romero, a psychiatric hospital in Buenos Aires, to participate in the process of collecting genetic material from patients diagnosed with bipolar disorder. Lakoff highlighted that Argentine psychiatrists did not routinely diagnose bipolar disorder and that in order for the joint venture to proceed, they would need to adopt diagnostic practices utilizing the *DSM-IV*. Lakoff observed that this created "an unfriendly ecology of expertise—one in which the politics of knowledge militated against the adoption of a model of mental illness that was associated with biological reductionism, with the dismantling of public health, and with North American hegemony" (p. 5).[17]

The adoption of North American psychiatry was an extension of neoliberalism and all of its ramifications for public health, and the state of knowledge in Argentine psychiatry. As the legacy was dismantled by this fundamentally economic process, the entire value system of Argentine psychiatry, and its relationship with the state, changed.

Values and Argentine Psychiatry

We conducted an empirical study of Argentine psychiatrists to establish a model of their value system.[23] We speculated that the recent transformation of Argentine psychiatry seemed to provide insights into the contextual influences upon the moral agency of this group of psychiatrists. In conducting this study, we interviewed Argentine psychiatrists about their work with traumatized patients. From the qualitative analysis of the interviews, we evolved a model of values that emerged from the data (Figure 12.1).

In the first instance, Argentine psychiatrists valued a notion of justice. Justice had a number of perspectives, including rectifying social inequalities, assisting with legal or economic constraints faced by patients, and fostering access to necessary treatment services. Argentine psychiatrists valued each patient's individual story and often acknowledged that, unlike the reductive application of *DSM* diagnostic criteria, their patients' formulation of their difficulties may simply reflect the mundane realities of social and economic circumstances. As one of the psychiatrists argued of the reductive biologism of northern hemisphere psychiatry:

> The problem is inside the skin … in the brain. This is never connected with the social problem or the strategy and for that reason, I think we have difficulties to create solutions for the people.[23]

Argentine psychiatrists value efforts overcome the intrinsic problems of psychiatry in Argentina—professional divisions, archaic treatment and diagnostic practices, and political rivalries. The recent modernization of the profession involved the embrace of the apparent benefits of northern hemisphere scientific progress in psychiatry, while retaining some form of professional autonomy. Moreover, the modernization of psychiatry in Argentina

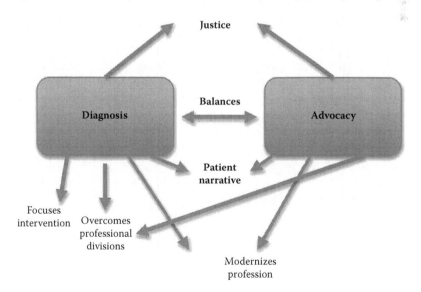

Figure 12.1 The value system of Argentine psychiatrists.

required both the development of specialized fields of expertise (such as child psychiatry and general hospital psychiatry) and the judicious use of medication and structured psychotherapies on the basis of effectiveness and appropriateness to patient need rather than economic constraint.

In terms of the moral agency in relation to these values, Argentine psychiatrists utilized two main strategies for dealing with these obligations, the diagnostic act and advocacy. The background issue in modern Argentine psychiatry is the North American system of classification. Tensions exist, related to the perils of submission to the *DSM* system balanced against the value achieved by doing so in the realm of advocacy and efficacious treatment. American psychiatrist John Sadler defined this tension, generally, as one between "ethnographic particularism" (p. 15) and the generalizations of *DSM*.[24]

The second strategy, advocacy, is one with a variety of contexts. Advocacy for the profession, in terms of its social role and its ongoing development in the light of advances in the profession broadly, was a theme virtually all of the subjects nominated. Advocacy on behalf of the patient in the face of a radically transformed health system was equally prominent in the minds of most of the subjects. Broad social advocacy, particularly in terms of poverty and access to education and other social goods, was a similarly prominent issue and one that has a strong tradition in Argentine psychiatry.

Moral Agency in Argentine Psychiatry

In this chapter, we have sought to provide an account of moral agency in a group of psychiatrists in a particular context. There are many distinct and interesting aspects to the history of Argentina and Argentine psychiatrists. The direct relevance of this to our thesis is how to integrate these aspects into a plausible formulation of moral agency by a group of psychiatrists. In doing this, we have integrated the varied background theoretical constructs—the noumenal self as moral agent, the socially constituted moral agent, and the professional moral agent working within the dual-role dilemma. The current value system of Argentine psychiatrists involves conceptions of justice, advocacy, and acknowledging the complex psychosocial situation of the patient and his or her distinct set of challenges. Argentine psychiatrists find themselves amid many dual-role tensions, including the preservation and evolution of their discipline, advocacy for their patients in the light of dramatic social and economic transformations, and their own ontological and financial uncertainties in the light of changes in Argentina since the Malvinas War in 1982.

Having surveyed the varied themes in Argentine psychiatry and recent Argentine history, we have evolved a model of moral agency of Argentine psychiatrists (Figure 12.2).

While any generalization has limitations, we argue that it is reasonable to consider that the Argentine narrative—political and economic instability and the risks these pose for the individual—approximates a common experience. Argentines are characteristically political in their views, whether at a level of political activism or a particular disposition to the kind of society their European enclave in the antipodes should be.

As members of a professional group with such a troubled and politicized history, Argentine psychiatrists arguably deliberate and act morally in light of this history. The epistemic and ontological tensions between the *salud mental* and northern hemisphere paradigms of psychiatry play out in the clinic, in professional interactions, and in the community. As one of the Argentine psychiatrists argued of their divided discipline:

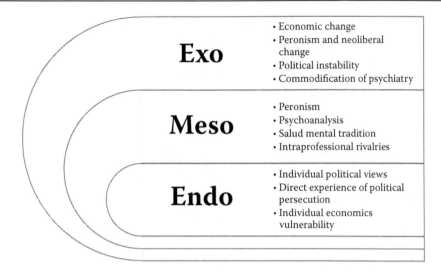

Figure 12.2 Moral agency and Argentine psychiatry.

We need to join in order to create better conditions because we have psychiatrists who use medication, and psychological treatment is in another way, divided—"dissociated."[23]

To illustrate how moral agency in Argentine psychiatrists is determined by this social constitution, the narrative of one of the psychiatrists who participated in the study is illuminating. The quotes come directly from an interview we conducted in Buenos Aires.

Dr. Diego worked in a psychiatric clinic in suburban Buenos Aires. His hospital faced financial pressure, and Dr. Diego had been directed to reduce his psychotherapy list and refer patients to shorter psychotherapies or medication review. Dr. Diego accepted the referral of a female patient, Katerina, who was in her early 40s. Katerina was a single mother of an adolescent son and received welfare benefits. She and her son had escaped a violent relationship and were forced to live in a barrio with a high crime rate. She had been sexually abused by a male relative from age 7 to 12. The perpetrator died six years ago, precipitating a marked deterioration in Katerina's mental state.

Katerina had seen a psychoanalyst for 5 years three times a week. She had to opt out of her insurance plan and could not continue her therapy.

Dr. Diego described that Katerina had been "diagnosed as a sexual addict; she was treated for a long period by another therapist as a sexual addict, and when she came to me I made a diagnosis of dissociation and I began to treat her as a separately traumatized patient." Katerina had displayed a propensity for sexualized acting out in addition to mood instability and periods of paranoid thinking. To a North American psychiatrist, her problems would meet criteria in the *DSM-IV* for borderline personality disorder. Dr. Diego had more sympathy with the approach of Katerina's previous therapist than with the reifying effects of the *DSM-IV*, but was fully aware that "there is pressure to use medication and briefer therapy. With lack of money, services are looking for more resolution-focused psychotherapy to achieve results .... Money is one of the biggest issues—20 or 30 years ago, it wasn't uncommon that a person was seeing their therapist two or three times a week; now that is rare."

Dr. Diego had been trained as a Freudian analyst although he was influenced by the work of Pierre Janet, particularly in relation to dissociation. Dr. Diego had recognized that much of Katerina's behavior had been dissociative in nature and noted that in recent times, "The first issue here in Argentina is that few people know about … dissociation. The second point is that they are usually treated as if they were psychotic." Dr. Diego understood that his assuming care of Katerina relied upon her problems being diagnosed along the *DSM-IV*, as he and his colleagues "used the *DSM* more in our dealings with the health system, the public health system, to offer some information, and they ask us to use these symptoms, but most of us didn't agree with *DSM*."

This dissonance was common among his colleagues. Dr. Diego, much to his chargrin, documented Katerina as suffering from cyclothymic disorder and suggested she trial lamotrigine to help her depressive and mood instability problems. He referred Katerina to a group-based dialectic behavior therapy program in lieu of her reengaging in psychoanalytic treatment. Dr. Diego justified his use of diagnosis as being a means of advocacy, as "the ethical problem is to defend patient rights, for the patient's needs."

The example of Dr. Diego highlights the nature of moral agency in Argentine psychiatrists. Facing a highly constrained economic situation and the need to rationalize healthcare, Dr. Diego had to abandon the traditions of his training and abide by the *DSM* system. He did this to advocate on behalf of a patient who faced gross social disadvantage and whose ongoing care necessitated the culturally alien recasting of her problems from a trauma-based dissociative process responding to a psychoanalytic method to a complex mood disorder managed by cost-effective means of drugs and structured psychotherapy.

References

1. Puig M. *Betrayed by Rita Hayworth*. New York: Vintage; 1981.

2. Plotkin M. *Freud in the Pampas*. Stanford, CA: Stanford University Press; 2001.

3. Baita S. Dissociation in Argentina. *Newsletter of the International Society for the Study of Dissociation*. 2005;23:2–5.

4. Pigna F. *Los Mitos de la Historia Argentina 4*. Buenos Aires: Editorial Planeta; 2008.

5. Goñi U. *The Real Odessa: Smuggling the Nazis to Perón's Argentina*. London: Granta Books; 2002.

6. Isabel Peron's arrest signals shift in Argentina. *Los Angeles Times*. January 13, 2007.

7. Knudson J. Veil of silence: the Argentine press and the Dirty War. *Latin American Perspectives*. 1997;24:93–112.

8. Sabato E. *Desde el silencio*. Buenos Aires: Sudamericano/Planeta; 1985.

9. Maechling C. The Argentine pariah. *Foreign Affairs*. 1981–82;45:69–83.

10. Lewis P. *Guerillas and Generals: The Dirty War in Argentina*. Westport, CO: Praeger; 2002.

11. *Nunca Más (Never Again): Report of CONADEP (National Commission on the Disappearance of Persons)—1984*. http://www.nuncamas.org/english/library/nevagain/nevagain_001.htm (accessed March 31, 2007).

12. Gomez-Cordoba. *The Psychosocial Approach to Truth Commissions*. 2001; http://www.ishhr.org/conference/articles/cordoba.pdf (accessed March 31, 2007).

13. Baita S. Dissociation in Argentina. *Newsletter of the International Society for the Study of Dissociation.* 2005;23:2–5.

14. Herman J. *Trauma and Recovery.* New York: Basic Books; 1992.

15. France M. *Bad Times in Buenos Aires.* London: Phoenix; 1998.

16. Baita S. Coping with childhood trauma and dissociation in Argentina. *Journal of Trauma Practice.* 2006;4:35–53.

17. Lakoff A. *Pharmaceutical Reason: Knowledge and Value in Global Psychiatry.* Cambridge: Cambridge University Press; 2005.

18. Abelard J. Law, medicine and confinement to public hospitals in 20th century Argentina. In: Plotkin M, ed. *Argentina on the Couch: Psychiatry, State and Society, 1880 to the Present.* Albuquerque: University of New Mexico Press; 2003:87–112.

19. Kretschmer E. *Physique and Character.* London: Routledge; 1931.

20. Plotkin M. Mental health and the Argentine crisis. In: Plotkin M, ed. *Argentina on the Couch: Psychiatry, State and Society, 1880 to the Present.* Albuquerque: University of New Mexico Press; 2003.

21. Guerrino A. *La Psiquiatra Aregntina.* Buenos Aires: Editores Cuatro; 1982.

22. Plotkin M. Psychiatrists and the reception of psychoanalysis 1919's–1970's. In: Plotkin M, ed. *Argentina on the Couch: Psychiatry, State and Society, 1880 to the Present.* Albuquerque: University of New Mexico Press; 2003.

23. Robertson M, Kerridge I, Pols H. Argentine psychiatry part 2: A pilot ethnomethodological study. *Journal of Ethics and Mentalh Health.* 2008;3:e1.

24. Sadler J. *Values and Psychiatric Diagnosis.* New York: Oxford University Press; 2005.

13

Protecting the People

Dangerous People

Michael Stone was well known to authorities. He had been convicted of his first acquisitive offense at age 12. By his early adulthood he had been imprisoned several times for violent crime and was addicted to heroin. Stone had been grossly emotionally and sexually abused as a child. At some point in his criminal career, Stone had been diagnosed as a psychopath.

On July 9, 1996, Stone attempted to rob a home in the town of Chillenden in Kent, England. In the course of the robbery, he killed Lin Russell and her 6-year-old daughter, Megan, with a hammer. Russell's 9-year-old daughter, Josie, survived the attack, despite suffering severe head injuries. She recovered and relocated with her father to Wales. Stone was arrested and charged with the murders a year later. He was convicted in 1998 and imprisoned for life. Stone's conviction and sentence were appealed as the Crown had relied on the testimony of a fellow prisoner to secure the verdict.

The horrific murders of Lin and Megan Russell, and the 2001 murder of Sarah Payne by Roy Whiting, another man considered a psychopath, provoked a rancorous and at times divisive disagreement between the psychiatric profession and the UK government at the time. At issue was what American psychiatrist Paul Appelbaum described as "an experiment in using psychiatry as an instrument for the control of dangerous persons."[1]

In the light of a prolonged coverage of the issue by the Fleet Street press, Home Secretary Jack Straw made numerous statements in the House of Commons on the matter. In February 1999, Straw stated:

> ... there is, however, a group of dangerous and severely personality disordered individuals from whom the public at present are not properly protected ... there should be new legislative powers for the indeterminate, but renewable detention of dangerously personality disordered individuals. These powers will apply whether or not someone was before the courts for an offence.

While the Mental Health Act (1983) recognized the specific entity of psychopathy as a mental disorder characterized by excessively aggressive or seriously irresponsible conduct, the detention and involuntary treatment of these types of patients was precluded by the treatability clause, Part 2, Section 3[2]a, of the act. In response to the Stone case and many similar instances, the UK government issued a white paper in 2000,[2] which proposed the removal of the treatability clause and the legislation of the proto-diagnosis[3] of dangerous severe personality disorder (DSPD). It was clear that the UK government, and Straw in particular, had lost patience with the psychiatric profession and its apparent refusal to take responsibility for the problem.[4]

Straw embarked on a public campaign to criticize psychiatrists in the UK, particularly in regard to their failure to protect the community against the danger posed by psychopaths. Straw was particularly critical of what he saw as the craven use of the treatability criteria of the act:

Twenty years ago [psychiatrists] were adopting what I would say was a commonsense approach to serious and dangerous persistent offenders. These days they have gone for a much narrower interpretation of the law. Quite extraordinarily for a medical profession, they have said they will only take on those patients they regard as treatable. If that philosophy applied anywhere else in medicine there would be no progress whatsoever. It's time, frankly, that the psychiatric profession seriously examined their own practices and tried to modernise them in a way that they have so far failed to do.[5]

Psychiatrists in the UK were at odds with the Home Office, and several prominent psychiatrists spoke out against the ethical and practical problems of the reform of the Mental Health Act in the light of the public debate. The 2002 draft revision of the act made no mention of DSPD, although the proposed definition of mental illness was diluted to address any situation where there was impairment or disturbance of mental functioning. The proposed revision of the law also diluted the notion of treatability to one of the provision of care. In July 2007, the Mental Health Act received royal assent. The new law introduced many innovations including supervised community treatment orders for people discharged from inpatient units. It also reclassified personality disorder as a mental disorder.

Prior to the modification of the UK mental health laws, the government sought to implement a program that identified persons with DSPD who posed a risk to the public and then detain them preemptively to enforce treatment for the condition. The Home Office and Department of Health had defined DSPD[3] in terms of the following:

1. They are more likely than not to commit an offense within five years that might be expected to lead to serious physical or psychological harm from which the victim would find it difficult or impossible to recover.
2. They have a significant disorder of personality.
3. The risk presented appears to be functionally linked to the significant personality disorder.

The program established four centers dedicated to the detention and management of DSPD including the special hospitals at Broadmoor and Rampton and prisons at Frankland and Whitemoor. In the 10 years to 2010, the DSPD program has cost £200 million and has been of dubious benefit. The UK government had considered the Dutch TBS system (*Terbesschikkingstelling*), which had been operating since 1928, managing high-risk violent and sexual offenders in secure community settings.[6] They opted for a program in prison hospitals or high-security psychiatric units.

The DSPD was an exquisite example of a socially constructed mental disorder. The teleological nature of determining potentially dangerous people as mentally ill in order to serve a social good has many parallels in the history of psychiatry. Advised by experts in the field, the Home Office provided a description of DSPD by integrating an Axis II diagnosis from the *Diagnostic and Statistical Manual of Mental Disorders, Fourth Edition (DSM-IV)* with a suprathreshold score on the Hare Psychopathy checklist PCL-R[7] significant of severe personality disorder.[8] A battery of risk assessment tools determined the adjectival aspect of the disorder. Prior to any systematic examination of the instrumental value of medicalizing, preemptively detaining, and forcibly treating violent criminals, it was estimated that five would need to be detained to prevent one violent act.[9]

Surprisingly, a committee-based, politically generated psychiatric disorder appeared to have some instrumental value. A study of 1,396 male prisoners serving sentences of 2 or more years for sexual/violent offenses was assessed for DSPD criteria and followed up over 2 years. The prevalence of DSPD in this cohort was 15 percent. Successful treatment of DSPD could reduce violent reconvictions among DSPD offenders by 71 percent and violent/sexual reoffenses in the prison population by 27 percent.[10]

The scientific literature in the area of DSPD is rich in ethical deliberation. Initial concerns about infringement of civil liberties in light of the imprecision of prediction of risk evolved into more elaborate articulations of the problem. A reflection on the DSPD experiment by a group of authors led by the personality disorders expert Peter Tyrer provided a balanced evaluation of the process.[3] Positive aspects of the program related to the stimulus of interest in a neglected clinical population, including service development and research focus. The negative aspects were the precedent of a specious diagnosis used for political ends, the triumph of public protection over individual liberty, the dilemma of financing and enforcing treatment of dubious benefit, and the warehousing of violent criminals in the mental health system.

DSPD as an Ethical Dilemma

The DSPD represents a significant challenge to the psychiatric profession in the UK. There is ample evidence of the Royal College of Psychiatrists, the British Medical Association, and rank-and-file members of the profession strenuously resisting a political process redolent of Soviet-era abuses of psychiatric diagnosis. Granted, it is much easier to have sympathy with a political dissident in a totalitarian regime than with a violent criminal; however, the fundamental dilemma of social justice remains.

In returning to the tenets of moral agency, the DSPD issue is a most apposite example, which integrates many of the themes in this book. British psychiatrists practice within a society and culture with a profoundly influential media and an overreactive political class. Generations of deprivation, welfare receipt, and social depredation have created a truly antisocial cohort of citizens, addled by social disadvantage, dysfunctional personality, and substance misuse. The musings of the social commentator and prison doctor Antony Daniels (writing under the *nom de plume* Theodore Dalrymple) highlight that through a process of well-intentioned but utterly misguided social welfare and medicalization, this underclass has not been socialized and does not know how to live.[11] Council estates have become factories of hopelessness, resentment, and despair. In the UK, mental health laws have been vague and have created a dilemma for psychiatrists burdened with the task of caring for the mentally ill and protecting the population. In Chapter 7 we highlighted the effects of neoliberalism on healthcare, and it is arguable that the whole DSPD experiment represents a triumph of managerialism in the process of medicalizing and commodifying a social problem with an associated financial solution.

In applying our deliberative method of moral reasoning, an argument can be made that the paradigm case should be the opposite of the gold standard—a clear circumstance where psychiatric diagnosis and treatment is a moral wrong. In the case of British psychiatrists and the DSPD, the starting point would be the Soviet-era diagnosis of "sluggish schizophrenia." Other examples might include the alleged persecution of Falun Gong by Chinese authorities (see the following section in this chapter), the pathologizaton of homosexuality in the period prior to the *DSM-III*, or the use of psychiatric diagnoses such as *amok* as a means of coercion by colonial powers.

As with sluggish schizophrenia, DSPD is a socially constructed diagnosis aimed at a political end. Both diagnoses lead to preemptive detention and appear to serve a social good rather than being a direct benefit to the patient. Unlike sluggish schizophrenia the DSPD has some content and predictive validity and a degree of inter-rater reliability, ironically due its social construction. Treatment interventions, in a significant number of cases, appear to reduce recidivism; and apart from hostile attitudes to the treatment program in secure hospitals rather than prisons,[12] the subjects of intervention see some merit in reducing their potential for reoffending.

In the final analysis, the conclusion from this approach to deliberation is that the DSPD program is not morally analogous to Soviet psychiatric abuses. It is in no one's best interests to be allowed to offend violently, and the whole affair has seen increased investment in clinical services for such a problematic group of patients. Psychiatrists who work in this program do not seem by this reckoning to be practicing in the same moral universe as the Soviet psychiatrists, and in the same vein, the DSPD debate does not reflect the kind of failure of the sovereign as evidenced in the Soviet example. There is, however, a broader issue of psychiatrists needing to insulate their practice against a reactionary political class and a carping, anti-intellectual media. As with many groups, severely personality-disordered patients require advocacy for such services, in addition to the appropriate degree of informing of public policy debates about the apparent social injustices that underlie the problem.

Psychiatric Abuses in China

By the time of Mao's victory in the Chinese Civil War in 1949, there was only a small number of psychiatrists in China. Many of them were Western trained and therefore were either rejected or persecuted by the Communist victors. In his reconstruction of postwar China, Mao turned to the Soviet Union for scientific and technical support, until the falling out between Mao and Khrushchev in the early 1960s. The Chinese writer Li Xintian noted, "With the arrival of advanced Soviet medical science, China's psychiatric workers were liberated from the ideological influence of the reactionary academic doctrines of Europe and America."[13] The Maoist doctrines of the cultural revolution attributed psychological and behavioral disturbance to a failure to appreciate the class struggle. Mao's *Little Red Book* became the de facto psychotherapy of the era. Those with established mental illness were taken from psychiatric facilities and incarcerated in labor camps and prisons for "counterrevolutionary" behaviour. Deng Xioping ceased this practice after Mao died in 1976.

This was by no means a liberation for psychiatry. Under Deng and later Jiang Zemin, the Soviet-era abuses of psychiatric diagnosis and treatment as a means of suppression of political dissent were revived. Enemies of the state were labeled mentally ill on the grounds of specious, politically motivated psychiatric diagnoses and detained and "treated" in special psychiatric hospitals, known as *Ankangs* (meaning peace and health), operated by the Ministry of Public Security. According to the Human Rights Watch:

> China's recently established Ankang system appears to be performing a role much the same as that of the Soviet Interior Ministry-run "Special Psychiatric Hospitals," which were used to incarcerate, in a medically unjustifiable way, hundreds and possibly thousands of peaceful Soviet dissidents.[14]

An official encyclopedia of communist Chinese psychiatry published in 1990 explains the three types of psychiatric diagnoses of people who were taken by police into psychiatric custody, and thence to the *Angkangs*. The first are those commonly known as *hua fengzi* (romantic maniacs), who are typical of the chronically homeless mentally ill found in most large cities. The *zhengzhi fengzi* (political maniacs) are essentially dissidents and reactionaries. The third group, *wu fengzi*, exhibit antisocial or criminal behavior.

The Hong Kong–based academic and human rights activist Robin Munro has been active in highlighting the reinvigorated Soviet-style abuses of psychiatry in China.[15-17] In 2000, Munro published an article in the *Columbia Journal of Asian Law*, highlighting the abuse of psychiatric diagnosis as a means of repressing political dissidents, or enemies of the state.[17] Munro noted:

> Arrested political dissidents and others in similar categories brought for assessment by the State's forensic psychiatrists are often officially treated as ranking among the most "serious and dangerous" of all alleged mentally ill offenders, and are thus prime candidates for compulsory committal in such institutions.

In April 1999, an obscure spiritual community in China, Falun Gong (Cultivation of the Wheel of the Law), mounted a demonstration outside an important Communist Party building in Beijing. This was the largest public demonstration held in China since the Tiananmen Square massacre in May 1989. Jiang Zemin, then Communist Party president, found his motorcade swamped with 15,000 Falun Gong protestors. Jiang was reportedly troubled by the fact that the protestors, all practitioners of Falun Gong, were not the typical student prodemocracy activists but from all ages and social groups. Jiang saw this movement as a threat to the status quo and promptly outlawed Falun Gong. Jiang created "The 610," an office with the authority to eradicate Falun Gong from China.[18]

Falun Gong is considered by Chinese authorities to be a cult. Their leader, Master Li Hongzhi, claims to be divine, superior to Jesus and the Buddha. He is thought to have preternatural powers—that he can fly and walk through walls. The Falun itself is the traditional Buddhist swastika. Practitioners of Falun Gong believe Master Li has implanted the Falun into their abdomens; the more accomplished of them proclaim they can feel it rotating. Falun Gong practitioners apply the *qigong*, a traditional form of Chinese physical and mental exercise.

After the Falun Gong movement was outlawed, its leaders and many followers were arrested and imprisoned. Like Stalin with Grigorenko, the mere imprisonment of Falun Gong members was not sufficient to quell the movement. A psychiatric diagnostic label then appeared, the "*qigong* related mental disorder."[19,20] This was used as a pretext to detain Falun Gong followers in *Ankangs*. Chinese psychiatrists defend the *qigong*-related mental disorder as a culture-bound syndrome—the core disturbance of this condition is the delusional belief that a person has a swastika implanted in his or her abdomen.[21] *Qigong*-related mental disorder has since subsided as the expedient psychiatric diagnosis for problematic Falun Gong followers, who are now diagnosed with "evil cult-related mental disorder." Figures from the Beijing University of Medical Science indicate that the number of patients with psychiatric disorders caused by practicing Falun Gong accounts for between 10 and 42 percent of all psychiatric diagnoses in China.[22]

Robin Munro estimated that at least 3,000 people charged with some kind of political crime in the past two decades were referred for psychiatric evaluation by police, and that most of them were deemed mentally ill and confined in the *Ankang* system. The Soviet numbers are small by comparison—only 200 to 300 Soviet dissidents were ever sent to psychiatric hospitals during the Soviet era.

In May 2000 the American Psychiatric Association's (APA's) Committee on Abuse of Psychiatry and Psychiatrists urged the World Psychiatric Association (WPA) to begin an investigation of charges that Chinese psychiatrists were taking part in human rights violations perpetrated against Falun Gong members. In 2001 the British Royal College of Psychiatrists voted to urge the WPA to send an investigative team to China and assess the validity of charges of psychiatric abuses related to Falun Gong members. In August 2002, at a meeting in Japan, the WPA passed a resolution to send a team to China to investigate the charges about psychiatric abuse. The Chinese Psychiatric Society agreed to cooperate with an investigation that was to begin in April 2002. Several days before it was to start, the Chinese Psychiatric Society sent the WPA a letter in which it indicated that it was, at the Chinese government's insistence, postponing the visit indefinitely. In May 2004 the APA held its annual meeting in New York. The WPA and Chinese Psychiatric Society came to a compromise agreement that denied the systematic psychiatric abuse of Falun Gong practitioners by psychiatrists in China. As it stands, the narrative around this issue is that the abuse of psychiatric power in suppressing the Falun Gong is sporadic and conducted of the misguided practices of rogue psychiatrists.

Despite Munro's detailed arguments, a number of prominent psychiatrists remain unconvinced that the alleged abuses of Chinese psychiatry parallel those of the USSR. Two prominent academic psychiatrists from Harvard, Alan Stone and Arthur Kleinman, are skeptical of the notion of the Chinese government prevailing upon Chinese psychiatrists to use specious psychiatric diagnoses to suppress Falun Gong. Stone led an APA task force and had some access to Chinese psychiatric facilities. He found Chinese psychiatrists and the Chinese Society of Psychiatrists to be both cooperative and concerned about the issue. Stone noted that Falun Gong practitioners in secure hospitals had not been admitted by malefactor psychiatrists; many had been conveyed following torture or detention by authorities.[23] Kleinman and a co-writer, Sing Lee, saw Munro's methods of study as flawed and the claims of systemic abuse of psychiatric power in China highly implausible.[24] Even Munro concedes it is difficult to justify the conclusion of widespread human rights abuses by Chinese psychiatry.[19]

Conclusion

Both of these recent dilemmas confronting psychiatrists in the UK and China have particular and socially distinct aspects and speak to universal notions of human rights. In both cases, psychiatrists face pressure from government and the community to deal with a challenge from a particular group. What remains the subject of debate is the degree to which a moral relativist position can be justified in both circumstances.

If we return to our model of social justice and the dilemma of professional ethics, the fundamental question is whether the sovereign has failed in directly persecuting a group and, by extension, whether the common good presents an affront to the values of psychiatrists. In the case of the UK, a liberal democracy that is signatory to international covenants of human rights and functions within the rule of law presents a credible face of the sovereign. The DSPD project may present as the pretext to violation of human rights, particularly in regard to preemptive detention on the basis of a socially constructed psychiatric disorder of people who pose a public menace, yet the aspiration is to provide interventions that reduce recidivism through clinical improvement. The distasteful aspects of psychiatrists participating in an agenda of social control are not new problems, yet it is in no one's interest to allow a patient with a severe personality disorder to commit a violent offense.

In the case of China, the assessment of the problem strays into broader and more complex considerations of China's approach to civil rights generally and the desirability of political reform in the eyes of the West. By no means does the liberal West hold the franchise on moral rectitude, and the approach to allegations of abuse of psychiatric power collide with similar dilemmas over China's alleged treatment of its own citizens, racial minorities such as Huigurs, or its approach to its near neighbors such as Tibet. In returning to the moral relativism of David Wong,[25] the question is whether the sovereign role of the Chinese government provides for its population. By many measures, China continues to grow economically and many of its citizens stand to benefit—as does much of the rest of the global economy. China is politically stable, and while the rule of law in China may seem harsh through Western eyes, Chinese citizens are in large part able to go about their lives. Unlike the DSPD program, the balance of opinion appears to indicate that the persecution of Falun Gong by psychiatrists is not part of a government-initiated process. Chinese psychiatry under more totalitarian periods of government in postwar China had a distinctly Soviet flavor, and it would seem reasonable to assert that some aspects of Chinese psychiatry under Mao and Deng were in some way morally equivalent. This does not appear to be the case in present-day Chinese psychiatry, and all evidence indicates that the Chinese psychiatric profession, despite the sensitivity of their political masters to Western scrutiny, seeks the same resolution to the issue as their international colleagues.

In the final analysis, psychiatrists in China and the UK face a similar dilemma. Their professional contract with their societies, manifest as a specific interaction with government and those who formulate public policy, necessitated involvement in serving the common good in reducing the threat posed to public safety by certain citizens assumed to be acting under the influence of a mental illness. In this chapter, we have grappled with analyses of these two quandaries from various perspectives. Regardless of one's own conclusions about these issues, it is clear that both Chinese and British psychiatrists, as socially constituted and contextualized moral agents, face a challenging incarnation of the dual-role dilemma.

References

1. Appelbaum P. Dangerous severe personality disorders: England's experiment in using psychiatry for public protection. *Psychiatric Services.* 2005;56:397–399.

2. Department of Health. Reforming the Mental Health Act. London: Stationery Office; 2000.

3. Tyrer P, Duggan C, Cooper S, et al. The successes and failures of the DSPD experiment: the assessment and management of severe personality disorder. *Medicine, Science and Law.* 2010;50:95–99.

4. Maden A. Dangerous and severe personality disorder: antecedents and origins. *British Journal of Psychiatry.* 2007;190(Suppl 49):S8–11.

5. Aquinas T. *Summa Theologica.* 1947; http://www.sacred-texts.com/chr/aquinas/summa/index.htm.

6. Mangan J. An historical analysis of the principle of double effect. *Theological Studies.* 1949;10:41–61.

7. Hare R. *The Hare Psychopathy Checklist-Revised (PCL-R).* Toronto: MHS; 1991.

8. Home Office & Department of Health. *Dangerous and Severe Personality Disorder (DSPD) High Secure Services for Men: Planning and Delivery Guide.* London: Home Office; 2005.

9. Buchanan A, Leese M. Detention of people with dangerous severe personality disorders: a systematic review. *The Lancet.* 2001;358:1955–1999.

10. Ullrich S, Yang M, Coid J. Dangerous and severe personality disorder: an investigation of the construct. *International Journal of Law and Psychiatry.* 2010;33:84–88.

11. Dalrymple T. *Life at the Bottom.* Lanhaml, MA: Ivan R Dee; 2001.

12. Sinclair J, Willmott L, Fitzpatrick R, et al. Patients' experience of dangerous and severe personality disorder services: qualitative interview study. *British Journal of Psychiatry.* 2012;200:252–253.

13. Xintian L. One decade of the clinical application of artificial hibernation therapy in China. *Zhonghua Shenjing Jinshenke Zazhi (Chinese Journal of Nervous and Mental Diseases).* 1959;6:351.

14. Human Rights Watch and Geneva Initiative on Psychiatry. Dangerous minds: political psychiatry in china today and its origins in the Mao era. 2002; http://www.hrw.org/reports/2002/china02/.

15. Munro R. Political psychiatry in post-Mao China and its origins in the cultural revolution. *Journal of the American Academy of Psychiatry and the Law.* 2002;30:97–106.

16. Munro R. *Dangerous Minds: Political Psychiatry in China Today and Its Origin in the Mao Era.* New York: Human Rights Watch and Geneva Initiative on Psychiatry; 2002.

17. Munro R. Judicial psychiatry in China and its political abuses. *Columbia Journal of Asian Law.* 2000;14:1–128.

18. Lu S, Galli M. Psychiatric abuse of Falun Gong practitioners in China. *J Am Acad Psychiatry Law.* 2002;30:126–130.

19. Lyons D, Munro R. Dissent as a symptom: why China has questions to answer. *The British Journal of Psychiatry.* 2002;180:551–552.

20. Lyons D. Soviet-style psychiatry is alive and well in the People's Republic. *British Journal of Psychiatry.* 2001;178:380–381.

21. Lee S. Who is politicising psychiatry in China (Letter)? *British Journal of Psychiatry.* 2001;179:178–179.

22. Shi J. *Li Hongzhi and His "Falun Gong": Deceiving the Public and Ruining Lives.* Beijing: New Star Publishers; 1999.

23. Stone A. The plight of Falun Gong. *Psychiatric Times.* 2004;21:13.

24. Lee S, Kleinman A. Psychiatry in its political and professional contexts: a response to Robin Munro. *J Am Acad Psychiatry Law.* 2002;30:107–111.

25. Wong D. Relativism. In: Singer P, ed. *A Companion to Ethics.* Oxford: Blackwell; 1991:442–449.

14

The Wretched of the Earth

Introduction

Throughout this book, we have identified examples of psychiatric moral agency in a variety of challenging circumstances. Whether it be British psychiatrists grappling with legislation targeting personality-disordered patients, American psychiatrists practicing under unrestrained market forces and internecine arguments over the state of psychiatric knowledge, or Argentine psychiatrists adapting to a rapidly changing social context, the psychiatrist's moral behavior has been profoundly influenced by context. In this last chapter, we return to the issue of social justice and how psychiatrists can enact moral agency in the face of a seeming failure of the sovereign. The broader focus of this chapter is the dilemma over how Australian psychiatrists respond to the treatment of asylum seekers by their Commonwealth government. This is not a distinctly Australian problem, although in the context of Australian psychiatry it is an apposite example of the multiple contextual influences upon the moral agency of Australian psychiatrists. This example involves Australian psychiatrists—the colleagues of the authors of this book. While our consideration of the challenges faced by our fellow psychiatrists can be handled in an objective manner, our examination of an ongoing challenge to the ethical practice of psychiatry in Australia is by nature more a participant–observer process than our quasiethnographic considerations of other areas. In a sense, our consideration of the issues raised in this chapter and the conclusions we argue speak to the social constitution of our moral agency and our own personal dual-role dilemma.

Themes in Australian History

Identity

The historian John Hirst argued for a thematic approach to an "Official History of Australia."[1] Hirst's themes include convict settlers, a harsh country, Diggers, economy and politics, sport, nation, and Aboriginal people. According to the sociologist Catriona Elder, the narratives of being Australian are created in relation to other nations and cultures, which creates a situation of binary opposites of Australian versus non-Australian.[2] This process arises out of the unfamiliarity of the original European settlers with the Australian landscape and the need to impose European symbolic order upon its alien features.[3] These narratives are often created in times of war, such as the Australian and New Zealand Army Corps

(ANZAC)* story and Australia's relationship with New Zealand, or the Vietnam War and the relationship with the United States. The binary narrative is linked to being white and, according to Elder, creates a sense of otherness within society. This nonwhite otherness traditionally includes indigenous Australians and, more recently, new arrivals (migrants, refugees, or asylum seekers) of Asian or Middle Eastern descent.

Aboriginal Australia

The relationship between Aboriginal and white Australia has been a perpetually traumatic one. The arrival of white settlement in Aboriginal Australia resulted in dispossession of traditional lands, degradation of Aboriginal culture, and a sporadic program of murder, all of which have been equated with the genocides of other native populations by Europeans in the nineteenth century.[4] Frequent instances of virtual "ethnic cleansing," either through mass murder or attempts at assimilation of Aboriginal people with mainstream white Australia, betrayed a social Darwinist agenda, which viewed Aboriginal Australians as inferior beings, possessed of a primitive culture and unworthy of the lands they had lived in for millennia.[5]

A more recent and troubling issue was the recognition of the policy of forced removal of children of Aboriginal and Torres Strait Islander families in the period 1869–1969.[6] Such a policy was based upon legislation in different jurisdictions and involved the state forcibly removing such children from their families and placing them in the care of church missions or state-run facilities. While the removals were argued to have been based on concern for children of mixed-race background, there is clear evidence that this was, in essence, a policy based upon Darwinist ideology, eugenics, fears of miscegenation, and a desire to maintain Caucasian racial purity in the face of mixed-race children.[7] Apart from the effect of traumatic separation on the children and their families, and the frequent instances of abuse and maltreatment in care, the truly abhorrent nature of the practice was that it represented a form of ethnic cleansing. Moreover, such intellectually bankrupt notions of racial purity paralleled those in 1930s Germany, inviting the assumption of a moral equivalence between two different forms of ethnic cleansing.[8] The racist motivations of this policy were not lost on the survivors. This process posed an existential threat to indigenous Australia of the "devaluation of Aboriginal parenting, state paternalism devalu(ing) distress of the family, forced geographic, cultural and emotional isolation, devaluation of Aboriginal culture."[9] While the Australian Prime Minister Kevin Rudd (2007–2010) referred to this systematic violation of human rights as a blemished chapter in our nation's history, the country remained polarized along political lines on the issue. An acrimonious debate occurred in the media between those who saw the specter of the "stolen generation" as a national disgrace and those who advocated polemic denials of the policy's existence or its negative impact.[10]

Historically, the approach to the relationship between indigenous and nonindigenous Australians was predicated upon the assumption of *terra nullius*. In 1992, the High Court of Australia determined in the "Mabo case" that pastoral leases did not extinguish native title in common law, which was tied to the long-standing and unique relationship between the Aboriginal population and the land. This decision was seen to herald a new era of reconciliation with indigenous Australia. However, in 1996 the *terra nullius* issue was resuscitated when the High Court ruled in the "Wik" decision that competing claims

---

* In the First World War, Australian and New Zealand troops were combined into a single force termed *the ANZAC*. The ANZACs took part in the disastrous Gallipoli campaign in Turkey in 1915. Many regard this as the foundation myth of the Australian identity.

between native title and pastoral leases could coexist. The newly elected conservative federal government subsequently implemented the Native Title Amendment Act 1998, which undermined much of the progress in reconciliation. A parallel cultural process emerged in the so-called "history wars," where questions were raised about the historical accuracy of the accounts of the genocide of Aboriginal peoples in the nineteenth century.[11]

Australian Militarism

The one enduring cultural icon in the Australian narrative is that that of the ANZAC. The anniversary of the ANZAC landings at Gallipoli in 1915 is a national day of remembrance. Great War battlefield sites (and increasingly sites from other wars such as the Kokoda Track in Papua New Guinea) have become sites of pilgrimage for Australians. From the original European convict settlement and the establishment of a military garrison in Sydney Cove in 1788, there has been a military narrative in the Australian story. While it may have reached an apotheosis in the carnage of the Great War, this narrative has passed through several eras. In modern times, the national approach to ANZAC day and Australian militarism has seen dramatic shifts in perspective in the community. In the aftermath of the divisive Australian involvement in the Vietnam War, there was, at best, ambivalence toward Australian militarism. In the early twenty-first century, there has been a virtual renaissance in Australian militarism. This may be, in part, due to the passage of time from both the Vietnam War era and the death of the last surviving ANZAC, although the revival of Australian militarism has been argued to have been cultivated in the light of the so-called war on terror and as a political expedient.[12]

Themes in the History of Australian Psychiatry

Early Influences

The psychiatric profession in both Australia and New Zealand was originally established as an extension of British psychiatry.[13] In the mid-nineteenth century various "lunatic acts" were established in different jurisdictions.[14,15] The most important themes in early Australian psychiatry were alienism and mental hygiene. As in Argentina, alienism and mental hygiene in Australia manifested in a latent xenophobia and fear of importing medical and psychiatric illness through uncontrolled immigration. Australian psychiatrists in the early twentieth century identified the significance of what they termed the *eugenic imperative*, indicating a synergy between the themes of mental hygiene, alienism, and immigration policies.[16] Many Australian psychiatrists became vitally interested in eugenics in the first three decades of the twentieth century,[17] coincident with the policy of the removal of Aboriginal children on the same philosophical grounds.

As in other settings, the asylum system was the dominant paradigm of psychiatric care in Australia.[18,19] Such asylums suffered the same limitations as in other countries, although Australian psychiatry celebrates the modernizing influence of Frederick Norton Manning, the inspector general of the insane for the New South Wales colony. Among Manning's many achievements, he is noted for his specific attention to indigenous mental health.[19] The other celebrated figure in Australian psychiatry is John Cade, whose 1949 paper on the use of lithium salts was profoundly influential in the management of severe mental illness.[20]

Australian psychiatrists in the nineteenth and early to mid-twentieth centuries practiced with British specialist qualifications. The Australasian Association of Psychiatrists was founded in October 1946 and the Australian and New Zealand College of Psychiatrists (later Royal) (RANZCP) was incorporated on October 28, 1963. The RANZCP is now the main professional organization of psychiatrists in Australasia and has an influential role in advising governments on many aspects of mental health policy and practice.

Aboriginal Mental Health

Racist attitudes toward indigenous Australians were evident in early writings of Australian psychiatry. Aborigines were characterized as "crude and simple, childish and devoid of reasoning, and often sexual and animal in nature," and as such, "Aboriginal insanity was interpreted as the most exaggerated expression of their innate primitiveness and savagery."[21] The emergence of serious consideration of the unique issues of Aboriginal mental health are credited to the psychiatrist John Cawte.[22,23] In addition to meticulous ethnographic studies, Cawte's work placed Aboriginal mental health in the context of the tension between old- and new-world influences.[24] Indigenous mental health emerged as a substantive area of expertise internationally due to the wave of decolonization and a dedicated World Health Organization report into the mental health of indigenous peoples.[25]

The ongoing situation of injustice faced by indigenous people in Australia manifests as physical and mental illness and social discord.[26] Arguably, disrespect and a sense of inferiority become physically manifest as immune suppression, inflammation, and acute and chronic illness. Externally, these social processes emerge as substance misuse, risk-taking, violence, and social discord.[26,27] It also indicates that for indigenous populations, physical health, mental health, and social deprivation are inseparable. This profoundly influences help seeking among indigenous people, whose relationship with healthcare professionals from nonindigenous society is often characterized by problematic power relationships.[28] There are frequent breakdowns of order in indigenous communities, leading to demoralization and anomie.[29] This has created a discourse in indigenous mental health that has realized the need for culturally respectful and sensitive mental health services.[30]

Scandals

Two scandals loom large in the psyche of Australian psychiatrists—the death of numerous patients at Chelmsford Private Hospital in Sydney and the abuse of patients in Ward 10B of Townsville Hospital in Queensland.

The Chelmsford Hospital scandal involved the criminally negligent use of the discredited practice of continuous narcosis, or deep sleep therapy (DST). Under the direction of a psychiatrist, Dr. Harry Bailey, and a local general practitioner, Dr. Ian Herron, DST was performed at Chelmsford from 1963 until the mid- to late 1980s. Patients were induced into continuous profound sedation with barbiturates, fed through naso-gastric tubes, and administered electroconvulsive therapy (ECT). Those who had not responded clinically to Bailey's satisfaction were referred to a local teaching hospital for cingulotractotomy. Apart from severe medical negligence, Chelmsford Hospital was also culpable in its use of inexperienced nurses in the care of such patients. Moreover, when the hospital's medical board prohibited the use of DST, Bailey subverted the process by admitting patients under Herron's name. After a series of complaints, a Royal Commission was established in 1988[31] and concluded that, at the very least, 24 patients had died as a result of DST at Chelmsford. Another 19 patients who had undergone DST committed suicide within a year of their admissions to Chelmsford. Much of the agitation about Chelmsford had been by the Church of Scientology's Citizen's Commission of Human Rights. Bailey committed suicide in 1985. Unrepentant, his suicide note stated, "Let it be known that the Scientologists and the forces of madness have won."[32]

The ultimate impact of Chelmsford on the Australian psychiatric profession was a loss of a degree of professional autonomy. Subsequent mental health legislation in the state of New South Wales prohibits private psychiatric hospitals from admitting patients on an involuntary basis, psychosurgery has been outlawed, and independent tribunals now closely regulate the administration of ECT.

Just as the Chelmsford scandal was resolving, another emerged in the state of Queensland. Dr. John Lindsay, the director of the psychiatric ward of Townsville Base Hospital (Ward 10B), had run the inpatient unit along the lines of a therapeutic community. By 1986, 123 complaints had been made to the Townsville Hospital's Board about Lindsay and Ward 10B,[33] including allegations of sexual and physical abuse and gross medical negligence. In 1991, the Queensland government established a commission of inquiry.[34] The commission received testimony that patients in Ward 10B were subjected to cruel and inhumane treatment and identified 65 deaths attributable to either suicide or iatrogenic causes. As did Chelmsford, 10B affected psychiatry in Australia in that

> although (Townsville Ward 10B) suggests that problems at Townsville can be attributed to Lindsay's desire for innovation, and refusal to recognise mistakes, further investigation reveals that this is not an unusual problem within psychiatric practice in Australia.[33]

Contemporary Failures

There is a weight of opinion that indicates that Australian psychiatry has a self-image problem. Australian historian Milton Lewis highlighted that since the 1950s Australian psychiatry was not only "divorced from the mainstream of medicine … but it was also not a very highly regarded area of medical specialisation" (p. 99).[18] Two historians have highlighted that the official history of the RANZCP[19] has a tone of negative self-assessment.[35] Moreover, psychiatry in Australia has endured a series of scandals, involving either moral lapses on the part of individual psychiatrists resulting in sexual abuse of patients, or in one extraordinary incident, the murder of a senior psychiatrist, Dr. Margaret Tobin, by a disgruntled colleague in 2002.[36]

In the 1960s, the global trend to community care led to a process of deinstitutionalization in Australia,[18] although the process resulted in those suffering mental illness being "removed from one form of incarceration only to end up in another."[37] The period from the 1960s saw significant levels of divestment of government in community mental health services and the defaulting of many services to poorly funded nongovernment organizations.[38] Rather than see the blossoming of community psychiatry, Australian psychiatrists witnessed a process of transinstitutionalization of the mentally ill from large psychiatric hospitals to overcrowded low-cost accommodation, homelessness, and increasingly, prisons. In Australia, much like the rest of the developed world, the prevalence of psychiatric disorder is significantly higher in the prison population than the community,[39] inviting the critique that prisons have become the de facto psychiatric institutions.[40]

Values and Australian Psychiatrists

The presumed values of Australian psychiatrists are expressed in the Code of Ethics elaborated by the RANZCP. We conducted an empirical study of the values of Australian psychiatrists and identified that four main values emerged from our analysis of the study data—the value of the patient, the value of sophisticated understanding, the value of reflexivity, and the value of advocacy.[41] The value of the patient integrates psychiatrists' concerns to value the patient's narrative above other forms of defining the patient's experience, placing his or her experience in a broad sociocultural context and acknowledging how different individuals and those around them may define their experience in both clinical and existential terms (the patient's construction of meaning).

Sophisticated understanding is the valuing of the complex, pluralistic, and integrative approach psychiatrists take to their discipline. Reflexivity refers to the value psychiatrists place on a form of reflection in their practice, including the need to consider personal and professional value systems in their clinical and nonclinical roles as psychiatrists, an awareness of the historical failings of the psychiatric profession in the Australian and international contexts, an awareness of the potential for harm to arise from psychiatric diagnosis and intervention (including stigma and iatrogenic harm), the potential adverse consequences of desiring for certainty or omnipotence manifesting in rigid or inflexible approaches to patient care, and actions that may be self-serving or promote harmful divisions within the profession.

Advocacy involves the provision of the best care for the patient including the judicious use of clinical practice guidelines, balancing tension between scientific rigor, and tailoring the treatment to the patient's circumstances. This value also addresses complex themes such as the relationship between psychiatrists and the psychiatric profession with institutions, the limits of political activism, and the use of the media as a form of advocacy.

The Asylum-Seeker Debate

Background

The Australian experience has long been tied to otherness. Since European settlement, the Australian psyche has always been other-regarding, particularly in relation to migration policy.

From the late 1970s, Australia received an influx of refugees from Indochina. Laws determining the mandatory detention of unauthorized arrivals of refugees in Australia were introduced in 1992. While the legislation specifically disallowed judicial review of detention, it imposed a 273-day limit on detention. In 1994, the Migration Reform Act 1992 removed the 273-day limit and broadened the scope of mandatory detention to any person who did not hold a valid visa.

In 2001, the then-conservative federal government developed a policy termed the "Pacific Solution," whereby many areas previously considered under Australian jurisdiction were excised from Australia's migration zone. The policy also involved asylum seekers being removed to detention camps in other countries (usually small, economically disadvantaged Pacific nations) while applications for asylum were considered. Despite the term being reminiscent of the Nazis' Final Solution, the Pacific Solution was a popular policy among the electorate. The policy was terminated in February 2008, although in 2010 the federal government sought to resuscitate it by having asylum seekers detained in Malaysian camps while their applications for asylum were processed. Since then, off-shore detention centers have reopened, and most alarmingly, children have been placed back into circumstances of indefinite detention. This policy was deemed illegal by the High Court in 2011.

The emotive and highly political issue of asylum seekers represents a significant challenge to Australian psychiatrists. While the issue of border protection and treatment of asylum seekers is highly political and has figured as a significant issue in federal elections,[42] there is considerable evidence of psychological harm arising from the policy of mandatory detention[43,44] and indefinite periods of uncertainty about immigration status.[45] As such, the policy represents a public health issue.

It is abundantly clear that the social dislocation arising from escaping violence in one's home country is profoundly injurious to mental health.[46,47] It is also evident that the current practice of detaining refugees who have entered sovereign lands in an unauthorized fashion is as traumatic as the persecution or warfare they fled.[43–45,47–49] While the experience of being a refugee and sociocultural displacement requires specific cross-cultural considerations in treatment,[50,51] an emergent ethical issue is how psychiatrists or other mental health professionals position themselves within a society where public policy is tolerated or even encouraged by the polity.

In Australia, many psychiatrists chose to involve themselves in the plight of the asylum seekers. The issue of children being held in what were essential to concentration camps was an anathema to many in the profession. Involvement of psychiatrists varied from the provision of clinical services for those in detention to very public advocacy. The dilemma, simply put, was the virtual futility of trying to alleviate the psychological distress arising from traumatic imprisonment in the face of persisting social injustice. As one psychiatrist noted of tending to children in detention:

> Treatment of much of the disease and distress was meaningless without addressing the causes (indefinite mandatory detention, family separation, impermanent protection). Prevention always being better than cure, the options were limited. It was not enough to be sympathetic, to sit with, to listen and to nod. The only choice was advocacy. (p. 218)[52]

The issue of advocacy was the pivotal issue. Several prominent psychiatrists signed a formal letter of protest at the Australian government's treatment of asylum seekers.[53] Such public forms of advocacy created tension within the RANZCP membership, frequently along partisan political lines. This led to an at times rancorous debate in scientific literature[54,55] and popular media,[56] including allegations of government interference in some psychiatrists' research into the mental health of asylum seekers.[57] In the course of our study, one psychiatrist spoke of the dilemma faced in considering the perils of advocacy for asylum seekers:

> And in that particular arena what happened from very early on was that there was denigration of the individuals from doing that advocacy, there was ignoring of recommendations … and in the media as well there was use of the media by politicians and bureaucrats to stigmatize and denigrate asylum seekers for political gain, so it was extremely politicized.

The debate over asylum seekers prompted consideration of the role of psychiatrists in such social debates, with one published survey identifying the majority of the RANZCP's constituency supporting some form of activism.[58]

Analysis

In Chapter 2 we considered the issue of social justice in relation to psychiatry and its centrality to the moral agency of psychiatrists. In the instance of the asylum-seeker debate, there is a failure of the social contract in regard to a particular group. Allowing for discussion over rights of sovereignty, even the most self-interested perspective would acknowledge that the vast majority of those seeking asylum in Australia would ultimately secure refuge and become members of the community suffering from severe mental illness. To force these future members of the community to endure trauma at the hands of their future government invites all manner of problems downstream and represents, if nothing else, an increased future demand on health services. In the face of the psychologically injurious practice of mandatory and indefinite detention or indeterminate immigration status, Australian psychiatrists confront an issue of social justice.

In considering our onion-skin model of advocacy, the primary focus of this moral quandary is the issue of advocacy. In this section we will apply our methodology to arrive at a reasoned position on this issue of advocacy on behalf of asylum seekers.

Reflective Phase

The various components of the reflective phase of deliberation are shown in Figure 14.1.

The clinical issues in relation to the policy of mandatory detention are primarily in the domain of the evidence of the deleterious effects of the policy on the mental health of asylum seekers and the subsequent implications for treatment once they join the community. More significantly, the context of the discussion integrates complex themes such as the stance taken by the RANZCP in similar issues such as indigenous mental health, the historical anxieties about immigration and the history of strong alienist themes in Australian psychiatry, and the framework in which asylum seekers' claims to refugee status and entitlements under law are considered. The partisan and at times emotive tone of the debate and its prominence in political machinations by elected officials are also profoundly influential.

In the domain of values, psychiatrists abide by a value of advocacy in the face of apparent social injustice in addition to the value of each individual patient for whom they perceive a

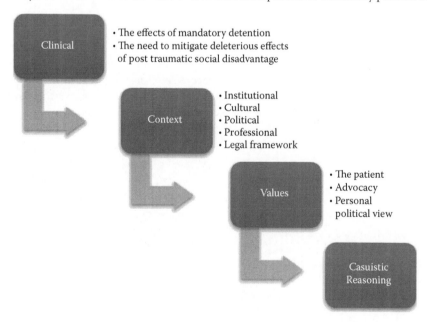

Figure 14.1 The reflective phase of moral reasoning in relation to advocacy in the asylum-seeker debate.

responsibility as a physician. This is balanced by their own party political views, which will affect their perception of the scope of the challenge and the need for advocacy.

Deliberative Phase

The deliberative phase is shown in Figure 14.2. A careful consideration of the qualitative aspects of the dilemma refines the focus to that of advocating against a law on the basis of robust evidence of the psychological harms such a law brings. In this case, there would be moral justification to speak out in the popular press to influence public opinion, in addition to direct representation to government. In this deliberation, the paradigm case is the proposed public policy of the legalization of marijuana. In the case of the proposed legalization of marijuana (as opposed to decriminalization), the issue of a law making the drug accessible to young people represents a significant threat to public health in that increased exposure of younger people to cannabis has dire implications for mental health including exacerbation of existing mental illness, a gateway effect to other substance use, and the unmasking of latent vulnerability to mental illness. These concerns are well supported by the scientific literature. The issue does not have broader implications for other policy, does not in itself invite partisan political debate, and has a direct clinical relevance.

Other pretexts for advocacy on public policy by psychiatrists in recent times have included arguing for increased funding for community mental health services, advocating on behalf of policies that aim to mitigate climate change, and arguments against legalization of same-sex marriage.

In regard to the case under consideration, there is ample evidence of the harmful effects of the policy of mandatory detention on the mental health of those affected. Unlike the

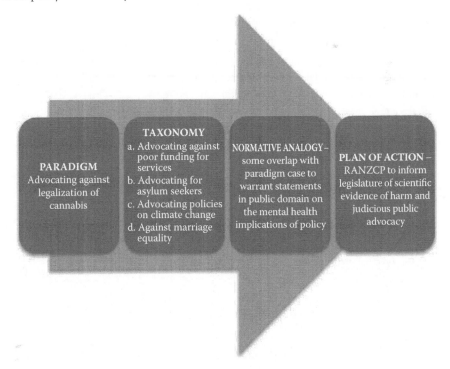

Figure 14.2 The deliberative phase of moral reasoning in relation to advocacy in the asylum-seeker debate.

paradigm case, the issue of ending mandatory detention stumbles into partisan politics, other policy areas such as border security and immigration policy, and an emotive debate in the lay press.

Arguments for advocacy in regard to laws relating to climate change or same-sex marriage do not have a compelling case that they adversely affect mental health in the light of the scientific literature and are clearly partisan political debates with highly emotive public discourses. As such, they are further removed from the paradigm case and would seem to be issues for psychiatrists as private individuals, rather than as members with a profession that is empowered with a public voice.

Thus the issue of advocacy against laws enforcing mandatory detention of asylum seekers is less proximate to the paradigm case than advocacy against funding cuts for services, yet still provide scope for advocacy. The golden mean would seem to be the scope of advocacy being direct submissions to government on the apparent mental health implications of the policy with judicious communication within the public domain, mindful of the incendiary nature of the debate.

Conclusion

Australian psychiatrists, like their international colleagues, face complex dilemmas in their relationship with the community. In the asylum-seeker debate, the historical, cultural, and political implications of the dilemma are as influential as the clinical aspects. To arrive at a defendable conclusion, our method of moral reasoning concludes there is a scope for advocacy within a specific limitation of informing public policy decisions as to the implications for the mental health of those affected. The dual-role dilemma in such an emotive and very politicized debate is between the moral agent as member of a professional group and the private citizen with complex values and political views. While Australian psychiatrists (and their international colleagues confronted with similar dilemmas) would do well to not overestimate the influence of their social power in such matters, it is nonetheless an issue of the use of power and therefore needs careful moral deliberation.

References

1. Hirst J. Australia: the official history. *The Monthly.* 2008; http://www.themonthly.com. au/tm/node/781 (accessed May 1, 2008).

2. Elder C. *Being Australian: Narratives of National Identity.* Sydney: Allen & Unwin; 2007.

3. Rutherford J. *The Gauche Intruder: Freud, Lacan and the White Australia Fantasy.* Melbourne: Melbourne University Press; 2000.

4. Kiernan B. *Blood and Soil: A World History of Genocide from Sparta to Darfur.* New Haven, CT: Yale University Press; 2007.

5. Lindqvist S. *Terra Nullius: A Journey Through No One's Land.* London: Granta; 2007.

6. Australian Human Rights and Equal Opportunity Commission Report of the National Inquiry into the Separation of Aboriginal and Torres Strait Islander Children from Their Families. 1997; http://www.hreoc.gov.au/pdf/social_justice/bringing_them_home_report.pdf (accessed April 8, 2007).

7. Anderson W. *The Cultivation of Whiteness: Science, Health and Racial Destiny in Australia.* Melbourne: Melbourne University Press; 2003.

8. Foley G. *Australia and the Holocaust: a Koori perspective.* 1997; http://www.kooriweb.org/foley/essays/essay_8.html (accessed June 14, 2008).

9. Petchkovsky L, San Roque C. *Tjunguwiyanytja,* attacks on linking: Forced separation and its psychiatric sequelae in Australia's "stolen generations." *Transcultural Psychiatry.* 2002;39:345–366.

10. Bolt A. *Still Not Sorry: The Best of Andrew Bolt.* Melbourne: News Custom Publishing; 2005.

11. Windschuttle K. *The Fabrication of Aboriginal History, Volume One: Van Diemen's Land 1803–1847.* Sydney: Macleay Press; 2002

12. Birmingham J. *Quarterly Essay 20—A Time for War: Australia as a Military Power* Melbourne: Black Inc; 2005.

13. Kirkby K. History of psychiatry in Australia, pre-1960. *History of Psychiatry.* 1999;10:191–204.

14. Dax E. Crimes, follies and misfortunes in the history of Australasian psychiatry. *Australian and New Zealand Journal of Psychiatry.* 1981;15:257–263.

15. Dax E. The first 200 years of Australian psychiatry. *Australian and New Zealand Journal of Psychiatry.* 1989;23:103–110.

16. Coleborne C, Mackinnon D. Psychiatry and its institutions in Australia and New Zealand: An overview. *Internationnal Review of Psychiatry.* 2006;18:371–380.

17. Garton S. *Medicine and Madness: A Social History of Insanity in New South Wales 1880–1940.* Sydney: UNSW Press; 1988.

18. Lewis M. *Managing Madness: Psychiatry and Society in Australia 1788–1980.* Canberra: Australian Government Publishing Service; 1988.

19. Rubinstein W, Rubinstein H. *Menders of the Mind: A History of the Royal Australian and New Zealand College of Psychiatrists, 1946–1996.* Melbourne: Oxford University Press; 1996.

20. Cade J. Lithium salts in the treatment of psychotic excitement. *Medical Journal of Australia* 1949;36:349–352.

21. Murray C. The "colouring of the psychosis": interpreting insanity in the primitive mind. *Health & History.* 2007;9/2:7–21.

22. Cawte J. Assimilation and its discontents: case histories illustrating problems of Aboriginal mental illness. *Australasian Psychiatric Bulletin.* 1963;4:17.

23. Cawte J. *Cruel, Poor and Brutal Nations.* Honolulu: University of Hawaii Press; 1972.

24. McMahon E. Psychiatry at the frontier: surveying Aboriginal mental health in the era of assimilation. *Health & History.* 2007;9:22–47.

25. Duke M. The dawn of Aboriginal psychiatry. *Australasian Psychiatry.* 2007;15:305–309.

26. Wilkinson R. *The Impact of Inequality: How to Make Sick Societies Healthier*. New York: The New Press; 2005.

27. Marmot M. Health in an unequal world: social circumstances, biology and disease. *Clinical Medicine*. 2006;6:559–572.

28. Baskin C. Conceptualizing, framing and politicizing Aboriginal ethics. *Journal of Ethics in Mental Health*. 2007;2:2.

29. Spencer D. Anomie and demoralization in traditional cultures: the Australian model. *Transcultural Psychiatry*. 2000;37:5–10.

30. Eley D, Young L, Hunter K, et al. Perceptions of mental health service delivery among staff and Indigenous consumers: it's still about communication. *Australasian Psychiatry*. 2007;15:130–134.

31. New South Wales Royal Commission into Deep Sleep Therapy. Report. Chair: J.P. Slattery, Commissioner. 362.2109944/10 RL, Med, Pu. Parliamentary Paper: 304/1990–1991 (NSW) 1990.

32. Chandler J, MacDonald J. The battle to control the mind. *The Melbourne Age*. 1991 (April 22); http://www.xenu-directory.net/news/19910422b-themelbourneage.html (accessed February 2010).

33. Watson E. Eccentric and idiosyncratic treatment philosophies: the therapeutic community at Townsville's Ward 10B, Queensland, 1973–87. *Health & History*. 2003;5/2:60–74.

34. Queensland Commission of Inquiry into the Care and Treatment of Patients in the Psychiatric Unit of the Townsville General Hospital. Report. (W. J. Carter, Commissioner). Brisbane: Government Printer; 1991.

35. Coleborne C, MacKinnon D. Psychiatry and its institutions in Australia and New Zealand: an overview. *International Review of Psychiatry*. 2006;18:371–380.

36. Sweet M. *Inside Madness*. Sydney: Macmillan; 2006.

37. Coleborne E. Introduction: deinstitutionalisation in Australia and New Zealand. *Health & History*. 2003;5/2:1–16.

38. Mental Health Council of Australia. *Not for service: experiences of injustice and despair in mental health care in Australia*. 2005; http://www.mhca.org.au (accessed June 10, 2008).

39. Butler T, Andrews G, Allnutt S, et al. Mental disorders in Australian prisoners: a comparison with a community sample. *Australian and New Zealand Journal of Psychiatry*. 2006;40:272–276.

40. White P, Whiteford H. Prisons: mental health institutions of the 21st century? *Medical Journal of Australia*. 2006;185:302–303.

41. Nussbaum M. *Women and Human Development: The Capabilities Approach*. New York: Cambridge University Press; 2000.

42. Marr D, Wilkinson M. *Dark Victory*. Sydney: Allen and Unwin; 2003.

43. Silove D, Steel Z, Watters C. Policies of deterrence and the mental health of asylum seekers. *Journal of the American Medical Association*. 2000;284:604–611.

44. Steel Z, Silove D. The mental health implications of detaining asylum seekers. *Medical Journal of Australia*. 2001;175:596–599.

45. Steel Z, Silove D, Brooks R, et al. Impact of immigration detention and temporary protection on the mental health of refugees. *British Journal of Psychiatry.* 2006;188:58–64.

46. Silove D, Steel Z, McGorry P, et al. Trauma exposure, postmigration stressors, and symptoms of anxiety, depression and post-traumatic stress in Tamil asylum-seekers: comparison with refugees and immigrants. *Acta Psychiatrica Scandanavica.* 1998;97:175–181.

47. Sinnerbrink I, Silove D, Manicavasagar V, et al. Asylum seekers: general health status and problems with access to health care. *Medical Journal of Australia.* 1996;165:634–637.

48. Sinnerbrink I, Silove D, Field A, et al. Compounding of premigration trauma and postmigration stress in asylum seekers. *The Journal of Psychology.* 1997;131:463–470.

49. Steel Z, Silove D. Science and the common good: indefinite, non-reviewable mandatory detention of asylum seekers and the research imperative. *Monash Bioethics Review.* 2004;23:93–103.

50. Garcia-Peltoniemi R. Clinical manifestations of psychopathology. In: Westermeyer J, Williams C, Nguyen A, eds. *Mental Health Services for Refugees.* Washington DC: US Government Printing online; 1991:42–55.

51. Westermeyer J. Cross-cultural care for PTSD: research, training and service needs for the future. *Journal of Traumatic Stress.* 1989;2:515–536.

52. Mares S. First, do no harm. In: Mares S, Newman L, eds. *Acting from the Heart.* Sydney: Finch; 2007:217–222.

53. Dudley M, Jureidini J, Mares S, et al. In protest. *Australian and New Zealand Journal of Psychiatry.* 2004;38(11–12):978–979.

54. Samuell D. Speaking on behalf of the college: the politics of children or childish politics? *Australasian Psychiatry.* 2003;11:121–122.

55. Boyce P, Lammersma J, Miles W. Comment. *Australasian Psychiatry.* 2003;11:123.

56. "Our work has been undermined, researchers say." Lateline Reporter: Margot O'Neill. Australian Broadcasting Corporation Broadcast. 09/02/2005; http://www.abc.net.au/lateline/content/2005/s1299518.htm (accessed 13 June 13, 2008).

57. Wroe D. Canberra paid $30,000 for report to discredit studies. *The Age.* February 12, 2005.

58. Rey J, Walter G, Giuffrida M. Should the RANZCP comment about the political and social issues of the day? The opinions of Australian fellows and trainees. *Australasian Psychiatry.* 2003;11:124–126.

Epilogue: Whither Psychiatry?

Ms. H was a woman in her early 30s who was born to Turkish parents and lived in a large U.S. city. She had experienced a harsh upbringing due to her problematic behavior as an adolescent, leading to her being expelled from school. She had used cannabis and stimulants and fled home on several occasions due to what was later considered the prodromal phase of schizophrenia. During a period of intravenous drug use she acquired hepatitis C infection, which led to a moderate degree of cirrhosis and portal hypertension, including splenomegaly. Ms. H was finally hospitalized with a psychotic episode at age 22, and throughout the next five years her illness appeared treatment refractory. She was alienated from her family, isolated from her community, homeless, and unemployed.

Her mental state improved dramatically when she took a combination of clozapine and valproic acid. This came at great cost, as she gained 50 kg in weight and developed a diabetic state, dyslipidemia, and severe obstructive sleep apnea. The valproic acid unmasked polycystic ovary syndrome, which virilized her appearance. Regardless, such was the severity of her schizophrenic illness that she and her psychiatrist resolved that she stay on clozapine.

A year into her clear remission, she developed neutropenia. While such a delayed onset was unusual, it was detected by the clozapine monitoring system, and the medication had to be discontinued. Further investigation of her deranged white cell counts indicated that she had long-standing baseline neutropenia and mild thrombocytopenia, presumably due to hypersplenism. Regardless, the clozapine monitoring authority insisted the treatment be ceased. Within a month, Ms. H's mental state deteriorated catastrophically and she was rehospitalized in a profoundly disorganized, regressed state. Retrials with alternative antipsychotic drugs and a course of electroconvulsive therapy (ECT) did little to resolve her situation.

With little credible alternative to clozapine, Ms. H's psychiatrist made a case to stimulate a leukocytosis with lithium therapy. This decision was based on a number of case reports in the scientific literature and discussion with the patient, her family, and colleagues. Ms. H's neutrophil count normalized and she recommenced clozapine. Over time, Ms. H's mental state approximated the previous improvement and she participated in a long-term rehabilitation program. One particular improvement was her adherence to the management of her diabetes, her polycystic ovary syndrome, and her proper use of a continuous positive airway pressure (CPAP) machine for her obstructive sleep apnea. She was able to engage with her psychiatrist in a supportive psychotherapy that allowed her to address some of the traumatic events she had experienced in the course of her illness. Ms. H's psychiatrist also took the opportunity to meet with her family to better involve them in Ms. H's life.

Who else could have managed this situation? Could a clinical psychologist with rights to prescribe medication have managed the complexities of Ms. H's problem? Could a mental health nurse practitioner have been able to integrate so much complicated internal medicine and engage either the patient in psychotherapy or the family in constructing a narrative over the trauma of Ms. H's illness, its meaning to the family, or the broad cultural significance of it for her family and their relation to their cultural community?

The complex needs of people such as Ms. H and her family require a skilled physician. If she were dealing with cancer, ischemic heart disease, or severe epilepsy, it would be unthinkable that she would not have a medical specialist to care for her. Is psychiatry in crisis, and what will it be in the near future? More relevant to this book, how will psychiatrists manage the moral challenges in their future?

Problem of Knowledge

Michel Foucault emphasized that medicine had evolved from an episteme of a process of observation of the external manifestation of illness in the patient to an episteme of the observation of the internal state of the patient through the discipline of pathology.[1] Had he lived long enough, he would undoubtedly have added a new episteme of the laboratory or the computerized observation of the patient.

What is psychiatry's episteme or paradigm? The impressive progress of neuroscience promised much to psychiatry but delivered little. As we have argued, the neuroscience revolution served as a Trojan horse for the infusion of neoliberalism into psychiatry, manifesting in profound alterations of the conceptualization of psychiatric disorder and treatment. The notions of the commodification of healthcare and medical technoluxe discussed in Chapter 7 have emerged from the current neuroscience episteme in psychiatry. With these have arrived specific moral challenges for psychiatrists. Yet neuroscience has proven a false prophet in psychiatry. Despite the complexity of the solutions to the problems of Ms. H, the lot of someone like her has not changed since George H. W. Bush's presidential proclamation of the Decade of the Brain.

Consider an uncontested focus of psychiatry, severe mood disorder. In recent times, the Scientific debate in the field of severe mood disorder has focused upon the dimensional aspects of bipolarity; i.e., how can complex presentations of mood disorder be conceptualized as variations of bipolar spectrum disorders?[2] Despite decades of research, there are no replicated genetic, structural, or functional neuroimaging findings to enlighten us on the question, nor has there been a definitive treatment to emerge from the research conducted. Indeed, the whole field remains in the realm of the external gaze of the physician of the patient; the current *Diagnostic and Statistical Manual*'s diagnostic system remains based upon the clinical gaze.

This is not a new process in psychiatry. In the first or second century AD, Aretaeus of Cappadocia provided the first clear description of bipolar disorder. Aretaeus's writings fell into obscurity in the Dark Ages but were revived by seventeenth century English scientist Robert Burton in the *Anatomy of Melancholy*.[3] In Chapter 6 of his book *On the Causes and Symptoms of Chronic Diseases*, Aretaeus describes acute psychotic mania followed by a postpsychotic depression[4]:

At the height of the disease they have impure dreams, and irresistible desire of venery, without any shame and restraint as to sexual intercourse; and if roused to anger by admonition or restraint, they become wholly mad. Wherefore they are affected with madness in various shapes; some run along unrestrainedly, and, not knowing how, return again to the same spot; some, after a long time, come back to their relatives; others roar aloud, bewailing themselves as if they had experienced robbery or violence. Some flee the haunts of men, and going to the wilderness, live by themselves ... If they should attain any relaxation of the evil, they become torpid, dull, sorrowful; for having come to a knowledge of the disease they are saddened with their own calamity.

This description has not been bettered by any contemporary mood disorder experts, and the words of Aretaeus represent the same grounds for diagnosis of bipolar disorder by a present-day psychiatrist.

Persian and Arabic scholars were heavily involved in translating, analyzing, and synthesizing Greek texts and concepts in the Muslim world. Arab texts from this period contain descriptions of disorders that are essentially unchanged in the *DSM* criteria.[5] To Arab scholars, mental disorder was essentially an irrational state and acknowledged the complex interaction between symptoms, meaning, and spirituality.[5] The work of Arab scholars reverberates in the biopsychosocial model of the formulation of diagnosis and treatment outlined by George Engel.[6] The Qur'an advocated what most Western psychiatrists would recognize as moral treatments and elements of social justice. The world's first dedicated psychiatric ward appeared in eighth century Mesopotamia (modern-day Iraq). Arab doctors used many naturally occurring medicines, including the potentially beneficial psychotropic properties of cannibidiol.[5]

In light of these reflections, it is arguable that the scientific basis of psychiatry does not provide a comprehensive or even credible account of the daily activities of psychiatry. In the midst of the flourishing of neuroscience, there were several calls for psychiatry to morph into a subspecialty of neurology.[7,8] The current epistemic basis of the discipline of psychiatry has remained unchanged for millennia. There is little indication that the current flurry of neuroscience activity will alter this. To any student of the philosophy of mind, this comes as no surprise. Understanding the infinite complexity of the brain is unlikely in the foreseeable future to resolve the dilemmas first identified in antiquity and given their modernist form by Enlightenment philosophers such as Descartes, Berkeley, or Locke. As physicians of the mind, psychiatrists have not been well served by their quest for ontological security in the bosom of neuroscience.

So Whither Psychiatry?

Several psychiatrists have attempted to grapple with this question and recast psychiatry and its future moral dilemmas. The most cogent and compelling of these reflections is offered by American psychiatrist and philosopher David Brendal.[9-11] Brendal writes in the tradition of American pragmatism and Karl Jaspers. He sees the science–humanist divide in psychiatry and the folly of privileging of theory over practical results as the main ethical challenge of a profession attempting to "heal itself" (p.3).[9] Brendal acknowledges the community demand for commoditized answers to life's questions and the complicity of psychiatrists in indulging this, but seeks to recast the role of psychiatry in contemporary society as integrating multiple sources of understanding in both a dialogic and dialectic process. These ideas approximate those of Ghaemi we discussed in Chapter 11.

In a more polemic vein, American psychiatrist Daniel Carlat sees psychiatry's crisis as resulting from the literal embrace of the flawed *DSM* system of classification and its foreclosure on the tradition of "talking" to the patient. Carlat argues that the 15-minute medication review is in part a product of the limited access to psychiatrists and the need to rationalize their time as a limited social good, but sees the process as ultimately ruinous to the status of psychiatry and its future.

Throughout this book, we have sought to establish the communitarian position that psychiatrists as moral agents function within a complex contextual framework and as a profession practice their craft within a form of social contract. We have argued that the moral challenges faced by psychiatrists integrate a complex synthesis of epistemic, ontological, and values-based problems. We have emphasized that as a moral enterprise, the practice of psychiatry is fundamentally a social process, both in the construction of psychiatric disorder (not *disease*) and its treatment. Our thesis is that most moral challenges faced by psychiatrists can be concretized as a form of dual-role dilemma and an ethical, values-based plan of moral agency can be formulated using a method that integrates reflection on the complexities of a situation with a practical, transparent, and instrumentally valuable means of deliberation.

Future dilemmas in psychiatric ethics will relate to the patient, the profession, and the community. At the time of writing, the emotive and internecine exchanges over the nature of the *DSM-V* portend a crisis in psychiatry. The likelihood is that *DSM-V* will be condemned, boycotted, or discredited by many groups, including psychiatrists. This crisis mirrors growing discontent with the reductionist and hegemonic influence of northern hemisphere biological psychiatry and is likely to lead to a renaissance in antipsychiatry and the evolution of moral challenges to psychiatrists more on questions of knowledge, politics, economics, and culture. To resolve such problems, the future psychiatrist will need to both revisit and embrace the truly interdisciplinary nature of the field. Psychiatrists ignore knowledge of philosophy, ethics, sociology, and history at their peril. In justifying his argument for philosophy as being a core concept of psychiatry, Nasser Ghaemi quotes the Australian psychiatrist Aubrey Lewis, "'The psychiatrist [is] confronted, whether he likes it or not, with many of the central issues of philosophy'."[12]

This book began by considering the crimes of Irmfried Eberl. Eberl was motivated by the one big idea of social Darwinism and the sacred task of psychiatry to rid the *volk* of impure blood. The origin of Eberl's crimes was complex, but his failure to reflect on the broad contextual influences upon his profession begot his unspeakable acts through the fool's gold of a reductive single idea as the basis of psychiatry and an unreflective discharge of duty to a social contract with a criminal government and a community mesmerized into a moral quagmire.

We ignore this at our peril.

References

1. Foucault M. *The Birth of the Clinic: An Archaeology of Medical Perception*. Sheridan Smith A, trans. New York: Vintage Books; 1975.

2. Akiskal H, Bourgeois M, Angst J, et al. Re-evaluating the prevalence of and diagnostic composition within a broad clinical spectrum of bipolar disorders. *Journal of Affective Disorders*. 2000;59:S5–S30.

3. Burton B. *The Anatomy of Melancholy* (Project Gutenberg Ebook#10800); 2004. http://www.gutenberg.org/ebooks/10800 (accessed June 2012).

4. Aretaeus. Causes and symptoms of chronic diseases (English). *Greek Texts and Translations*. http://perseus.uchicago.edu/perseus-cgi/citequery3.pl?dbname=GreekTexts&getid=1&query=Aret.SC (accessed June 2012).

5. Youssef H, Youssef F, Dening T. Evidence for the existence of schizophrenia in medieval Islamic society. *History of Psychiatry*. 1996;7:55–62.

6. Engel G. The clinical application of the biopsychosocial model. *American Journal of Psychiatry*. 1980;137:535–544.

7. Bergström J, Andersson G, Karlsson A, et al. An open study of the effectiveness of Internet treatment for panic disorder delivered in a psychiatric setting. *Nord J Psychiatry*. 2009;63:44–50.

8. Andersson E, Ljótsson B, Hedman E, et al. Internet-based cognitive behavior therapy for obsessive compulsive disorder: a pilot study. *BMC Psychiatry*. 2011;11:125.

9. Luo J. Health information technologies for practicing psychiatrists. *Psychiatric Times*. 2010;27:16–18.

10. Brendal D. Reductionism, eclecticism, and pragmatism in psychiatry: the dialectic of clinical explanation. *Journal of Medicine and Philosophy*. 2003;28(5–6):563–589.

11. Brendal D. The ethics of diagnostic and therapeutic paradigm choice in psychiatry. *Harvard Review of Psychiatry*. 2002;10:47–50.

12. Ghaemi N. *The Concepts of Psychiatry: A Pluralistic Approach to Mind and Mental Illness*. Baltimore: Johns Hopkins University Press; 2003.

Author Index

Subject Index